Pelican Book A685

Law in a Changing Society

Wolfgang Friedmann was born in Berlin in
1907, and received his Doctor of Jurisprudence
degree from the University of Berlin. He is also
a Doctor of Laws and a Master of Laws from
the University of London, and a Master of
Laws from the University of Melbourne,
Australia. He was Reader in Law at the
University of London from 1938 to 1947 and
during the same time worked for the Allied
Military Government of Germany. From 1947
to 1950 he was Professor of Public Law at the
University of Melbourne, and from 1950 to
1955 Professor of Law at the University of
Toronto in Canada. Since 1955 he has been
Professor of Law and Director of International
Legal Research at Columbia University in New
York City. He has also been a United Nations
Consultant and a Member of the Executive
Council of the American Society of
International Law. He is a Fellow of the
American Academy of Arts and Sciences, and
a Barrister at Law, Middle Temple.

Among his other books are *Legal Theory*, now
in its fourth edition, *Introduction to World
Politics*, about to appear in a fifth edition,
*The Allied Military Government of Germany*, *Law
and Social Change in Contemporary Britain*, and *The
Changing Structure of International Law*. He has
written or edited many other books and articles.

W. Friedmann

# Law in a Changing Society

Abridged Edition

Penguin Books
Baltimore · Maryland

Penguin Books Ltd, Harmondsworth,
Middlesex, England
Penguin Books Inc., 3300 Clipper Mill Road,
Baltimore 11, Md, U.S.A.
Penguin Books Pty Ltd, Ringwood,
Victoria, Australia

First published by Stevens & Sons 1959
This abridged edition published in Pelican Books
1964
Copyright © Stevens & Sons, 1959, 1964

Made and printed in Great Britain by
Cox and Wyman Ltd,
London, Reading, and Fakenham
Set in Monotype Baskerville

To May

# Contents

# Preface to Pelican Edition

The present edition is an abbreviated version of the writer's *Law in a Changing Society*, published in 1959 by Stevens and Sons. The cuts necessary to make this book available to a wider public in paperback form, have been distributed throughout the book, so as to leave the main thesis and line of reasoning untouched. No single chapter has been omitted; all the cuts concern matters of detail, elaborations which appear to be of greater importance to the specialized student of jurisprudence than to the general reader.

No substantive changes have been made, except for a discussion in Chapter 2 of the decision of the House of Lords in *Shaw* v. *Director of Public Prosecutions*, a decision which seemed too important – and in this writer's opinion, too dangerous – a contribution to the role of the courts in the evolution of law to be ignored. Reference is also made to the important new decision of the House of Lords in *Hedley Byrne* v. *Heller*.

The main purpose and approach of the book is stated in the preface to the original edition, which follows this introductory statement. The intervening years have, if anything, reinforced the crucial importance of mature reflection on the interrelation between social and legal change. In the United States, the implementation of the Supreme Court's desegregation decision in *Brown* v. *Board of Education* continues to raise a multitude of problems in the adjustment of the law to new social postulates. The pending civil rights legislation is the principal, though by no means the only, expression of this problem. In practically all the emergent and developing countries, one of the paramount problems is the adjustment, principally through legislative, administrative, and judicial means, of traditional and static social and legal institutions to the needs and demands of societies aiming at economic development and social advancement. The stated aims of these new societies are often incompatible with the existing structures of land law, of tribal, village, or family organization. It is in this type of society that the role of the legislator, as an initiator of social change, becomes most evident.                                                    W. F.

*January, 1964*

# Preface

In 1951, I published a book entitled *Law and Social Change in Contemporary Britain*, which attempted to analyse the impact of social change – mainly on contemporary English law, though with a number of comparative observations. As this book has now been out of print for some time, I was faced with the alternatives of letting it rest there, of preparing a new edition, or of writing a basically new book on the same theme. Eventually, I decided on the last of these alternatives.

The present book shares with the former mainly the approach[1]: the conviction that the law must, especially in contemporary conditions of articulate law-making by legislators, courts, and others, respond to social change if it is to fulfil its function as a paramount instrument of social order. While most of the reviews of the earlier book have accepted this premiss – though by no means all of the conclusions – some distinguished critics have expressed doubts. The traditional reluctance of English lawyers – not shared by men such as Dicey or Maitland – to analyse and rationalize the effect of social changes on contemporary law, as distinct from legal history, is reflected in Professor Hart's question whether the picture of the impact of recent economic and social changes upon English law was 'drawn too soon'.[2]

It is certainly a serious question, how far it is possible to be either adequately informed or sufficiently objective in an appraisal of the impact of social change on a contemporary legal system, in the midst of which the author lives, works, and fights – as he must, if he is a responsible citizen – for certain views as against others? In both respects, *Law and Social Change in Contemporary Britain* had, no doubt, its share of errors and prejudices. If I now venture, nonetheless, to submit a similar book, considerably wider in the scope of subject-matter as well as in the range of comparative treatment, it is certainly not without a consciousness of the very serious inadequacies of knowledge and vision from which such an attempt is bound to suffer. Yet the conviction that it must be made has been strengthened by the additional experience that I have gained, since the publication of the earlier book, through teaching and living in Canada and the United States. The difficulties of the undertaking are, indeed, immense. The material to be analysed is almost limitless. Yet, if a book of this kind is not to fail entirely in its purpose, it must keep a balance between too much detail – which would turn it into a series of minor and inadequate textbooks – and unsubstantiated generalities.

I have therefore concentrated in each of the areas surveyed on what appear to me to be the most significant challenges of social change, and illustrated them by corresponding responses – or failures to respond – in legislation, case law, and legal thinking. The comparative treatment is also inevitably selective, within the limitations of this writer's knowledge. Comparative analyses are mainly based on the different common-law systems on the one hand, and some civil-law systems (mostly French and German) on the other hand. The rapidly increasing literature has enabled me to make fairly extensive references to Soviet law. Except for occasional references, I have not attempted to include non-Western systems, save in so far as they are fashioned upon Western patterns. This is not due to any lack of sense of their importance, but to lack of adequate knowledge.

A very brief survey of the outline and contents of the book may clarify both its purposes and its limitations.

The introductory part has some general reflections on the inter-relation of legal and social change, against the background of different political systems and social pressures. This is followed by an analysis of the role of the courts in the adaptation of the law to social change.

The second part is concerned with the impact of social change on our principal legal institutions, i.e. property, contract, tort, criminal law, and family law. As all these chapters attempt to show, social change sometimes affects the concept itself, of property or contract, for example; sometimes, the concept remains outwardly unchanged, but it is put to new purposes, and eventually comes to represent something entirely different from its earlier meaning. In the field of property – where a comparison between Continental and Anglo-American developments is particularly fruitful – the concept of property has gradually widened, while the principles governing the power and the use of property have been profoundly modified under the impact of new social ideas. In the field of contract, it is evident that the *Idealtyp*, the contract as an instrument of free bargaining between parties on the basis of equality, has been largely displaced by the standardized contract, the collective agreement, and the impact of public law, either through the imposition of statutory conditions or the – still insufficiently analysed – phenomenon of the public-law contract, which is further treated in the public law chapter.

In the field of tort, the gradual change in principles of tort liability, and, in particular, the transformation of the concept of negligence – which goes together with, and partly overlaps, the shift from fault liability to strict liability – is analysed, in conjunction with the decisive impact of both public and private insurance on the position of the law of tort. This is divided into two aspects: the implications of the shifting of the burden of liability from the defendant to an insurer, and the substitution of public or private compensation by way of insurance, for the damage action in tort.

The criminal law chapter traces the impact of three major phenomena of modern society on the concepts and functions of criminal law: the relativization of guilt through modern psychoanalytical research; the profound changes in the philosophy of punishment; and the growth of the modern 'administrative' or 'public-welfare' offence, with purposes and functions largely different from those of traditional criminal law.

The chapter on family law brings together matters usually dealt with under different headings, such as marriage and divorce, the treatment of the right to life in criminal law, and the place of the family in the modern State. This includes such matters as the problem of indissolubility of marriage and divorce, the various attitudes towards the legitimacy of birth control, abortion, and artificial insemination, and the profound changes in the social and legal position of married women and children.

The next major part of the book traces the impact of some important changes in the social structure of contemporary society on legal ideologies. The metamorphosis and partial eclipse of the ideal of freedom of trade is traced, against the background of both common law and statutory developments, in the field of anti-trust, and other public controls. One of the most important phenomena of our time, the growth of corporate power, is analysed in its dual impact on the position of the corporation in relation to the State and to the individual. In the same vein, the threefold pressure to which the individual is exposed, through the commercial corporation, the labour union, and the demands of State security, is analysed.

The next part of the book consists of an outline of the principles of public law as they are developing in the common-law world. The justification for this attempt is the excessive attention still paid to procedural safeguards, as compared with the principles of relations between public authority and the individual, in the common-law jurisdictions. In this chapter, therefore, an extensive comparison with the principles and institutions of the Continental systems of administrative law has proved particularly important.

The next part attempts a corresponding analysis for the changing international society of our time. A survey of the international legal institutions and relations, which are affected by the divergences of social organizations within the family of nations, is followed by a brief estimate of the kind of international society into which our deeply troubled world – both more interdependent than ever and more deeply divided by political and social tensions – appears to be moving.

A final chapter seeks to reassess the meaning of the rule of law in our time, again taking as its theme the triangular tension between the claims of individual, group, and State.

It is obvious that, even if the book should succeed in its main purpose – to outline some of the principal problems and challenges to law in our dynamic and turbulent society – it can at best be a prolegomena, a challenge to others to elaborate the many themes adumbrated in this book. To the best of my ability, I have attempted to isolate major social changes in our society from merely personal beliefs. One learned critic of the earlier book[3] has accused it of being 'tendentious, without being frankly so'. While this criticism was not shared by many other eminent reviewers, I have taken it seriously. Value assumptions should be stated frankly. My major assumptions are, first, that law is, in Holmes's phrase, not a 'brooding omni-presence in the sky', but a flexible instrument of social order, dependent on the political values of the society which it purports to regulate, and, second, that the paramount value of Western society remains the free and responsible individual. But the legal conditions of such freedom have to be constantly reassessed against the changing social framework.

Granted these premisses, there remains much room for disagreement. He who believes in the sacramental indissolubility of marriage will reject any attempt to widen the grounds of divorce and to depart from the concept of guilt, no matter how overwhelming the evidence of discrepancy between the theory of the law and the practice of contemporary divorce may be. To the upholder of undiluted *mens rea* in criminal law, the sympathetic consideration of the public welfare offence as a largely different type of sanction will be objectionable. Evidence of the disastrous dangers of over-population will not move those who regard birth control as inherently evil. The ardent champion of private enterprise will not admit that public enterprise – efficient or otherwise – is any, even partial, answer to the evils of excessive private economic power. And so on. The reader will have to make his decision. I claim no more than to have dealt with major social phenomena of our time, as a challenge to which we must seek a solution, and which we cannot ignore by pretending that they are not the lawyer's province, but that of the legislator, the politician, the sociologist, or the economist.

For better or worse, the creative and moulding power of the law has never been greater than in our highly articulate society. And it has never been more important that lawyers – as legislators, judges, teachers, or practitioners – should be more than highly trained craftsmen.

W. F.

*August, 1959.*

# Acknowledgements

The author of a book like the present is, to a particular degree, dependent on the scholarship of those who have specialized in the many fields here brought together. My debt will be apparent from the bibliographical references. I have, however, had the additional and invaluable help of friends and colleagues, who have been generous enough to read and criticize various chapters falling within their field of expertise. Otto Kahn-Freund of the University of London, Fleming James Jr of Yale University, William C. Cary, Walter Gellhorn, Gerald Gunther, Paul Hays, Philip Jessup, Harry W. Jones, and Monrad Paulsen – all of the Columbia Law School – have read various chapters and, by their criticisms and suggestions, have greatly helped me, without having any responsibility for the remaining errors, let alone the views expressed in this book.

I have also had valuable assistance from Mr Samuel Cohen, M.A., LL.M. (who has prepared the Bibliography and Index), Mr Richard C. Pugh, LL.B., and above all, from my secretary, Miss Lini S. May, M.A., for which I am most grateful.

The completion of the final draft of the book during the summer of 1958 was facilitated by a grant from the Rockefeller Foundation, which also enabled me to obtain some research and secretarial assistance. I am grateful to the Foundation for their support.

I am obliged to the editors of the *American Journal of International Law*, the *Canadian Bar Review*, and the *Columbia Law Review* for permission to use all or part of articles published in these reviews (Chapters 2, 9, 14).

I should like to express my gratitude to Mr Robert Stein, LL.B., for his help in abridging this book for the purposes of the Pelican edition.

# Acknowledgments

Part One

# Theory of Legal Change

# The Interactions of Legal and Social Change

## SAVIGNY AND BENTHAM

The controversy between those who believe that law should essentially follow, not lead, and that it should do so slowly, in response to
clearly formulated social sentiment – and those who believe that the
law should be a determined agent in the creation of new norms, is
one of the recurrent themes of the history of legal thought. It is
tellingly illustrated by the conflicting approaches of Savigny and
Bentham.[1]

For Savigny, a bitter opponent of the rationalizing and law-
making tendencies spurred by the French Revolution, law was
'found', not 'made'. Only when popular custom, in part articulated
by lawyers, had fully evolved, could and should the legislature take
action. Savigny particularly deprecated the trend towards the
codification of law, inaugurated by the Napoleonic Codes, and
spreading rapidly over the civilized world.

By contrast, Bentham, a fervent believer in the efficacy of rationally constructed reforming laws, devoted a great part of his life to the
drafting of codes for a large number of countries, from Czarist
Russia to the newly emergent republics of Latin America. While
most of these efforts were not immediately successful, notably in his
own country, whether in the field of civil law, criminal law, evidence, or poor law, his philosophy became increasingly influential as
the nineteenth century progressed. It was Bentham's philosophy,
and that of his disciples, which turned the British Parliament – and
similar institutions in other countries – into active legislative instruments, effecting social reforms, partly in response to, and partly in
stimulation of, felt social needs.[2] It is essentially the judge-made
law that, in the countries of the common-law world, has still in large
measure resisted legislative – as distinct from judicial – reform,
although even in the traditional fields of the common law, legislative
activity is steadily increasing. In most other fields – of which elec-
toral reform, social welfare legislation in the broadest sense, tax
law, and the reform of the machinery of justice are examples – the
Bentham philosophy triumphed in the practice of States, as the
urbanization and industrialization of nineteenth-century Western

society proceeded, and long before the political and social cata-
clysms of the twentieth century posed a series of new challenges
with which this book is essentially concerned.

### EHRLICH

Savigny's theory is today a matter of history, too much out of
tune with the basic condition of modern society to be a matter
of serious discussion. But the far more subtle and realistic theory
proposed a century later by the Austrian jurist Eugen Ehrlich,
forms a convenient starting point for the reflections offered in this
chapter.[3]

The similarity of Ehrlich's to Savigny's approach lies in his
emphasis on the 'living law of people', based on social behaviour
rather than the compulsive norm of the State. Norms observed by
the people, whether in matters of religious habits, family life, or
commercial relations, are law, even if they are never recognized or
formulated by the norm of the State.[4] For Ehrlich, the main sphere
of the compulsive State norm is in the fields specifically connected
with the purposes of the State, i.e. military organization, taxation,
and police administration. While he admits that the sphere of essential State activities, and, therefore, of the norms created for their
protection, has expanded in our time, it still remains for him an
ancillary part of the law, and one he separates from the 'living law'
of the community.

It is this basic differentiation between a main body of the law,
which develops from the social life of the 'people', living as nations,
church congregations, business communities, or families, and a
limited sphere of 'State norms', created for purposes of organization
and protection, that has lost its validity and meaning in the increasingly industrialized and articulate society of our time. Today, the
legislature is everywhere heavily at work, flanked by a multiplicity
of administrative agencies on the one side and a variety of judicial
institutions on the other side. It actively moulds and regulates the
scope of business enterprise as well as the property relations of
families and even breeding habits. Hire-purchase legislation
strongly affects purchasing habits, while zoning and town planning
legislation has a decisive influence on the pattern of land ownership
and other property rights. A highly urbanized and mechanized
society, in which great numbers of peoples live close together and are
ever more dependent upon each other's actions and the supply of
necessities outside their own sphere of control, has led to an increas-

ingly active and creative role of the conscious law-making instrumentalities of the State.

## THE INTERPLAY OF STATE ACTION AND PUBLIC OPINION

It is only certain organic theories of State – which found their climax
in the Hegelian philosophy of law and State, carried to ultimate
frenzy in the Fascist theories of twentieth-century Germany and
Italy – that have turned the State into an abstract and mystical
entity, moving and acting with a mind and soul of its own. The
State is indeed the organized power of the community, equipped
with a steadily increasing armoury of instruments of action, and, as
such, it is opposed to the unorganized groundswell of public opinion.
The power of those who control the machinery of the State has been
multiplied manifold, absolutely and relatively, by the development
of the modern legislative and administrative machinery as well as
the growing concentration of physical and technical power, and the
means of communication. But it is still the *people*, groups and individuals, who control the machinery. They are, themselves, to a
greater or lesser extent, the representatives of the social forces which,
in turn, they seek to mould and control through the instrumentalities of the State. At the one extreme, a ruthless individual or a small
group, holding in their hands a concentrated power which the
modern Fascist and Communist systems have demonstrated, may
seek to impose their will, in the form of laws, regulations, and police
action, on an apathetic or cowed community. At the other extreme,
prevalent in primitive communities, but increasingly infrequent in
our time – a government may be essentially representative, taking
the minimum of action, when required by overwhelming pressure
to do so. But whether we are concerned with the abolition of secret
police powers, the creation of legal remedies against administrative
action, the enactment of an anti-trust law, or the introduction of
new divorce grounds, there is always some inter-relation between
the State machinery which produces these changes, and the social
opinion of the community in which they are intended to operate.
The kind of inter-relation that obtains in any given situation is
essentially determined by two factors: (a) the type of political
system that controls legal action; (b) the type of social interest
which is the object of the legal regulation in question.

## CONSTITUTIONAL PATTERNS AND
## LEGAL CHANGE

Modern dictatorship resembles older forms of absolutism in its hostility to any form of separation of powers, and in the concentration of as many functions of government in as few hands as possible. It is distinguished from older forms of absolutism by the sophistication and refinement of the legislative, administrative, and judicial techniques, developed in intermediate centuries. A system of government that controls, directly or through faithful henchmen, the machinery and all levels of executive power subject to no judicial supervision, and that, through a combination of political appointments, insecurity of tenure, and direct instructions, also controls the administration of justice, has an apparently unlimited power to make whatever laws the ruling junta deems necessary. As such a government has, among its many other powers, complete power over all forms of education and the media of communication, it may, in due course, be able to mould and condition the minds of the people which it controls to such an extent that they will meekly, or even enthusiastically, accept whatever laws the masters impose upon them – either by direct decree or by using the trappings of a pseudo-democratic legislative process. Twelve years of Nazi government in Germany showed the length to which such a process, ruthlessly and fanatically pursued, may go.

More significant, perhaps, is a study of the inter-relation of law and social change in the Soviet Union.[5] For the Soviet system has now been in operation for well over forty years, long enough to re-fashion the entire political, economic, and legal system of the country as well as the education and growth of an entire generation. The Soviet legal revolution has gone much further than the Nazi legal revolution. Unlike the latter, it has not confined itself to the constitutional structure and the system of political power, but basically changed the conditions of production and commercial transactions and, with it, the structure of legal ownership and contract. It has also effected basic changes in family relationships, by approximating the making and dissolution of marriages to the conclusion and discharge of contracts, by creating complete equality between men and women, by drastically improving the status of the illegitimate child, and by the legalization of abortion.[6] Like the Nazi system, the Soviet system has entirely subordinated the rights of the individual and of groups to the State, using for that purpose the para-legal powers of a powerful secret police, with its own quasi-criminal procedure, the political pressures of the ubiquitous Communist Party, and mass detention and deportation without trial.

But the survival and consolidation of the Communist régime in the Soviet Union is in large measure due to its positive achievements. Whereas the Nazi Government despised education and educated people and, during its short régime, largely lived on the intellectual achievements of former generations of Germans, the Soviet Government strove successfully to turn a backward into an educated nation, albeit to the exclusion of free thought in political matters. The result of this process is, it seems, that the Government can no longer impose the most ruthless forms of civil oppression upon a new and better educated generation. This would seem to explain the drastic curtailment of the once almost unlimited powers of the M.V.D. and several other reforms in the judicial process, although they do not basically affect the concentration of legal and political power in the hands of the Government.

Equally significant is the fact that after more than forty years of Soviet law, despite many basic differences between the Soviet and other legal systems, no basically new concepts or legal relationships have developed. The machinery of justice operates in forms and procedures comparable to those of other systems, although, of course, not in the independence cherished by democratic forms of government. Groups within the State, such as churches or trade unions, survive, the former tolerated despite the basic hostility of the Marxist philosophy and the official doctrine of the Soviet State to any organized religion; the latter an essential part of the State, but with very limited functions and without the essential autonomy that is part of the liberal concept of freedom of association. Marriage survives as a monogamous institution, and although it is in theory a much less strict union than, for example, the American marriage, comparison of the practice of marriage in both countries would make this assertion very doubtful.[7] Contracts continue to be concluded and enforced, although the most important contracts are those between Government-owned corporations, which operate the main branches of industry and commerce. Private property exists and is recognized, although on a much more limited scale than in non-Socialist countries. Tort actions prosper and are dealt with very much as in other industrialized countries. The social insurance system is closely comparable to that of Great Britain or the Scandinavian countries.

A totalitarian government can, indeed, use its monopoly of the law-making and executive powers for the re-shaping of law, in disregard of the democratic processes of opinion, to a far greater extent than other systems, but it is limited by the need to secure at least the acquiescence and, where it produces an educated minority, the willing acceptance of its law. It is, on the other hand, limited by the permanence of certain categories of social relationships, dictated by the conditions of human life and society rather than by a specific political ideology.

In a democracy, the interplay between social opinion and the law-moulding activities of the State is a more obvious and articulate one. Public opinion on vital social issues constantly expresses itself not only through the elected representatives in the legislative assemblies, but through public discussion in press, radio, public lectures, pressure groups, and, on a more sophisticated level, through scientific and professional associations, universities, and a multitude of other channels.

Because of this constant interaction between the articulation of public opinion and the legislative process, the tension between the legal and the social norm can seldom be too great. It is not possible in a democratic system to impose a law on an utterly hostile community.[8] But, a strong social ground swell sooner or later compels legal action. Between these two extremes, there is a great variety of the patterns of challenge and response. On the one hand, the law may at length, and tardily, respond to an irresistible tide of social habit or opinion. Such is the case with the gradual enlargement of divorce grounds in the great majority of non-Catholic Western countries – either through the addition of new divorce grounds (cruelty, incompatibility, etc.) or the judicial extension of existing grounds for divorce or annulment (e.g. annulment for fraud in the State of New York). The extension of legitimate divorce is a response to the increasing freedom of movement of the married woman in modern Western society, a loosening of religious ties and social taboos, and the development of social habits which lead to the dissolution of a vastly increased number of marriages, with or without the sanction of law. Here the alternative for the legislator is to permit an increasing gap between legal theory and social practice to develop, or to respond to an overwhelming change in the social facts of life.[9] Again, suicide which is still in theory a crime in the common-law jurisdictions, has in fact ceased to be so, not through an act of the legislator, but through an all but universal practice of regarding suicide *ipso facto* as committed 'while of unsound mind'.

On the other hand, a determined and courageous individual or small minority group may initiate and pursue a legal change, in the face of governmental or parliamentary lethargy, and an indifferent public opinion. Such legislation as now exists in many countries for the preservation of forests or wild life, or the conservation of other vital resources, has been the belated result of the determined efforts of small groups of men who saw beyond the immediate interests not only of vested interests but of the ordinary legislator and government executive. A much needed liberalization of the English divorce law effected in 1937 was the result of the almost single-handed efforts of an individual Member of Parliament, Mr A. P. Herbert. But while the determination of far-sighted individuals is often an indispensable factor, it cannot become effective in a democracy unless there is a minimum of acceptance by public opinion. When President Franklin Roosevelt carried through the legal revolution in American labour relations, symbolized by the National Labour Relations Act, he enjoyed the unusual combination of a brilliant political mind and a large Congressional majority – although the opposition of a majority of the Supreme Court judges retarded the process for a while. But he could not have carried through the change unless far-reaching changes in industrial organization, on the side both of employers and labour, had made the acceptance of collective bargaining as the essential instrument of negotiation a vital necessity, and unless the convulsions of the great depression of the early thirties had greatly weakened both the power of the employers and the ideological strength of extreme economic individualism. Town planning legislation in England, and zoning legislation in the United States, has been the belated, and far from sufficient, response to the social and aesthetic chaos created by generations of unplanned speculative building and urban development. But the pioneering efforts of what was originally a small group of town planners and sociologists would not have come to fruition until the point had been reached when even the ordinary citizen and the average national and local legislator had at last been impressed with the immediate urgency of the conditions which it was sought to remedy. In recent years, the Indian Constitution of 1949 has abolished both the polygamous marriage and the caste system, in the face of age-old social and religious custom. How far this legal revolution will be successful, is still a matter of some uncertainty. That it has a reasonable prospect of succeeding is, in itself, a sign of the greatly increased power of modern State action as against old social custom. But not even the prestige of a

Nehru, or the predominance of the Congress Party in organized political life in India, could have attempted such far-reaching reforms, unless the impact of Western ideas had effected a far-reaching change in educated public opinion.

Similar problems arise in the transformation of long-standing and, until recently, unalterable personal status laws in the Muslim world. The sacrosanctity of the Sharī 'a – the canon law of Islam – derived partly from its predominantly theological origin[10] and partly from the static character of overwhelmingly rural, nomadic, and autocratically governed societies. But while the hold of Islamic religion remains as strong as ever, the majority of Islamic States are in a process of rapid economic and social change, leading to increasing commercialization and industrialization. The first and major legal impact has been in the field of civil and commercial law, where a majority of Islamic States have introduced codes based on the leading Western (particularly French) systems or a blend of Sharī 'a and Western principles.[11] But more recently, the effect of this transformation and the closer contact with other systems has increasingly affected family law and, in particular, the 'miserable lot of Muslim wives'.[12] Egypt, Iraq, Jordan, Lebanon, Pakistan, and the Sudan have at least begun to introduce reforms which give some rights to the wife. Here, as in India, legislative action could not have been attempted unless social changes, such as urbanization, and intellectual influences (from Western ideas absorbed by the younger educated generation) had prepared the soil. The transformation of personal status law is, however, likely to be far slower and more difficult than the introduction of Western-modelled modern principles of obligation and commercial transactions.

Examples have already been given of the response of the law to social change not through legislation, but through judicial reinterpretations.[13] When the Supreme Court of the United States, in 1954,[14] after a series of preparatory judgements, upset the interpretation of the 14th Amendment on the equality of races, given nearly half a century earlier, it partly responded to, and partly led, public opinion. It certainly could not have made the attempt – how successfully, is still an open question – unless the intervening period had brought a great change in the economic and educational status of the American negro, and a corresponding evolution in the attitude of responsible individuals and important social groups, such as the armed forces, churches, universities, and at least part of organized labour.

### STATE POWERS AND THE CONTROL OF PERSONAL LIBERTIES AND ECONOMIC RIGHTS

The rights of business and labour to organize, concentrate, and monopolize, social security legislation of all kinds, matters of education, and of the political and civic status of religious and racial groups within the State, all these are matters of such general impact on the life of the community that they call sooner or later for legislative, administrative or, in some cases, judicial action. By contrast, the so-called 'lawyers' law' is generally concerned with matters of more technical and limited import. They are essentially within the sphere of the traditional common law, regulated by a gradually evolving judge-made law in the common-law jurisdictions, and the civil codes in most other jurisdictions. In this sphere, there is a more strictly defined interplay of social change, legal evolution by judicial interpretation, and legislative action, which varies from country to country and from time to time. Professional groups and the technical training of the lawyer play a predominant role, and it is in this field that the courts are still largely expected to carry on the process of legal evolution in response to social change, although, as we shall see, they have often failed to rise to the challenge. In matters of contract, tort, definition of property rights, form and validity of wills, matrimonial rights, and the like, the interaction between law and social change, while often of considerable social and economic importance, is predominantly a matter of give and take between relatively small and highly trained professional opinion on the one side, and the courts or, in certain cases, the legislature, on the other side. In this field are such matters as the erosion of the contributory negligence rule evolved by the common law, the recognition of comparative negligence in England and a number of American jurisdictions, and the consequent apportionment of damages in proportion to the respective fault of the parties; liability of occupiers of land to various categories of visitors, formal validity of wills made abroad, or changes in the rule against perpetuities. These matters are generally the jealously guarded preserve of the trained lawyer, and they have a subordinate place in the attention of the legislative bodies which are preoccupied with matters of more obvious and popular concern to the community at large. But while the necessary corollary should be the adaptation of the law by an interplay of social pressure and judicial response, the courts have often been handicapped, notably in the common-law jurisdictions, by their adherence to precedent and a frequent disinclination to take note of changes in public opinion.[15] After the English House of Lords had resolutely refused to effect the necessary simplification and rationalization of the liability of occupiers of land to visitors, despite the fluid state of the precedents and a great deal of professional writing on the subject, it was necessary to appoint a Royal Commission and, subsequently, to enact legislation to reform this branch of the law. The same was true some years earlier of the law of comparative negligence, which, in the United States, still varies from state to state. In some fields, the courts are unable to effect the necessary reform of the common law not only because of long tradition, but because the interests of governments are too closely involved. The British Crown Proceedings Act of 1947 and, less extensively, the American Federal Tort Claims Act of 1946 have abolished most of the archaic and socially untenable rule of immunity of governments from suit in contract and tort, but in the majority of the American jurisdictions the rule survives, wholly or in part.[16] While the courts with few exceptions feel unable to abolish it, State legislatures and governments seldom feel impelled to take action. In the field of family law, some relations are capable of judicial adjustments; others are too fundamental to respond to any legislative change. Generally, legislative reform has been necessary to effect the adjustment of the property rights of the married woman to her drastically changed position in the modern Western world. Sometimes, a matter of what is normally 'lawyers' law' becomes entangled with State policy in a different field. One of the most fundamental differences between the civil and the common law is that between the various systems of community property – embodied, in one form or another, in all contemporary civil codes – and the system of separation of property enshrined in the common law. But some of the western and southern jurisdictions in the United States have community-property systems based on former French or Spanish affiliations. When some years ago, these states applied the community-property system to income-tax law by enabling husbands and wives to split their total joint income for income-tax purposes, a number of common-law jurisdictions proceeded to introduce community property solely for the purpose of legislating corresponding tax concessions. When the Federal Tax Law made the joint income-tax return universal, they speedily reverted to their traditional common-law system. Again, there are certain branches of family law in which only legislation can create a new status. The adoption and legitimation of children responds to a widely felt need, and it is overwhelmingly approved by contemporary public opinion. It is only legislative action which can create the status of an adopted or legitimated child, for such a status requires a specific regulation of the respective rights and duties, as between the various parties concerned, and administrative machinery, which cannot be effected by judicial adaptation.[17]

## THE VARIOUS PATTERNS OF DEMOCRACY, AND LEGAL CHANGE

The contemporary Constitutions of France, Great Britain, India, West Germany, and the United States can all be characterized as democratic, but such are the differences in their constitutional structure that the interchange between social opinion and the legislative process is greatly affected. In the parliamentary system developed by Great Britain, and adopted by the major Dominions of the British Commonwealth, a two-party pattern prevails. The government formed by the victorious party almost invariably controls a safe majority for a number of years, and is therefore usually able to push through important legislative measures. Cabinet leadership and government initiative are decisive, in relation to the law-making role of the private Member of Parliament, who is only occasionally able to put through a major legislative measure, with a mixture of luck and dogged persistence.

The importance of government leadership and predominance in the legislative process is further enhanced where a parliamentary system of the type just described goes together with the overwhelming – and more than temporary – predominance of one party. This is the case in contemporary India, or in Burma, where the Government Party has not only been the architect of political independence, but has, since attainment of independence, enjoyed an overwhelming majority.

Where, as in the French Fourth Republic or in the Weimar Republic, the parliamentary régime is built upon a plurality of parties – some representing sectional interests rather than national political movements – none of which is able to govern singly, so that governments are formed by shifting and unstable coalitions of a number of parties, the scales are more heavily weighted against the translation of new social developments into legislative reform. For such reforms demand positive action, and the difficulty of obtaining agreement among coalition partners, usually united only in a *'mariage de convenance'* and deeply divided over major issues, means, in effect, a veto power of any one of the partners. Thus, French Socialists and Popular Republicans have found themselves usually united over questions of international policy and social reform, but deeply divided over questions of educational policy. On the other hand, Left and Right are sharply divided over questions of foreign and colonial policy. There are deep conflicts between the various parties over questions of tax policy and social services. The result is more often than not a maximum of debate and a minimum of legislative action.

It should, however, be pointed out that the unofficial veto power of minority groups obtains in all democracies, to a greater or lesser extent, and that it need not necessarily find organized expression in any one political party. In terms of legal and social reform, democracy means implementation of the will of the majority only with very severe restrictions. Thus a well-organized and influential minority can delay changes to which it objects strongly almost indefinitely, even though a majority of the people might favour it. There is, for example, a widespread movement for the establishment of public birth-control and family advice centres, as one means of reducing the countless thousands of illegal abortions performed annually in all industrialized countries where abortion is not legalized or put under public guidance. In many of the American states, e.g. in the State of New York, determined Catholic opposition to any form of official sanction of birth-control makes the establishment of such centres virtually impossible, even though a majority of the people might favour them. As long as we are concerned with criminal sanctions, e.g. for suicide, infanticide, abortion in cases of extreme necessity, such as imminent danger to health or rape,[18] it is somewhat easier to effect a tacit legal change by abstention from prosecution, by verdicts of acquittal, or by a permanent judicial fiction such as that of the state of 'unsound mind', invariably presumed nowadays in the case of suicide. This, however, affords no relief where positive action is required, for example, by the establishment of birth-control clinics, or a change in the legal status of illegitimate children.

## Legal Change in Federal Systems

Many obstacles to the translation of social into legal change are offered by federal constitutions. A federal system is predicated on a balance of power. Although there are significant differences between various federal States, the preponderant effect of the system of balances is to reduce the power of government and, with it, the power of positive action.

While each federal structure has its particular composite of checks and counter-checks, many of them based on historical and local characteristics, three major factors, each tending to retard legislative action and response to new social needs, are built into the federal system as such:

First, the distribution of powers between Federation and States. As recent history has shown, it does not make much difference whether the Federation or the States have the residuary legislative power. In Australia, it is the Commonwealth, in Canada it is the Provinces which have enumerated legislative powers. Yet, the constitutionality of the so-called Canadian New Deal legislation of the early thirties was invalidated by the Privy Council, then the highest constitutional tribunal for Canada, by a narrow interpretation of the power of the Dominion to legislate for 'peace, order, and good government' in the light of the provincial powers to legislate for 'property and civil rights'.[19] On the other hand, the Australian High Court limited the apparently unambiguous power of the Commonwealth to legislate in respect to banking by extending the meaning of another clause of the Constitution, guaranteeing the free flow of trade, so as to turn it into a protection of individual freedom to trade, as an implied constitutional prohibition of the nationalization of banking.[20] During the decade following the initiation of the 'New Deal' in the United States, a considerable proportion of the social-service legislation, in regard to collective bargaining, protection of children and women, minimum standards, etc., was effected and judicially upheld by means of the Inter-state Commerce Clause. The power of the Federation in matters of inter-state commerce was read so as to include compliance with certain social standards.[21]

Overwhelmingly, however, the distribution of powers between the Federation and the States acts as a brake. As there is almost invariably an interlocking of various subject-matters, which are seldom united either in Federal or State hands, it is often possible, as we have just seen, to emphasize either the one or the other aspect. In cases of serious doubt, necessary legislation will not be initiated. Even the approval by a constitutional organ specially constituted to safeguard the interest of the States, such as the United States Senate or the German *Bundesrat*, will not bring about a change which any one of the States may challenge as being an infringement of its reserve. Thus, the States of the 'deep South', today, claim, in effect, that any legislative or judicial federal power in regard to the constitutionally guaranteed equality of races is implicitly limited by the State power in regard to education.

The second major built-in brake lies in the separation of functions between the three branches of government. In the typical modern federation, such as the United States, Australia, Canada, India, and West Germany (but not Switzerland), the principal restraining function is exercised by the Supreme Court of the country, which passes the final verdict on the constitutionality of both Federal and State legislation. The immense influence which the exercise of this power can have on the social structure of a country is illustrated by the effective postponement of social-security legislation in the United States, through the interpretation given by the Supreme Court for many decades to both Federal and State Acts enacting compulsory social standards as being an unconstitutional violation of the 'due process' clauses; a parallel, of shorter duration, is the invalidation of the social-security legislation of Canada, until an amendment of the British North America Act was passed. Given the general pattern of distribution of functions between Federal and State governments, the court can decisively influence the national pattern of social welfare, transport and communications, trade and business, education, and many other vital fields.

The power of the court – acting negatively, through the striking down of legislation, not positively through the stimulus to new legislation – is greatly increased where a constitution embodies a 'Bill of Rights'.[22] This is the case, notably in the Constitution of the United States, and the post-war Constitutions of West Germany and India, but not in the Federal Constitutions of Australia and Canada. The basic freedoms usually enshrined in such Bills of Rights – of worship, speech, association, movement, property, and trade – and the equalities guaranteed in regard to race, sex, religion, are inevitably of such sweeping and general character that the role of interpreter comes close to that of the legislator. The judicial function merges with the policy-making function. This is hardly a matter of choice for the court, but of necessity. A court which, as in *Plessy* v. *Ferguson*,[23] interprets the constitution as guaranteeing 'separate but equal', but not integrated, facilities of education for whites and negroes is as much a policy-maker as a court which interprets the constitution as guaranteeing complete equality in every respect, including the integration of schools.[24] The constitution is the basic law of the country, designed to endure for a long time, and notoriously difficult to amend. If, as is claimed by some, the interpretation of the court should strictly accord with the intentions of the makers of the constitution at the time of its enactment, this would mean, for example, that a clause such as the Inter-state Commerce Clause has the same meaning in the 1950s as in the pre-industrial eighteenth century.[25]

As we have seen, the British parliamentary pattern, as it prevails in the Federations of Australia and Canada, shows a high degree of conformity between the executive and legislature. By contrast, the United States Constitution imposes a further vital check on the adaptation of law to social change by the rigid separation of the executive and legislature. Even in the not too frequent cases of coincidence of Presidential and Congressional control, executive initiative meets with a multitude of obstacles in the legislature. In the American system of government, these checks operate, first, through a multitude of legislative committees, often controlled by a majority hostile to the executive; and, secondly, through the duplication of the legislative process in the two Houses of Congress, where one of them, the Senate, incorporates the federal element. The federal element is, in some federations, notably the United States, further reinforced by the weighting of votes and influence in favour of the smaller states.[26] In the United States Senate, each of the fifty states is represented by two Senators. Although, in due course, the progressive industrialization and urbanization of the country may diminish the gap between the outlook of the highly industrialized, densely populated major states on the one part, and the smaller, rural states on the other part, it is still significant. The social problems, for example, of Vermont or Nebraska, are not the same as those of New York or California. But the influence of the smaller states – which will usually, though not invariably, feel far less impelled than the larger industrialized states to enact legislation in response to social demands coming from urbanized and industrialized regions – will, in the Senate, be disproportionately large. It is usually only in times of major emergencies – war, major economic depressions, or natural catastrophes of nation-wide proportions – that these divergent pulls can be overcome, as, for example, in the early years of the New Deal. Normally, the factors of conservatism and inertia will retard or impede positive action, e.g., in the field of economic aid for foreign countries, the reorganization of the armed services, or the extension of federal aid to schools and other educational institutions.

### CONCLUSIONS

We have seen that in a democratic system of State organization there is a great variety of interactions between social evolution and legal change. The stimulus may come from a variety of sources, some of which have been briefly surveyed. There may be the slowly growing pressure of changed patterns and norms of social life, creating an increasing gap between the facts of life and the law, to which the latter must eventually respond. There may be the sudden imperious demand of a national emergency, for a redistribution of natural resources or a new standard of social justice. There may be a far-sighted initiative of a small group of individuals, slowly moulding official opinion until the time is ripe for action. There may be a technical injustice or inconsistency of the law demanding correction. There may be new scientific developments calling for new forms of legal evidence (such as acceptance of blood-group tests for the negative proof of paternity).

The law responds in various ways, too. The speed and manner of its response is usually proportionate to the degree of social pressure. It is also influenced by the constitutional structure. But circumstances and personalities may hasten or retard the response. In the sphere of 'political law' or where a new status is created, legislative action is required. In other fields, there is a give and take between legislative and judicial remedial action, in part determined by the subject-matter but in part by the changing and diverse attitudes of legislators and judges.

# The Courts and the Evolution of the Law

Every legal order, federal or unitary, whether of civilian or common-law background, faces the problem of the role of the court in the evolution of law.

This problem has become increasingly articulate and complex in the present century. Until the turn of the century the opinion prevailed in theory and practice that there was a clear-cut division between the spheres of the legislator and the judiciary. It was the function of the former to make the laws, and of the latter to apply them. Perhaps this simple doctrine, propounded by the analytical jurisprudence of both English and Continental provenance, would have been less self-confident if it had had a closer acquaintance with, and understanding of, the role of the Supreme Court in the United States. However, despite the natural-law flavour of many of the decisions of that latter Court, it seemed, itself, predominantly convinced of the absence of any intention on its part to interpret the Constitution according to any but self-evident principles of construction.

It is difficult to say whether it was primarily the increasing challenge of new social problems, or a gradual revolution in thinking, or – as the present author would be inclined to think – an interaction of these factors, that, towards the turn of the century, led writers and, subsequently, courts in the leading countries of the Western world to challenge the assumptions so easily held during the nineteenth century.

When the French jurist, Gény, in a work first published in 1899,[1] looked back on nearly a century of legal developments under the Code Civil, he found that the courts had transformed the Code through creative interpretation in many vital respects. French courts have, for example, adapted the delict provisions of the Code Civil (articles 1382–6) to the new realities of industrial accidents, of railway traffic, motor-cars, and aeroplanes. The results of such thought were apparent in the German Civil Code of 1900, whose general clauses have enabled the German courts to cope with such tremendous upheavals as the great inflation following the First World War or to develop a comprehensive law of unfair competition.[2]

Even more clearly, the Swiss Civil Code of 1907 directs the judge to decide as if he were a legislator when he finds a gap in the law, guided by 'approved legal doctrine and judicial tradition'. A more recent version of the same idea is article 3 of the Italian Civil Code of 1942, which directs the court, in cases that remain doubtful after the exhaustion of normal methods of construction, to decide 'according to the general principles of the jurisprudential organization of the State'.

From very different premises, English and American jurists came to conclusions not very different from those of the Continental jurists and legislators. Dicey, in his *Law and Public Opinion in England during the Nineteenth Century*,[3] analysed the transition from the liberal premises of Benthamite philosophy to the increasing importance of active social-service legislation, and the beginnings of the collectivist society which is now in full blossom.

In the United States, over half a century ago, Roscoe Pound started to examine law and legal problems from the point of view of conflicting interests and values. The examination, not only of problems of constitutional law, but of common law, labour law, criminal law, and other fields, led Pound, and the many jurists who developed and modified his approach, to see law predominantly as an instrument of social engineering in which conflicting pulls of political philosophy, economic interests, ethical values, constantly struggle for recognition against a background of history, tradition, and legal technique. Mr Justice Cardozo formulated the result of a life-time of reflection and practical experience in the following terms[4]:

. . . logic and history, and custom, and utility, and the accepted standards of right conduct, are the forces which singly or in combination shape the progress of the law. Which of these forces shall dominate in any case, must depend largely upon the comparative importance or value of the social interests that will be thereby promoted or impaired. One of the most fundamental social interests is that law shall be uniform and impartial. There must be nothing in its action that savours of prejudice or even arbitrary whim or fitfulness. Therefore in the main there shall be adherence to precedent. There shall be symmetrical development, consistently with history or custom when history or custom has been the motive force, or the chief one, in giving shape to existing rules, and with logic or philosophy when the motive power has been theirs. But symmetrical development may be bought at too high a price. Uniformity ceases to be a good when it becomes uniformity of oppression. The social interest served by symmetry or certainty must then be balanced against the social interest served by equity and fairness or other elements of social welfare. These may enjoin upon the judge the duty of drawing the line at another angle, of staking the path along new courses, of marking a new point of departure from which others who come after him will set out upon their journey.

If you ask how he is to know when one interest outweighs another, I can only answer that he must get his knowledge just as the legislator gets it, from experience and study and reflection; in brief, from life itself. Here, indeed, is the point of contact between the legislator's work and his.

Even before the First World War the growing pressure of new industrial and technical developments, of new social and political philosophies, had led jurists of many countries, independently of each other, to think about law in new terms: to see it primarily as an instrument of social evolution. Legal logic and techniques came to be seen as elements, but by no means the sole, or even the predominant factor, in the unending race between law and new social problems.

### PRECEDENT AND SOCIAL CHANGE IN THE COMMON LAW

Since the First World War the tempo of social change has accelerated beyond all imagination. With it, the challenge to the law has become more powerful and urgent. We have seen that many years ago, leading jurists and judges concurred that it was not only the right but the duty of the judge to take note of fundamental changes in public opinion. Indeed, it is almost certain that the common law would no longer exist if great judges had not from time to time accepted the challenge and boldly laid down new principles to meet new social problems. The decisions which reflect such judicial revolutions are relatively few in number, but they stand out as landmarks. Every one of them symbolizes a new social epoch and has laid the foundations on which hundreds of elaborations or routine decisions can be built up. A few examples may suffice to illustrate this point.

When Blackburn J. formulated the rule in *Rylands* v. *Fletcher*,[5] he began to adapt the principles of tort liability to the era of expanding industrial enterprise in a once predominantly agricultural society.[6] The technique by which that great judge accomplished this feat was the collection, synthesis, and remoulding of several instances of liability which, in Dean Wigmore's language,

wandered about, unhoused and unshepherded, except for a casual attention, in the pathless fields of jurisprudence, until they were met by the master-mind of Mr Justice Blackburn who guided them to the safe fold where they have since rested. In a sentence epochal in its consequences this judge coordinated them all in their true category.

Another judgement of Blackburn J.[7] laid the foundations for the principle of legal liability of public authorities, now of outstanding importance in the age of government enterprise.

The twentieth-century counterpart of the rule in *Rylands* v. *Fletcher*,[8] the juridical creation of a direct action by a user or consumer against the manufacturer of a faulty product, is technically simply an abandonment of the principle that *A*, if contractually liable to *B*, cannot simultaneously be liable in tort for the same action or omission to *C*. But sociologically, it means the judicial recognition of the age of mass manufacture and standardized products, an age in which the economic position of the retailer is vitally changed. In the field of contract, the development of the doctrine of frustration was stimulated by the upheavals of the First and Second World Wars. The doctrine has, in English and American law, not yet assumed the same significance as on the Continent, mainly because the social and economic upheavals have not been as great. The main impetus was given to it by the requisitioning of the British Merchant Navy in the First World War, an event of basic economic importance in a maritime nation. It was the shattering inflation following the First World War which led the German courts to develop the doctrine of frustration of contract from certain general clauses in the German Civil Code. It became an instrument for the judicial adjustment of obligations which had become grossly unjust as a result of drastic currency devaluation. This doctrine has had great influence on other Continental systems such as French, Swiss, and Greek law. That its significance in English law has also increased is shown by some recent decisions of the Court of Appeal.[9] While the doctrine of frustration is accepted in American law, its practical impact has been small, because the economy of the United States has not so far been basically shaken by wars or inflations. The two most interesting decisions on the subject were characteristically provoked by a priority system for automobiles established during the Second World War,[10] and a severe shortage of certain materials caused by the Korean War.[11] In neither case was the disturbance of the contract situation found drastic enough to justify exoneration of the party affected.

The principle of *stare decisis* has set certain limits to judicial lawmaking which are apparent in the fate of the doctrine of common employment. Invented at a time when judges thought in terms of patriarchal households and small-scale business,[12] it has long been found utterly unsuited to the facts of modern industrial employment. In a number of decisions, the House of Lords whittled down the doctrine, but was unable to abolish it.[13] This was eventually accomplished by the legislator through the Law Reform (Personal Injuries) Act, 1948.

Another area in which the courts have played an important role in the adjustment of law to new social realities is the field of matrimonial relations. Here, English courts have, in recent years, introduced certain ideas of community property into the settlement of property issues between husband and wife.[14]

Yet the majority of the British and Commonwealth judges still take the view that there is a difference, not only of degree, but of kind, between the making of the law – which is the legislator's field – and the application of the law, which is the judge's domain. This view was put in blunt terms by Lord Jowitt L.C. on the occasion of the Seventh Legal Convention of the Law Council of Australia[15]:

Please do not get yourself into the frame of mind of entrusting to the judges the working out of a whole new set of principles which does accord with the requirements of modern conditions. Leave that to the legislature, and leave us to confine ourselves to trying to find out what the law is.

These observations were occasioned by the discussion of a learned paper by Mr Justice Fullagar of the High Court of Australia, dealing with the problem of 'Liability for Representations at Common Law', a problem recently underlined by the decision of the Court of Appeal in *Candler* v. *Crane, Christmas & Co.*[16] The discussion showed up clearly the main weakness in Lord Jowitt's contention: the extreme difficulty, in many cases – for example, in regard to the present scope of the rule in *Donoghue* v. *Stevenson* – of discovering what the law is. It is the uncertainties of the law which have compelled the courts to develop the law in some direction. As a result, the law of tort of today bears little resemblance to that of fifty years ago. The clear-cut division between the law as it is and the law as it ought to be does not exist.

The history of the common law has been a constant give and take between consolidation and progress, between the legal technicians and the creative jurists. In the past, the tempo of social change was very much less rapid than it is today, and it cannot be assumed that the 'lawyer's law' will always remain a prerogative of the professional lawyer, a backwater removed from urgent social and political problems. What could once be regarded as more or less technical 'lawyers' law', may today be a matter of urgent economic and social policy. There is no more telling illustration of this shift than the recent transfer of the whole field of restrictive trade practices from the common-law domain – where it has rested, in England, for centuries – to a statutory regulation which entrusts the administration of this vital sphere of national economic policy to a mixture of administrative commissions, governmental authorities, and, more recently, a special tribunal composed of a majority of non-lawyers instead of the law courts.[17] Nor can this transfer of emphasis and responsibilities simply be attributed to a kind of 'parvenu' intrusion of modern regulatory and Welfare State policies into the sacred domain of judge-made law.

As will be shown later in this book, it is essentially the stubborn refusal of the English courts to face the economic and policy issues inherent in the field of restrictive-trade covenants and practices that is in large part responsible for recent British statutory developments.

Those who oppose the notion that law courts should take an active part in the adaptation of law to social problems usually argue that to do so would sacrifice certainty, the primary virtue of the law, to utility. If adhesion to legal technique and the inclusion of value-judgements had achieved certainty, the contention would have force. Certainty is one of the paramount objectives of law. It is usually achieved in the thousands of routine decisions which quantitatively make up the bulk of the law. But in the relatively small number of leading cases which give direction to hundreds of others, stability and certainty have seldom been either aimed at or achieved. The distinction between *ratio decidendi* and *obiter dictum*, the differentiation of cases on facts, the reliance on one or the other judgement in a decision by a higher court, and many other factors give a choice vastly wider than is apparent on the surface. The divergences outlined in the cases mentioned earlier cannot be accounted for by technical arguments or legal logic. These are indispensable but highly flexible instruments of legal reasoning. They are the servants, not the masters. When they are built up into the position of masters, it is by choice, not by necessity.[18]

Nor is the inevitability of the creative function of the courts in the interpretation of the law challenged by the leading modern representatives of analytical jurisprudence. The Vienna School, led by Merkl and Kelsen, has long recognized, in its Stufentheorie, that the judicial function, while far more circumscribed in the freedom to create law than the legislature, nevertheless involves the making of law in the process of applying the norm to individual facts. However, the Vienna School refuses to indicate the principles by which this creative judicial process should be guided, since this is held to be outside the task of a 'pure legal science'. Similarly a modern English analytical jurist, who has concentrated on the elucidation of the meaning of legal concept, has this to say in his most recent contribution[19]:

> There must be a core of settled meaning, but there will be, as well, a penumbra of debatable cases in which words are neither obviously applicable nor obviously ruled out. . . .
> We may call the problems which arise outside the hard core of standard instances of settled meaning 'problems of the penumbra'; they are always with us whether in relation to such trivial things as the regulation of the use of the public park or in relation to the multi-dimensional generalities of a constitution. If a penumbra of uncertainty must surround all legal rules, then their application to specific cases in the penumbral area cannot be a matter of logical deduction, and so deductive reasoning, which for generations has been cherished as the very perfection of human reasoning, cannot serve as a model for what judges, or indeed anyone, should do in bringing particular cases under general rules. In this area men cannot live by deduction alone. And it follows that if legal arguments and legal decisions of penumbral questions are to be rational, their rationality must lie in something other than a logical relation to premises. . . .
> . . . instead of saying that the recurrence of penumbral questions shows us that legal rules are essentially incomplete, and that, when they fail to determine decisions, judges must legislate and so exercise a creative choice between alternatives, we shall say that the social policies which guide the judges' choice are in a sense there for them to discover; the judges are only 'drawing out' of the rule what, if it is properly understood, is 'latent' within it. . . .

Once it is admitted that there is an area of uncertainty in the interpretation of (common-law or statutory) concepts, the question whether the solution to a doubtful situation is found by drawing out 'a latent meaning', or by a creative intepretation, becomes mere verbal quibbling.[20] No serious student of the problem has ever disputed that certain terms, such as 'bankruptcy' or 'vehicle' have a greater area of settled interpretation than others, such as 'freedom of speech' or 'clear and present danger'. The freedom, and the agony, of choice does, indeed, greatly differ from case to case. This increases the urgency of our task to formulate rational guiding lines whether or not this is defined as part of the process of finding the law as it is, or an infusion of the law as it ought to be.[21]

The analysis of recent trends in the common law thus underlines the theoretical observations made earlier in this chapter. The Swiss and Italian Civil Codes, the conclusions reached by Gény in France, by Holmes, Stone, or Cardozo in America, by Dicey or Lord Wright in England, express the same thought in different ways. In his application of precedent, as in the interpretation of statutes, the judge must take note of major shifts in public opinion and social policy, of development sufficiently fundamental to be accepted by the consensus of public opinion and to be expressed by the general trend in legislative policy. The theoretical formulation of such an approach must always remain somewhat vague, for the ways in which changes in public opinion express themselves in a democratic society are many and it is not an easy task for a court to fix the borderline between accepted evolutions in public opinion, on the one hand, and personal philosophy or prejudice, on the other.

It is, however, not difficult to illustrate by concrete examples the distinction between personal idiosyncrasy and the incorporation of new social policies in the administration of the law.[22] Any court of a contemporary industrialized country must, for example, recognize collective bargaining and labour organization as a legitimate and commonly accepted instrument of social action. One result is the shrinking of the tort of conspiracy. What was, fifty years ago, regarded as personal malice, is now juridically recognized as a legitimate weapon in the economic struggle between organized social groups.[23] The Supreme Court of the United States, as late as 1936[24] regarded a minimum wage act as an unconstitutional interference with the freedom of property. Twenty years later such a denial would not be seriously contemplated. As one problem is solved, a new one opens up. Trade unions are no longer outlaws, or underdogs, but powerful and often monopolistic organizations. Today, the problem of the closed shop shows the clash between two equally accepted legal principles: the right to bargain collectively and the freedom of the individual to choose his place of work and his associations. Again, contemporary British and American courts must base their decisions on the principle of the equality of races, religions, and sexes. Practical expressions of this trend are the recent decisions of the United States Supreme Court prohibiting discrimination against negroes,[25] or the award of damages by an English court for violation of a common-law right[26] to a coloured person who had been refused admittance to a public hotel. A corresponding evolution in the field of public law is the increasing rejection of crown privileges in the field of civil liabilities, privileges which are incompatible both with the rule of law in a democracy and the growing role of government in commercial and industrial enterprise. Unfortunately, both British and American courts, but particularly the former, have signally failed to apply the logic of universally expanding government functions to the important problem of government immunities in international law.

## STATUTORY INTERPRETATION AND THE CONFLICT OF VALUES

The clash of values and interests, the conflict between different judicial approaches, is no less marked in the interpretation of statutes that it is in the common law. The controversy between the 'literal' and 'liberal' theories of statutory interpretation corresponds closely to that between the adherents of a static and a dynamic interpretation. The former regard the interpretation of a statute as essentially an exercise in grammar, based on a strict distinction between the legislative and the interpretative function. The latter regard it as a process of purposeful collaboration based on an understanding of the legislative purpose, for which the rules of *Heydon's Case* (1584) or Plowden's celebrated note on *Eyston* v. *Studd*[27] can still serve as a guide:

And in order to form a right judgement when the letter of a statute is restrained, and when enlarged, by equity, it is a good way, when you peruse a statute, to suppose that the law-maker is present, and that you have asked him the question you want to know touching the equity; then you must give yourself such an answer as you imagine he would have done, if he had been present. . . . And if the law-maker would have followed the equity, notwithstanding the words of the law . . . you may safely do the like. . . .

To illustrate the problem by a few recent cases in different fields: In a recent Canadian case,[28] the fortuitous profits of private trading clashed with the claim of government – a non-Socialist government – to redistribute profits caused by governmental price regulation in the interest of the community. This conflict was barely hidden by a grammatical controversy about the meaning of a clause in the National Emergency Transitional Powers Act. The English Court of Appeal,[29] some years ago, had to decide whether ministerial powers under a new Town and Country Planning Act superseded the terms of an agreement between a local authority and a private company concerning the development of an estate, a decision which plainly hung on the evaluation of the relation between old contractual ties and new legislative powers.

The Appeal Court of Wisconsin was recently faced with a choice between two conflicting statutory provisions – one authorizing the receivability of blood-group tests in evidence to determine the parentage of a child, the other burdening a party asserting the illegitimacy of a child born in wedlock with 'proof beyond all reasonable doubt' – when a mother, who had had intercourse with her husband eight months before delivery, swore that he was the father, while blood tests excluded all possibility of his fatherhood.[30] The decision depended on a balancing of the respective weight of two conflicting legislative directives, not on a logical choice.

Most important of all, the interpretation of constitutions constantly brings up conflicts of social principles. This conflict may appear in the interpretation of the 'property and civil rights' clause in the British North America Act, of the 'due process' clauses of the American Constitution, or of the 'freedom of trade, commerce, and intercourse' clause in the Australian Constitution; the basic social problems which appear in different legal forms are essentially the same.

Can we – as is so often contended – dismiss these social issues from our legal conscience by adhering to a 'strict' or 'technical' interpretation of statutes? This problem divides itself into two. First, is it correct to speak of statutes as a genus for purposes of interpretation? Do the same rules of interpretation apply to a written constitution and to a bankruptcy Act, a taxation Act, or a criminal statute? Second, if one set of rules is to be applied to all statutes, are they sufficiently clear and certain to eliminate conflicting interpretations? The assumption that, for purposes of interpretation, statutes are all of one kind is clearly implicit in the following observations recently made by a former President of the Canadian Bar Association[31]:

We have been fortunate in Canada, too, in the establishment of a tradition which has looked in the main to the legislatures rather than to the courts for the development of the law to meet novel conditions. Inevitably, under our federal constitution uncertainty has arisen on many occasions as to the competent legislative authority to deal with a particular subject-matter, but the courts have interpreted the statute which allocates legislative authority, the British North America Act, as a statute and have thus given certainty to our basic law at the sacrifice, of course, of elasticity. To lawyers who must advise clients certainty is the great virtue.

In an earlier analysis,[32] I have suggested that statutes are by no means all of one kind and that both judicial practice and principle indicate important differences between the rules of interpretation appropriate to different types of statutes. An eminently political and general document, such as a constitution, is not and cannot be treated in the same way as a statute concerned with the registration of land or with criminal procedure. Lord Jowitt, Lord Wright, Lord Greene, Mr Justice Dixon, and Mr Justice Frankfurter are among the eminent judges whose views were quoted for confirmation of such a differentiation.[33]

But even if it were assumed that there are uniform rules of interpretation for all types of statutes, the further question remains whether these rules are so clear, so technical, and so unpolitical in their character as to avoid any conflict of values. Technical rules are to a large extent self-contradictory, and in decisions of fundamental importance the issue has seldom turned on them. The House of Lords – generally more attached to 'strict' or 'technical' interpretations of statutes and precedents than any other high court of the common-law world – has not hesitated to depart from literal interpretation or established canons of construction when the problem at issue appeared sufficiently important to justify it.

In *Roberts* v. *Hopwood*,[34] a London Borough Council had fixed a minimum wage of £4 a week for all its employees, male and female. This, one should have thought, it had a clear power to do, under a statute which empowered local authorities to allow such wages 'as [they] may think fit'. Yet the House of Lords added the word 'reasonably' to this phrase, and then proceeded to quash the action of the council as unreasonable. On the other hand, in *Liversidge* v. *Anderson*,[35] the House was concerned with the interpretation of Defence Regulation 18B, which gave the Home Secretary certain powers of detention, where he had 'reasonable cause to believe' certain persons to be of hostile associations. This formulation had been adopted, after a parliamentary debate, in order to provide some check on the Home Secretary's discretion. But the majority, anxious this time to help the executive in a time of great emergency, refused to examine whether the Home Secretary had, in fact, had reasonable cause. In effect, 'where . . . . he *thinks* he has reasonable cause to believe' was substituted for 'had reasonable cause', a construction which Lord Atkin had little difficulty in showing was contrary to all precedent and to the usual canons of interpretation. In a post-war decision,[36] the Privy Council confirmed Lord Atkin's view when, in a clause virtually identical with 18B, it affirmed the right of judicial scrutiny as to whether an administrative authority had, in fact, acted reasonably, and all but dissented from *Liversidge* v. *Anderson*.

## SOCIAL CHANGE AND THE
## INTERPRETATION OF CONSTITUTIONS

The belief that the Privy Council and the Canadian courts have
avoided the political problems and tensions of the United States
Supreme Court by interpreting the British North America Act as a
'statute' is in conflict with the views of many eminent Canadian
constitutional authorities. Thus, Mr Justice MacDonald in his
survey of the *Constitution in a Changing World* had this to say:

> The impact of external change upon judicial decision, however, has
> not been as great as the character of that change might suggest or require;
> for, in the main, the Constitution has been approached as if it were –
> what it palpably is not – an ordinary statute; and one, moreover, to be
> interpreted by the evidences of the intention of its makers collectible
> from its own terms and scheme, rather than from authoritative guides
> to that intention known to every educated Canadian. Thus, in but few
> cases has the Privy Council sought for the meaning of terms rather than
> intention; and in still fewer has it allowed to such terms a meaning
> other than that which they bore in 1867.[37]

The interpretation of the British North America Act, especially
by the Privy Council, has been as fraught with political meaning as
that of the American Constitution by the Supreme Court of the
United States, and as far reaching in its social consequences.[38] And
this approach has not ensured certainty either of principle or of
precedent. The decisions on such matters as the Dominion's
residuary power, the treaty-making power, and the regulation of
trade and commerce are neither more consistent nor more certain
than those of any other court which interprets a document of a
political or social character.

A decision of the Supreme Court of the United States[39] illustrates
well the conflict of judicial approaches to a problem of constitutional interpretation which involves social and economic issues.
Under the Agriculture and Markets Law of the State of New York,
the Commissioner had refused a licence for an additional milk
distribution plant on the ground that the proposed expansion of the
petitioner's milk distribution facilities would reduce the milk supply
for local markets and result in destructive competition in a market
already adequately served. The approach to the problem revealed,
however, three distinct philosophies. The majority, led by Justice
Jackson, regarded the New York law as a violation of the principle
of free trade embodied in the commerce clause of the Federal Con-

stitution. A dissenting group (Justices Black and Murphy) regarded this view as an improper judicial interference with the legitimate regulating functions of government and as a revival of antiquated due process and *laissez faire* philosophies. A third group (Justices Frankfurter and Rutledge) took an intermediate position, regarding the issue as on balance between competing interests to be adjudged from case to case.

The three opinions in this case express the conflicting interpretations of state power and individual economic freedom, as reflected in the American Constitution. Such conflicts are inevitable where independent judges have to interpret static clauses in a dynamic society. It is not only the conflict of values and philosophies in a free society which produces such clashes, but also the frequent divergences in the application of general principles to concrete issues. Where the power of government is divided between a federation and its member states, advocacy of planning or *laissez faire* alone cannot resolve the conflict; for the further constitutional question arises whether, in a federation, there is an inviolable minimum of state powers which a federation cannot infringe by an expansive interpretation of taxing power, inter-state commerce, and of other powers to which modern social conditions give a meaning vastly different from the one it had at the time of the Founding Fathers. Moreover, judges in a free society will often deliberately check their own preferences because they regard even the appearance of a biased decision as more harmful than a result which they personally disapprove.[40] Even when the issue of principle is clear, the question remains, as in *Hood*'s case, how the exercise of a specific power should be classified. The discussion of principles can lead to a clarification of issues. It cannot eliminate the responsibility of decision in a given issue.

The much attacked judgements of the United States Supreme Court, whether unanimous or divided, reflect and interpret a real world, a world of conflict and tensions, of uncertainties and divided opinions. They do not pretend that the application of the general formulas of the Constitution to the complexities of a concrete problem is a simple task. True to the tradition of Holmes, Brandeis, Cardozo, Stone, the Court no longer confuses – as it once did – the duty to be as impartial and detached as the conflicts of human minds permit with the illusion that political problems are not political problems, an illusion to which British courts are so often prone.

The New Deal period served as the main catalyst for the Court's thinking. For a few years, the conservative majority of the Court prevailed in its stubborn adherence to its well-entrenched due-process philosophy, invalidating the main pieces of the new edifice of social legislation. The reappraisal came when the dissident minority, for which Justice Stone had become the principal spokes-man in succession to Justice Holmes, was converted into a majority, through the accession of Chief Justice Hughes and Justice Roberts. In a famous trilogy of decisions in 1937,[41] the Court upheld the collective-bargaining principle of the new labour legislation, the new social-security legislation, and a minimum-wage statute. It not only abandoned the attitude, which it had maintained for so long, that such regulatory interferences on the part of the elected legisla-ture constituted a violation of 'due process', which it had elevated from a procedural safeguard into a natural-law principle of *laissez faire*. What is more important, it came to adopt the attitude of restraint long advocated in regard to measures of social and econo-mic reform by Holmes, Stone, and others, that the Court could not substitute itself as a non-elected legislator for the will of the elected legislator, except in cases of manifest violation of the Constitution.[42] Through all the subsequent vicissitudes and controversies, the Court has generally maintained this attitude of respect for the expressed will of the legislator. It has not, however, been able to escape other and no less bitter ideological battles. The intensity of the 'cold war', and the often hysterical accusations levelled in the less responsible Press and in Congressional committees against persons and organi-zations alleged, with more or less reason, to be subversive, have forced the Court to draw a line between the legitimate concerns of national security and the irreducible minimum safeguards of individual liberty in a Constitutional democracy.

The issue of equality, regardless of nation, race, or colour – an issue over which the Civil War was fought and which is enshrined in the Bill of Rights of the United States Constitution – has been another vital matter in which the Supreme Court has been com-pelled to reappraise the hierarchy of values explicit or implicit in the Constitution. Here the Court has, over the last fifteen years, acted with remarkable unanimity, at the cost of bitterly alienating some sections of public opinion, especially in the deep South. It has steadily reversed the priority of constitutional values by according to government and legislature the right to experiment in social affairs, and, on the other hand, affirming far more strongly than at any previous time the substantive meaning of racial equality. Proceeding from the condemnation of discriminatory practices and laws in elections, including primaries, to the condemnation of separate university facilities for whites and Negroes, the Court finally, in 1954,[43] condemned the system of separate public schools for whites and Negroes, prevalent in the South, and with it, specifically over-ruled its own previous 'equal but separate facilities' doctrine of *Plessy* v. *Ferguson*.[44]

Normally, controversies about the proper canons of interpreta-tion of a constitution remain a matter of essentially professional concern. But when they touch vital political and social questions they may have far deeper repercussions. The prolonged refusal of the Supreme Court, during the early phase of the New Deal reforms, to recognize the constitutionality of some of its most impor-tant statutory measures led President Roosevelt to his – fortunately unsuccessful – attempt to alter the law governing the composition of the Court, so as to be able to fill the newly arising vacancies with nominees of his choice. The crisis was eventually solved by the above-mentioned change in the attitude of the Court. At the present time, a succession of decisions, which have re-interpreted various aspects of the Constitution, in such matters as the constitutionality of 'separate but equal' facilities for the education of whites and Negroes[45] or the relation of Federal to State power, in criminal prosecutions,[46] or the constitutionality of various state statutes deal-ing with 'subversive activities', as being improper interferences with the constitutionally protected liberties of the citizen,[47] or the limits put to Congressional investigation by the First Amendment,[48] have led to a nation-wide discussion, both in professional and non-professional circles, of the proper function of the Court in the interpretation of the Constitution. Unfortunately, though not sur-prisingly, a dispassionate approach to the infinitely complex prob-lem of balance in constitutional interpretation has, in the great majority of cases, given way to partisanship for or against the particular decisions involved. Some of those who, before the Court's change of posture in 1937, condemned judicial obstruction of legisla-tive reforms as an improper infusion of reactionary political beliefs into the arbitral function of a Constitutional Court, now see in the Court a vital bulwark of basic liberties against popular hysterias and administrative or legislative pressures. On the other hand, many of those who, in the middle thirties, regarded the Supreme Court's sweeping interpretation of the due process clauses, and the conse-quent invalidation of the New Deal legislation, as the only solid bulwark of a 'government under laws' against the arbitrary will of legislators, consider the Court's present emphasis on constitutional liberties as an intolerable interference with the will of the legislator.

Serious lawyers as well as laymen have again advanced the proposition that the Court must stick to the interpretation of the Constitution as it can be deduced from the actual or presumed intention of the Founding Fathers.[49] This patently absurd proposition can best be answered in the words of the most honoured of contemporary American judges, himself a critic of some of the recent judgements of the Supreme Court[50]:

> Not only is it true that, 'if by the statement that what the Constitution meant at the time of its adoption is what it means today it is intended to say that the great clauses of the Constitution must be confined to the interpretation which the framers, with the conditions and outlook of their time, would have placed upon them, the statement carries its own refutation', but it is also impossible to fabricate how the 'Framers' would have answered the problems that arise in a modern society had they been reared in the civilization that has produced those problems. We should indeed have to be sorcerers to conjure up how they would have responded.

Far more serious is the revival of the time-worn thesis that the Court should 'apply', but not 'make', the law, that it should not intrude into the field of policy-making; for this has found the qualified approval of the Conference of Chief Justices held in August, 1958. In a resolution adopted by 38 votes against 8 dissenters, the Conference resolved, *inter alia*:

> That this Conference, while recognizing that the application of constitutional rules to changed conditions must be sufficiently flexible as to make such rules adaptable to altered conditions, believes that a fundamental purpose of having a written constitution is to promote the certainty and stability of the provisions of law set forth in such a constitution.
>
> That this Conference hereby respectfully urges that the Supreme Court of the United States, in exercising the great powers confided to it for the determination of questions as to the allocation and extent of national and state powers, respectively, and as to the validity under the federal Constitution of the exercise of powers reserved to the states, exercise one of the greatest of all judicial powers – the power of judicial self-restraint – by recognizing and giving effect to the difference between that which, on the one hand, the Constitution may prescribe or permit, and that which, on the other, a majority of the Supreme Court, as from time to time constituted, may deem desirable or undesirable, to the end that our system of federalism may continue to function with and through the preservation of local self-government.

Neither the Conference nor any responsible critic advocates that the Supreme Court of the United States should adopt the strict doctrine of *stare decisis*, in accordance with that of the British House of Lords – which does not interpret a federal constitution. In the elaborate Report accompanying the resolution,[51] one looks in vain for any guidance on the distinction between application of law and policy-making, other than a criticism of specific decisions and a general admonition to caution:

> It is our earnest hope which we respectfully express, that that great Court exercise to the full its power of judicial self-restraint by adhering firmly to its tremendous, strictly judicial powers and by eschewing, so far as possible, the exercise of essentially legislative powers when it is called upon to decide questions involving the validity of state action, whether it deems such action wise or unwise.

The vagueness and, indeed, emptiness of the attempted distinction between interpretations, alleged to apply existing law, and those alleged to make policy, was pointed out by one of the dissenters, the Chief Justice of New Jersey (Weintraub c.j.):

> It would hardly be a justifiable criticism to say the Supreme Court engages in a process of evaluation and judgement. The Constitution does not offer a literal, definitive answer to the awesome problems which confront the Court. One may read the commerce clause, the due-process clause, the equal-protection clause, a thousand times and still not detect the slightest clue to the proper decision. The answer must be found elsewhere. The constitutional framework, as we all know, is a mere skeleton expression of governmental power and individual rights. The actual contours of those powers and rights must be determined in the context of changing conditions, by a process which is more than a mere mechanical application of a constitutional phrase to a set of facts.

We have already stressed in a different context that, in a constantly changing society, in which, for example, the status, education, and the public estimation of the Negro component of the American people have greatly changed as compared with the end of the last century, a decision to preserve 'separate but equal' facilities is as much a policy decision as one aiming at gradual integration. At most, it can be conceded that a change of interpretation should, as far as possible, be confined to matters of major and fundamental importance, and rest on the greatest possible consensus of judicial opinion. This was, indeed, the case in the desegregation decisions[52] which were given by a unanimous court.

In a federal constitutional system, any attempt to cut off the courts from the power to reflect major evolutions in public policy, would possibly be more fatal even than in unitary systems, where legislative change is easier. Ultimately, the proper balance between the conflicting values of stability and change can only be struck by judicial tact rather than abstract principle. To quote Judge Learned Hand again[53]:

No doubt it is inevitable, however circumscribed his duty may be, that the personal proclivities of an interpreter will to some extent interject themselves into the meaning he imputes to a text, but in very much the greater part of a judge's duties he is charged with freeing himself as far as he can from all personal preferences, and that becomes difficult in proportion as these are strong. The degree to which he will secure compliance with his commands depends in large measure upon how far the community believes him to be the mouthpiece of a public will, conceived as the resultant of many conflicting strains that have come, at least provisionally, to a consensus.

That this prescription will leave many cases of divided courts, as well as of bitter political attacks upon judicial decisions, is an inevitable reflection of the strains and stresses of a changing society. Any attempt to solve this problem by restricting the Court to a static, i.e. conservative, interpretation,[54] will not solve the problem of the judicial process, while it is likely to dam up one of the constitutional outlets for gradual legal evolution. As another distinguished American lawyer has said in a recent survey of the policy-making powers of the Supreme Court[55]:

The difficulty in modification of the Constitution makes the Supreme Court a very powerful body in shaping the course of our civilization. In dealing with the constitutional guarantees of human dignity, it often has the application of the national conscience in its keeping. It is a sort of diplomatic priesthood. . . .

We live under a federal government which cannot exist as such without an umpire. In particular is an umpire necessary as between the states, otherwise the Constitution might have many different meanings in different states. Looking over our history, which agency would the American people prefer as an umpire: The President, acting through some commissions; the Congress; or the Supreme Court?

Where the limits of the judicial adaptation of law to new circumstances lie, we have attempted to outline earlier.[56]

But we are still left with the question what principles are to guide the umpire in the agonizing choice between values, inevitable in a Constitution that seeks to regulate the principles of life in a vast and constantly changing society – and that not over years or decades, but over centuries.

Does the sway of the battle leave us with anything more than the resigned acceptance of changing political tides and pressures, of individual preferences dictated by the conflicting beliefs of individual judges and resulting in shifting and accidental majority decisions?

The difficulty is illustrated by the attempt to articulate the choice of values in the so-called 'Preferred Freedoms' doctrine.

The proposition that certain freedoms in the United States Constitution, i.e. those guaranteeing the basic personal liberties, might be more fundamental than any concerned with changing processes of economic and social organization, was first tentatively mooted by the late Chief Justice Stone[57]:

Regulatory legislation affecting ordinary commercial transaction is not to be pronounced unconstitutional unless in the light of the facts made known or generally assumed it is of such a character as to preclude the assumption that it rests upon some rational basis within the knowledge and experience of the legislators. There may be narrower scope for operation of the presumption of constitutionality when legislation appears on its face to be within a specific prohibition of the Constitution, such as those of the first ten amendments, which are deemed equally specific when held to be embraced within the Fourteenth.

This approach has been enthusiastically supported by Justices Black and Douglas and, in effect, though perhaps not in words, by Chief Justice Warren in a number of decisions or dissents where the inviolability of freedom of speech and expression was asserted against the encroachments of national-security legislation or of other legislative efforts. On the other hand, a judge as strongly in the tradition of Holmes and Stone as Justice Frankfurter has criticized the doctrine as being incompatible with the need for self-restraint by a non-elected Court.[58] While acknowledging that 'those liberties of the individual which history has attested as the indispensable conditions of an open . . . society' have greater weight than liberties deriving from 'shifting economic arrangements' – which acknowledges a hierarchy of constitutional values, Frankfurter seems to regard any 'preferred freedom' philosophy as a dangerous over-simplification of a complex process of legislative experimentation.[59]

The doctrine has been unconditionally criticized by another eminent judge in the following words[60]:

I cannot help thinking that it would have seemed a strange anomaly to those who penned the words in the Fifth to learn that they constituted severer restrictions as to Liberty than Property, especially now that Liberty not only includes freedom from personal restraint, but enough economic security to allow its possessor the enjoyment of a satisfactory life. I can see no more persuasive reason for supposing that a legislature is *a priori* less qualified to choose between 'personal' than between economic values; and there have been strong protests, to me unanswerable, that there is no constitutional basis for asserting a larger measure of judicial supervision over the first than over the second.

In the 1959 Holmes lecture,[61] Professor Wechsler accepts both the inevitability of a judicial choice between conflicting values, and the impossibility of interpreting a Constitution in an inflexible historic context. But he criticizes with Frankfurter the 'preferred freedoms' doctrine as being unclear and oversimplified. He believes that a solution must be sought in adherence to 'rational' and 'neutral' principles. Certainly, giving preference to the 'Bill of Rights' (the first ten amendments) and to the Fourteenth Amendment does not necessarily solve the dilemma, for there may be a conflict between, for example, freedom of association or contract and racial non-discrimination, as in the 'restrictive covenant' cases.[62] But if, as Professor Wechsler concedes, a value choice is inevitable and the Court should not be strictly bound by precedent, a 'principled' approach can mean little more than that the conflict of values should be frankly articulated and that the Court should not simply be guided by its preference in the case before it, but by consistency of reasoning.[63]

The conflict can perhaps be confined, but it cannot be eliminated. We may agree that the Supreme Court must hesitate to substitute its own will for that of the elected legislator, that it cannot, consistently with the Constitution, legitimate the socialization without compensation of all private property any more than it can today deny the legitimacy of collective bargaining. But a Constitution, and even the sum of legislative and articulated public opinion can be no more than the framework, which judges must seek to fill out, seeking to find, in Learned Hand's words, 'the resultant of many conflicting strains that have come, at least provisionally, to a consensus'.

Much of the remainder of this book will be concerned with the determination of both the possibilities and the limits of such consensus in the various fields of law.

## JUDICIAL LAW-MAKING AND THE CRIMINAL LAW

The approach to judicial creativeness in the field both of common-law development and statutory interpretation needs considerable modification in the application of criminal law. The basic reason for this differentiation is that the private law – whether common-law developed or statutory – is essentially concerned with an adjustment of economic relations, with the shifting of a financial burden or liability from one party to another. Criminal law, on the other hand, lays down on behalf of the community at large a set of sanctions against the individual offender, ranging from monetary fines to long terms of deprivation of liberty and, in extreme cases, capital punishment. According to the scales of values generally predominant in civilized legal systems, this is a far more serious matter than the adjustment of financial losses, and the application of sanctions must therefore be surrounded with stricter safeguards against the extension of sanctions to the detriment of the individual.

This general proposition is embodied in the maxim *nullum crimen sine lege*. This maxim is a cherished pillar of individual freedom, often embodied in a bill of constitutional rights. It means that an offender should not be punished for any action, without a clear and definite legal basis. This excludes in particular the retroactive effect of a penal statute. The basis of this maxim is the concept of individual guilt as the foundation of criminal law. An offender should be punished only for an action for which he can be held morally responsible, because he is aware of its illegality. The application of this maxim divides itself into two parts: the construction of penal statutes, and the interpretation of common-law offences, the latter a problem essentially confined to the common-law jurisdictions where the criminal law is not, or not fully, codified. In both respects, it is subject to substantial qualifications.

In the first place, the maxim assumes that the protection of the individual is generally, in the hierarchy of values, superior to the interest of the community in preventing or punishing a certain socially objectionable conduct. This, however, is dependent on the scope and purposes of criminal law, which have in many contemporary systems been either substantially modified or widened. In the form that is most objectionable to a liberal system of values, the power to punish is widened by statutory authorization of judicial extension of offences, in accordance with the predominant policy of the State. This is the real meaning of the notorious clause introduced into the German criminal law by an Act of 1935 (under the Nazi régime), under which: 'Any person who commits an act which the law declares to be punishable or which is deserving of penalty according to the fundamental conceptions of a penal law and sound popular feeling, shall be punished . . .' Similarly, the R.S.F.S.R.

Penal Code of 1926 provides that 'a crime is any socially dangerous act or commission which threatens the foundations of the Soviet political structure and that system of law which has been established by the Workers and Peasants Government for the period of transition to a Communist structure'.[64] Such clauses, introduced into totalitarian systems where the essential independence of the judiciary from the policy-making bodies has been curtailed or abolished, are a thinly disguised invitation (which, in such systems, means a command sanctioned by a variety of harsh penalties) to the judge to pervert the Code, or to extend it in line with current political directives.

The practical significance of these spectacular and dangerous clauses is not nearly as great as appears on the surface, for in totalitarian systems many other means exist to undermine or destroy the legal protection of the individual. Important crimes are taken away from the jurisdiction of the ordinary courts and subjected to special political tribunals, while a special police, controlled not by the judiciary, but only by the political authorities, exercises para-legal powers of punishment, altogether outside the sphere of the criminal law proper.

In the common-law sphere, many of these offences were, like the rest of the common law, originally judge-made and judge-developed (e.g. homicide, rape, larceny, arson). The Court of Star Chamber played a prominent part in the creation of new offences. But it was the Court of King's Bench which, in 1616, declared that

to this court belongs authority, not only to correct errors in judicial proceedings, but other errors and misdemeanours extra-judicial, tending to the breach of peace, or oppression of the subjects, or to the raising of faction, controversy, debate, or to any manner of misgovernment; so that no wrong or injury, either public or private, can be done, but that it shall be reformed or punished in due course of law.[65]

As late as 1774, Lord Mansfield, for many years Lord Chief Justice of England, declared that:

Whatever is *contra bonos mores et decorum*, the principles of our law prohibit, and the King's court, as the general censor and guardian of the public manners, is bound to restrain and punish.[66]

Gradually, as the principle of legality increased, together with the body of statutorily defined offences, the pace of further development of common-law crimes slackened. How objectionable it had become to predominant opinion in the course of the nineteenth century, is shown by the dictum of one of the most famous of English criminal lawyers, Stephen L.J., in a case, deciding whether the burning of a corpse could be declared a criminal offence, without statutory basis:

There are some instances, no doubt, in which courts of justice have declared acts to be misdemeanours which had never previously been decided to be so, but I think it will be found that in every such case the act involved great public mischief or moral scandal. It is not my place to offer any opinion on the comparative merits of burning and burying corpses, but before I could hold that it must be a misdemeanour to burn a dead body, I must be satisfied not only that some people, or even that many people, object to the practice, but that it is, on plain, undeniable grounds, highly mischievous or grossly scandalous. Even then I should pause long before I held it to be a misdemeanour, for many acts involving the grossest indecency and grave public mischief – incest, for instance, and, where there is no conspiracy, seduction or adultery – are not misdemeanours, but I cannot take even the first step. . . . The great leading rule of criminal law is that nothing is a crime unless it is plainly forbidden by law. This rule is no doubt subject to exceptions, but they are rare, narrow, and to be admitted with the greatest reluctance, and only upon the strongest reasons.

Because it had become more or less accepted that courts would not invent new offences, an English decision of 1933 stirred up deep opposition. In *R.* v. *Manley*,[67] the Court of Criminal Appeal declared that a false allegation of robbery made to the police and causing them to make unnecessary investigations was a public mischief, and therefore a criminal misdemeanour. More objectionable than the judgement as such was the statement by Lord Hewart C.J.: 'We think that the law remains as it was stated to be by Lawrence J. in *R.* v. *Higgins*[68]: "All offences of a public nature, that is, all such acts or attempts as tend to the prejudice of the community, are indictable."'

Protests against this sweeping statement, which, in view of the vague and ubiquitous meaning of the phrase 'acts or attempts as tend to the prejudice of the community' lends itself to gross abuse, were so universal,[69] that it seemed highly unlikely that this decision would form the basis of a new wave of judicial crime-making. It is representative of contemporary thinking on this problem that the new Canadian criminal code of 1954 has specifically excluded common-law crimes,[70] while creating a new statutory offence covering the *Manley* situation (s. 120).

However, the judicial power to create new offences, by means of a sweeping interpretation of an allegedly surviving common-law offence called 'conspiracy to corrupt public morals' was revived by the House of Lords in the much discussed decision of *Shaw* v.

*Director of Public Prosecutions.*[71] In this case the appellant had published a magazine called *Ladies Directory* which contained the names, addresses, and other particulars of prostitutes, with the object of assisting prostitutes to ply their trade. For this the appellant received fees from the prostitutes concerned and he also derived profit from the magazine.

Against the vigorous dissent of Lord Reid, the House specifically held that an offence of conspiracy to corrupt public morals existed at common law and that conduct calculated and intended to corrupt public morals – such as the appellant's conduct – constituted an indictable offence of this character.

After protesting that he was no advocate of the right of the judges to create new criminal offences, Lord Simonds observed as follows:

I am at a loss to understand how it can be said either that the law does not recognize a conspiracy to corrupt public morals or that, though there may not be an exact precedent for such a conspiracy as this case reveals, it does not fall fairly within the general words by which it is described . . . The fallacy in the argument that was addressed to us lay in the attempt to exclude from the scope of general words acts well calculated to corrupt public morals just because they had not been committed or had not been brought to the notice of the court before. It is not thus that the common law has developed. We are, perhaps, more accustomed to hear this matter discussed on the question whether such and such a transaction is contrary to public policy. At once the controversy arises. On the one hand it is said that it is not possible in the twentieth century for the court to create a new head of public policy, on the other it is said that this is but a new example of a well-established head. In the sphere of criminal law, I entertain no doubt that there remains in the courts of law a residual power to enforce the supreme and fundamental purpose of the law, to conserve not only the safety and order but also the moral welfare of the state, and that it is their duty to guard it against attacks which may be the more insidious because they are novel and unprepared for.

The opposite approach to the creation of new criminal offences by contemporary courts was expressed by Lord Reid. He pointed out that the offence of criminal conspiracy was the creation of the Star Chamber, but that 'its methods and principles were superseded and what it did is of no authority today'. Lord Reid further drew a distinction between the possible extension of tort liability, e.g. through the widening of the categories of negligence, and the creation of new criminal offences by the courts. Finally, he referred to precedent for the view that the courts cannot create new offences by individuals, and deduced that 'every argument against creating new offences by an individual appears to me to be equally valid against creating new offences by a combination of individuals . . . Even if there is still a vestigial power of this kind, it ought not, in my view, to be used unless there appears to be general agreement that the offence to which it is applied ought to be criminal if committed by an individual. Notoriously there are wide differences of opinion today how far the law ought to punish immoral acts which are not done in the face of the public. Some think that the law already goes too far, some that it does not go far enough. Parliament is the proper place, and I am firmly of opinion the only proper place, to settle that.'

The observations made earlier in this section, on the respective functions of law courts in the evolution of civil and criminal law, can leave little doubt as to the present writer's view on the respective merits of the majority opinion, and of Lord Reid's dissenting judgement. The House of Lords, which has so often refused to adjust the fields of the common law that are concerned with the balance of economic and social rights and obligations – and none more emphatically than Lord Simonds[72] – affirms such a power in sweeping terms, in the very field in which democratic and liberal conceptions of justice are said to differ from totalitarian concepts of justice, by refusing to extend criminal offences by analogy, and thus to make them, in effect, retroactive. Indeed, one critic[73] has rightly pointed out that the nearest counterpart to the doctrine of the House of Lords enunciated in *Shaw*'s case is to be found in the universally condemned German statute of the Nazi period (1935) which empowered courts to punish accused persons if they were deserving of punishment according 'to the fundamental conceptions of penal law and sound popular feeling'. For reasons discussed in the preceding two chapters, it is in the field of the civil aspects of the common law that the courts have a vital function in the continuous evolution of the law, whereas it is in the field of criminal law that the legislature must now be taken to have the exclusive power to formulate new offences. It is no doubt understandable moral indignation which led the majority of the House to the reverse conclusion. But moral indignation does not make good legal theory.

But while this more blatant form of creation of new crimes by the judges in development of the common law will probably remain exceptional, a far more complex problem arises in the case of certain common-law crimes, notably those of conspiracy and sedition, which are so sweeping that they are subject to many divergent interpretations, in the light of changing political and social conditions.[74] But apart from these relatively few, though potentially dangerous, offences, which, in the American jurisdictions, have been defined by statute, there remains the more complex problem of the application of a precedent to a new situation. The main significance of this problem, has, however, in modern times, shifted from the pure common-law interpretation to the judicial interpretation of penal statutes.

While the great majority of the older offences are now defined by statute, whether in the form of a codification or not,[75] new offences are created by statute all the time, especially in the fields of public communications, transport, and welfare standards. In all of these, the problem of 'strict' or 'liberal' interpretation arises. Even if we accept as still valid the maxim, *nullum crimen sine lege*, this is no answer to the question whether a given penal statute should be construed narrowly or liberally. It is a policy choice in either case. To construe a statute narrowly is simply to assume on the part of the legislator one purpose rather than another. Thus, no basic value of democracy or liberty is involved in the construction of the expression 'self-propelled vehicle' in a penal statute as excluding rather than including an aeroplane.[76] Is it required by the democratic canon of values to make a notorious child kidnapper's conviction for murder 'turn on whether the window in the nursery was open or shut, with the law until comparatively recently unsettled if the window were partly open'?[77] Is it an essential application of *nullum crimen sine lege* to hold that the statute punishing larceny of 'cows' does not include heifers?[78]

It is, of course, a *petitio principii* to say that the maxim *nullum crimen sine lege* demands a 'strict' construction of a penal statute, i.e., a construction which, in the face of two or more alternatives and, in terms of logic or grammatical construction, equally admissible interpretations, must choose the one that narrows the scope of the criminal offence. For the tacit assumption, the 'inarticulate premiss', of such contention is that, whenever a statute contains a penal sanction, the intent of the legislator and the general principles applicable to the interpretation of statutory language do not apply. The effect of such a widely held view – which was attacked strongly by Dean Pound half a century ago,[79] has been to produce, in the United States, a number of specific abrogations of the common-law rule, either in special statutes or through the adoption of a general liberal construction rule for statutes. Thus a number of states have adopted the suggestion of the Field Draft Penal Code, originally prepared for New York in 1864, that all penal statutes 'are to be construed according to the fair import of their terms, with a view to effect their objects and to promote justice'. Other states have abolished the distinction between the construction of civil and penal statutes, and substituted for all statutes a general direction 'to carry out the intention of the legislature'.[80]

Clearly, the crux of the problem lies in the generality of the term 'penal statute', and in the continued application to modern conditions of a principle developed under entirely different circumstances. While the older common-law offences survive, a vast variety of new offences has been added, essentially as one of many ways in which the modern Welfare State must ensure the maintenance of social standards required by the community. Just as modern penal statutes and judicial constructions have, for a large proportion of these offences, accepted the principle of strict liability,[81] so we shall have to differentiate in the construction of penal statutes. There is certainly no justification for throwing out the strict construction principle, lock, stock, and barrel, in so far as it serves the reasonable protection of citizens from arbitrary punishment. In cases of grave offences, where the construction of a statute is in reasonable doubt, not only should the accused be given the benefit of the doubt, but the principle of strict *stare decisis*, generally adhered to by the English courts, should be mitigated. In the same spirit, it would seem reasonable to acquit a defendant who has committed an offence in reliance on a decision, e.g. on the invalidity of a statute which is subsequently overruled. An American court has held in such a case that the overruling decision can only have prospective effect for future cases.[82] Here, the ratio of *Taylor*'s case applies even more strongly. The defendant should not be penalized for reliance on an official declaration, even if it is later departed from. The same principle was, unfortunately, rejected in favour of a far more casuistic ground by the House of Lords.[83] Here, at a time of prevailing official licences and restrictions arising from the war situation, the defendant had been given oral permission by a competent public officer to carry out certain ship repairs, which were, in fact, illegal because a written licence was required. In the Court of Appeal, Denning L.J. had characteristically sought to rationalize the obviously desirable acquittal of the defendant by restating the principle which he had formulated in an earlier decision that, 'whenever government officers in their dealings with a subject take on themselves to assume authority in a matter with which the subject is concerned, he is entitled to rely on their having the authority which they assume'. The House of Lords, while rejecting this rationalization, chose instead a rather strained construction to the effect that the written licence, which was later granted, could operate retroactively.

The confusion prevailing in this field extends to the wider domain of an honest mistake of law as a defence to a criminal offence.[84] While there has been an increasing departure from the rigidity of the 'strict construction' principle for penal statutes, it is very difficult to formulate an alternative principle. Here, as in other fields of law, it is a matter of reasonable balance between the conflicting interests of the community in fighting certain social evils or maintaining certain social standards, and in protecting the individual from punishment for acts where it is unreasonable to expect punishment. This is not identical with the principle of fault, for as we shall see later, many statutes of an essentially public-welfare character with a predominant interest in maintenance of standards have led to the partial discarding of the fault principle. Neither is a solution possible on the lines that the courts should avoid all but strictly grammatical construction of a statute, for this is patently impossible and contrary to universal judicial principles and experience.[85]

The following guiding principles would be in accord with the general approach to judicial interpretation as portrayed in this chapter:

(1) It is beyond the proper province of the courts to create basically new offences. These are properly the province of the legislator.

(2) Where a court is faced with conflicting interpretations of the language of a statute, either of which is compatible with reasonable canons of construction, it must balance the legislative purpose of the statute, in the light of the object matter and the policies at stake, with the principle that a person should not be convicted of an offence which he can reasonably regard as a non-criminal action.[86]

Such an approach does not separate the modern criminal law, with its variety of purposes and policies, from the rest of the law in an artificial and socially unjustifiable manner, while it preserves the sound substance of the principle that in a free society the citizen should not be punished for acts that he cannot reasonably construe as criminal.

### JUDICIAL LAW-MAKING IN INTERNATIONAL LAW

Although, as we have seen, even the highly organized legislative machinery of the modern state demands an active and constructive participation of the courts in the evolution of the law, the scope of such judicial law-making should, at first sight, be far greater in international law. Contemporary international society is still loosely organized; it lacks legislative and executive organs with power to make decisions, other than by consent of the member States. Substantive international law is still a collection of fragments rather than an integrated system of rules governing the conduct of nations in their mutual relations. The highest judicial organ of contemporary international society, the International Court of Justice is, in article 38 of its statute, directed to apply to its decisions of disputes, next to international conventions and international custom, 'the general principles of law recognized by civilized nations', and 'judicial decisions and the teachings of the most highly qualified publicists of the various nations, as subsidiary means for the determination of rules of law'.

The field for judicial development of the law is, therefore, wide and open, and the challenge presented to the Court by its own statute to create new law while deciding cases, seemingly irresistible. However, the same causes which account for the relative weakness and incompleteness of contemporary international law also restrain the highest international court as well as other international judicial organs, in the exercise of such a creative function. International law is still based upon the principle of State sovereignty, and international obligations derive from the consent of the States to restrict their freedom of action by certain specified commitments. Thus the principle of consent still controls the interpretation of legal obligations in international law, and this strongly restrains the International Court in its attempt to develop international law through judicial decisions. For any creative interpretation is likely to be resented by the party against whom judgement is given, as an encroachment on the principle of sovereignty and the limited character of the obligation by virtue of which the Court is called to give a decision. This is apt to be the case, whether the decision is given under a specific agreement between two States to submit a dispute to the Court, or under the so-called 'optional clause' by which a large number of States have agreed to submit certain types of legal disputes generally to the jurisdiction of the Court.[87]

The precarious position in which an international judicial organ finds itself in a society still dominated by (an increasing number of) sovereign States and national conflicts of interest, therefore drastically curtails the scope of judicial law-making in international law, even though the necessity for such creativeness is urgent, and the field immense.[88] The inevitable dependence of the effectiveness of legal institutions on the degree of social cohesion in the society which

they serve and represent, is demonstrated. The composition of the
Court itself reflects to a large extent the divergent national interests
that impede its creative function. Yet, the role of the Court in the
evolution of international law is far from being purely passive or
negative. The very creation of such an institution – now forty years
old – represents, for all its limitations, an advance in the social
cohesiveness of the family of nations, a small step from a society to a
community of nations. The number of cases in which the International Court has felt able and willing to push international law
forward boldly, either by way of a judgement or an advisory
opinion, is small but important. Outstanding, in this writer's
opinion, is the Advisory Opinion in which the international Court,
by a strong majority, bestowed full international legal personality
upon the United Nations as a condition of its capacity to demand
reparation for injury suffered by one of its servants (Count Berna-
dotte). In going beyond the wording of article 104 of the U.N.
Charter, which cautiously refrained from declaring such international legal personality, the Court firmly established the advance
from a system of international law in which States are the sole
subjects, to one in which international organizations, without being
super States, live and function as personalities in their own right.[89]
Hardly less important for the advance of international organization
is a more recent Advisory Opinion,[90] where the Court, again by a
substantial majority, held that the General Assembly of the United
Nations, once having created an independent tribunal with power
to make final awards in the determination of disputes between the
United Nations and its employees, was not free to overrule or disregard its awards simply because it had been the creator of the
tribunal. This Opinion powerfully advances the principle of judicial integrity and independence in international organization,
while it indirectly also strengthens the status of the individual as
against both States and the international organizations of which
they are members. In another field, the Court, this time in a judgement on a dispute between two States,[91] made an important contribution to the highly controversial and fluid problem of the limits of
territorial waters, by holding that economic conditions as well as
historical tradition and geographical peculiarities, justified the
delimitation of Norwegian territorial waters by a series of straight
base lines connecting points on the islands off the coast, instead of
the base line following the actual low-water mark, and not exceeding four miles from the shore at any point.

In the development of 'general principles of law recognized among civilized nations', the Court has generally been extremely cautious.[92] In this field, it seems that more important judicial advances will continue to come from special international tribunals, or from regional judicial institutions. Such institutions as the mixed Arbitral Tribunals created between the Allied States and Germany after the First World War, or the General Claims Commission established by the United States and Mexico have made important contributions to the principles of restitution and reparation for injuries suffered by nationals of one State at the hands of another.[93]

It is a corollary to the close interdependence of social cohesion and legal development that much of the development of international law through judicial law-making is likely to continue to come from the judicial institutions of more closely knit communities of States, such as the Court of Justice of the three West European Communities, or the Court of Human Rights established by the Council of Europe. The creation of a supra-national judicial institution, such as the European Court of Human Rights, being empowered to pass on claims raised by individuals and groups against their own States, is likely to mark a revolutionary advance not only in the international law prevailing among the member States, but in the development of general international law.[94]

While the judicial development of international law is thus inevitably lagging very seriously behind the necessities of contemporary society, it is likely to function, together with the increasingly numerous international conventions between States, as an important agent in the gradual transition from international anarchy to international law.

### JUDICIAL DILEMMAS IN MODERN DEMOCRATIC SOCIETY

In modern democratic society, the judge must steer his way between the Scylla of subservience to government and the Charybdis of remoteness from constantly changing social pressures and economic needs. There is little need to point out the dangers of complete political subservience which the judiciary has experienced under both Fascism and Communism. The administration of law under these systems becomes a predominantly political function and an instrument of government policy. Under Fascism and Communism certain spheres of social and commercial law are left relatively intact because the government does not consider them as sufficiently important to interfere or regards it as desirable that citizens should enjoy some security of rights in spheres not directly touching government policy.

In democracies, on the other hand, the illusion is still widespread, despite the warnings of many jurists, that the judge can ignore the social and political issues on which he is asked to adjudicate. It was Lord Justice Scrutton, one of the most conservative as well as one of the most learned of English judges, who warned in the following terms against confusion of prejudices with objectivity:

. . . the habits you are trained in, the people with whom you mix, lead to your having a certain class of ideas of such a nature that, when you have to deal with other ideas, you do not give as sound and accurate judgements as you would wish. . . . It is very difficult sometimes to be sure that you have put yourself into a thoroughly impartial position between two disputants, one of your own class and one not of your class.[95]

Part of the illusion still current among many lawyers is an antiquated conception of the separation of powers. In its absolute and rigid formulation, the doctrine of the separation of powers has never been a correct reflection of politics.[96] The independence of the judiciary from both executive and legislature remains a cornerstone of democratic government, but it cannot be absolute. The notion of 'quasi-judicial' has been extended by a judiciary anxious to maintain some control over the executive, through the prerogative writs.[97] When law courts have felt doubtful about the wisdom of bringing too many ministerial actions under judicial control, they have tended to narrow down the concept of quasi-judicial functions.[98] On the other hand, the English law courts have recently proceeded to widen drastically the scope of judicial review of the decisions of 'domestic tribunals'.[99]

Certainly the problem of the proper scope of judicial control of the executive or of social groups, such as professional associations or trade unions, cannot be solved by categorical absolutes. It is futile to demand the abolition of government regulation in the kind of society in which we live. Discretion, and even arbitrariness, is no monopoly of the executive. Offenders as well as prison administrators are keenly enough aware of the vast discrepancies in the scale of punishment inflicted upon motor-car owners for speeding offences, or for crimes committed under the influence of alcohol.

Much of the confusion has resulted from a false conception of the separation of functions between the three branches of government. It is now increasingly recognized by contemporary jurists that borderlines are fluid, and that cooperation rather than separation, in a constant interchange of give and take between legislature, executive, and judiciary, reflects the reality of the legal process.

The statute lays down a principle which must be applied in cases and circumstances not yet in being. Obviously, while it is difficult enough to determine the rule for transactions which have arisen, it is all the more difficult to do the same for transactions that have yet to occur. Hence, a legislature must speculate more perilously as to how future cases will arise and what contingencies they will involve.

Because perfect generalization for the future is impossible, no generalization is complete. Aware of this impossibility, legislatures often do no more than purport to lay down the most general statements of law, intending that the courts and other law-applying agencies shall creatively adapt the general principle to specific cases. Thus, every time a statute uses a rule of reason, or a standard of fairness without specification, there is conscious and deliberate delegation of this responsibility to the courts. . . . [100]

The task of the modern judge is increasingly complex. Hardly any major decision can be made without a careful evaluation of the conflicting values and interests of which some examples have been given in the preceding pages. Totalitarian government eliminates much of the conflict by dictating what should be done.

The lot of the democratic judge is heavier and nobler. He cannot escape the burden of individual responsibility, and the great, as distinct from the competent, judges have, I submit, been those who have shouldered that burden and made their decisions as articulate a reflection of the conflicts before them as possible. They do not dismiss the techniques of law, but they are aware that by themselves they provide no solution to the social conflicts of which the law is an inevitable reflection.

We live in an age of uncertainties and dangers, an age in which it is only too tempting to seek escape from the responsibility of decision in some kind of mythology. Millions have succumbed to authoritarian systems of government or emotional formulas which help to absolve the individual from decision and moral responsibility, and which afford an escape from the hard facts of life. In the administration of law it is also tempting to seek escape from the burden of decision. The law must aspire at certainty, at justice, at progressiveness, but these objectives are constantly in conflict one with the other. What the great judges and jurists have taught is not infallible knowledge, or a certain answer to all legal problems, but an awareness of the problems of contemporary society and an acceptance of the burden of decision which no amount of technical legal knowledge can take from us.

# Part Two

# Social Change and Legal Institutions

Property

That property and its distribution occupies a central – and in the view of many a decisive – position in modern industrial society is a view shared by legal and political philosophers from the extreme right to the extreme left. The right to property as an inalienable, 'natural' right of the citizen, immune from interference by government or other individuals, becomes a central element in the legal philosophy of Locke, of the Founding Fathers, of the '*Déclaration des Droits de l'Homme*', while it permeates the interpretation of the United States Constitution, and the Neo-Scholastic political and legal philosophy of the Catholic Church.[1]   Land ownership had, of course, played a dominant role in feudal society. But it was *tenure* of land, based on the hierarchical order of feudalism that characterized the role of property in medieval feudal society. The detachment of the right of property as such accompanies the rise of modern Western commercial and industrial society.

At the other end of the scale, Marxist analysis clearly regards property as the key to the control of modern industrial society. The capitalist, by virtue of his ownership of the means of production, effectively controls society. He exercises the powers of command which ought to be vested in the community. Hence, Marxist theory demands a transfer of the ownership and the means of production to the community, which, in the initial stages, exercises its control through a dictatorship of the proletariat and the coercive power of the State, until the latter 'withers away'. This key function of property and the establishment of a social order remains, almost without qualification, part of modern Soviet philosophy. It still maintains that, with the transfer of ownership in substantially all means of industrial and agricultural production to the community, the problem of social justice has been substantially solved in Soviet society.[2] Ideologically and politically, the property philosophy of the American Constitution and the Catholic Church is bitterly opposed to that of modern Communism, and of all forms of Marxist interpretation of history. But they share the heritage of modern Western political philosophy: the controlling significance of property in the social order. In that, they differ from earlier phases of occidental civilization as well as from other civilizations.

## DIFFERENT CONCEPTS OF PROPERTY

In its political and sociological – and, indeed, in its popular – sense, 'property' is clearly not confined to ownership in 'things' (*Sachen*). It comprises not only the realty and personalty – or, more precisely, immovable and movable objects – but also patents,[3] copyrights, shares, claims. In this respect, Anglo-American conceptions of property are closely in line with the sociological and popular meaning, whereas civilian concepts of property still labour under an artificial analytical division inherited from Roman jurisprudence, and out of step with the reality of modern industrial society. The French Civil Code of 1804, the German Civil Code of 1900, the Swiss Civil Code of 1907, and the Italian Civil Code of 1942 – but also the Soviet Civil Code of 1923 – agree in confining ownership, in a legal sense, to 'things', movable and immovable. There cannot be, technically speaking, an ownership of mortgages or of copyrights. There has even been much elaborate and futile discussion of the question whether such a commodity as electricity can be classified as a '*Sache*' and, therefore, be the object of ownership.

The common law is mercifully free of these distinctions which artificially divide things that economically and sociologically belong together. In this field, at least, the empirical development of the common law, its aversion to theoretical definitions of legal concepts, its preference for thinking in terms of legal relationships, of powers and liabilities, rights and obligations, types of action rather than of abstract concepts, has proved an advantage. 'The English lawyer does not find it incongruous to say that the claim for the repayment of a loan, a mortgage on another man's land, or a share in a limited company, belongs to a person's "property".'[4] Property, as the same learned author says, is 'a bundle of powers'. Similarly, an American writer has recently defined property as a 'bundle of rights' by which one claimant is enabled to exclude others, and therefore property is not limited to corporeal things.[5] Not only is Anglo-American law untroubled by conceptual limitations of ownership; it also knows degrees of ownership. This may, perhaps, be attributed to two characteristic features of Anglo-American legal development: on the one hand, the evolution of the trust concept has attuned the common-law mind to the division of property between different parties, each endowed with certain parts of the property right which, in the classical Continental definition of article 544 of the French Civil Code is '*le droit de jouir et de disposer des choses de la manière la plus absolue. . . .*' The trustee and, to a certain degree, the settlor, has the power to dispose; the beneficiary has the right to enjoy. On the other hand, the predominance of land law in the formative era of the common law, and its impregnation with a feudal concept, under which only various degrees of estate are held, while the residue – and theoretically the only full right of property – is vested in the Crown, has resulted in the establishment of various 'estates' in land rather than full ownership. While some contemporary jurists[6] regard the survival of the theoretical ownership by the Crown of all land as a mere fiction to be disregarded, and therefore describe the fee simple as full ownership, others[7] strongly criticize such a conception as unhistorical and contrary to the spirit of English law, and maintain that in English law there are only various forms of 'estate' in land, ranging from the near-absolute fee simple to limited tenancies with correspondingly more or less far-reaching degrees of protection of possession in relation to others. A similar, though not identical, conception underlies the formulation in the American Restatement of the Law of Property of 1936, which defines an estate as 'ownership measured in terms of duration'. Whether or not there is, theoretically, a full ownership in land in the common law, does not greatly affect the social realities of modern land tenure. It is probably less important than the fact that common law conceives of the substratum as well as the dimensions of property in terms of function rather than of definition.

The artificiality of a definition of property which confines it to the complete control over a 'thing', has been modified to some extent by giving 'similar' or 'quasi-proprietary' rights, such as copyrights or patents, the same legal protection as property, for instance, in the law of torts.[8]

But it is not only the development of the physical sciences and the increasing importance of sources of energy, such as electricity or nuclear power, which makes the romanistic distinctions between 'things' and 'non-things' archaic. The economic significance of intangible property rights such as patents, copyrights, shares, or options has revealed the dogmatic aridity of the civilian definition of property; even more important is the increasing realization that in modern industrial and commercial society, property is not an exclusive relation of dominance, exercised by one person, physical or corporate, over the thing or even a number of 'quasi-things', but that it is rather a collective description for a complex of powers,

functions, expectations, liabilities, which may be apportioned between different parties to a legal transaction. The most significant
expression of this trend is, perhaps, the modern French concept of
'*propriété commerciale*'.[9] Under modern French legislation, both
businessmen and farmers, who rent their premises and land respectively, enjoy certain rights as against the owner, which are generally
described as '*propriété commerciale*'. The essence of this right is a
claim of the occupier against the owner for renewal of the lease,
except in certain strictly defined circumstances. The owner is to
that extent deprived of his legal power to dispose of his property, in
favour of the lessee's right to the continuity of his enterprise. In the
words of Ripert[10]:

> The businessman has over the immovable property a right which per-
> mits him the utilization of the asset for his benefit, a right which he can
> oppose to the owner of the land as to any third party.

In Ripert's view, the fact that this right is derived from a contract
has disguised the property-like character of this right. But another
jurist has, perhaps, more accurately observed that the right of the
*commerçant* over the land on which he conducts his business has not
the character of a property right. It is rather a concomitant of the
legal protection given him for his other assets, his '*fonds de commerce*'.
The owner can refuse renewal against proper compensation.[11]
Whatever the analytical solution may be, here, as in the English
trust, the powers and rights once concentrated in the owner of the
land are now divided between owner and user. Unlike the common-
law trust, civilian systems cannot dissect property into its various
components, but they have transferred certain functions of property
from the owner to others, responding to new economic needs and
social policies. Legislation protecting tenant farmers as against the
owners is known in many countries, in France[12] as in the United
Kingdom[13] and elsewhere. The scarcity of housing may demand a
quasi-property protection of the tenant; the national needs of food
production may demand the strengthening of the right of the tenant
farmer against the absentee owner. Such social pressures produce an
evolution in the concept of property. The romanistic definition
remains at best a point of departure, of decreasing significance in the
modern social context. The necessary correspondence between
changes in the function and the concept of property is brought out
in the analysis of a contemporary Danish jurist.[14] Kruse considers
the right of property in contemporary society as 'the driving force in
the economy of the community, of its widely diffused economic

mechanism, of the production, distribution, and credit of society, with their numerous carefully enumerated sections'.[15] In such a society, a 'division of labour' takes place in the 'internal economy of the property'. Rights of use, easements, rentcharges, mortgages, and claims arise through a division of the right of property. These 'partial' rights of property must be included in the definition of property not only because they form part of its total function, but also because they are protected against expropriation by others, and because the holder enjoys the same powers over them as over the complete right of property.[16]

Thus, slowly, modern Continental law is arriving at a more elastic and functional concept of property, similar to that of the common law. This development clearly makes the nation of property more adaptable to the constantly changing demands that modern society makes upon it.

The function of property in modern industrial society is a problem which transcends the historical and conceptual differences between civilian and common-law thinking. The comparative study of this problem will therefore be facilitated by the evolution that has narrowed the gap between Continental and common-law analysis. One important consequence of this is the possibility of developing property concepts in international law acceptable to all civilized nations. Much attention has recently been devoted to the scope of protection of property interests in international law. There is at least no conceptual obstacle to the recognition of economic interests such as concessions, licences, and contractual promises of various kinds as being included in 'property' for purposes of international legal regulation.[17]

### PROPERTY LAW AND THE EVOLUTION OF INDUSTRIAL SOCIETY

Whether in the restricted definition that dominates Continental civil codes, or in the wider meaning traditionally given to property in the common law, property denotes the most complete form of control that the law permits. The definitions of the various civil codes from the French to the Soviet code, agree on this point, although all these codes make, with varying emphasis, the obvious reservation that this absolute control operates within the limits of the law. The impact of this reservation varies, of course, in accordance with the prevailing social philosophy and economic conditions, a fact which has enabled the definition of the French civil code to survive through radical changes in the *actual*, as distinct from the *theoretical*, role of property in society.[18] While the more modern German and Swiss civil codes exclusively emphasize the power of the owner to *dispose* of the object of property, the older French civil code, more comprehensively and accurately, underlines the two aspects of property: '*la propriété est le droit de jouir et de disposer des choses* ...' It is indeed this dual aspect of property: the power to enjoy and the power to control – which any contemporary analysis of the function of property in society must take as its point of departure. For it is the increasing divorce of these two, once normally united, aspects of property which is the most characteristic feature of modern evolutions of property. Correspondingly, the legal restrictions on the rights of property are different in impact and social significance, according to whether they seek to restrain the power to enjoy or the power to control.

In a primitive and essentially self-supporting society, property coincides broadly with the sphere of work of an individual – at least if we include with the head of the household his family. 'Property, ... the central institution of private law, fulfilled, in the system of simple commodity production, the functions of providing an order of goods and, in part, an order of power.'[19] In a broadly accurate simplification, the owner of a farm or a workshop in such a society owns the land, the stock, the tools, which he needs to live or to produce in exchange for certain elementary commodities. Hired labour or trade in commodities are generally ancillary rather than essential complements of property. Power and enjoyment of property and the capacity to work are not too far apart from each other.

Although even pre-industrial society shows an increasing tension and separation between these different functions of property, the decisive break comes with the industrial age. In the earlier phase of industrial society, the power aspect of property becomes immensely extended. The ownership of physical assets enables the early capitalist entrepreneur to multiply not only his power over things – factories, commodities, or products – but also over men. The power to make contracts, to hire and fire, becomes, perhaps, the most important function of property. In the earlier days of industrialism, before trade unions were legitimate and powerful, this power enabled the owner of industrial assets to become, in Renner's analysis,[20] a 'commander'. He exercises, by arrogation or toleration, a quasi-public authority over people and social relationships that ought to belong to public authority only, and in the theory of democracy, to a public authority responsible to the people as a whole. There are industrial empires, parallel to autocratic political empires, although domination is disguised by the theoretical equality of contract under the civil law, an equality as little concerned with the differences of economic power between the parties as the law that, in Anatole France's famous phrase, in majestic impartiality permits rich and poor alike to sleep out on embankments.

Renner's analysis stops at a point where ownership is still the exclusive key to control in modern capitalistic society. It is true that the means of exercising this control has become diversified through the 'Konnexinstitut', such as the power to rent, to hire and fire, and other complementary institutions to which we have referred earlier.[21] But legal ownership still remains, as in earlier Marxist analysis, the key to economic power. The owner keeps the title to the surplus value. He surrenders only the use of his property, 'an item in which he never was interested'.

This analysis neglects the decisive and dominant function which the modern large-scale corporate enterprise is exercising in contemporary capitalism (under private capitalism as well as State ownership). In the present century, corporate enterprise has taken control of all the major fields of industrial and business operations, and the structure of corporate enterprise itself has drastically changed in the process. The development of the modern corporation is characterized by an increasing divorce of ownership and control, a phenomenon analysed by a now classic American treatise published a few years after Renner published the last edition of his work.[22]

Renner saw capitalist ownership as an octopus whose numerous tentacles – contracts of service, loan, hire or instalment purchase, etc. – enveloped more and more victims. But in the overwhelmingly important field of corporate enterprise, the nominal owner, that is the shareholder, is becoming more and more powerless. He turns into a mere recipient of dividends, often barely distinguishable from the bond or debenture holder. In the analysis of Berle and Means, control has been wrested from the shareholder owner by five different devices: first, control through almost complete ownership; secondly, majority control; thirdly, control through a legal device without majority ownership; fourthly, minority control; fifthly, management control. Of these, only the last four are of major sociological importance. Some of the forms of control, especially those achieved through a voting trust, are peculiar to Anglo-American law, although the delegation of votes to banks or other agents can achieve very similar results in Continental company law. But, on the whole, the devices which vest control either in a minority directed by interests outside the company itself, or in the management, at the expense of scattered and passive shareholders, are the same in Continental or Anglo-American law, for the social and economic factors which account for this transformation are similar: the increase in the vastness and complexity of modern industry in most fields, the dispersal of shares among multitudes of small shareholders whose joint influence does not compare with that of a single compact minority interest, and the increasing importance of the managerial as against the financial element, owing to the technical and administrative complexities of modern large-scale enterprise.

Among the devices for separation of ownership and control discussed by Berle and Means, two seem particularly significant. A group of entrepreneurs – industrial or financial – may build up a pyramid of corporations. They need the ownership of a majority or near-majority of shares, at most at the top of the pyramid, preferably in a holding company. The holding company acquires a controlling interest in a series of operating or other holding companies, each of which acquires a controlling influence in the company next below in the pyramid. By this device, the original group of entrepreneurs can acquire a decisive or even monopoly control over an entire industry.[23] Ownership and control are even more completely divorced where the management of a vast and complex corporate enterprise can either govern undisturbed because of the dispersal of shareholdings among multitudes of small owners, or because it can, if necessary, stir up the majority of shareholders in order to fight the dominant minority.

The powers formerly necessarily attendant on property have now largely passed to those who, without necessarily being owners, can control and direct a variety of owners of shares or assets in an enterprise, whether this be the result of diffusion of ownership, of apathy, of skilful manipulation, of the centralization of know-how and administrative control in the hands of management, or a combination of all these factors.

### PUBLIC RESTRAINTS ON THE RIGHTS OF PROPERTY

Although many of the major powers flowing from property rights have now passed from the property owner to others, notably the managers of corporations, such power still *derives* from property.

While the social demand to restrain the power of the 'over-mighty subject' is no longer necessarily directed against the legal owner of such property, the need for social restraint on private property is as urgent as it has ever been. In accordance with the analysis given earlier, we shall survey the various moves which have, over a century, led to an increasing range as well as a growing intensity of public restraints on property from two aspects: restraints on the *enjoyment* of property designed to mitigate the privileges which it confers in the enjoyment of the things that life has to offer; and restraints on the private *power* to use the control of industrial property as a 'delegated power of command', as a means of a quasi-governmental private control over the major assets of a nation.

The distinction between these two aspects of property rights is both legally and sociologically important. It is possible for a legislator to concentrate on one or the other aspect. Social welfare and Socialism (or even State supervision of private industry) are not the same. Indeed, modern capitalism as applied, for example, in the United States, has a multitude of legal restraints on private property designed as alternatives to Socialism. Social obligations have often become the price to be paid for continued private control over the productive assets of the nation. On the other hand, a legal restraint on property may, and often does, affect both the enforcement and the power aspects of property. Thus, legislation against the abuse of patents is directed against the dangers of excessive financial benefits as much as the dangers of a stranglehold over industrial development. Progressive taxation primarily aims at mitigating the inequalities in the access to commodities flowing from unequal accumulations of property. But driven to extremes, it may affect the conduct of industry and business as such.

## Restrictions on the Use and Enjoyment of Private Property

*Abuse of Rights.* In recent years, comparative lawyers have devoted attention to the problem of abuse of rights. They have contrasted the attitude of modern Continental civil codes with that of English law, still dominated by a decision of the House of Lords of 1895.[24] Continental legal systems such as the French, German, and Swiss, make the abuse of property rights a good defence where the predominant objective of the exercise of a property right has been chicanery, or the intent to do injury to another party.[25] English law still basically adheres to the principle that a person can do with his property what he likes, except for specific statutory restrictions. Some isolated decisions in nuisance cases have, however, given preference to the plaintiff's reasonable economic interests against the defendant's unsocial use of his private-property right.[26] This approach has been carried somewhat further in American law. It is now settled in the great majority of jurisdictions that, where a defendant erects a fence for the sole purpose of shutting off the plaintiff's view – as distinct from putting up such a structure for a useful purpose, even if a malicious motive has played a part in the action – he may be restrained from doing so.[27] Again, there is abundant authority for holding that a drilling of a well, not in order to procure water on the defendant's premises, but to cut off the plaintiff's underground water, is unlawful.[28] But where – as was the case in *Bradford* v. *Pickles* – a landowner digs a hole in his ground so as to abstract water from a neighbouring property, in order to raise the purchasing price of his property wanted by a local authority, it may be doubted whether, at least in a primarily private-property-oriented legal system, there is not a legitimate, though ruthlessly pursued, economic objective.[29]

The practical significance of the whole doctrine is very much smaller than its theoretical interest. In the practice of American, French, German, or Swiss courts, it means little more than that the very unusual kind of landowner who creates obstacles out of spite for his neighbour, or who prefers to leave a piece of land unused rather than grant a right of passage, may be restrained by the courts.[30] Continental courts have understandably refrained from developing the principle into a more fundamental social doctrine by which the use of property is subject to the needs of the community. It is in this wider sense that the principle of *abus de droit* has sometimes been used to justify (together with the principle of unjust enrichment) the *propriété commerciale*, i.e. the right of a lessee to demand continuation of his lease from the owner of the premises. But here the principle loses all legal precision and becomes a moral precept rather than a juristic concept.[31]

Again, the 'abuse of rights' stands for a completely different social philosophy of property as applied in article 1 of the Soviet civil code, which withholds protection from private rights 'exercised in contradiction to their social and economic purpose.'[32]

## Statutory Restraints on the Use of Property

An increasing array of statutory duties affects the freedom of property of landowners, factory owners, employers, retailers, public utilities, in a multitude of ways.

*Restraints on Producers and Employers.* There are provisions for the safety of machinery or mines, for sanitation and drainage, for the purity of foods and water. They enjoy the sanctions of criminal and civil law; statutory penalties for these 'public welfare' offences[33] do not normally require a *mens rea*. The protection of civil law is often a twofold one: the extension of the obligations of the manufacturer towards the consumer[34] has greatly widened the scope of protection of the public against deficient products. English courts have also increasingly awarded damages to individuals for the breach of statutory duties as such, for example, to a third party injured in a car which, contrary to statute, had no third-party insurance,[35] or to a ratepayer poisoned by impure water supplied by a local authority.[36] In the United States the position is complex because of the large number of jurisdictions and the infinite variety of statutes.[37] Many statutes have been construed as only imposing a public duty (e.g., most statutes providing for compulsory licensing). But many private claims have been granted (e.g. to employees against the employers for violation of a statutory obligation to fence dangerous machinery, or to children injured by the failure of a railway to comply with a fencing statute).[38]

Official Acts and regulations increasingly not only forbid but also prescribe. Economic emergencies have greatly accentuated this development. The State lays down utility standards for a wide range of consumers' products; or it allocates scarce raw materials or foreign currencies according to priorities. The most powerful and dangerous of State powers, the right of direction of labour, has so far been sparingly used in democratic systems, except in war, for freedom to choose one's occupation is a far more elementary aspect of human freedom than liberty to do with one's material property as he likes. But a grave economic crisis which makes a nation dependent on its essential resources always increases the pressure for compulsory direction or freezing of certain forms of labour, such as coal mining or agriculture, which, in normal times, tend to lose more labour than they attract.

*Restraints on the Ownership and Use of Land.* Defence needs, economic emergencies, and the need for conservation and the best possible utilization of existing land and mineral resources have been the principal causes of far-reaching public interferences with the private uses of land. They have led to powers of dispossession and, in certain cases, even to legislative restrictions on the amount of land that can be privately owned by any single individual. The emphasis and intensity of these restrictions on private land-ownership vary from country to country. They are conditioned by the need for the available national resources, by the degree of economic emergency which natural conditions or human-made catastrophes such as war impose; they are, of course, also influenced by the distribution of power between different social groups within the country. What is common to all these developments, especially in the last decade, is a growing awareness of the prior claims of the *utilization* of land, as against its mere status. As a French jurist has expressed it: '*l'human-ité a pris conscience de ce que la propriété qui est seulement matière ne fructifie que par le travail de l'homme*'.[39]

It is not surprising that, in France, where the political power of the small farmer is greater and better organized than in any other Western country, the protection of the rights of the tenant farmer has taken pride of place. We have previously mentioned the *propriété commerciale*, a short and not altogether accurate description of the rights enjoyed by the small businessman – another powerful political force in France – against the owner, on the premises of which he conducts his business. The rights of the tenant-farmer (*fermiers et métayers*) go further. Under legislation which has developed over the years and which was consolidated – after the war – in 1945 and 1946,[40] the tenant farmer is virtually irremovable from the land which he farms, at the termination of the lease. The duration of the lease and the rent are fixed by law. After the statutory duration of nine years, the lease can be indefinitely renewed at the option of the lessee. Nor can the owner of the land terminate the lease against the payment of an indemnity. He can reoccupy the land only if he wants to cultivate it personally, or through his children. Furthermore, the tenant farmer has a right of pre-emption whenever the owner wishes to sell the land. While the parties may abrogate from the terms of the law in certain details, they cannot abrogate by contract the essential principles of the law which, in the French legal terminology, is *d'ordre public*.

In Great Britain, where the social power and economic influence of the farmer do not compare with that of his counterpart in France, war emergencies, food shortages, and an increased need to rely on native produce have nevertheless strengthened the legal position of the farmer and superimposed a public power of dispossession over the private rights of parties. Under the British Agriculture Act of 1947, the Minister of Agriculture has the power to dispossess inefficient farmers in certain contingencies, by either compulsory purchase or an order directed to the owner to let the farm to an approved tenant. The Agricultural Land Commission manages and farms land vested in the Minister and placed by him under the control of the Commission. Coupled with this are statutory standard terms for agricultural tenancies.[41] This is of course a most significant restriction of the rights of private property in the interest of the community. It expresses the recognition of agricultural land as a national asset, which private owners and tenants must use to the advantage of the community. The power exercised by urban or agricultural landowners through tenancy and the power of the mortgagee to appropriate the substance of the power deriving from landownership plays a considerable part in Renner's analysis.[42] This type of legislation shows a new technique: positive administrative action now displaces private terms of contract, instead of negative administrative measures (clearance orders) as used by the Housing Acts.

Another type of public interference with the private use of land is illustrated by the powers of the Minister under the Town and Country Planning Act. Under this legislation, the competent Minister can withhold permission for private development of land in the interests of town and country planning. In a case where, under a previous Act, a local authority and private landowners had agreed on private development of the land, and laid out certain moneys toward this purpose, the Minister was confirmed by the Court of Appeal in the withholding of his permission for further development under the new Act. The statutory power was held to be a limiting factor in any private agreements previously entered into.[43]

Yet another aspect of the shift of emphasis from private to public uses of land is illustrated by the New Towns Act, 1946, the major piece of legislation incorporating a planned policy of decentralization, and an attempt to draw a small portion at least of the population of the major British cities into smaller communities in outer surrounding belts. Under the Act, public corporations called New Town Development Corporations have powers to expropriate private land after certain hearings of an administrative and quasi-judicial character.

The United States has hitherto been only slightly affected by the disorders of wars and economic upheavals, which have shaken all of Europe, with the exception of a few smaller neutral countries. Moreover, it is a country of abundant resources, vast spaces, and its history and political philosophy is permeated by distrust of State interference in property and economic enterprise. Yet, even American land law has witnessed a remarkable evolution.[44] Since the entry of the United States in World War II, extensive rent control legislation imposes major restrictions on the ability of the landlord to evict tenants. Both legislation and court decisions have, since the great depression of the early thirties, substantially restricted the rights of creditors against land which served as security for debts.[45] More gradually, the courts have developed concepts of good husbandry and increased the concept of waste by owners of possessory interests in land, reflecting changing patterns of land utilization. The increasing urbanization of living, reducing the percentage of rural population from 60·3 per cent in 1900 to 37·3 per cent in 1950, has accounted for a steady increase in public regulation of urban land-users, mainly through zoning legislation.[46] By a wider interpretation of the 'police power' inherent in both Federal and State governments, the courts have generally upheld official attempts to regulate land use by laying down minimum sizes and minimum floor space for homes.[47] The great majority of States now also have enabling legislation authorizing various local and county authorities to regulate subdivision practices. Through such control, subdividers may be required to provide adequate road networks and public utilities, space for parks, playgrounds, and schools as a condition of acquiring lots. Conservation legislation in many States now seeks to prohibit the waste of natural resources, such as natural gas, thus restricting the right of the landowner to do with his property what he likes. Perhaps the most remarkable illustration of the extent to which natural and social conditions may modify the prevailing ideology is the legislation prevailing in certain western areas of the United States, which are chronically short of water. Here, no owner is permitted to possess or control more than a certain area of land if he wishes to qualify for water supply from public irrigation projects.[48]

### Taxation and Credit Control as a Means of Redistribution of Property

Taxation is one of the most important weapons by which the State can mitigate the two objectionable aspects of unrestricted private property: first, the inequalities of wealth, and secondly, the power to use property for private profit, and without regard to community purposes. In popular consciousness the first aim still predominates. By graded taxation and surtax on high incomes, gross inequalities of wealth are evened out more easily than by the equalization of incomes or the abolition of private property. But the second aspect of taxation policy is becoming increasingly more important. On the one hand, taxation is a cheap means by which the State finances its costly social service schemes. Under the British National Health Service Act, 1946, medical services are free for all. The cost of medical services is no longer met by millions of contributions of varying magnitude from private pockets, but out of public revenue. This means that income and property taxes largely pay for the medical services of the poorer classes. To the extent that the State contributes to the cost of national insurance (National Insurance Act, 1946) the same applies.

On the other hand, differential taxes and customs duties form part of national economic planning. The import of non-essential goods is penalized by higher duties. A purchase tax is put on luxury goods, which are earmarked for export instead of home consumption. Some countries, Sweden for example, finance their comprehensive health and social services by State-controlled high prices for alcoholic drinks, which are sold through a State-supervised monopoly. The law of taxation is gradually revolutionizing private as well as public law. The incidence of taxation will be one of the main considerations determining the lawyer's advice on the form of a settlement or a will, or the formation of a subsidiary company. The rise of the incorporated charitable foundation[49] is largely a result of the incidence of taxation on large estates.

Public control of financial credit is another means by which the State curtails privately financed capital. Low interest rates may limit the income from private credit and other banking transactions, but by far the more important aspect of official credit restrictions is the curtailment of the power of private capital to influence the national economy through the expansion or restriction of credits. Agricultural banks in Germany and other Continental countries have, through their mortgaging policy, greatly influenced the structure of the national economy.[50] In Britain, credit policy is controlled through the nationalized Bank of England. The raising or lowering of discount rates by the U.S. Federal Reserve Bank is used as a means of controlling inflation and either quickening or slowing the pulse of the national economy. In Australia, the Banking Act, 1945, gives to the Governor-General, acting with the advice of the Federal Executive Council, and to the Commonwealth Bank important supervisory powers over gold and foreign exchange reserves and, above all, over interest rates to be charged by banks.

## CURBING THE POWER OF PROPERTY

It is not surprising that the many different devices by which the contemporary property owner is checked and restrained by the law in his *droit de jouir et de disposer des choses* are of an essentially restrictive and regulatory character. The *abus de droit* as a defence to an action, the compulsory licensing by administrative order or judicial decision of a misused or non-used patent, the numerous duties imposed by statute upon factory owners, employers, and others, the restrictions on the use and disposition of land, these and many other legal innovations attempt varying degrees of restraint and redistribution of property, with the object of distributing the benefits of property over wider sections of the community.

By contrast, the more serious countermoves against the *power* aspects of property in modern industrial society have been of an essentially *institutional* character. These new institutional developments represent either organized countervailing power, matching and curbing the formerly unrestrained power of the property owner in early industrial society, or they provide new institutions as a substitute for private property.

The power aspects of property in contemporary industrial society result overwhelmingly from the concentration of industrial assets. It is as owner and controller of industrial assets that, in Renner's terminology, the industrial owner becomes a 'commander'. But in the twentieth century, the industrial property owner is hardly ever in form – and very seldom in substance – a physical individual. The owner and controller of industrial assets is the corporation. And it is with the impact of corporate ownership and corporate power that modern legal and social countertrends are overwhelmingly concerned.

We have seen that the power to contract is in industrial society a most vital aspect of property. It is, therefore, the countervailing influence of trade-union organization and the institution of collective bargaining which constitute by far the most important restraint on the power of the industrial property owner to command the services of people through his control over industrial assets. We will deal with this aspect of restraint of the power of property in connexion with the evolution of the contract.[51]

As all these devices and developments are overwhelmingly the result of the growth of *corporate* property and power, we shall deal with them under this aspect in a later chapter.

### DECLINE OR REBIRTH OF THE RIGHT OF PROPERTY?

Surveying the many restraints which new public policies have imposed upon the untrammelled use of property rights, both in private and public law, many – and most articulately the upholders of a conservative philosophy of property – have decried the passing of property. This philosophy, articulated in the earlier, and now discarded, interpretations of the 'due process' clauses by the United States Supreme Court, sees property menaced or even destroyed by statutory welfare obligations, curbs on the employers' freedom in labour contracts, taxation, zoning or conservation legislation, not to speak of powers of expropriation in the public interest. It is certainly true that the right of property, in its traditional limitation to the more or less unlimited use and enjoyment of things, such as land, industrial assets, and quasi-corporeal rights, such as patents, has been severely curbed. But it is at this point that the redefinition of the concept of property, outlined earlier in this chapter, shows its philosophical and social significance. Thus, as has always been inherent in the common-law concept of property, and as is increasingly recognized in the civilian legal systems, property is not confined to the control of 'things', but extended to the whole field of legitimate economic interests and expectations. The protection of property rights today is spread over the community as a whole, where it has, in the past, essentially benefited the very limited class of owners of land and commercial property. The effect of the law was to give excessive protection – often at the expense of the essential necessities and liberties of the rest of the community – to the owners of large estates and industrial assets. Today, the balance is being restored, by a wider conception of property. Gradually, new social and economic philosophies are influencing the legal concepts. For the vast majority of people, the most essential economic interest is the right to use one's labour and skill, and to be protected in the exercise of these capacities.

The big landowner or the industrial entrepreneur is unquestionably today far more restricted in the free use of his property than in earlier times. But from the standpoint of the average person, who disposes of limited physical assets and mainly depends for his own and his family's livelihood on the ability to work, on fair conditions of trade, and on the enjoyment of minimum standards of living, it is truer to say that 'the notion that private property is an essential condition of human freedom is still accepted. We are perhaps giving the idea a greater practical effect than did our predecessors.'[52]

The social function of contract in the formative era of modern industrial and capitalist society may be summed up in four elements: freedom of movement; insurance against calculated economic risks; freedom of will; and equality between parties. These four elements are closely linked, and to some extent, overlapping, but each has a distinct meaning. The problems of legal adjustment and interpretation, however, which they have posed in a rapidly changing society, are not of the same order. The first two of our four elements are essentially formal in character, the latter two also express political and social ideologies. The difficulty of bridging the gap between the formal and substantive aspects of both freedom and equality is evident in the pathetic contrast between the law of contract as it is taught in most textbooks, and modern contract as it functions in society.

## THE CORNER-STONES OF CONTRACT IN THE 'CLASSICAL' ERA

### *Freedom of Movement*

For a developing industrial society contract supplied the legal instrument which enabled men and goods to move freely. It is this aspect of contract above all which is expressed by Maine's theory that progressive societies have developed from status to contract. As against a legal status determined by ties and conditions outside personal decisions, contract allows the individual to change his country or employment. In the American Civil War, the contest between status and contract stood behind the ideological struggle between slavery and personal freedom. The static rural and patriarchal society of the South wanted a hierarchical immobility. The slave, as part of the estate, was at the bottom of the social scale, although, as the future showed, his economic and social lot was often better than under the mobile and free economic society which the industrialized and commercialized North wanted and achieved. Freedom to hire and fire, and the unrestricted mobility of labour, were essential to this society, which regarded economic bargaining value as the main standard by which the demand for labour was regulated.

The evolution from status to contract, from immobility to mobility, gradually pervaded all spheres of life, beyond the fields of commercial and labour contracts. It invaded family relations, and the law of succession. It became the basis of club and union membership. Gradually it penetrated even into the law of land tenure, sale, and succession. In the English property legislation of 1925, the right of free disposal over land, including the power to disentail, is finally recognized.[1] In some respects, this movement from status to contract still continues, especially in so far as the modern state gradually abandons its ancient legal privileges, as the price to be paid for the vastly increased functions of modern government. The British Crown Proceedings Act of 1947, and corresponding legislation in the Dominions,[2] abolishes petition of right as the form of proceedings between subject and Crown, as well as the immunity of the Crown from liability in tort, based on the feudal and absolute status of the Sovereign. It introduces instead ordinary actions in contract, tort, and property, as between subject and Crown.[3]

But this aspect of contract is increasingly overshadowed by a return to a new kind of immobility resulting from the profound changes produced by the social welfare responsibilities of the modern state, by group organization and collective bargaining in industry and commerce, and, last but not least, the state of industrial mobilization into which international strife has forced Western states since the outbreak of the First World War.

## Insurance Against Calculated Economic Risks

The economic correlate of common-law contract in its formative phase is a free enterprise society, in which the economic rewards for enterprise or speculation are restricted only within very wide limits, if at all. The functioning of such an economic system depends on the guarantee of the law that enterprise or speculation, in so far as it implies contracts for labour, goods, or shares, will be protected by the award of damages or specific performance. At this stage, we need not discuss the various theories of contract, especially the controversy between those who see the essence of contract in the legitimate expectation of its performance, and those who see it in the guarantee against loss by damages.[4] On either assumption, the sanctions of contract enable the hirer of services, the manufacturer of goods, the speculator in land, or the purchaser of shares, to engage in calculated economic risks. This part of contract has been comparatively free from difficulties of ideology or adaptation to social change. It is a significant application of the Aristotelean principle of distributive justice, which demands the equal treatment of those equal before the law. It assumes that parties entering into a contract are equal before the law, and therefore entitled to the same remedies for breach of contract. It need not enter into the problem of social or economic equality between the rich and poor, capitalists and workers, groups and individuals. The courts have been mainly concerned with working out the comparatively technical, or to some extent logical, problems of possession, of remoteness of damage, and of 'positive' and 'negative' interest. Occasionally, social and economic problems intrude. The *Liesbosch* case[5] arose in tort, but might equally have arisen in contract. The owners of a dredger, under contract to a third party to complete special work in a given time, were put to much greater expense in fulfilling this contract because they were too poor to buy a substitute for the dredger sunk by the negligence of the defendants. Was this poverty too remote a consequence to be taken into consideration? The House of Lords held that it was, and assumed that, for the purposes of the law of damages, poverty is a misfortune for which the law cannot take responsibility. A similar philosophy was adopted by the English courts during the few years when 'expectation of happiness' played an exciting though slightly fantastic role in English law.[6] As Lord Simon put it, in *Benham*'s case, 'Lawyers and judges may ... join hands with moralists and philosophers and declare that the degree of happiness to be attained by a human being does not depend on wealth or status.' But on the whole, the problem of sanctions for breach of contract, while vital to its function in modern industrial society, has remained relatively technical.

## Freedom of Will

In one sense, freedom of will is only another way of expressing the essential mobility of contractual obligation. But freedom of contract has acquired a wider and more problematic significance, because of its philosophical and political connotation. Freedom of will goes both to the making and to the terms of contract. It means that a servant, an agricultural or an industrial worker, must be free to change his employer and his job. It means, on the other hand, that an employer can hire and fire at will, according to economic motives or personal dislikes, or for other reasons for which he is not generally accountable to anybody but himself. It means that a landowner can give notice to quit to a farmer-tenant whether his husbandry is good or not, and whether the land will go to waste or not. Freedom to make or unmake a contract also implies that a person cannot tie himself indefinitely to another. In other words, contract must not become a disguised form of status. This issue has not often come before the courts, but in *Horwood* v. *Millar's Timber and Trading Co.*,[7] the Court of Appeal held a contract illegal by which a man had, without any limitation of time, assigned his salary to a money-lender, contracted with him never to terminate his employment without the moneylender's consent, never to obtain credit, move from his house, and in several other respects to restrict his personal movements.[8]

This freedom also applies to the terms of contract. The parties, it is assumed, are free to bargain out among themselves the conditions and terms of agreement. The classical theory of contract assumes the legal individual also to be a physical individual. The foundations of the theory were shattered when corporations increasingly displaced physical persons as legal individuals, and as parties to commercial and industrial contracts. Because the theory was that two or more individual persons freely bargained with each other, control over the terms of contract was limited to a few categories of illegality. The idea that the State on behalf of the community should intervene to dictate or alter terms of contracts in the public interest, is, on the whole, alien to the classical theory of common-law contract. It is true that contracts in restraint of trade are supposed to be void if they are 'unreasonable', and reasonableness is measured by the interests of the parties as well as the interests of the public. Yet, in the long series of cases in which English courts have dealt with contracts in restraint of trade, there is only one case[9] in which consideration of the public interest produced a decision different from that resulting from a consideration of the interests of the parties. It was used to deny the plaintiff a pension which the defendants had promised him, on condition that he would not compete against them in the wool trade. Although the plaintiff did not plead restraint, but was anxious to comply and take the pension, the contract was held void as against the public interest.[10]

## Equality

To some extent, the concepts of freedom and equality in contract are interchangeable. Lack of freedom to make or unmake a contract, or to bargain on its terms, also implies lack of equality. As long as we restrict both concepts to the limited meaning which the orthodox theory of contract gives them, one usually implies the other. In so far as a person is free from physical restraint or other direct compulsion to make and unmake a contract, he is also assumed to be in a position of equality. Because the law will impartially award damages or an injunction according to the same principles of distributive justice to the employer and to the employee, it is not generally concerned with the inequality resulting from the fact that one may be a corporation, controlling the entire oil or chemical industry of the country, and the other a worker on weekly wage and notice. And formal equality, to vote, to make contracts, to migrate, to marry, was regarded by early utilitarianism and democratic theory as automatically conducive to social liberty and equality.

The increasing gap between this theory and the reality of developing capitalist society, which led to the gradual reversal of the earlier Benthamite theory,[11] had its particular effect on the law of contract, the legal symbol *par excellence* of this society. It is the main purpose of this chapter to analyse the extent to which a mixture of legislative developments and judicial interpretations have bridged the growing gap between the early philosophy of contract and the reality of contemporary society. It will become apparent that the evolution of the law of contract in response to fundamental social changes has overwhelmingly occurred outside the court room. Unfortunately, cases still form the almost exclusive material for English textbooks.[12] By contrast, American students of the law of contract have become increasingly conscious of the importance of 'contracts of adhesion' and the inclusion of standard terms in the materials of contract law.[13]

It would not, however, be correct to infer that the courts have been entirely blind to the discrepancy between the formal postulates of freedom and equality in contract and the social reality. There are, of course, well into recent times, judges who continue to uphold the assumptions of the early nineteenth century, either believing that they are still a true reflection of society, or that the law should not attempt to take note of any social evolution.

Perhaps the most telling expression of this view is that of Justice Pitney in *Coppage* v. *Kansas*.[14] But the majority of judges have striven, in however haphazard a way, to mitigate at least some particularly blatant consequences of the early theory. If they have not achieved very much, this is to some extent due to judicial conservatism, but to a far greater extent, to the organic weakness of judicial-law reform. It is easy enough to detect inarticulate premisses or prejudices, or ignorance of economic and social realities, in English and American case law. It is far more difficult to suggest an alternative. Vital developments of modern contract, especially in the sphere of collective bargaining, have largely proceeded outside the law courts. But even in so far as law courts can and wish to take into account the social implications of legal concepts, how far are they to go? Within the framework of the American Constitution, the Supreme Court has, since 1936, reversed the priority of values. It has, on the one hand, departed from the long line of decisions by which the court had interpreted the due-process clauses, so as to invalidate, for example, maximum hour legislation, or the legislative prohibition of 'yellow-dog' contracts. In this way, the court recognized that the main responsibility for translating the postulates of equality, freedom, and other political values into legal reality, was normally the job of the legislator in which the court ought not to interfere except in extreme cases. On the other hand, the court has, in recent years, emphasized the provisions of the constitutions which guarantee political and social equality, regardless of race and religion. It has, to some extent, but by no means clearly or unanimously, adopted a 'preferred freedoms' philosophy, a hierarchy of values, in which basic personal freedoms are more immune from legislative interference than economic freedoms.[15] What Professor Corwin has described as a 'Constitutional Revolution Limited', is a judicial revolution made possible as well as limited by the political principles incorporated in a written constitution and accessible to judicial interpretation. Even so, the American courts can only play a minor part in the fundamental changes in the function of contract which are taking place all the time. The judicial function is far more limited in Britain, where the courts have no specific catalogue of political rights to interpret.

## Equality between Parties

Neither in the common law nor in any other developed system of law has there ever been absolute freedom of contract, or complete passivity in the face of patent inequality between the parties. It is largely as a result of the early constructive influence of equity that the protection of infants and of beneficiaries under trusts has been extended, that remedies against both innocent and fraudulent misrepresentation and undue influence have been developed, and that, generally, property rights of persons suffering legal disabilities such as married women or infants, have been protected against the encroachments of rapacious husbands or parents. But equity shows even more clearly the strict limitations of such judicial interference. Anyone who approaches the study of equity by looking at its twelve maxims must beware of reading too much into such noble phrases as 'equality is equity', or 'equity will not suffer a wrong to be without remedy'. Their scope does not extend much beyond the adjustment of property rights, such as the rights between joint tenants, co-mortgagees, or co-sureties.

A much bolder attempt to apply the maxim that equality is equity to a modern contract between a Government agency and one of the most powerful corporations in the country was made when the U.S. Government sought to recover from the Bethlehem Steel Corporation vast profits claimed under wartime contracts made in 1918 between Bethlehem Steel and the U.S. Steel Corporation.[16] Bethlehem Steel undertook to build a number of ships to meet the emergency caused by German submarine warfare. The Government claimed that the agreed profits averaging over 22 per cent of the computed cost were excessive, and, due to the exploitation by Bethlehem Steel of a wartime emergency, the Government was compelled to accept the terms of the country's leading shipbuilder. The majority of the U.S. Supreme Court (deciding against a similar background during the Second World War) rejected this attempt to apply, as 'corrective justice', the principle of 'social solidarity' in wartime to a commercial contract, partly because it rejected the suggestion that the U.S. Government was in a position of bargaining inferiority, partly because it held that it was for Congress, not for the Court, to determine the proper method of obtaining war supplies from the citizens. But Frankfurter J., in a powerful dissenting judgement, held that 'the Court should not permit Bethlehem Steel to recover these unconscionable profits and thereby make the Court the instrument of injustice'. Had the majority followed this view, the Court would have made itself the arbiter of 'just profit' and, to some extent, of the proper distribution of the social product.[17] From such a task – which has faced the United States courts more frequently and directly in the interpretation of the Sherman Anti-Trust Act[18] – it shrank. It thereby agreed with the great majority of judges in all countries with a developed legal system, who refuse to use the judicial function for measures of social or economic redistribution. In that interpretation, the maxim of equity retains a limited significance of technical, not social, adjustment.

The prevailing attitude of the courts has been to protect freedom and equality of contract against physical coercion, inequality, or the use of 'unlawful' means. But what are unlawful means? In the *Crofter* case,[19] the House of Lords finally recognized that group pressure, applied for economic or social ends, as distinct from personal malice, and carried out by means not in themselves unlawful, was a legitimate weapon of modern economic and social conflict.[20]

Common-law courts have thus gradually come to sanction judicially the restoration of a rough equality in the economic and social conflicts, by recognizing group pressure as legitimate. They have gone somewhat further in counteracting social or economic inequality in twentieth-century decisions on restraint of trade. Going back to the *Nordenfelt* case,[21] they have held that restrictive covenants are generally valid, if entered in consideration of the sale of a business goodwill. The parties in such situations are presumed to be generally equal in economic power. On the other hand, since *Mason*'s case,[22] a covenant by which an employee engages himself not to use his skill and labour, has been held to be void, because the employee is presumed to be in a weaker bargaining position, and the restriction on his main or only capital, that is, labour and skill, is not to be encouraged.[23] Here the courts have touched at least the fringe of that great and dominating problem, the gap between the formal equality of parties free to make contracts as they wish, and the actual inequality and lack of freedom caused by stark differences of economic bargaining power. Yet it is obvious that the courts can only go a very limited distance along that road. The sphere of law which is not actually or potentially touched by the legislator is steadily shrinking. Over a century ago, English courts invented the doctrine of common employment. A century later, its abolition though favoured by the judiciary, had to be left to the legislator.[24] Judicial temperament, and beliefs, will make some courts go much farther than others in the reform of injustices through the discriminating use of precedent or the manifold other devices of judicial reform.[25]

The inevitable limitations of judicial reform in the field of major economic and social adjustments were underlined by the legislation immediately following the decision in the *Bethlehem Steel Corporation* case. Resulting from voluntary negotiations between various defence procurement agencies and private contractors for price adjustment by so-called 'renegotiation clauses', the United States enacted the Renegotiation Act of 1943. The basic conception of this Act was that wartime contracts for vital defence supplies, between the government on the one part, and private contractors on the other, could not be left to the free play of supply and demand or to the unchecked 'profit motive'. It provided for 'renegotiation' of certain categories of contracts, with special emphasis on excessive profits.

### THE MAIN SOCIAL CAUSES OF THE TRANSFORMATION OF CONTRACT

Four major factors may be regarded as being mainly responsible for a transformation in the function and substance of contract, which is creating a widening gap between legal reality and the traditional textbook approach. The first is the widespread process of concentration in industry and business, corresponding to an increasing urbanization and standardization of life. Its legal result is the 'standard' contract, or 'contract of adhesion'.

The second factor is the increasing substitution of collective for individual bargaining in industrial society. Its legal product is the collective contract between management and labour, with a varying degree of State interference.

The third factor is the tremendous expansion of the welfare and social-service functions of the State in all common-law jurisdictions; its legal product is twofold: on the one hand, it has led to a multitude of statutory terms of contract, substituted for, or added to, the terms agreed between the parties; on the other hand, it has led to a vast increase of contracts where government departments or other public authorities are on one side, and a private party on the other. The effect of this on the law of contract, though as yet little explored, is profound.

All these developments affect the theory and practice of contract, but in different ways. The social-security ideology means emphasis on stability and a corresponding lack of mobility, especially in employment contracts. The standardization of contract greatly restricts the freedom of the weaker party, and is usually accompanied by inequality of bargaining power. Collective bargaining, on the other hand, has substantially restored equality of bargaining power between employers and employees, though increasingly at the cost of individual freedom, as the legal or practical compulsion to join employers' associations and trade unions progresses. The imposition of statutory duties in the interest of social justice largely sacrifices mobility for stability and security. The increasing participation of public authority in contract creates the wider and as yet generally unexplored problem of the dual function of the state, as a superior and as an equal.[26]

Lastly, the economic security aspect of contract, the elaboration of remedies for breach, is increasingly affected by the spread of such political, economic, and social upheavals as war, revolution, or inflation. Its legal result is the doctrine of frustration of contract, with its consequent extension of legal excuses for the non-performance of contract.

## *Standardization of Contract*[27]

In extreme cases, a single corporation controlling an entire industry or business can impose its conditions upon an unorganized multitude of individual parties. In the vast majority of cases the firms operating in a particular industry or business are organized in an association, through which they formulate general conditions, which, by virtue of their membership, they are under an obligation to incorporate in their individual transactions. Most contracts which govern our daily lives are of a standardized character. We travel under standard terms, by rail, ship, aeroplane, or tramway. We make contracts for life or accident assurances under standardized conditions. We rent houses or rooms under similarly controlled terms; authors or broadcasters, whether dealing with public or private institutions, sign standard agreements; government departments regulate the conditions of purchases by standard conditions.[28] In many ways, this standardization of contract terms simplifies business; indeed, it is an inevitable aspect of the mechanization of modern life. The working out of thousands of individual contract terms for substantially similar transactions would be as uneconomical as the use of antiquated machinery. It has even been suggested that 'By standardizing contracts, a law increases that real security which is a necessary basis of initiatives and tolerable risks.[29] At the same time, it is certain that the standardization of contracts affects both freedom and equality of bargaining, except where groups of approximately equal strength confront each other. This is seldom the case in the type of transaction mentioned earlier. Freedom is affected in so far as the individual has a purely fictitious alternative to accepting the terms presented to him. The traveller may have a choice between different airlines or shipping companies, but it will hardly ever be a choice between different terms. The same applies to those who wish to insure themselves, mortgage their houses, or buy goods on hire-purchase. A shipping company or a government department will not agree to individual modifications of terms where a standard voyage or purchase is in question. In a recent case which concerned the effect of conditions printed on the back of a railway pass, Scott L.J. spoke of a 'misuse of contract which makes the legislature tend to substitute status'. [30] The absence of such freedom is, however, important mainly because of the ensuing inequality of bargaining power. Standard terms invariably detract from common-law rights: by limiting or excluding liability[31]; by making the landlord the judge of whether the tenant has infringed certain terms of the tenancy agreement[32]; by making a government department as contractor the sole judge of whether it is justified to terminate a contract because of altered circumstances.[33] Courts, or even the legislature, can do very little to alter this situation, which is inherent in modern conditions of life. It is difficult to see how it would be practicable for courts to 'enforce only those terms to which a reasonable offeree would have agreed if he had enjoyed equal bargaining power with the offeror'. [34] An alternative approach to the problem of standardized terms of contract imposed on all comers by a party of overwhelming economic power is that of deconcentration by legislation, as attempted by the American anti-trust legislation in civil or criminal law.[35] But it is fair to say that, while a certain degree of competition may be restored or preserved by such legislation and jurisdiction, its effect on the standardization of terms as between industry and the customer is small. The legislator and the courts have been somewhat more active in countering another form of inequality, that resulting from the fact that one party draws up terms of contract as a result of experience, long consideration, and expert advice, while the other party has no more than a hasty opportunity to scrutinize the terms. In some cases, the legislator has attempted to counter this inequality, for example, in the English Hire-Purchase Act, 1938, which makes the enforceability of a hire-purchase agreement dependent upon the delivery to the hirer of a note which sets out the essential terms of the agreement, and contains a legible note of the hirer's rights in a form prescribed by the Act. The so-called Ticket Cases have also touched this problem, although, as it appears, with inconclusive results, in both English and American law.[36] To some extent, at least, the courts have recognized that the customer is not bound by terms of which he cannot reasonably be expected to have taken notice, because they were unusual, inconspicuous, or unreasonable on some other ground. But again, it would go much too far to pretend that this haphazard and occasional legislative and judicial control has substantially altered the position for the great majority of people. A significant exception is, in English law, provided by section 97, Road Traffic Act, 1930, which, in the case of public-service vehicles, invalidates any contractual limitation of the carrier's liability.

As regards the lack of real, as distinct from nominal, freedom to refuse to enter a contract where the other side holds the monopoly or overwhelming power, a modification of this position would again require a fundamental alteration in the economic and social organization. Only a return to large numbers of fiercely competing railways, shipping lines, or insurance companies, not legal prohibition, would alter the position. Some attempt has, however, been made to counter this lack of freedom by a corresponding compulsion on the other side to offer a contract to all comers. To some extent, legislation imposes an obligation upon the providers of vital utilities to make services available under certain statutory conditions, or regulates the minimum terms from which they cannot derogate in the provision of services. Thus the British Road Traffic Act, 1930, and the British Transport Communication Passenger Charges Scheme, 1954, prohibit the exclusion or limitation of liability in contracts for the conveyance of passengers on public-service vehicles.[37] American courts have developed similar principles without legislation. 'The law seems well settled that a common carrier, owing a duty to serve all proper persons who apply, cannot, when acting in its public capacity, validly exempt itself by contract from liability for negligence.'[38]

Similar stipulations by private contractors are discouraged, at least where the user is dependent on the contractor's services.

Moreover, American courts have developed a theory by which a party holding a practical monopoly of service is assumed to have incurred a duty to render public service, and cannot therefore arbitrarily refuse to contract. Yet 'the field of genuine compulsory contract has not, on the whole, transcended that of public utilities and compulsory insurance'.[39] It is this problem of squaring the *de facto* exercise of public functions with the private-law liberty of making or refusing to make a contract, with all its ensuing powers of discrimination and abuse, which has, in some countries, led to the demand for the socialization of public utilities and insurance.[40]

## *Public Control over Terms*

The variety of impacts of public law on contract is almost infinite, but four broad methods of public control over the terms of contract may be sufficient for our purposes[41]:

(1) Public policy, through statutory or judicial prohibitions, may declare contracts void, either wholly or in part, in so far as they offend against certain principles of social or economic equality. Reference has already been made to the line of cases which have invalidated restrictive covenants between employers and employees purporting to restrict the exercise of the employee's skill and labour. This is a relatively rare instance of judicial correction of an inequality of bargaining power. A statutory parallel may be seen in the Truck Acts prohibiting the payment of wages in goods instead of money.[42] These Acts invalidate contracts by which an employer undertakes to pay any part of a workman's wages otherwise than in current coin, or lays down conditions as to the manner or place in which the workman had to spend his wages (e.g. by having to buy at the employer's store). Subject to certain exceptions laid down in the Act, the employer cannot make any deduction from wages in respect of meals or other benefits in kind.[43] The practical importance of these forms of legislative or judicial protection has, of course, been greatly diminished by the far-reaching restoration of equality of bargaining power through collective bargaining. They retain importance mainly in regard to unorganized employees.

(2) Of greater practical importance are the many forms of compulsory terms incorporated in contracts for the enforcement of certain social policies. The most frequent way of incorporating social duties in contracts is by means of statutory duties, which come into existence as by-products of the master-and-servant relationship. Technically, the breach of such statutory duties will usually be sanctioned either by penalties or by actions for damages akin to tort actions. For example, the breach of a statutory duty to fence dangerous machinery, or provide minimum standards of sanitation, may result in an action for damage by the person injured through neglect of these provisions. Workmen's compensation legislation – now replaced in Britain by the comprehensive National Insurance (Industrial Injuries) Act – provides a statutory obligation, regardless of fault, for compensation in the case of accidents suffered in the course of employment. Sometimes, legislation of this type imposes statutory duties of a quasi-contractual type, added to a contract

proper, for example, between landlord and tenant. A familiar example in English social legislation is the Housing Act of 1936, by which lessors of houses below a certain rateable value incur a statutory warranty of 'fitness for human habitation'. The relation of this statutory provision to the contractual terms has been the subject of some judicial differences of opinion. All the judgements expressed strong doubt whether contractual conditions such as notice of defects should be imported into statutory terms added to the contract in the public interest.

Another type of compulsory term imposed upon private contracts is that resulting from minimum-wage legislation. Two kinds of minimum-wage legislation have recently gained importance in English law. The first type makes it compulsory for contracting parties in a number of industries to incorporate 'fair wages' standards, that is, to negotiate wages in accordance with recognized standards. These principles have been embodied in particular in a large number of Acts, which provide assistance to industries and public authorities, by way of grant, loan, subsidy, guarantee, or licence.[44] This means that contracting parties are compelled to adopt minimum conditions determined by reference to standards outside their own volition and control. The second type of minimum-wages regulation directly imposes statutory minimum standards on a number of industries. Wage fixing is normally done through boards or councils, known as 'wage-regulating authorities', which make their orders after having heard the parties concerned. In substance, this is sometimes much like a process of collective bargaining, but in form it is a State Act which, by means of a statutory order, imposes terms on the parties themselves. In Britain, this machinery is used in a few industries where collective organization is weak, notably in agriculture, catering,[45] and in the retail trade.

(3) Another way of imposing public law upon private agreements is the variation of certain terms of contract by public authority, that is, either automatically by statute, or more frequently, by ministerial order. In so far as collective agreements are made automatically binding on individual contracts between employers and employees, the terms of the collective agreements are automatically substituted for those of the individual contract, to the extent that it derogates from the collective terms.[46] The English Agriculture Act, 1947, provides an interesting example of a ministerial variation of contractual terms in the name of national agricultural policy. Section 36 empowers the Minister, either on the application of the landlord or the tenant, or otherwise, to vary a contract which provides for the

maintenance of certain land as permanent pasture, by directing that certain parts of the land shall be treated as arable land. In this way the State ensures that the land is cultivated according to what appear to be paramount national interests, in preference to the agreement of the parties. Another section of the same Act empowers the Minister to make regulations about the maintenance, repair, and insurance of fixed equipment, which shall be deemed to be incorporated in every contract of tenancy concerning an agricultural holding. The Landlord and Tenant (Rent Control) Act, 1949, provides another example of modification of contractual terms in the public interest. Either the landlord or the tenant of a dwelling-house, subject to the Act, may apply to a Rent Tribunal for determination of a reasonable rent, and such rent is substituted for that agreed between the parties.

(4) An increasingly important type of official interference with contract is the statutory frustration of certain contracts which occur consequent upon the nationalization of an industry. Thus, the British Coal Industry Act, 1949, s. 3, gives the corporation power to terminate certain long-term contracts, for the sale of products as well as for the employment of a person 'if the board is of opinion that they are, or are likely to be, hampered in the efficient performance of their functions by the operation of provisions of a contract'. If the board exercises this power, it is liable to pay compensation, which, in default of agreement, is determined by arbitration. If the contract is effectively terminated, provisions of the Law Reform (Frustrated Contracts) Act, 1943, apply.

## Public Authorities as Parties

The modifications of the traditional principles of contract discussed so far are familiar to all common-law countries. Moreover, it is their frequency and importance, rather than their existence, which is a fairly recent development. By far the most important modification of the law of contract, however, results from the increasing role played by the government, by local authorities, and the growing number of incorporated public authorities as owners and managers of industry, as providers of public utilities, administrators of social services, or in some other capacity which requires the making of contracts. It is perhaps not surprising that this problem has as yet been so little explored in the common-law systems. It is a familiar problem in Continental systems, where the relations between public authority and the citizen have, for many decades, been the concern of the science of public law. The legal classification of conflicts between public authorities and the citizen is also indispensable for the allocation of a particular dispute, either to a civil court or an administrative tribunal. In the common-law systems, on the other hand, public law has crept in gradually and by stealth. As all common-law countries now have highly developed government machineries, social services, public utilities, and publicly owned industries, the significance of public law in these countries is steadily growing. But public law has to be developed mainly out of the categories of common law. The impact of public law on common law concepts, however, is of at least equal significance. It presents itself in two forms. First, government departments or other public authorities are employers, buy and sell goods or services, manage factories, grant loans, repair dykes, or regulate watercourses, and exercise a multitude of other activities which bring them into legal contact with the citizen. On the other hand, public authorities contract with each other. The British Transport Commission must buy coal from the National Coal Board, and the National Coal Board uses nationalized railways. This theme will be developed further in a later chapter, assessing the growth and place of public law in the common-law world.[47]

So far as the conditions imposing social and economic policies are concerned, no bargaining takes place; the contract clauses embodying those policies are prescribed and printed in advance, becoming standard 'boiler-plate' in the contractual document.

To a large extent, accordingly, the Government contract is an instrument of a power relationship, and only vaguely resembles the consensual agreement extolled by Maine and relied upon by Adam Smith. The significant decision is that of the Government in setting the terms and conditions of the proposed agreement. . . .[48]

## Contract in a Socialized Economy

To an increasing extent, government departments or incorporated authorities now deal with each other. The greater the sector of socialized industry, the more important is this type of transaction. Against a different legal background, it has become the predominant form of contract in the Soviet system, where all industry is nationalized. Through the establishment of the different industries as quasi-autonomous legal corporations, Soviet law has treated them as separate legal managerial and accounting units which are able to make contracts. But contracts between State-owned corporations working under an overall economic and political plan are obviously different in substance, if not in form, from the private-law contract of both common law and the civil law systems, which are based on the principle of individual ownership and free economic enterprise.

In modern Soviet jurisprudence, contract has been restored as the chief legal instrument in the relations between State enterprises. Earlier Soviet jurists who, under the leadership of Pashukanis, relegated all law, and contract in particular, to the scrap-heap as an instrument of bourgeois society have been castigated as 'wreckers'. But the restitution of contract to a place of honour serves mainly the purpose of administrative decentralization, and of the accountancy of State enterprises to the political planners. 'The two – contracts and plans – bear a polar relation to each other.'[49]

In general, the Soviet Civil Code of 1922, which is in many ways modelled upon the modern civil codes of Continental Europe, applies to the transactions between State enterprises. Liability for breach of contract depends upon fault; the familiar rules of civil law regarding mistake, impossibility, unjust enrichment, illegality, are applied.[50] Special commercial courts, the *Gosarbitrazh*, adjudicate on disputes between State enterprises. Though separate from the ordinary courts and closely linked with the administrative branch of government, these courts have been increasingly directed to apply law rather than general equity or policy principles.[51] Yet the interpretation and enforcement of contracts between Soviet enterprises – which are above all instruments of national planning – account for at least two distinctive features: first, in the decisions of the *Gosarbitrazh* administrative and penal sanctions are coupled with civil sanctions. Where the court regards a particular breach of contract as injurious to the national economy, it will report to the superior authorities.[52] Secondly, the ability to fulfil a contract is often influenced by policy and planning decisions outside of the control of the parties. This is perhaps only a difference of degree as compared with the present position in Britain or the United States, where the official allocation of raw materials, the prohibition of certain transactions, the imposition of price controls and other aspects of a semi-planned economy are becoming increasingly frequent. The Soviet commercial contract is of necessity part of an overall plan laid down by the superior authority. The latter enter annually into general contracts on the basis of which the subordinate enterprises conclude local contracts.[53] An unjustified delay in the conclusion of a local contract will expose the defaulter to penalties.[54] But where a cartographical factory had ordered seventeen million pieces of tin stamp from the plaintiff trust and then refused to accept the goods because its planned task only called for eight million pieces, the *Gosarbitrazh* held the defendant liable.[55]

In non-Socialist society, the penalty of miscalculation is a financial one, although the increasing intervention of government considerably cushions such effects of a *laissez faire* economy, by guarantees, compensation clauses, and other means. In Soviet law the sanctions of contract are used as a whip. Damages will show up in the accounts of the enterprises concerned; penalties will bring it into bad odour; court reports to the superior authorities will expose the management to disciplinary measures. Even though the form and sanctions of contract are largely similar to those of non-Soviet law, its social function is different.

Where the predominant type of legal transaction is between public authorities, law becomes far more closely linked with and dependent upon State policy and planning.

## Economic Upheavals

Before the First World War, physical or legal impossibility was the only means by which contract could be discharged, apart from breach of contract. The First World War produced the problem of frustration of contract, as a result of political, social, or economic upheavals. A further impetus was given to the doctrine by the post-war inflation in Germany, which led to important judicial developments, especially to the doctrine of 'foundation of contract'. The French doctrine of *imprévision* in administrative contracts also had considerable influence. What emerged was a doctrine which, in civil, commercial, and industrial relations, supplemented the strict categories of impossibility by 'frustration' of contract, where war, devaluation, major social unrest, or similar factors beyond the control of the parties had vitally affected the ability of one or both parties to perform. By now the doctrine of frustration is an established part of most civil-law and common-law jurisdictions.[56] This is mainly a reflection of the vicissitudes and uncertainties of a period of wars, international tensions, social revolution, and economic upheavals. The law recognizes that these factors, due to national or international policies, go beyond reasonable calculations of economic risk, to safeguard which is the function of the law of contract. This is not the place to discuss in detail the extent to which the doctrine of frustration has now been incorporated in the law of contract of the Western systems, both in the common-law and the civil-law[57] systems. Frustration of contract is still predominantly a judicial doctrine, although it has been incorporated in a recent civil code.[58] A vital change of circumstances may lead sometimes to the complete discharge, and sometimes to the judicial modification of the terms of contract.[59] The doctrine of frustration has recently gained increased importance in English law. This is a natural consequence of the upheavals of war, inflation, and any such social and legal changes as are produced by the nationalization of industries. Reference has already been made to the instances of statutory frustration, where the boards of nationalized industries are empowered to disclaim certain contracts and leases. In English law the doctrine owed its main expansion to the First and Second World Wars. But the courts stopped short of varying the terms of contracts, until in a recent decision[60] the Court of Appeal followed some Continental models and boldly revised the terms of contract. A contract between the Commissioner of Works and a private firm had stipulated that the sum to be paid to the contractor 'should not be greater than the actual cost plus a net profit remuneration of £300,000'. The parties had contracted for about £5,000,000, but extra work ordered brought the total cost up to £6,683,000. The court awarded the contractors extra remuneration in proportion to the excess cost. In another recent case,[61] a contract for the supply of newsfilms made during the war was to continue until a Cinematograph Film Order, made in 1943, under the Defence Act, 1939, was cancelled. When the Defence Act expired after the war, the order was continued under the Supplies and Services Act, 1945. The Court of Appeal considered the circumstances which had led to the agreement and came to the conclusion that the order had been continued for reasons different from those leading to the original Cinematograph Film Order, and it discharged the defendants from further performance of the contract, despite its clear wording.

Lord Justice Denning regarded this as more than a matter of construction.

In these frustration cases, as Lord Wright said, the court really exercises a qualifying power – a power to qualify the absolute, literal, or wide terms of the contract – in order to do what is just and reasonable in the new situation, and it can now by statute make ancillary orders to that end. Until recently the court only exercised this power when there was a frustrating event, that is a supervening event which struck away the foundations of the contract. In the important decision of *Sir Lindsay Parkinson & Co., Ltd* v. *Works & Public Building Commrs,* however, this court exercised a like power when there was no frustrating event, but only an uncontemplated turn of events.[62]

But the House of Lords, in reversing the decision, went out of its way to repudiate the suggestion that courts had a broad qualifying power in regard to contracts. The decision in *Parkinson*'s case was reduced to one of construction, following from the language of the contract.

On the basis of a comprehensive comparative analysis, a recent American study[63] suggests the 'gap-filling doctrine' as a suitable rationalization:

Where circumstances occur, neither foreseen nor reasonably foresee-able at the time of the promise, it follows from application of the proper standard of interpretation that the promise may not reasonably be construed to express an intention to be found also in the unanticipated situation. Broad terms do not cover unforeseen contingencies. Since, therefore, in regard to the unforeseen circumstances, the contract shows a gap, supplementation with provisions ensuing from reasonableness is required.

Such a rationalization can, however, only serve as the framework within which courts, guided by the intensity of the upheaval, will supplement, modify, or supersede the intentions of the parties expressed at the time of the making of the contract. Despite such judicial emphasis on *pacta sunt servanda* and other traditional aspects of contract, the character of contract as a legal instrument of contemporary society is undergoing profound changes, in which elements of the old mingle with the new. The normal commercial contract – between individuals or corporate persons – can still be handled with the traditional categories and approaches. But whenever elements of public policy enter into the making of a contract, either through the status of one or both of the parties, or through the terms of the contract itself, the policy aspects of contract increase. In a private-enterprise economy, like that of the United States, war procurement is still largely handled through contracts between governmental authorities and private contractors. It is nevertheless an instrument of policy, and as the various Renegotiation Acts show, they are subject to considerations that do not apply to the normal commercial contract.

### Collective Bargaining

The increasing substitution, in all the common-law jurisdictions, of collective bargaining for individual contract, is steadily supplanting, for the vast majority of employees, the traditional master and servant relationship. In Britain, neither legislature nor courts have had a major part in this development.[64]

In England the growth of collective bargaining has proceeded almost unnoticed by the law. The term is only briefly mentioned in the most recent textbook on industrial law.[65] The overwhelming legal significance of collective bargaining in modern English law would be almost unknown except for the work of a German-trained jurist.[66] Collective bargaining is taken for granted in England as a predominant method of regulation of conditions in industry and agriculture, but despite the tremendous growth of State intervention in recent legal history, governmental interference in the regulation of labour conditions has been extremely cautious and, on the whole, exceptional. Where it has happened, it has been done mainly in the form of minimum-wage legislation, that is, through the compulsory determination of minimum terms of remuneration in the relevant contracts.[67] Indirectly, collective bargaining is recognized through 'fair wages' clauses, incorporated in many statutes or directives to enter into collective bargaining. Moreover, the Nationalization Acts enjoin the boards of the public corporations managing the nationalized industries 'to enter into consultation with organizations, appearing to them to represent substantial proportions of the persons in the employment of the board', for the purpose of negotiating terms and conditions of employment. The validity of the 'closed shop' as a contractual term has never been legally tested in Britain.

The actual strength of trade unionism in most major industries is such that the practical compulsion of union membership is sufficient, and also preferable to legal compulsion. Occasionally, a single trade union is recognized as exclusively entitled to bargain on behalf of the employees.[68] But on the whole, the collective-labour agreement, for all its tremendous importance in the lives of millions of people, has remained outside the sphere of the English law courts, and that means it is still on the bare fringe of interest for the legal profession and writers of textbooks. Strictly, the collective contract is not enforceable before an English law court. Section 4 of the Trade Union Act, 1871, says that 'nothing in this Act shall enable any court to entertain any legal proceeding instituted with the object of directly enforcing or recovering damages for the breach of. . . . Any agreement made between one trade union and another' (this includes employers' associations). Thus there is no direct enforcement of what, in a Continental terminology now increasingly familiar in

the common-law jurisdictions, is termed the contractual or obliga-
tory aspect of collective agreement.[69] But the lack of direct legal
enforceability compares starkly with its social strength in a society
in which group bargaining has almost entirely displaced individual
bargaining. As to the 'normative' aspect, that is, the question how
far an individual contract of employment must conform with the
terms laid down in the collective agreement as to wages, holidays,
and other important matters, the only English decision on the
point[70] decided that no individual member of an association could
bring an action on the terms of an agreement made between that
association and another. But the legal effect of collective agreements on individual employment contracts is greatly strengthened
by the Terms and Conditions of Employment Act, 1959, which
became law on 30 April 1959. Under this Act if there are 'recognized
terms and conditions', i.e. terms of collective agreements or awards
concluded by or rendered between substantially representative
organizations, and an employer, whether a party to such agreements or awards or not, does not observe them, the Minister, upon a
report by a substantially representative organization, may take
any steps to secure a settlement of the claim. If he does not succeed,
he must refer it to the Industrial Court, and the Industrial Court,
unless satisfied that the employer is granting not less favourable
terms, must make an award requiring the employer to observe the
recognized terms or conditions as respects all workers of the relevant
description.

Thus, a court award will be compulsorily implied in the relevant
employment contracts. English law appears to be moving closer
towards the Continental concept of legal – instead of merely social –
sanctions for collective bargaining.

The growth of collective bargaining in the U.S.A. is of far more
recent origin.[71] The suddenness and the size of its growth, as well
as its association with the New Deal legislation, have brought it far
more within the purview of legal discussion and adjudication than in
Britain. The National Labour Relations Act, 1935, made it compulsory upon employers to bargain collectively with the chosen representatives of the employees. The National Labour Relations Board,
established under the Act, and the courts deciding on appeal from
that Board, have given hundreds of decisions trying to elucidate
what type of action by the employer complies with the direction of
the Act. It is not necessary in our context to pursue that question.[72]
The Labour Management Relations Act of 1947 made collective
agreements specifically the subject of suits for enforcement in the

Federal Court. The position therefore now differs from that in English law, where collective agreements are still not directly enforceable. As regards the normative force of collective agreements on individual contracts of employment, the attitude of the courts is not unanimous.

Precedents can be found for almost any conceivable view: that collective agreements impose a mere moral obligation upon the parties[73]; that collective agreements create a usage, the incorporation of which into labour agreements is a question of fact[74]; that collective bargaining agreements are void for want of consideration[75]; that collective agreements give both parties the full armoury of equitable remedies, especially injunctions and specific performance[76]; that the violation of a collective agreement is an unfair labour practice[77]; that individual employees may assert rights under collective agreements, either because the union has acted as their agent,[78] or as third party beneficiaries.[79] On the whole, there has been a definite development towards full legal status and enforceability of collective agreements. They are increasingly given statutory recognition and protected by various private as well as public-law sanctions. The public-law aspects are further underlined by the important role of the arbitrator, who, in United States and Canadian industrial labour practice, almost universally interprets disputes under the agreements, and whose creative role in the interpretation of comprehensive collective-labour agreements as living instruments of order, rather than as individual commercial contracts, has been stressed by authoritative commentators.[80]

The legal position in Canada is, as in many other fields, a blend between British and American legal developments. Substantially the same view as in *Holland*'s case is taken in a decision of the Judicial Committee, on appeal from a Canadian court.[81] In that case, the plaintiff had sued a railway company for damages for wrongful dismissal, basing himself on a collective agreement between the Canadian Railway Board and a division of the American Federation of Labor. The Judicial Committee did not exclude that such an agreement might establish directly enforceable rights for an individual but held that, in this case, the collective agreement appeared 'to be intended merely to operate as an agreement between a body of employers and a labour organization. . . . If an employer refused to observe these rules, the effect would be, not an action by any employee, not even an action by the Union against the employer for specific performance or damages, but the calling of a strike until the grievance was remedied' A number of later Canadian cases have also held that an individual workman cannot derive actionable rights from a collective agreement.[82] Subsequent Canadian legislation, both Federal and provincial, has put collective agreements on a statutory basis and given them definite legal effect, as between the parties to the agreement.[83]

A third type of collective bargaining is represented by Australia and New Zealand, where the machinery of collective bargaining entirely dominates labour conditions, but with a significant difference in that the terms of collective bargaining can be hardened, and thus be turned from group law into State law, by an award of the Arbitration Court.[84] This may be either by a consent decree, or an award adjudicating between contesting points of view. Here the machinery of group bargaining is the basic factor, but the State machinery, in a capacity half-judicial, half-legislative, is super-imposed upon it.

The vital significance of collective bargaining for the law of contract thus lies in its following aspects: first, it resembles a standard contract of business and industry in that standardized terms regulate the conditions of employment of millions of individuals. Secondly, it is a most important instance of a public-law function delegated, by the permissive or even imperative authority of the State, from government to social groups. Thirdly, the freedom of the individual to bargain on his terms of employment is inevitably curtailed by the prevalence of collective bargaining. It is even excluded where the 'closed shop' is recognized either legally or *de facto*. Fourthly, this lack of freedom is compensated by a substantial restoration of equality of bargaining power. It is not the individual employee who has regained equality, but the trade union negotiating on his behalf. Although the trade union is not, strictly speaking, the agent, it has, in effect, absorbed and consolidated the bargaining power formerly vested in the individual.

The future of the collective contract in the common-law jurisdictions is ultimately dependent on the degree to which group autonomy can survive in the planned society. In the completely planned State, as represented by Soviet Russia, the collective contact between management and labour survives, but it is overwhelmingly an instrument of planning and social solidarity, leaving only limited scope to complementary bargaining by individual plants or industries.[85] There are model collective contracts with all the emphasis on maximum production and labour discipline. Supplementary plant collective contracts mainly concentrate on social aspects, such as schools, nurseries, clinics, and houses. In the

Soviet State, management and labour can represent conflicting interests only within very strict limits, in complete subordination to the State plan. It is more than doubtful whether these collective contracts create any legally enforceable obligations.[86] By contrast, the individual rights of workers, in regard to wages, dismissal, holidays, are protected by an elaborate administrative and judicial procedure.[87] This position is not far removed from that of Nazi labour law which merged all collective workers' organizations in a compulsory State labour front, but preserved the labour courts for the protection of individual rights. The modern totalitarian 'organic' State destroys the autonomy and freedom of its workers, but gives them security and protection in return. Anglo-American society is still far removed from such a State, but the ever-growing emphasis on defence and production, and the increasing responsibilities of government for the economic well-being of the people, are steadily increasing the public policy and planning elements and reducing the autonomy of groups.

### CONTRACT AND THE REALIZATION OF ECONOMIC EXPECTATIONS

The mixture of heterogeneous factors that make up the complex picture of modern contract and have turned it into something rather different from the chief commercial guarantee of a private enterprise society, is best illustrated by the problem of sanctions.

The controversy whether the primary sanction of contract is actual performance or a promise to make reparation for non-performance is of old standing. Oliver Wendell Holmes long ago proposed the view that 'the only universal consequence of a legally binding promise is that of the law making the promisor pay damages if the promised event does not come to pass'.[88] This view has been widely criticized, mainly on the ground that the law does not leave the promisor the freedom to choose between performance and the payment of damages where he is able to perform.[89]

The history of the common law tends to support Holmes's view, in so far as the common-law sanction for breach of contract is damages, whereas equity supplies the supplementary sanctions of specific performance and injunction, as additions or alternatives to the basic remedy of damages in meritorious situations. By contrast, the Civil Codes of the civilian systems regard performance as a primary, and damages as a secondary, remedy.[90] In practice, the difference is far less marked than in theory. Under both systems, the normal remedy for a breach of contract is pecuniary compensation, i.e. damages, whereas in appropriate situations where the individualized character of the transaction makes pecuniary compensation inadequate,[91] specific performance of injunction will, under both types of systems, take preference.

The proportion of public and private elements in a given contract determines the degree to which the traditional sanctions of contract apply. The normal commercial contract is still predominantly an insurance against economic risk. Its primary sanction is pecuniary compensation, including the loss of profits to be expected from the carrying out of the agreed transaction. In a minority of cases, it is specific performance.

But in a case like the *Bethlehem Steel* case,[92] contract fulfils a substantially different function, although it is still cast largely in the traditional mould of an ordinary commercial contract. Mutual rights and obligations are fixed, times of delivery are specified, prices and profits are agreed, etc. But, at the same time, a contract of this type is a public transaction. In this case, the government and a powerful firm enter into a kind of partnership for the delivery of vitally needed commodities. It is this factor which induced a minority of the U.S. Supreme Court to regard the Court as justified in a *post factum* adjustment of profits, in regarding, in other words, the contract to some extent as the discharge of a public duty. Even though the majority of the Court disagreed, and left this kind of adjustment to subsequent legislation, a transaction of this type still retains its public character. The participation of an administrative authority in the adjustments of terms under the Renegotiation Act shows that this kind of transaction resembles the classical commercial contract in name rather than in substance.

## CONCLUSIONS

It has not been possible, in this attempt at synthesizing the various changes in the structure and function of contract, to give more than a general picture of developments which require the most detailed study. It should, however, suffice to justify some general conclusions. First, it is clear that contract is becoming increasingly institutionalized. From being the instrument by which millions of individual parties bargain with each other, it has to a large extent become the way by which social and economic policies are expressed in legal form. This is another way of saying that public law now vitally affects and modifies the law of contract.

In so far as the basic industries and economic commodities are now subject to standardized regulation by private insurance, transport, or public utility undertakings these exercise functions of public law. Because of the inability of the other party to bargain effectively on terms, such private enterprises exercise, by permission of the State, a quasi-legislative power. Where 'the sense of injustice'[93] is strongly aroused, public law intervenes further, either by the imposition of statutory conditions, by the compulsory restoration of competition, by the 'renegotiation' of defence contracts, or, in the last resort, by the transfer of the industry or utility concerned into public ownership.

The exercise of public-law functions through nominally private-law groups is even more marked in the position of collective bargaining. By permitting or even directing the regulation of industrial conditions through collective contract, the State transfers a vital law-making function to the recognized organizations of employers and employees. Sometimes it formally strengthens this position by making the terms of representative collective agreements compulsory, sometimes it modifies them by State award.

In another way, collective bargaining narrows the gap between the mobility of contract and the stability of status. The paramount purpose of collective bargaining on an industry-wide or nation-wide scale is the stabilization of industrial conditions. The more successful the collective bargaining, the greater the approximation of the status of the employee to that of an official. Recently American collective agreements in industry have been preoccupied with the stabilization of conditions for a period varying from three to five years. A number of collective agreements between industrial giants and the most powerful labour unions – General Motors, Ford, or United States Steel on the one hand, and the Automobile or Steel Workers' or Coalminers' Unions on the other hand – provide for rates of pay, with escalator clauses, holidays, seniority rights, pensions, and grievance machinery, in return for no-strike promises. They go further than any previous agreement towards giving employees an assured status in exchange for a limited surrender of mobility.

Lastly, the increasing use of contract as an instrument of economic State policy, through the extension of government functions and the socialization of industries, makes contract largely the legal expression of economic and social policies. This weakens the degree to which contract can any longer fulfil the function of security against calculated economic risks. This is further emphasized by the development of the doctrine of frustration, which allows for the statutory or judicial consideration of circumstances beyond the control of the parties. To that extent, contract becomes the foundation for a broad adjustment of risks in which private agreement and public policy are mingled.

The law of tort or delict is concerned with the adjustment of risks, with the extent to which the manifold injuries to person and property caused by the contacts between people and things should be the subject of pecuniary compensation. As Oliver Wendell Holmes put it many years ago[1]:

> Be the exceptions more or less numerous, the general purpose of the law of torts is to secure a man indemnity against certain forms of harm to person, reputation, or estate, at the hands of his neighbours, not because they are wrong, but because they are harms. . . . It is intended to reconcile the policy of letting accidents lie where they fall, and the reasonable freedom of others with the protection of the individual from injury. . . . As the law, on the one hand, allows certain harms to be inflicted irrespective of the moral condition of him who inflicts them, so, at the other extreme, it may on grounds of policy throw the absolute risk of certain transactions on the person engaging in them, irrespective of blame-worthiness in any sense.

It is obvious that this branch of the law must strongly reflect changing social conditions. The type and significance of risks incurred in social contact varies with the type of society in which we live. The principles of liability governing the readjustment are greatly influenced by changing moral and social ideas.

In the formative stage of the common law – and, indeed, of other legal systems – the law of torts is mainly concerned with the infringement of protected interests in land. Commerce and communications are ill-developed, towns and other close congregations of people are scarce and small, and the type of economic asset which predominates by far, in quantity and in legal esteem, is land. Consequently, the early law of tort is largely concerned with the protection of property in land. It is dominated by trespass to land, from which other actions upon the case branch out that are closely modelled upon trespass.

Urbanization, industrialization, and, in particular, since the last century, the ever-growing development of fast-moving traffic, shift the emphasis gradually from injury to land and related interests to other and broader forms of property interests, and even more to reparation for personal injury. Although negligence has in recent years gone far to displace trespass or nuisance even as a remedy for injuries to property, it owes its main growth to the phenomenal multiplication of personal injuries due to modern conditions of living. As emphasis shifted from definition by the kind of *interest* injured (as in the older torts) to the kind of *conduct* which engenders liability, negligence was obviously better fitted to become the modern tort action *par excellence*.[2]

The change in the type of interest with which the law is primarily concerned, and in the kind of injury that occurs most frequently, is accompanied by a struggle between conflicting theories of civil liability. There is not a single modern legal system in which principles of strict and fault liability are not closely intermingled, partly as a result of statutory intervention, and partly as a result of judicial law-making. A brief survey later in this chapter will attempt to analyse the conflicting trends and pulls as they appear to shape the contemporary common law in this field. In any attempt to bring some order into the mixture of conflicting ideas, theories, and decisions, two major determining factors have to be borne in mind: delictual liability is firstly determined by a choice of moral philosophies which have deeply influenced the law. As some writers have pointed out,[3] the change from emphasis on liability for harmful acts regardless of fault, to liability for fault only – which dominated the eighteenth and the major part of the nineteenth century – is parallel to the movement from status to contract, and both affect the philosophy of the free will, symbol of the self-reliant individual who makes and unmakes his legal engagements freely and who bears responsibility for his behaviour in society because he has a choice between good and evil. A great deal of this philosophy is still with us; indeed it could not be otherwise in any society that has not completely abandoned the ideal of individual responsibility for social conduct. But this philosophy has been increasingly countered by growing emphasis on the responsibility of the community for the accidents that befall the individual. And the growth of the new policy is due largely to the social transformation of modern Western society, a society in which more and more vicissitudes threaten a multitude of individuals whose liberty to avoid them shrinks steadily. The steady growth of the principle of social responsibility for injuries is not due to any cynical abandonment of the principle of individual responsibility but to the extent to which millions of individuals find themselves exposed to accidents arising in factories, on the roads, in aeroplanes, or the threat of unemployment.

The advance of the idea of social responsibility against that of individual fault has not, however, entirely expressed itself in the substitution of strict liability, or even of insurance, for individual liability. It has, to a large extent, expressed itself in a gradual transformation of the idea of fault itself, in what one might call the objectivization of fault liability. Thus the question which still greatly exercised Sir John Salmond in his treatise on the law of torts – whether negligence is a state of mind or a standard of conduct – is no longer a serious issue. The countless thousands of negligence cases which arise from traffic or factory accidents or similar causes, are not concerned with the individual state of mind of the defendant but with standards of conduct measured by that of the 'reasonable man'. Beyond that, the courts in many countries have gradually widened the concept of negligence – e.g. regarding the responsibilities of employers to employees, of manufacturers to consumers, or of motor-car drivers to pedestrians – by a series of judicial creations in such a way that modern writers can speak of 'negligence without fault'[4] or of 'negligence in name only'.[5]

The transformation of the meaning of negligence, the almost complete elimination of moral factors in favour of objective standards of conduct – and these mostly affecting corporate rather than individual persons – have done as much to change the character of fault liability in the most important area of the law of tort as the advance of strict liability as such.

But with the further progress of industrialization and the structure of modern enterprise, another factor now affects civil liability even more profoundly: the shift of civil liability from the immediate tortfeasor to a third party, who for a variety of reasons is considered to be better fitted to absorb the risk of compensation.

The first significant development in that direction was, quite a long time ago, the acceptance of the principle of vicarious liability of the master for the torts of his servant. Seen from the standpoint of the master, this appears as an example of strict liability. He is held responsible for a wrong which he has not himself committed but which is imputed to him. But seen from the standpoint of relationship between the injured and the wrongdoer, vicarious liability means a transfer of the primary responsibility from the immediate tortfeasor to a third party: the employer. The justification for this development is the power of control and direction exercised by the master over the servant. The enterprise rather than the individual cog in the wheel is seen as presenting certain risks to the community for which it must assume responsibility. Such oddities as the now generally discarded 'fellow-servant' or 'common employment' rule only serve to underline the significance of the shift from personal to enterprise liability.

But this shifting of the burden – of which vicarious liability was the first significant token – is now occurring on a vastly wider scale, mainly as the result of the progress of insurance. Tort liability is affected by the progress of private as well as of social insurance, though not in the same way.

The impact of private insurance on tort liability has become most obvious and socially significant in the growth of insurance against automobile accidents. Liability insurance does not as such – at least in the practice still prevailing in the common-law countries – undermine tort liability. The insurer is normally substituted for the insured in any tort claims that may arise. It is therefore outwardly a change of parties rather than any modification of the principles of tort liability which occurs as a result of liability insurance.[6] Far more important, though less easily ascertainable in terms of legal principle, is the psychological effect of liability insurance, especially where the civil jury still predominates in accident cases.[7] The knowledge of the existence of liability insurance is likely to affect the jury both in the allocation of responsibility and in the assessment of damages. Just as damages in defamation actions have often been grossly inflated where a motion-picture company or a big newspaper is the defendant, so the knowledge that an insurance company stands behind the defendant may influence the assessment of responsibility, especially where the plaintiff is a pedestrian and thus not normally insured. It also affects the amount of damages, especially where it is possible for the plaintiff's lawyer to dramatize the contrast between the poor victim of the accident and the powerful companies that adjust damages as a matter of routine business. It is not, therefore, surprising that trial lawyers in those common-law countries where the civil jury still predominates, bitterly oppose not only the possible abolition of juries in tort cases, but even a reduction of their number.[8]

Especially in the many countries which have introduced compulsory liability insurance for motor-car operators, the effective shift of liability from the motor-car driver to the insurer has increasingly raised the question whether liability insurance should not be openly turned into loss insurance.[9] Loss insurance means an abandonment of the principle of individual tort responsibility and the frank substitution of compulsory insurance for loss incurred as a result of certain operations. Administration replaces to that extent civil litigation, and an element of social insurance is injected into this sphere of private relationships. As will be shown, there is increasing support for the idea that the social importance of traffic accidents[10] justifies the transfer of this complex of legal relationships from the private to the public sphere. Insurance against traffic accidents, in that conception, becomes assimilated to insurance against industrial accidents which has for many years been separated, in all common-law countries, from general tort liability and turned into a social insurance scheme. The main social justification for such a transfer

is the massive and complicated network of negligence doctrines which by virtue of their administrative intransigence work to the advantage of the insurance carrier so that most of the victims of the highways are left outside the protection of the law altogether. With only a small percentage of the total traffic claims subject to the litigation process, the courts in the large centres are so congested as to defeat many meritorious cases. Insurers gain great advantage from this congestion while claimants suffer great losses. Liability insurance still falls far short of being either universal or adequate in amount, but even if it were both, the pattern of litigation is so forbidding as to deny many claimants access to the courts; hence they accept what is offered in settlement, or, if nothing is offered, decline to risk the hazards of litigating their claims.[11]

It is not, however, essential to this idea of loss insurance that it should be administered by or on behalf of the Government (as it is done under the Saskatchewan legislation). Alternative forms of administration, e.g. by the automobile insurers, by a joint autonomous body formed by those concerned, or by a public-trust fund, does not impair the idea of loss insurance.

A much more limited application of the idea of the pooling of risks, through distribution among a wider group, is the Unsatisfied Judgement Fund. Under this scheme – now adopted by six of Canada's ten provinces, in a number of American states, and since 1952 in France[12] – all these are countries that do not have compulsory liability insurance – a special Board, or sometimes a government department, administers the Fund, to which automobile owners as well as the insurance companies contribute. Its purpose is in no way a replacement of tort liability, but a guarantee that judgements obtained against a tortfeasor, but unexecuted, usually because the tortfeasor has not been insured, will be satisfied. The great difference between this scheme and the various private- or social-insurance schemes lies in this: the responsibility remains with the individual wrongdoer, but a section of the community, specially concerned in this matter, assumes a small part of the burden by way of subsidiary guarantee. The Unsatisfied Judgement Fund principle thus in no way displaces tort liability; it tries to make it more effective.

As will be seen from the foregoing analysis, there are various stages in the development from individual responsibility through tort liability to social insurance. Compulsory-liability insurance, and even more clearly loss-insurance schemes, lead towards the idea that either the community as a whole, or a limited section of the community, should take over responsibility from the individual wrongdoer. But it is only where this idea is fully developed into one of social insurance that the problem of the relationship between insurance and tort liability arises clearly and inescapably. In one field – that of industrial accidents – the principle of social insurance is now almost universally recognized, in common-law jurisdictions as well as in many other countries. The idea of workmen's compensation started out as an application of strict tort liability in substitution for fault liability.[13] The history of the relevant English legislation also confirms that the original purpose, first expressed in the Employers' Liability Act of 1880, was to lighten the injured workman's burden in proving the employer's negligence. This served at first to exclude the defence of common employment but was soon found insufficient and superseded by a series of periodically amended Workmen's Compensation Acts. But the English Workmen's Compensation legislation still centred on the individual responsibility of the employer although it became a strict responsibility. The financial responsibility was his individual concern, against which he might or might not insure. Liability could be contested before the courts, which until the abrogation of the legislation led to a fantastic mass of contested cases; nor did the legislation abolish private action in tort. The injured workman was left with an election between the alternative remedies, a situation which in its turn led to much litigation and many social injustices, as well as administrative inconvenience. The national-insurance legislation of 1946–9 substituted for the principle of individual compensation by the employer an overall system of national insurance, for industrial as well as other accidents. Apart from certain improvements in the definition of accidents coming under the Act, administration has been vested in the Ministry of National Insurance, i.e. it has become a matter of administrative rather than private law, and the appeal procedure does not involve the ordinary courts. Contributions are now jointly made by employers, workmen, and the State. This legislation, which turned an important sector of individual responsibility for injuries into a matter of social insurance, also raised squarely the problem of the relation between tort and social insurance.[14] Although British legislation did not take the ultimate step of abolishing tort liability, it could not avoid any longer an open legislative regulation of this relationship.

In Canada, following the model of the Ontario Workmen's Compensation Act of 1915, the insurance character of workmen's compensation became obvious much earlier, for here the common-law remedy was entirely abolished. A scale of statutory tariffs is administered by a public Board under complete exclusion of the law courts, and there is no alternative common-law remedy. The Accident Fund is supplied by contributions made by the employers, in classes or groups of industries, and in the great majority of cases the employers are therefore collectively liable. Where an employer is individually liable, he may be required by the Board to insure himself (e.g. the national railroad systems). Thus a group of the community assumes responsibility for a certain type of injuries caused as an incidence of modern industrial life. In the United States, the pattern is far more complex and less uniform. All American states, like French and German legislation,[15] preclude a common-law action supplementary to workmen's compensation, but many, though a decreasing number, permit election between compensation and common-law action.[16] But in the United States, as elsewhere, the social insurance character of Workmen's Compensation is becoming increasingly evident.

Workmen's compensation is not to be thought of as merely a way of disposing of a private quarrel between employer and employee about a personal injury; it is not a branch of strict liability in tort; it is not simply a substitute for common-law litigation between parties to a personal contest over private rights. Workmen's compensation is one segment or department in the overall pattern of income-insurance, which includes unemployment insurance, sickness and disability insurance, and old age and survivors' insurance.[17]

The foregoing survey has shown that the widening of the area of strict liability and tort – itself partly a result of judicial and partly of legislative developments – is only one stage in a gradual process of socialization of risks.[18] Not only have the two lines of development – the widening of tort liability, and the shifting of the burden from the tortfeasor to third parties, mainly by way of insurance – overlapped and supplemented each other. They have also interacted on each other, and this in turn is part of the complex story of the relation between judicial and statutory law-making. The remainder of this chapter will be concerned with a brief analysis of recent trends in tort liability in the common law. This will be followed by an analysis of the problem of relationship between tort liability and insurance as it has become articulate in recent statutory developments and discussions of the problem. From a consideration of the interaction between these two lines of development certain conclusions will follow as to the future of the law of torts.

## THE RETURN TO JUDICIAL CONSERVATISM

The rule in *Donoghue* v. *Stevenson*, like the corresponding American decisions, opened up a new field of liability, of potentially vast significance. If the manufacturer of a standardized mass product was liable to any potential consumer for a defect which would only in extraordinary circumstances not be imputable to him, why should this rule not be developed further into a general rule of responsibility of those who behave towards the public in such a manner as to raise certain legitimate expectations, if such reliance leads to injury?[19] The law of torts has long ceased to regard bodily injury or injury to tangible property as the only type of recoverable damage. Where then is the difference between the physical injury caused to a consumer of ginger beer, or the user of underwear on the one hand, and the economic injury suffered by reliance on the report of a qualified accountant on the prospects of investment in a company,[20] or the nervous shock suffered as a result of a careless statement made in a newspaper about an accident alleged to have killed the plaintiff's relatives?[21] Such an extension would be a further step in the redistribution of risks, by protecting the consumer of foodstuffs, the user of machinery, the small or big investor, and other sectors of the public against damage caused by enterprises and professions.

The rationale of such an extension of the economic interests to be protected by tort liability is somewhat different from that which has led to the extension of negligence liability in outstanding cases. Responsibility for injury to life – bodily integrity or tangible property – raises no problem as to the nature of the interest to be protected. It is just a question of the proper distribution of the burden. The principle of *Donoghue* v. *Stevenson* on the one hand, and its possible extension to the protection of economic expectations, such as reliance on the accuracy of an investment report, implies an extension of the concept of property, as discussed elsewhere in this book.[22] Although the widening of the concept of property interests to economic expectations is, today, occurring on a wide front, it still seems to present conceptual difficulties to the courts which they rationalize or evade by affirming strict adherence to *stare decisis*.

Some of these questions have, indeed, come before the courts in recent years and have revealed the somewhat erratic character of judicial law-making, influenced as it is by the uncertainties of case-law, the differences in temperament and philosophy between various judges and courts, and a number of conscious or unconscious inter-actions between legislative reformism and judicial conservatism. There has been a general tendency in the decisions of recent years to restrict the scope not only of the rule in *Donoghue* v. *Stevenson*, but of other potential foundations of strict or insurance-like liability, rather than to build upon them a general duty of care.[23] The conflict of philosophies was well illustrated in a decision of the English Court of Appeal.[24] Denning L.J. made a valiant attempt to extend the principle of *Donoghue* v. *Stevenson* to the negligent preparation of accounts by a firm of accountants who knew that the plaintiff was relying on their statement to decide whether to invest in a company or not. He saw no reason to refuse to legitimate economic interests the protection granted to the consumer of an edible product. A similar judicial advance had been made in 1789 when *Pasley* v. *Freeman*[25] first protected, by a tort action, the interest of pecuniary advantage against fraudulent misstatement. Nor was Denning L.J. deterred by the argument of novelty of the action.

It has been put forward in all the great cases which have been mile-stones of progress in our law, and it has nearly always been rejected. If one reads *Ashby* v. *White* (1703) 2 Ld.Raym. 938, *Pasley* v. *Freeman* (1789) 3 T.R. 51, and *Donoghue* v. *Stevenson* one finds that in each of them the judges were divided in opinion. On the one side there were the timorous souls who were fearful of allowing a new course of action. On the other side there were the bold spirits who were ready to allow it if justice so required. It was fortunate for the common law that the progressive view prevailed. . . .[26]

But the majority disagreed with equal vigour, pointing out that it was not the function of the courts to remedy gaps or defects in the law as they had developed for better or worse. This is, however, precisely what a differently composed House of Lords did in 1963[27] when despite dismissal of the action because of an express disclaimer of liability, it held, in a series of speeches clearly given *per curiam* that there could be recovery for financial loss caused by a careless statement where the 'special relationship' between the parties gave rise to a duty of care.

In American law, the position is less definite. The majority in *Candler*'s case had sought some support in the decision of the Court of Appeals of New York in *Ultramares* v. *Touche*.[28] In that case the New York Court of Appeals denied liability where the defendants, accountants employed as auditors by a corporation, had given the latter a number of copies of their report for whatever use the corporation might see fit to make of it. The plaintiff advanced money to the corporation, whose assets were considerably less than reported by the defendant, and consequently lost money. The court, speaking through Cardozo C.J., denied liability for negligence, since the defendants had not made a representation directly to the plaintiffs. It has been pointed out[29] that this decision is not nearly as strong an authority against liability for negligent misstatements as the English Court of Appeal supposed. The difference between the *Ultramares* case and the *Candler* case was that, in the latter, the plaintiffs clearly relied, to the knowledge of the defendants, upon the statements made. Support for this interpretation comes from the fact that in an earlier decision[30] the same American court had granted an action where a public weigher had given the purchaser a certificate which erroneously overstated the amount of beans delivered. There is much judicial support for this decision, enough to have enabled the American *Restatement of Torts* to state the following rule:

One who in the course of his business or profession supplies information for the guidance of others in their business transactions is subject to liability for harm caused to them by their reliance upon the information if (a) he fails to exercise that care and competence in obtaining and communicating the information which its recipient is justified in expecting, and (b) the harm was suffered (i) by the person or one of the class of persons for whose guidance the information was supplied, and (ii) because of his justifiable reliance upon it in a transaction in which it was intended to influence his conduct or in a transaction substantially identical therewith.[31]

In criticizing both the result and the approach of the majority decision in *Candler*'s case, Professor Seavey observes that 'the court missed a golden opportunity to accept an interpretation of the rule of *stare decisis* which, by and large, has enabled the common law of England to do justice during centuries of change'.[32]

In a related field, the House of Lords in 1947 deliberately and explicitly halted any tendency to widen the rule in *Rylands* v. *Fletcher* further so as to include responsibility for 'ultra-hazardous activities' on the part of the manufacturer or other controllers of premises to those injured on their premises. In *Read* v. *J. Lyons & Co.*[33] a factory had in wartime manufactured high-explosive shells on behalf of the government. The plaintiff, who had been directed by the Minister of Labour and National Service to work in the factory as an inspector, was injured by the explosion of a shell through no negligence on the part of the defendants. The plaintiff brought an action for damages, alleging applicability of the rule in *Rylands* v. *Fletcher* and liability for things dangerous in themselves. In the Court of Appeal, Scott L.J. compared the American Law Institute's *Restatement of the Law of Torts*, which imposes strict liability for activities which 'necessarily involve a risk of serious harm to the person, land, or chattels of others which cannot be eliminated by the exercise of utmost care', and which are 'not a matter of common usage',[34] with the absence of a general principle of strict liability for ultra-hazardous activities;[35] in English law moreover, the rule in *Rylands* v. *Fletcher* did not apply to accidents occurring inside the defendant's land or premises.[36]

Whereas the law of tort has been generally adjusted to the advent of industry and modern technical inventions, and the actions in negligence, nuisance, and trespass in particular have been so developed as to impose upon the occupier of land a general responsibility for damage to the public which he could have avoided by reasonable control, the House of Lords refused to impose similar duties on the landowner and farmer as keeper of animals. From the general angle of a reasonable distribution of burdens in modern economic society there is no reason for this differentiation between industry and agriculture in the age of farm subsidies, guaranteed prices, production quotas, and import tariffs. Farmers invoke State insurance against risks no less than industry.

The decision of the House in *Searle* v. *Wallbank* led to the appointment of a special committee to consider civil liability for damage done by animals. The report of the committee issued in 1953 recommends the modification of the rule as reaffirmed by the House of Lords largely on the lines of the criticism voiced by Lord Greene M.R. in *Hughes* v. *Williams*. But this has not so far been adopted.

It would have been no more difficult for the House of Lords to modify the old rule than it was for the same court in *Donoghue* v. *Stevenson* to abandon the old rule of non-liability of a manufacturer towards a consumer. Indeed, if the principle that all modification of the law must be left to the legislator had been applied logically, the law of torts would have stood still throughout the tremendous changes caused by the industrial revolution and the urbanization of contemporary society.

It is in the field of liability of owners and occupiers of property to visitors that both British and American courts have most conspicuously failed to contribute to the rationalization and modernization of the law by the gradual modification and abolition of categories and distinctions that have lost sense and meaning.

Gradually, under the influence mainly of the decision in *Indermaur* v. *Dames*,[37] a bewildering multiplicity of categories of visitors was developed, each shading into the other, and each giving rise to a different degree of responsibility. There are persons entering as of right, contractees, invitees, licensees, and trespassers, with certain tendencies to place children into a separate category altogether.[38] The complexity and artificiality of these distinctions – which have been much criticized[39] – became both more apparent and less necessary as the action for negligence, and with it, the general duty of care developed. This made, for example, the distinctions between visitors coming for business or other economic purposes of the occupier (invitees) and those coming for social purposes (licensees), or the corresponding distinctions between a duty of reasonable care, a duty to warn against dangers of which the occupier ought to have known (invitees) and against those of which he actually knows (licensees), more and more arbitrary. In England, the matter came to a head after the House of Lords, in two decisions, had reaffirmed the old distinctions, with very unsatisfactory results.

In *Jacobs* v. *L. C. C.*,[40] the House of Lords denied the claim of a plaintiff whose foot was caught in the stop-cock of a forecourt of a number of shops which, due to the sinking of the stones in the forecourt, projected above the stones. The plaintiff was held to be only a licensee in her capacity as a prospective visitor to the tenants of the premises, and the tenuous distinction between actual knowledge and means of knowledge was revived in all its glory. Yet in a number of respectable cases, defendants carrying on the business of a dock or railway undertaking had been held liable to plaintiffs who were injured while lawfully on their premises. While the layman might find it difficult to appreciate the distinction between these cases and those of visitors to other premises, Lord Simonds was content to say that he did not wish to and was not compelled to disturb the authority of those cases.

In *London Graving Dock, Ltd* v. *Horton*,[41] the House of Lords followed a similar approach, by refusing to approximate the duties owed by the owner of a ship to an invitee to the general duty of care in negligence. In this case, an electric welder was engaged in work for a sub-contractor on the defendant's ship. The defendants provided the necessary staging boards placed on angle irons for the plaintiff and other workmen, who had repeatedly but unsuccessfully complained to the defendants about the insufficiency of the staging. The plaintiff, in the course of his work, slipped and sustained injury. His action for negligence was denied by a bare majority of the House. The judgement of the majority is based on three grounds. First, the House refused to consider the duty of an occupier of a structure to a visitor as part of a general duty of care, on the lines of *Donoghue* v. *Stevenson*. This had been suggested in the Court of Appeal whose judgement was reversed. Second, the House reaffirmed a somewhat dubious interpretation of the ambiguous phrase 'damage from unusual danger of which he knows or ought to know' by saying that the duty was not to prevent unusual danger, but to use reasonable care to prevent damage from unusual danger. Third, such danger was precluded because the plaintiff had protested against the deficiencies of the equipment so that it had ceased to be a trap. And, finally, the House went a long way towards reestablishing a long-discredited interpretation of *volenti non fit injuria*. As one of the dissenting judges (Lord MacDermott) pointed out, the majority view got perilously close to saying that a servant who knew of a danger had to be regarded as assenting thereto. This view had been virtually discarded since *Smith* v. *Baker*.[42]

At least, these almost universally criticized[43] judgements led to a Report by the Law Revision Committee, which proposed a reform substantially enacted in the Occupiers' Liability Act, 1957, by which the various standards of duties to be owed to various categories of visitors are replaced by a 'common duty of care' owed to all except trespassers. Thus, the elastic and comprehensive concept of negligence has, at last, in English law, absorbed most of this branch of the law; but in the other common-law jurisdictions, the complexity and confusion continue as before.

The foregoing illustrations of a return to judicial conservatism are too numerous to be regarded as isolated freaks. They do not suffice to reverse the general trend in the development of the law of torts;[44] an objectivization of fault liability, in the sense that objective standards of conduct rather than individual behaviour are made the principal test of fault liability; a far-reaching shift of responsibility for reparation for injuries, to the 'enterprise', i.e. the master, employer, manufacturer, or owner of premises, not only from the victim but often from the person primarily responsible for the injury.

It would, however, be difficult to detect any consistent or scientific theory behind the gradual shift towards enterprise liability. In a suggestive short article,[45] Clarence Morris has suggested that 'those engaged in dangerous activities sometimes are and sometimes are not better risk-bearers than those injured by the prosecution of the activities. . . . The discussion does justify the conclusion that a general rule of absolute enterprise liability or liability for hazardous undertakings is bound to saddle some kind of defendants with losses they can bear no better than the kinds of plaintiffs compensated. Only courts discriminating wisely among classes of cases that are now lumped together can evolve a system in which losses are shifted only from classes of inferior risk-bearers to classes of superior risk-bearers.' The learned author concludes that, for the time being possibly *ad hoc* development of enterprise liability was the best solution, avoiding the pitfalls of either a system of absolute liability or one in which liability is tied to fault. Such an intermediate, empirical, and tentative adjustment of the spheres of fault and strict liability seems in fact to be the best summary of the present position in the common-law jurisdictions. The foregoing discussion seems to indicate that the great recent growing period of the law of torts, which produced such a substantial shift towards various forms of strict or semi-strict liability, may have come to a halt. Apart from a possible psychological reaction against the steady extension of statutory or insurance compensation for risks regardless of fault, the problem has, at least in certain spheres, become too big to be handled by the adjustment of principles of liability. At least in the spheres of industrial accidents and traffic accidents, involving many millions of people yearly in every major country, the problem of collective insurance, of the spreading of risk from the individuals concerned towards larger groups, has become steadily more pressing. The present-day function of tort liability cannot, therefore, be finally assessed, without a consideration of the various schemes of private and social insurance that have taken over, or are in process of taking over, broad spheres of liability for injuries caused.

### INSURANCE AND ALTERNATIVE TORT REMEDIES

Any attempt to adjust insurance and tort liability, where the two methods of compensation arise from the same incident, must steer between the Scylla of double compensation for the victim, and the Charybdis of immunity for the tortfeasor. The victim ought to be compensated adequately – as far as monetary compensation can do it – for the injury suffered, but he should not make a profit out of the situation. On the other hand, the growing incidence of insurance – private or social – should not serve to let the individual tortfeasor off. The latter consideration is supported by divergent policy motivations. Some emphasize the moral element: tort is moral wrongdoing, and the wrongdoer should not be relieved of his burden because of the victim's insurance, or the beneficence of the modern welfare state. Others emphasize the deterrent character of tort-liability. Absolution from liability would increase carelessness, and with it the incidence of accidents.

It is only in recent years that the problem has received more than usual treatment. Where it had arisen before, notably in the field of industrial accidents, solutions differed and still do differ widely.[46]

Before we consider the relation of tort liability and insurance more systematically, in the light of the British study made on the subject and resulting in the Law Reform (Personal Injuries) Act of 1948, it should be pointed out that both the 'double compensation' argument, and the 'moral wrongdoing' argument, have a much narrower scope than would appear at first sight. In most cases the double benefits that an injured person may derive are not truly double compensation but compensation from what in the United States are called 'collateral sources'. In the field of social insurance some American courts regard the statutory benefit of workmen's compensation as properly mitigating damages, others regard it as a collateral benefit not to be taken into account.[47] The Supreme Court of the United States has denied the government the right to recover from an entrepreneur for compensation paid to an injured soldier.[48] In the case of railroad retirement annuities, the American courts have vacillated between refusing any mitigation, mitigating damages in part in proportion of the contributions made by the employees through deduction of wages, and mitigating in full.[49]

In the field of private insurance, it is reasonably well settled that life or accident insurance are regarded as entirely separate transactions, creating separate interests, and not to be brought into mitigation of tort damages. On the other hand, fire and property insurance generally have subrogation clauses and thus exclude double recovery by the claimant.[50]

The 'moral wrongdoing' aspect has to be judged in the light of the foregoing discussion: the elimination of the moral element from the greater part of fault liability in tort. Both the alleged moral element in negligence liability and the argument that elimination or even reduction of tort liability in accident cases would increase the accident rate have been put forward time and again, often enough by those interested in the maintenance of a voluminous litigation in these fields, without either reflection on the nature of modern tort liability, or adequate statistical evidence. Neither the Saskatchewan experience nor American statistics appear to permit any conclusion that the degree of civil liability for the average negligence case has any relation one way or the other to carelessness and an increase in the accident rate.

The problem is thus somewhat less in dimension than might appear at first sight, but it remains of great importance. It is the advent of the comprehensive British National Insurance legislation after the Second World War which compelled a more systematic and thorough consideration of this problem.

Instead of mitigating certain specific evils, the British legislator now aimed at an overall insurance for the citizen. This has been implemented by a series of Acts, of which the most important are the National Insurance Act, 1946; the National Insurance (Industrial Injuries) Act, 1946; and the National Health Service Act, 1946. The relation between social insurance and tort liability was outlined in the Beveridge Report and discussed at length by a special departmental committee,[51] whose final report was published in July 1946, and was partly implemented by the Law Reform (Personal Injuries) Act, 1948.

The Act[52] adopted a compromise which some may regard as a model of Solomonic justice and others as a model of expediency. It contains the following clause:

In an action for damages for personal injuries (including any such action arising out of a contract), there shall in assessing those damages be taken into account, against any loss of earnings or profits which has accrued or probably will accrue to the injured person from the injuries, one half of the value of any rights which have accrued or probably will accrue to him therefrom in respect of industrial injury benefit, industrial disablement benefit, or sickness benefit for the five years beginning with the time when the cause of action accrued. . . . This subsection shall not be taken as requiring both the gross amount of the damages before taking into account the said rights and the net amount after taking them into account to be found separately.[53]

It also stipulated that, despite the comprehensive National Health Service which had since come into operation, it would still be legitimate to claim private medical expenses, though it is for the court to determine whether they are reasonable.

This compromise aroused remarkably little discussion either in the Commons or in the Lords. It was admitted that logically there was no more to be said in favour of allowing half the benefits to be set off than for any other proportion. As Lord Porter put it during the debate in the House of Lords, the compromise was effected 'rather by the rule of the thumb, which after all is the way in which juries arrive at their results'.[54] In a sense, the clause is a compromise between Left views and Right views. It saves for the time being the law of tort and makes common-law actions still worth while. On the other hand it concedes to the insured, among whom employees are the most powerful group, that the new national insurance is an additional benefit for which the insured pays, partly in the form of an insurance contribution, and partly as a citizen of a nation which has decided through its Parliament that the wealthier sections should by taxation help to mitigate the inequalities of the social system. That for the time being leaves both sides reasonably satisfied.

The general underlying problem cannot be solved purely by arithmetic, but only by a sociological valuation. The trade-union suggestion that benefits should be deducted in proportion to the contribution of the insured is not convincing, for the benefit received under national insurance is a standardized one and not dependent upon the rate of contribution. Having regard to the history of the Act and to its general scheme, there can be no doubt that it is dominated first by the objective of a general public insurance against the worst vicissitudes of life, and second by a desire to finance this insurance by a levelling procedure, that is to say, by throwing a relatively greater burden on the wealthier part of the population. In a system of graded taxation this follows from the fact that one-sixth of the contributions comes from the State, that is, from the taxpayer, but it also follows from the fact that the benefit is uniform, whereas contributions differ; for example, as between employed, non-employed, and self-employed persons. The logical conclusion from this argument would be that insurance benefits should not be taken into account at all, and this was in fact the argument of a minority not only of the committee but in Parliament. The concession to the other view that benefits should be taken into account is due to a balancing argument of expedience, not of logic. By allowing a partial offsetting of benefits against damages, the insured is reminded that part of the social insurance benefits is provided for him by a benevolent State, and the danger of the odd case in which a relatively light injury would be compensated out of proportion to the damages suffered is reduced. The Act steers a middle line between two conflicting philosophies.

So far, we have been concerned with the 'double compensation' aspect of social insurance. The Report also discusses the 'moral wrongdoing' aspect of the problem. Having recommended that civil liability in tort should continue to lead a legal existence independent of statutory social security, the committee was worried by the problem of how to differentiate the criteria of liability in tort from those of social-security obligations. The report made short shrift of the proposal that the common-law liability of the employer for a failure to take reasonable care for the safety of his workmen should be limited to cases of serious and wilful misconduct or gross negligence of himself or of persons exercising superintending functions on his behalf.[55] The committee devoted far more attention to the problem of absolute statutory duties. Both the Mines and Quarries Act, 1954,[56] and the Factories Act, 1937, impose upon employers statutory duties to observe safety provisions laid down in the Acts. Both Acts also provide penalties for offences, but qualify them by the requirement of due diligence to enforce the execution of this Act and of any relevant order or regulation made thereunder. In regard to civil liability, only the Mines and Quarries Act contains a provision that 'the owner of a mine shall not be liable to an action for damages as for breach of statutory duty . . . if it is shown that it was impracticable to avoid or prevent the contravention'. The Factories Act, inexplicably, contains no similar provision, thus making the employer's civil liability more extensive than his criminal liability. The malice of a servant acting outside the scope of his employment, or the interference of a stranger, is no defence.

Apart from the inconsistency between different statutes, the committee obviously felt that the extension of social-security benefits should go parallel with the reaffirmation of the fault principle in tort. It therefore recommended that

wherever any Act or Regulation imposes a duty on the defendant designed for the protection of workmen, and there is a failure to comply with that duty, the defendant shall be excused from liability in civil proceedings by the injured workman founded on that breach of statutory duty if he proves that it was not reasonably practicable for him or for his servants or agents, other than (i) the injured person, or (ii) another servant or agent who committed the breach while acting outside the scope of his employment, to avoid or prevent the breach.[57]

The Government at first accepted this recommendation but dropped it from the Bill in the second reading.[58] Government spokesmen did not attempt to provide juristic justification for this change of mind. It seems that the Government had been influenced by trade-union representatives objecting to any whittling down of industrial safety provisions.

### SOME COMPARATIVE APPROACHES

While there is not, as yet, any official study paralleling the Alternative Remedies Committee's Report for English law, some important studies have, in the last two years, been published on the relationship of tort liability and social insurance. A brief survey of these studies – made for legal systems as different in technical background and social policy as American law, Scandinavian law, and Soviet law – will serve to underline the common factors in the problem.

A few years ago, Professor Ehrenzweig published a remarkable little study entitled paradoxically *Negligence without Fault.*[59] In this study, he surveyed the various aspects of 'enterprise liability' and came to the conclusion that the bulk of so-called negligence liability in this field had become further and further removed from fault in its original moral sense. However, the lack of a clear distinction between the admonitory and compensatory elements of negligence liability had obscured the problem, and also the effect which insurance protection of the public against the hazards of modern enterprise was bound to have on this field of tort liability. More recently, this learned author has followed up this analysis with a positive proposal for the reorganization of automobile insurance.[60] This adopts many features of the Saskatchewan automobile accident insurance legislation – in turn based largely on the Columbia plan of 1932 – except for the American aversion to State management of insurance. Professor Ehrenzweig's 'full aid' plan suggests a statutory minimum 'full aid' accident insurance for operators of automobiles as the condition of relief from common-law liability for ordinary (in contrast to criminal) negligence. Any person injured by a car not so insured would be entitled to recover the same amount from an uncompensated injury fund administered by the automobile insurers licensed in the State. This fund would be fed from 'tort fines' collected from injurors or accident victims whose criminal negligence had contributed to the accident.

This scheme goes beyond the Saskatchewan legislation in excluding tort action, for the benefit of those who carry full aid and accident insurance, excepting cases of 'criminal' negligence. But to the state-operated Saskatchewan scheme it prefers a self-governing scheme administered by the automobile insurers.

Professor Fleming James has recently investigated the broader problem of social insurance and tort liability in American law.[61] The learned author suggests that there are four alternative solutions to the problem of relation between social insurance and tort liability: (1) the abolition of one of the remedies, (2) compulsion for the claimant to elect one and forgo the other, (3) allowing the claimant to have accumulative benefits of two or several remedies, (4) allowing the claimant to pursue all the available remedies but limiting his total recovery to the maximum amount he could recover from a single source.

In surveying the merits of these different solutions, Professor James first discounts the total abolition of the tort remedy, tempting though it may seem to those worried by the congestion of the courts in the larger cities and attracted by the simplification of administration. And there is, of course, precedent for such a solution in the Canadian workmen's compensation legislation, and in the corresponding legislation of some of the American states. However, Professor James is reluctant to recommend the abolition of tort largely for ideological reasons. He does not wish to 'rip any more of the threads of individualism out of the social and economic fabric than we must in order to take adequate care of the basic human needs of all our people'. Next, the election of remedies is a familiar pattern in workmen's compensation law but it has been widely found by those who have studied the problem to be a wasteful and socially undesirable solution, especially because of the delays and uncertainties involved, and the danger that a lump sum recovery in damages may throw out the purpose of the social legislation. It is for these reasons that recent British legislation has abolished the election. Next the learned author turns to the more complex problem of cumulative remedies. Professor James has doubts about the prevalent judicial practice to allow double recovery in accident insurance cases, though he believes the harm of such practice to be small because the beneficiaries of accident policies usually are willing to settle their tort claims for less than they otherwise would.[62] But contrary to a widespread opinion, he believes that accident insurance provides a weak analogy for social insurance. Social-insurance schemes are not intended to provide windfalls. At least the philosophy of the American legislation, unlike recent British legislation, does not seek to redistribute the wealth beyond the point that indemnity or compensation calls for. Similarly, he suggests that private group schemes, such as Blue Cross insurance, should also be treated as providing indemnity or compensation rather than a windfall.

On the other hand, Professor James is sceptical of the argument that the tortfeasor should not be let off free. In this respect he supports the analysis made earlier in the text of the change in the character of tort liability, and the various studies made on the relation of fault liability to accident rates which do not suggest tort liability for negligence as relevant one way or another.

Finally, Professor James discusses the problem of subrogation. This is widely suggested as a way to harmonize the two objectives of preventing double compensation and immunity for the tortfeasor, because it compensates the victim but substitutes the insurer for him against the tortfeasor. However, despite the obvious merits of this solution which is widely applied in both social and private insurance schemes, Professor James points out the administrative inconveniences of the subrogation machinery, as well as the difficulties of finding a proper basis of redistribution of accident losses. Some social-insurance programmes are based on the principle that society should meet certain economic losses to individuals and distribute them widely by taxation; others distribute the loss among the beneficiaries. In the latter case subrogation makes sense, in the former less so. Where, for example, disability benefits are paid from a fund recruited by general taxation, there would seem to be little to be gained by making the motoring public group pay back to the government (i.e. the taxpayers) the amount of the social-insurance benefits which the latter has paid the claimants. Generally, Professor James concludes with some doubts as to the merits of subrogation.

The problem to what extent insurance should take over the functions of tort law has been the subject of many studies in the Scandinavian countries. A distinguished authority in this field has recently given an analysis of Scandinavian developments and problems.[63]

. The Danish Act on Contracts of Insurance of 1930 provides that the liability of a tortfeasor is not affected by the existence of life, health, and accident insurance of the usual types, whereas it may be restricted in the case of fire insurance or other types of property insurance. But the important contribution to the general jurisprudence of the matter made by the Danish law is the authorization which it gives to the courts to exempt the tortfeasor from liability or to reduce the damages (1) if the liability is based on the defendant's negligence and the negligence was not gross or wanton, and (2) where the defendant was liable by virtue of the general rule of *respondeat superior*. Professor Ussing cites a number of cases to illustrate how the courts have used this discretion, broadly distinguishing between objectionable and less objectionable types of negligent conduct. This Danish law is not yet paralleled in the other Nordic countries.

In the field of social insurance, Sweden in particular has gone to such lengths in providing overall insurance benefits in case of illness, disablement, and accidents that a Swedish authority, Professor Ivar Strahl, has suggested that tort liability for harm to persons should in most cases be abolished.[64] Professor Ussing's own conclusion is that only for some situations ought tort liability to be maintained in order to restrain tortious conduct but that, apart from this rather narrow field, it would be preferable to have compensation made by means of insurance. Such insurance against third-party risk should be compulsory for those who conduct ultra-hazardous activities and probably also for operators of motor vehicles and keepers of animals.

Finally, a legal system as different in social concept as the Soviet law has met with very similar problems of adjustment between social insurance and tort liability.

Article 404 of the Soviet Civil Code provides for strict liability as follows: 'persons and enterprises, whose activities present special danger to the persons around them, such as railroads, street cars, factories and mills, vendors of inflammable materials, keepers of wild animals, persons engaged in the erection of buildings and other structures, etc., are liable for injury caused by the source of increased danger, unless they prove that the damage was caused as the result of *force majeure*, or as the result of a wilful act or gross negligence on the part of the injured party.' Article 413 of the same Code bears directly on the relation of social insurance and tort liability: 'A person or enterprise paying insurance premiums to protect an injured person under social insurance shall not be required to repair injury caused by the happening of the event against which the insurance has been purchased. . . . But if the injury is caused by the criminal act or failure to act of the management of the enterprise, the social-insurance agency which satisfies the injured person shall have the right to demand from the management of the enterprise an amount equal to the insurance benefits paid to the injured person (subrogation) . . . In such case, the injured person who has not received full reparation of his injury under social insurance has an additional claim against the entrepreneur.'

In his book on *Law and Social Change in the U.S.S.R.* (1953), Professor Hazard has discussed the implications of these provisions. Soviet law and practice have kept social-insurance benefits below full compensation. The right to bring suits in the courts against insured employers to recover the difference between insurance benefits and wages enables the courts to go beyond the report of the social-insurance medical commission but it may also enable them to correct any undue liberality on the part of the social-insurance administrators. More important is probably the second reason, namely, the desire to supervise, by the provision of actions for criminal negligence, employers in a non-capitalist society. Liability for damages in the State-administered Soviet industries gives the management a black mark in the administrative record. Thus 'tort law serves . . . as an instrument of policy in encouraging State economic administrators to give careful attention to the safety rules'. Soviet authors appear to be in several minds on the merits of utilization of tort law in fields covered by social insurance. Thus an author writing in 1950 suggests – very much like the American jurists discussed earlier – that vigilance and the observance of safety regulations is insured by precautions of public administration and law rather than by the maintenance of tort actions. There are other possibilities of penalizing carelessness, such as differentiated premium rates – as they are indeed applied in the practice of insurance companies. But where the defendant conducts an 'extra-hazardous activity', as defined in Article 404, fault does not have to be proved. Apart from that, however, Soviet law, like Scandinavian law, does operate with the concept of gross or criminal negligence as a means of limiting tort liability to the cases in which conduct is socially particularly reprehensible.

## SOME CONCLUSIONS

It is clear that no existing legal system, whether socialistically or capitalistically inclined, has so far shown any desire to abolish tort liability altogether. On the other hand, systems as divergent as those of Denmark and the U.S.S.R. have singled out criminal or gross negligence from that of negligence in general. It is submitted that the English Committee on alternative remedies was somewhat hasty in throwing out a similar suggestion as being incompatible with English law. The fact is that the concept of 'gross, criminal, or wanton' negligence does play a considerable part in the common-law system. The importance of the concept of gross negligence in criminal law is well known. In *R.* v. *Bateman*,[65] this was defined as 'such disregard for the life and safety of others as to amount to a crime against the State and conduct deserving punishment'. In *Andrews* v. *D. P. P.*,[66] Lord Atkin explained gross negligence in manslaughter in terms of recklessness. More recently the Irish Court of Criminal Appeal[67] distinguished negligence in manslaughter from tort negligence. In the former situation, 'a very high degree of negligence must be proved'.

Perhaps more apposite to the problem of civil liability is the adoption of the test of gross negligence in certain Canadian statutes of which the British Columbia Motor Vehicle Act of 1948 is representative. Under this legislation a gratuitous passenger in an automobile can recover damages from the driver who has caused an accident only where he can establish 'gross negligence'. 'No action shall lie against either the owner or the driver of a motor vehicle . . . unless there has been gross negligence on the part of the driver of the vehicle, and unless such gross negligence contributed to the injury, loss, or damage in respect of which the action is brought.'[68]

It is not suggested that the delimitation of 'gross' or 'criminal' or 'wanton' negligence from other forms of negligence is conceptually satisfactory or practically simple. It may well be argued – and it has been argued – that there can only be either negligence or no negligence. This argument, however, does not dispose of the practical policy question. It is obvious that among the thousands of cases which come under the general heading of negligence, there is a limited number which call for prosecution because of the relatively greater gravity of conduct. The same test can well be applied to tort actions. It is a matter of individual appreciation in the light of all the circumstances, and in this respect the distinction of gross negligence from other forms of negligence does not at all differ from such other judicial yardsticks as 'fair and reasonable' or the apportionment of guilt in comparative negligence.

The importance of this recent trend towards what Professor Ussing, in the above-quoted article, has aptly described as the effect of insurance on tort, namely, that it will bring about 'a certain broadening of tort liability', but at the same time 'a shrinking of the field of liability for tort', is that, after the dilution of the concept of fault in tort and the far-reaching inroad of insurance on tort liability, the admonitory function of tort is being reaffirmed in the more restricted sphere where it really has such a function. And this is a common rationale of the developments that have already taken place, among others in Scandinavia and in the Soviet Union, and as they are advocated by the American students of the subjects discussed earlier. The result would be that, for a very limited sphere, the law of tort would come closer again to criminal law in sanctioning immoral conduct, while for the vast number of accidents due to modern social conditions tort might either frankly become a matter of strict liability or be superseded by insurance.

It is difficult to attempt any general conclusions in a field so full of complexity and still so fluid. The following generalizations may, however, be attempted with some degree of confidence:

1. In those fields of tort which are socially most significant – traffic accidents, industrial accidents, responsibilities of employers, manufacturers, and other controllers of properties and enterprises — the fault principle has either been superseded by strict liability or lost its moral significance and become barely distinguishable from so-called strict liability.

The movement in this direction – which in the first part of the century in many different countries has received a powerful impetus from judicial legislation tending to extend the security for the under-dog by imposing liability on those thought best able to bear it – has probably been arrested, largely as a reaction to the spread of both social and private insurance.

2. Minimum compensation for the vicissitudes of modern life is a widely accepted principle, across borders and different legal systems. The need can be fulfilled either by (a) a comprehensive social insurance (United Kingdom, U.S.S.R., Sweden), (b) partial schemes of social insurance (Workmen's Compensation Statutes or the Saskatchewan automobile accident insurance legislation), or (c) compulsory private insurance schemes, in particular, compulsory third-party liability.

As forecast by Holmes in his *Common Law*, published in 1881, it is conceivable that the State may at some time take over completely the field of compensation for injury and replace tort altogether. But no country, however advanced in its social-insurance schemes, has as yet gone this far, partly as a matter of compromise with the existing legal system and partly as a matter of deliberate social policy.

3. The basic problem is the adjustment between the dilemma of double compensation and the dilemma of immunity for the tortfeasor. This dilemma is reduced by two factors: (a) many apparent cases of double compensation are really cases of collateral benefits where it is inequitable to offset insurance benefits against tort compensation; (b) partial or total relief for the tortfeasor is not as

objectionable as it appears at first because (i) the tortfeasor may pay his share of compensation in some other capacity (as a motorist, a worker, an employer, or generally, as a taxpayer), and (ii) because the moral significance of fault liability, as pointed out above, has become restricted to very few situations.

4. The true admonitory function of tort liability could be restored – and this is a clearly apparent trend in many different legal systems – by restricting, in fields covered by social or private insurance, tort liability to cases of 'gross' or 'criminal' negligence. The consequence of such restriction would be a drastic reduction of negligence cases with all the resulting economy, and an approximation of fault liability in tort to fault liability in crime – the relationship that once existed but has been diluted by contemporary developments.

For most lawyers in modern industrialized society, a preoccupation with the theory and practice of criminal law has receded into the background. The great majority of practising lawyers prefer the fields of corporation law, of drafting or civil litigation in matters of contract, tort, or property, of taxation, trade regulations, labour law, and the like. Not only do these fields generally bring far greater financial rewards; there is also a deplorable, but undeniable, tendency to regard criminal-law practice as carrying less social and professional prestige (except, perhaps, where private millionaires or corporation executives are indicted for fraudulent transactions and other white-collar crimes). In the popular image of the law, on the other hand, the criminal law continues to occupy an outstanding place, and that not only because of the headline significance of the sensational criminal trial, of emotional excitement caused by cases of murder, rape, or treason. The layman's image of the law is not only a survival from more primitive times, when criminal law and retribution occupied the central place.

The state of the criminal law continues to be – as it should – a decisive reflection of the social consciousness of a society. What kind of conduct an organized community considers, at a given time, sufficiently condemnable to impose official sanctions, impairing the life, liberty, or property of the offender, is a barometer of the moral and social thinking of a community. Hence, the criminal law is particularly sensitive to changes in social structure and social thinking.

While the definition of a crime has aroused the usual spate of controversies connected with any attempt to define a legal concept,[1] we may content ourselves, as a point of departure for the ensuing discussion, with the formulation of an eminent American authority on criminal law which is hardly open to challenge:

> The purpose of the penal law is to express a formal social condemnation of forbidden conduct, buttressed by sanctions calculated to prevent it. . . .[2]

Implicit in this formulation are three questions, to which different societies give very different answers:

First, what kind of conduct is 'forbidden'?

Second, what kind of 'formal social condemnation' is considered appropriate to prevent such conduct?

Third, what kind of sanctions are considered as best calculated to prevent officially outlawed conduct?

Social change affects criminal law in many ways: through developments in science, especially in biology and medicine: through changes in the predominant moral and social philosophy; through changes in the structure of society, especially in its transition from a rural, self-contained, and relatively sparsely populated, to a highly urbanized and industrialized, pattern. In the following discussion, we shall select, as particularly significant, four areas in which such changes have challenged, or are challenging, established concepts of criminal law.

The first two concern reappraisals of the responsibility of the individual for acts generally considered criminal by the law. The last two concern the scope and function of the criminal law itself, under the impact of the changing structure of modern society.

## MODERN PSYCHIATRY AND THE RESPONSIBILITY OF THE INDIVIDUAL

In the approach to a generally condemned act, such as murder, rape, or arson, the legal system may go from the one extreme of penalizing the act as such, without regard to subjective factors in the individual offender, to the other extreme of complete individualization, i.e. taking each individual as a composite of moral and intellectual faculties, genetic factors, social environment. Ultimately, this is a question of values, of the balancing between the interest in the safety and vigour of the community, and the consideration of the individual as a person. In no field has the conflict of these values been more dramatically, and often tragically, tested than in the treatment of insanity or mental deficiency. Persons thus afflicted are unquestionably a burden to society. And just as the Spartans killed by exposure weakling children so as not to impair the martial vigour of their State, so in recent times 'the suggestion has sometimes been made that the insane murderer should be punished equally with the sane, or that, although he ought not to be executed as a punishment, he should be painlessly exterminated as a measure of social hygiene'.[3] Such doctrines commended themselves to National Socialist Germany, which practised the extermination, confinement, or sterilization of whole groups of people, considered as inferior, objectionable, or useless, on a large scale. Overwhelmingly, the tradition of civilized nations, and of the criminal law, has been to take account of basic weaknesses of the individual as a defence against criminal prosecution, or at least in mitigation of punishment. But while some modern legal systems have gone a long way towards substituting alternative social sanctions for punishment, in the case of insane or mentally deficient persons as well as of juveniles, first offenders, and other special categories, none has held it possible to abolish the criminal law as a major and vital instrument of protection of society. Hence, the question remains at what point the borderline should be drawn, by what criteria criminal responsibility should be measured.

For more than a century, the basic test in the common-law jurisdictions has been supplied by the 'M'Naghten Rules', laid down by the House of Lords in the case of Daniel M'Naghten.[4] The essence of the directions given by the judges in that case to juries and for cases where the defence of insanity is raised is contained in the following passage:

The jury ought to be told in all cases that every man is presumed to be sane, and to possess a sufficient degree of reason to be responsible for his crimes, until the contrary be proved to their satisfaction; and that, to establish a defence on the gound of insanity, it must be clearly proved that, at the time of the committing of the act, the party accused was labouring under such a defect of reason, from disease of the mind, as not to know the nature and quality of the act he was doing, or, if he did know it that he did not know he was doing what was wrong.

This test – adopted throughout the British Commonwealth and almost universally in the United States[5] – rests on the criterion of knowledge. It assumes that a person who intellectually apprehends the distinction between the right and wrong of a given conduct must be held criminally responsible. As such, it was soon attacked, above all by members of the medical profession, but also by some eminent lawyers,[6] on the ground that 'insanity does not only, or primarily, affect the cognitive or intellectual faculties, but affects the whole personality of the patient, including both the will and the emotions'.[7] As long ago as 1870, it was abandoned in the State of New Hampshire,[8] in favour of the test whether the accused 'had the capacity to entertain a criminal intent – whether, in point of fact, he did entertain such intent'. In the light of modern psychiatric developments, criminological science, and changing conceptions of guilt, the criticism has assumed overwhelming proportions in recent years, both in England and the United States.[9] The gravamen of these criticisms can be summed up in the following formulation of an eminent American criminologist:[10]

These tests proceed upon the following questionable assumptions of an outworn era in psychiatry: (1) that lack of knowledge of the 'nature or quality' of an act (assuming the meaning of such terms to be clear), or incapacity to know right from wrong, is the sole or even the most important symptom of mental disorder; (2) that such knowledge is the sole instigator and guide of conduct, or at least the most important element therein, and consequently should be the sole criterion of responsibility when insanity is involved; and (3) that the capacity of knowing right from wrong can be completely intact and functioning perfectly even though a defendant is otherwise demonstrably of disordered mind.

In other words, a person must be seen in its entirety, and the faculty of reason, which is only one element in that personality, is not the sole determinant of his conduct.[11]

There is far less agreement on the alternative. It is almost universally conceded that some persons, who are perfectly capable of intellectually distinguishing between right and wrong, are yet driven to commit a criminal act by forces outside their control. This makes it improper to hold them criminally accountable in a legal system that bases criminal liability on personal responsibility. A widely accepted alternative, at least as a supplement to the M'Naghten Rules, has been the test of 'irresistible impulse'.[12] But a recent thorough investigation of the problem by a British Royal Commission, which, by a large majority, favoured the abolition or modification of the M'Naghten Rules, has described the concept of the 'irresistible inpulse' as 'largely discredited' and as 'inherently inadequate and unsatisfactory'.[13]

The real objection to the term 'irresistible impulse' is that it is too narrow, and carries an unfortunate and misleading implication that, where a crime is committed as a result of emotional disorder due to insanity, it must have been suddenly and impulsively committed after a sharp internal conflict. In many cases, such as those of melancholia, this is not true at all. The sufferer from this disease experiences a change of mood which alters the whole of his existence. He may believe, for instance, that a future of such degradation and misery awaits both him and his family that death for all is a less dreadful alternative. Even the thought that the acts he contemplates are murder and suicide pales into insignificance in contrast with what he otherwise expects. The criminal act, in such circumstances, may be the reverse of impulsive. It may be coolly and carefully prepared; yet it is still the act of a madman.

Instead, a powerful trend in modern psychiatric and legal opinion favours the adoption of a broader test, which correlates criminal liability with the capacity of the individual to control his conduct in conformity with the requirements of the law. Thus, a widely discussed decision of the United States Court of Appeals for the District of Columbia has formulated the rule 'that an accused is not criminally responsible if his unlawful act was the product of mental disease or mental defect'.[14] The majority report of the British Royal Commission suggests that:

the jury must be satisfied that at the time of committing the act, the accused, as a result of disease of the mind or mental deficiency, (a) did not know the nature and quality of the act or (b) did not know that it was wrong or (c) was incapable of preventing himself from committing it.[15]

A smaller majority preferred to abolish the M'Naghten Rules altogether 'and leave the jury to determine whether at the time of the act the accused was suffering from disease of the mind or mental deficiency to such a degree that he ought not to be held responsible'.

The tentative Draft No. 4 of the Model Penal Code, prepared by the American Law Institute, suggests the following formulation:

(1) A person is not responsible for criminal conduct if at the time of such conduct as a result of mental disease or defect he lacks substantial capacity either to appreciate the criminality of his conduct or to conform his conduct to the requirements of law.

(2) The terms 'mental disease or defect' do not include an abnormality manifested only by repeated criminal or otherwise anti-social conduct.

It should be noted that all these formulations not only supplement the purely intellectual appreciation of right and wrong of the M'Naghten Rules by a test of control over conduct as a guide for criminal responsibility, but that they also accept the findings of modern psychiatry in regard to mental 'disease' or 'deficiency', in addition to insanity. Mental deficiency generally connotes an 'intellectual defect, or defect of understanding, existing from birth or from an early age'.[16] Mental abnormality is a more comprehensive concept, but it is mainly concerned with two categories of abnormal persons who are neither insane nor mentally deficient: epileptics and psychopaths. It is the latter category which forms probably the main preoccupation of modern psychiatrists, but is also the most difficult to define. It comprises a vast variety of persons who, for emotional reasons, stand, permanently or temporarily, to a greater or lesser extent apart from the 'normal' member of society.

The almost infinite variety of psychopathic disturbances,[17] and the still continuing and widening scope of psychiatric study of mental disturbances adds to the complexity of the problem. The M'Naghten Rules not only greatly oversimplify the problem of criminal responsibility by the 'right and wrong' test, but they also leave nothing between black and white, no intermediate stage between responsibility and irresponsibility.[18] The doctrine of diminished responsibility was universally rejected in the law of England and in the common-law jurisdictions of the Commonwealth, until England accepted it for homicide in a recent statutory reform.[19] In the United States the position is somewhat obscure.[20] On the other hand, the law of Scotland, in regard to murder, and a number of Continental legal systems, have long accepted the doctrine of diminished responsibility as enabling the courts to mitigate the penalty. Perhaps, the most representative formulation is that of the Penal Code of Switzerland[21]:

1. The administrative authority of the Canton will put into effect the judge's decision ordering detention, treatment, or removal to hospital of offenders not responsible or only partially responsible for their actions.

2. The competent authority will order the termination of detention, treatment, or confinement to hospital as soon as the reason for it no longer exists.

The judge will decide if and to what extent the sentence passed on an offender only partially responsible for his actions is then to be carried out.

Clearly, the development in modern psychiatry which, between the fully normal and the fully abnormal person, recognizes an infinite variety of shades of disturbances lessening, to a varying degree, the emotional powers and capacities of self-control rather than intellectual discernment, calls for a corresponding elasticity in the legal approach to the problem of responsibility. But this very development makes it obviously very difficult to devise precise legal formulas, by either statutory or judicial legislation. Any attempt to elaborate a series of new additional criteria, superimposed on the M'Naghten test, in correspondence with the many types and grades of mental disturbance, would lead to casuistry and a multitude of interpretations by different judges and juries. Hence, the above-quoted reform proposals of the British Royal Commission, of the American Draft Model Penal Code, and others, suggest broad formulae correlating responsibility to control. It would seem not only logical but indispensable to extend this approach to the concept of 'diminished responsibility' as it has, by general consent, operated to general satisfaction in Scotland and in many Continental countries (where it is extended from murder to any criminal offence). In the evidence presented to the Royal Commission, preparatory to its Report, the British Medical Association suggested a reform to the effect that:

when a jury find that an accused person, at the time of committing the act, was labouring, as a result of disease of the mind, under a defect of reason or a disorder of emotion to such an extent as not to be fully accountable for his actions, they shall return a verdict of 'guilty with diminished responsibility'.[22]

The introduction of such a concept – which, in the sphere of private law, might be compared to differentiations between 'gross' and 'ordinary' negligence – would, of course, add to the individualization of each case, in the light of the medical evidence presented, and the estimate given in the judge's direction and the jury's verdict. It is clear that any solution compatible with modern thinking will place a wide measure of discretion, and a great burden of responsibility, on the court. But it has hardly been different under the M'Naghten Rules, for the decision whether a person is capable of distinguishing between right and wrong is no less arduous and difficult a task for a court than the proposed more general tests of control and responsibility. It is, however, as we have seen, entirely out of tune with modern scientific and social thought. The modern formulations give greater scope and proper weight to expert evidence on matters which call for scientific scrutiny.

Because of the inherent difficulty of finding any test that will not leave a great measure of individual discretion in the hands of the court, a good many critics have suggested the abandonment of the M'Naghten Rules altogether, without the substitution of an alternative legal formula,[23] so that the jury would be left to determine in any individual case whether the accused ought to be held responsible or not. This is a realistic recognition of the fact that, under the guise of a directing formula, judges and juries have, in fact, given widely varying interpretations to the rule.[24]

These tests do not, of course, pretend to give anything but a broad guide for an individual decision of a court or, as the case may be, of an administrative authority. As the Report of the British Royal Commission observed wisely,[25]

that a criterion of criminal responsibility is not necessarily to be rejected because it is imperfect and cannot be guaranteed to cover every case which it ought to cover. All legal definitions necessarily involve an element of abstraction and approximation, which may make their application difficult in marginal cases and may reasonably exclude cases which ought to be included; this is inevitable, since it is precisely the function of the law to draw clear lines for general guidance where there is no clear line in nature, and to deal with the difficulties and anomalies inherent in borderline cases by preserving a reasonable flexibility of interpretation.[26]

Modern legal theory has long recognized that general legal formulae could not or should not try to dispense with the individualizing application of justice to the case at hand. It is nevertheless of vital importance that the general directive should be in broad harmony with contemporary rather than outdated philosophy, morality, and social thought.

Yet, a translation of modern medical insight into law, the acceptance of the complexity of the human being, the understanding of the many forces and emotions that struggle in the breast of a human being and produce an almost infinite scale of variations, from 'normality' to 'abnormality', in turn raises serious problems. '*Tout comprendre, c'est tout pardonner*.' Somewhere, society must draw the borderline and hold a person guilty of a crime, even though psychiatrists may regard the offender as a very disturbed human being, and philosophers may deny the 'free will' to choose between right and wrong. Many of those who would be held not responsible for their actions under the amended M'Naghten Rule are unquestionably individuals highly dangerous to society, usually with a long record of dangerous actions.[27] The alternative is inevitably between punishment and compulsory confinement to an institution for the care of mentally-disturbed people. Where execution is ruled out, either because capital punishment has been abolished or is not applied, or because the defendant has been found 'guilty but insane', the choice is between the overcrowding of two sets of institutions, both of them inadequate, quantitatively and qualitatively, in the great majority of modern States. Above all, it is still the overwhelming opinion of modern criminologists and sociologists that punishment for the criminal is an essential outlet in modern, as in earlier, societies.[28] These needs of society might be threatened beyond danger point if the concept of 'mental defect' or 'mental disease' were stretched too far – if it were, for example, extended to the case of Mr Dallas O'Williams,[29] who, between 1932 and 1958, had been arrested more than a hundred times, convicted of eleven major crimes, ranging from assault to homicide. He had been judged criminally insane, but when committed to a mental institution, the psychiatrists were unable to find any evidence of mental disease or defect, other than propensity for crimes of violence. But if propensity for crime comes to be recognized as a mental disease as such, without any additional element indicating incapacity of the minimum degree of reasoning or control sufficient to prevent the commission of a crime, the way is open not only for a far-reaching frustration of the process of criminal justice, but for the obliteration of the borderlines of criminal law altogether.

The proposed reforms of the M'Naghten Rules do not abandon the basic criteria of a legal order, they simply attempt to draw the line differently. There is nothing sacrosanct in the particular test evolved over a century ago, and it is greatly preferable that law and social facts – of which medical knowledge is a part – should not be too far apart. At this point, the question of the treatment of the mentally disturbed person, from the insane to the emotionally disturbed incurable person, leads to the wider problems of punishment and its alternatives, in the light of modern social science.

## SOCIAL ENVIRONMENT AND THE MODIFICATION OF PENAL SANCTIONS

The limited area of the treatment to be meted out by society to the mentally-disturbed offender highlights a problem that is increasingly extending to the entire field of criminal law. The more enlightened attitude towards the mentally deranged has been the result both of a more humanitarian philosophy and of a deeper understanding of human personality in the light of modern psychiatric knowledge. A comparable dual challenge is gradually transforming the whole theory and practice of punishment and, with it, the theory of criminal law.

The characteristic of criminal law is the imposition of official sanctions calculated to interfere with the life, liberty, or property of the offender, for certain objectionable conduct classified as criminal, by statute or common law. On the purposes of such sanctions, there are a multitude of theories which shade into each other. The main traditional theories revolve, however, around three major philosophies[30]:

There is, first, the idea of atonement or expiation. Suffering punishment, the criminal expiates the sin he has committed.

This grim, clear cut, and simple doctrine of sin and atonement is close to, though not identical with, the philosophy of retribution. The latter emphasizes the position of the social group against which the criminal offends rather than that of the criminal himself. By imposing punishment, society exacts retribution or, in the dialectic language of Hegelian philosophy, it 'negates' the crime. The philosophy of retribution is often, though not correctly, identified with that of revenge. Through the infliction of punishment, society, in the latter conception, avenges itself for the wrong done to it. Often retribution and revenge are two sides of the same coin, but they need not necessarily go together. For a philosophy of retribution can be applied to punishment on a purely objective scale, without the subjective coloration of revenge.

Elements of all these philosophies certainly survive, both objectively in the scale and measurement of penalties inflicted for different categories of crime, and subjectively in the emotion aroused in the vast majority of people by certain criminal actions. Depending on the heinousness of the crime, and on the emotions aroused in us – which may or may not be in accordance with the objective gravity of the criminal action – we wish to see the criminal suffer and we wish to avenge ourselves, individually or collectively, for the wrong done to one, some, or all of us.

However, the science of criminal law has long departed from these somewhat primitive and abstract theories of punishment to one which emphasizes the social objective: the philosophy of deterrence. Punishment must be designed so as to deter as far as possible from the commission of similar offences. This again, divides itself into two aspects.[31] Appropriate punishment should deter the individual offender from a repetition of this, or similar kinds of, offence. It should also serve as a warning to other members of society. In both respects, deterrence should serve to protect society from crime.

Generally, the philosophy of deterrence still prevails in modern criminology. We continue to be concerned with preventing, by appropriate punitive sanctions, both the individual offender and other members of society from the repetition of crime, or the imitation on the part of others by similar actions. But the contemporary approach to the best way of achieving this general objective has undergone a profound transformation. We are no longer certain that the harshest punishment is necessarily the best way of preventing repetition of the offence. Where we have to concede that the harshest possible punishment – execution – will certainly prevent the particular criminal from committing this, or any other, offence again, we are no longer sure that this '*Spezialprävention*' will also have the effect of '*Generalprävention*,' i.e. that it will reduce the proportion of capital offences in the body politic. In the continuing controversy about capital punishment, one of the most powerful arguments of those who advocate the abolition of the death penalty is that 'there is no clear evidence . . . that the abolition of capital punishment has led to an increase in the homicide rate, or that its reintroduction has led to a fall'.[32]

When, as must be generally accepted in the light of recent thorough investigations, the statistical evidence does not support, for example, capital punishment on the ground of deterrence, the problem comes back to one of basic theory. Here, the older philosophies of retribution – in its various shades[33] – are increasingly inadequate although they continue to be supported by some eminent theologians, jurists, and others.[34] Modern civilized society has, in general, receded more and more from this philosophy of 'an eye for an eye, a tooth for a tooth'. The reason is for some, but only a minority, a revulsion against the arrogation by society of the right to take the life of a human being, a view which could be held consistently only by radical pacifists, and hardly by the great majority who justify killing *en masse* in case of war by order of the State. A more practical reason is the danger of an irretrievable error of justice. Both these arguments apply, of course, only to capital punishment, and not to the theory of punishment in general. What is of far greater importance to the theory of punishment as applicable to all major offences is the progress of social science in a manner parallel to that of modern psychology and psychiatry. We are far from having an exact estimate of the facts which modern urbanization and industrialization, with all the social disruption they entail, have on the rate of crime. We do, however, know beyond reasonable doubt that such factors as congregation of large families and, especially, juveniles in overcrowded slums have a considerable effect on delinquency, as has the diversion of vast numbers of married women in modern industrialized societies from domestic care to paid employment, or the disruption of family ties in estranged families. Individual and social psychology touch each other, when it comes to an appreciation of the effect of social environment or emotional upsets, in family, school, or elsewhere, on the mental balance and health of an individual. The more we understand of the complex web of conditions that go into the make-up of a person, the less can we accept the simple equations of sin and expiation, offence and retribution, and the like. But we are also faced again, as in the more specialized case of the mentally-disturbed individual, with the problem of the proper balance.

Generally speaking, the increasing understanding of the social and psychological causes of crime has led to a growing emphasis on *reformation* rather than deterrence in the older sense, as the best way to protect both the individual criminal from himself, and society from the incidence of crime. In practical terms, this has meant the increasing use of corrective and educational measures, either in addition to, or in substitution for, punishment proper. The consideration of such alternatives has gradually spread from specialized categories of offenders to criminal offenders in general.

In the case of persons adjudged insane – whether before trial, at the beginning of the trial (insane on arraignment), as the result of evidence during the trial (special verdict), or after sentence – it is obvious that alternative detention or care must be provided for, in the interest both of the individual and of society. This must be extended, as the categories of these persons widens from the 'insane' in the older sense to others adjudged 'mentally disturbed' or 'mentally deficient'.

A revolution of far greater proportion has, during the last generation, taken place in the treatment of juvenile offenders. Almost universally today, in civilized countries, the juvenile offender (usually a person between the ages of eight and eighteen), who not so long ago used to be subjected to the harshest penalties and thrown together with hardened criminals – is now subjected to a special procedure. The predominant pattern is that of the juvenile court – as introduced, during the last thirty years or so in England, Germany, the great majority of the American states, and many other countries – a court which differs radically, in procedure and the type of sanctions to be imposed upon the offender, from the ordinary criminal court. Probation and approved schools have become the substitute for imprisonment. A number of modern legal systems have gone further and removed the sanction power altogether from the courts, putting it instead into the hands of the child-welfare authorities.[35] In California the powers of the youth authority have been extended further. This authority now has power to deal with children below the age of juvenile criminality, and to mete out treatment in accordance with the diagnosis of their position.

From the juvenile offender, the substitution of corrective measures for punishment proper has spread to the adult offender. The principal emphasis is on probation for first offenders, as a conditional alternative to punishment.

But emphasis on the need for corrective measures is not confined to the first offender. At the other end of the scale, the recidivist, the habitual offender, is becoming increasingly the object of attention of modern penology. In the case of a first offender, it is felt that corrective measures of an educational and a reformative character will serve to deter him from further offences.[36] This follows in the footsteps of the pioneer work of Sheldon and Eleanor Glueck on juvenile delinquency, which has included a social prediction scale for proneness to delinquency.[37]

It is not our purpose – nor is it within the competence of this writer – to analyse and compare in detail the multitude of educational, corrective, and preventive measures that, in a growing number of countries are now applied not only to mentally-disturbed persons, juveniles, first offenders, but to all criminals. What emerges as a highly significant and critical fact is the increasing intermingling of the criminal and the administrative process in the modern science and practice of the criminal law. That the criminal offender is no longer seen as an isolated and guilty individual who, at a given moment, is brought before a court, duly sentenced by whatever term appears appropriate to the court within the often fantastically wide range of maximum and minimum penalties and then disappears forever from the sight of the judicial authorities, represents an evolution in the legal thinking on crime from which there can be no retreat. In a properly administered and enlightened modern legal system, the process, in which welfare, administrative, and criminal process elements are mixed, starts when the welfare of a child that lacks proper family care and attention, or otherwise shows symptoms that might, in the future, turn him into a criminal, is taken over by the appropriate public authority.[38] It continues when – either despite such measures or in their absence – a juvenile offender comes before a special juvenile court, which increasingly operates as an educational and corrective authority with judicial attributes. From there, administrative and welfare authorities take over again, in the shape of the probation officer, child-welfare board, youth authority, and of the various official institutions to which the juvenile offender is remanded in lieu of punishment. To these must be added a variety of medical, social, and educational experts who enter the process at some stage. Obviously, the old borderlines are becoming less distinct, and it is often uncertain at what stage the criminal process stops and the administrative process begins.

This vital and needed change raises, however, in its turn, some grave problems. In the first place, there must be a degree of co-ordination between the judicial authorities proper, i.e. the judge and jury, or the judge alone, and the various welfare and administrative

authorities, which is still often lacking. This appears to be particularly true of the length of present sentences – in the post-war
period it has significantly increased on an average both in Great
Britain and the United States[39] – which often bears no relation either
to the social usefulness of the sentence imposed, or to the administrative facilities available either in prisons or in other institutions. It is
probably still true – as it was certainly not so long ago – that a
majority of the judges have never visited a prison or one of the other
institutions now figuring in the punitive process.

Secondly, the distribution of functions between judicial authorities and various administrative and welfare officers emphasizes the
need for adequate training and social and professional status of the
latter, especially of the probation service, a relatively recent but
vitally important institution. The change from a purely repressive
to an educative function also emphasizes the need for properly
trained prison officers, whose arduous lot must be balanced by
adequate recognition in the social and financial scale. This, too, is
far from being the case.[40]

Lastly, and perhaps, most important, the blurring of the borderlines between the criminal and the administrative procedure holds
not only benefits, but also dangers for the effect on the individual.
The administrative process is in its essence discretionary, whereas
criminal procedure has, at least in the democratic scheme of values,
been surrounded with safeguards against arbitrariness.

As corrective and educational procedures have become intermingled with criminal or quasi-criminal processes, so the fear has
grown that benevolent but autocratic authority may be able to
deprive persons falling under its jurisdiction of liberty, for indefinite
periods, without the judicial safeguards attending criminal trial.
Criticism has been particularly vociferous in states which, like
California, have gone far in the substitution of corrective for criminal procedures in regard to juvenile offenders. The title of a recent
article,[41] is: 'We need not deny justice to our children,' while a
California judge has written that the juvenile court is 'fast developing into a complete system of Fascism, as dangerous to our institutions as Communism'.[42] Such complaints are based on the
vagueness or elasticity in the procedure of a juvenile court in
regard to such essential safeguards as the powers of the police to
arrest, the precise formulation of the offence, the right to trial
by jury, the right to refuse testimony, the acceptance of hearsay
evidence, or the right to counsel.[43]

Similar fears have been voiced in regard to the judicial power –

introduced in a number of countries[44] – to sentence habitual criminals to 'preventive detention', a procedure varying somewhat from
country to country, but definitely including corrective diagnosis,
treatment, and training (such as vocation training in a skilled trade),
in preparation for a return to normal life.[45]

The resolution of this dilemma can hardly be found in sweeping
and absolute formulas. Unless we wish to retreat from the entire,
laboriously developed process of preventive, educational, and
corrective methods, either in addition to or in substitution for
purely criminal trial and sentence, we cannot seek to wipe out the
necessary measure of administrative discretion that must rest in
responsible authorities supervising the treatment of the juvenile,
the habitual offender, the prisoner sentenced to an indeterminate
sentence, and the like. Yet, in all too many cases, the 'preventive
detention' or the institution to which a juvenile offender is sent,
resembles in fact, though not in name, the prison to which it is
meant to be an alternative. Certainly, it implies compulsory deprivation of liberty. Such interferences range, however, from the
supervisory powers of an officially appointed guardian to the compulsory retention, for an indefinite period, of an offender in a
strictly supervised and harsh institution. In regard to the juvenile
offender, the recent opinion of a District of Columbia Court has
attempted to draw the borderline in the following terms:[46]

Unless the institution is one whose primary concern is the individual's
moral and physical well-being, unless its facilities are intended for and
adapted to guidance, care, education, and training rather than punishment, unless its supervision is that of a guardian, not that of a prison
guard or jailor, it seems clear a commitment to such institution is by
reason of conviction of crime and cannot withstand an assault for violation of fundamental Constitutional safeguards.[47]

In practical application of this test, the court held that the
Attorney-General could not place a boy in the District of Columbia
jail for continued detention, nor could he designate the Federal
Correctional Institution at Ashland, Ky, as the place of confinement, because this institution is designed to rehabilitate youths
regularly convicted in the criminal courts. Instead, the Attorney-
General was ordered to designate 'the National Training School for
Boys or a similar institution not designed as a place of confinement
for those convicted of crime and where petitioner may not have
contact or communication with those convicted of crime'.[48] In
another recent case, a sex offender had been sentenced to an indeterminate term of imprisonment, in anticipation by the court of

proper psychiatric treatment, but had, in fact, received hardly any treatment in a state prison. A court which later became concerned with the case recommended transfer to an institution where the defendant would receive proper psychiatric treatment.[49]

On the even more difficult problem of sorting out the detention aspects from the penal treatment of the habitual offender the authorities appear to be divided. Some consider that, at least until completely different institutions are developed, preventive detention cannot be effectively distinguished from prison treatment,[50] but others believe that a genuine differentiation has already been achieved in the Scandinavian countries, and that preventive detention need not be, in effect, a punishment, provided it is administered in the proper spirit.[51]

The solution must be sought in further progress in the genuine distinction between penal and educational or corrective institutions, in substance rather than in name. The problem of the proper borderline between administrative discretion and individual right is not, after all, confined to this issue, but pervades the whole body of law.[52] The imposition of a new form of criminal procedure on the deliberately elastic welfare procedures of youth authorities, social welfare boards, and the like would largely defeat the object for which they were created. On the other hand, there is great merit in the attempt made by the above-mentioned judgement of the District of Columbia Court to draw a genuine distinction between corrective and penal institutions. In the wider sense, this problem borders on the more general one of the new relationship between authority and individual created by the enlarged functions of the modern Welfare State. It is, in many ways, easier for the 'negative' State (which confines itself essentially to the minimum functions of defence, police, and machinery of justice) to be just to the individual – at the expense of active concern for his social and economic welfare. Such active concern means of necessity interference. On balance, such interference is beneficial; otherwise it would not have been adopted by one State after another during the present century. Nobody seriously wishes to go back to the prison system of the time of Dickens. Instead, we should direct our attention to the working out of the safeguard against the abuse of welfare activities rather than against their substance. This applies to the field of criminology no less than that of administrative discretion in general.

Three major developments which, singly and in combination, deeply affect modern criminal law, will be considered. They are:

First, the necessity to protect the *public* economic interests and resources against depredations by individuals (physical and corporate).

Second, the growth of the corporation, largely in substitution for the individual, as a subject of rights and duties in modern society.

Third, the steadily increasing welfare functions of the modern State, which entail a protection of social standards by a combination of administrative and penal sanctions.

### ECONOMIC CRIMES AGAINST THE COMMUNITY

In a *laissez faire* economy, the waste of property is, like its accumulation, a matter of private concern. The rape of the earth, through ruthless deforestation, overgrazing, waste of water, dust-bowl farming, is a matter for the individual owner, who is presumed to suffer the appropriate penalty through the diminution of his crops and financial returns. The same applies to the neglect or non-use of machinery, such as power plants, tractors, or of mineral resources, even if such abuse should lead to scarcity and the impoverishment of the community. Such a philosophy is no longer held, except by a diminishing band of passionate believers in the absolute sacrosanctity of property, immune from any official interference or regulation. A major cause of the change in the public philosophy has been the incidence of total war in the twentieth century. Scarcity of food has made the careful use of land a vital necessity, in blockaded countries, such as Germany in the First World War, or densely populated, entirely industrialized countries, dependent largely on sea supplies, like England in both World Wars. This has meant at least a temporary change in legal values.[53] Similarly, waste or unauthorized use of precious resources becomes, in such situations, a criminal and social offence.

Outside the emergencies of war conditions, the growing recognition of the social function and use of property has led to more permanent changes in legal values.[54] The recognition of these changed evaluations of the relation of property and individual has gone furthest in socialized legal systems. Following the constitutionally enshrined concept of 'public, Socialist property as the sacred and inviolable foundation of the Socialist system . . . .', in the Soviet Constitution[55] the destruction, the theft, and the misuse of State-owned property – which embraces the bulk of the industrial, commercial, and agricultural assets of the nation – is attended with criminal sanctions. After various preliminary statutes, a decree of 1947 provided specially heavy penalties for theft of State-owned and cooperatively-owned property.[56] To a large degree, penal sanctions in a socialized system must serve as a substitute for the regulatory effect of financial incentives, the 'profit motive'. But the philosophy of penalizing waste and misuse of public property has deeper roots. Where the national philosophy is the development of the national economy to the general benefit by the planned use of resources, the intentional or careless waste of national assets acquires basic importance.

The growing consciousness of the need to preserve vital assets for the community, and to protect it from the rapaciousness or neglect of the individual, goes far beyond socialized systems of the Soviet pattern. We have seen that, in some western parts of the United States, scarcity of water has produced restrictive legislation not only on the use of water, but even on the ownership of land.[57] If, as many demographers and ecologists believe, the growth of the world's population will increasingly outstrip available resources, the conservation of agricultural, mineral, and other natural assets will become an increasingly vital social and legal value, fortified by harsh criminal sanctions.

Meanwhile, the protection of vital resources and commodities has, in non-Socialist societies, mainly developed through regulatory measures, attended with penal sanctions. Here, the most notable development has probably been in German law, the outcome of scarcity situations produced by two world wars, with intervening inflations, raw material, and currency shortages. Out of the multitude of statutes and decrees, controlling and regulating the supply of scarce commodities, and especially transactions in foreign exchange, has developed a whole body of *Wirtschaftsstrafrecht*. After the last World War, the West German Republic consolidated the concepts and offences gradually developed in a comprehensive *Wirtschaftsstrafgesetz*.[58] The law distinguishes between a graver type of economic offence called *Straftat* and a lesser type, called *Ordnungswidrigkeit*. In the former category is, above all, an action designed to 'retain, put aside, destroy, or deliberately or negligently allow to perish, objects of vital need, where the actor knows or must, in the circumstances, be deemed to suppose that he thereby endangers the satisfaction of these needs.'[59] Other important offences in this category concern violations of rationing and price controls. The *Ordnungswidrigkeit* covers essentially violations of officially imposed supervisory duties in the conduct of an enterprise. There is also a category of *Zuwiderhandlungen* which may be either a *Straftat* or an *Ordnungswidrigkeit*. It is the former where the action 'violates the interest of the State in the conservation and integrity of the economic order as a whole or in individual branches'.

These concepts have been adopted in the recent West German Anti-trust Law (*Wettbewerbsgesetz*) of 1957, which regards an offence against the provisions directed to the elimination of various restrictive practices, monopolies, and the like as an *Ordnungswidrigkeit*.

The most interesting aspect of this new classification of economic offences is its differentiation between what we might call the old-style type of criminal offence and the new type of administrative offence. The yardstick is both the gravity of the interest that has been injured, and the *mens rea* of the offender. There are new types of interest deserving of protection by the State and unknown to the older criminal law, but not all of these can be measured in terms of older concepts of criminal law.

Long before the development of these new concepts of economic crime in the Soviet Union, Germany, and some other countries, following the economic dislocation of the present century, Canada (in its Criminal Code of 1889) and the United States (in its anti-trust legislation of 1890) had attempted to utilize the criminal law for another type of economic offence, which marks an equally significant, though differently based, departure from the traditional scope and purposes of the criminal law. By making it a misdemeanour to contract or engage in any combination or conspiracy in restraint of trade or commerce among the several States or with foreign nations, or to monopolize such trade or commerce, the Sherman Act of 1890 clearly recognized that it was the function of criminal law not only to protect private property against unlawful interference, but also to protect the basic economic order of the nation, and the conditions of its existence, against unlawful interference by private subjects of the law. This was, indeed, a revolutionary departure from established concepts. It was, of course, based on an economic philosophy radically different from that later embodied in the Soviet Constitution, or even that of the German *Wirtschaftsstrafgesetz*. The interest to be protected was the maintenance of a competitive economy based on private enterprise. The State did not mean to become owner or entrepreneur, but it felt compelled to use its legislative, administrative, and judicial machinery for the protection of the economic well-being of the community as a whole – as conceived by a liberal economic philosophy – and to defend it against powerful industrial and commercial interests. This is no less a revolution in legal thinking than the establishment of economic crimes in the Soviet law, despite the radical difference in the economic philosophies underlying American and Soviet law. Moreover, United States anti-trust legislation, later supplemented by the establishment of the Federal Trade Commission, with powers largely parallel to those of the Department of Justice, envisages not only criminal action, but also a civil suit by the Department of Justice, either as an alternative or an addition to criminal action. Moreover, private litigants may bring the so-called triple-damage action, a procedure that has recently gained in popularity. The Federal Trade Commission, one of the major regulatory agencies that are essential to the American conception of government, has powers to issue 'cease and desist' orders for the enforcement of fair trade (including anti-trust offences), which may be sanctioned by a penalty. This, however, is a 'civil' penalty, what the Germans would call an *Ordnungsstrafe*, a means to enforce the authority of government, not a criminal sanction proper.

To this variety of proceedings must be added the possibility to terminate a pending suit by a 'consent decree' – a very frequently used procedure – and the many informal, behind-the-scenes negotiations by which, for example, the Department of Justice may give immunity to a contemplated action which might possibly violate the anti-trust laws.

The real effectiveness of legal sanctions depends, of course, above all, on the degree and methods of their practical implementation. In Canada, criminal sanctions comparable to those of the Sherman Act remained practically a dead letter until the reinvigoration of anti-trust enforcement after the Second World War.[60]

In the United States, on the other hand, the anti-trust law has become a basic reality of public and business life, a factor of major influence on the decisions and actions of the business community.

On the whole, it must be concluded that, in so far as the anti-trust law has been effective in the restraint or elimination of monopolistic conditions, it has been due predominantly to administrative and civil measures, or just to the general sense of awareness caused by the existence of the legislation and the possibility of its interference with business operations. It is significant that the various recent anti-trust laws of other countries – with the exception, in a limited sense, of the German *Wettbewerbsgesetz* – have entirely discarded the criminal sanction and relied on measures of publicity and administrative regulation rather than the deterrence of criminal offence.[61]

### THE CORPORATION AND CRIMINAL LIABILITY

Elsewhere in this book the impact of corporate power on the social and legal pattern of contemporary industrial society is discussed.[62] The fact that, today, the corporation is the predominant unit, and therefore a potential defendant, in actions of economic and commercial impact has a profound effect on this branch of the criminal law. A corporate body is, by the law, equated to a physical individual, but it is not an individual.[63] The characterization of the corporate body as a living organism is a symbolic gesture, even where it is not simply a disguise for the legitimation of omnipotence of the State over the individual. Except for the purely administrative or welfare offence – with which we shall deal below – the criminal law appeals to the individual. It can direct itself to the corporate body only by a further process of imputation. Accordingly, the problem of the criminal responsibility of corporations divides itself into several aspects[64]:

First, a clear distinction should be made between vicarious liability of the master for acts of the servant, and imputation of the actions of a person in the employment, or acting on behalf, of the corporation which are properly imputable to the latter. Imputed liability is not vicarious, but original, liability. The principle of vicarious responsibility has been developed in the law of tort, because it has seemed socially and economically necessary to hold the master – and that is in many cases a corporation – liable *vis-à-vis* third parties for acts committed within his sphere of operations. The master is held able to recover against his servant. The law of tort is, however, concerned with the economic adjustment of burdens and risks, and the principle of vicarious liability is applicable to the criminal law only in so far as the criminal law is approximated to the objectives of the law of tort, i.e. where the law is essentially concerned with the enforcement of certain objective standards of conduct, through the imposition of fines, rather than with the individual guilt of a person. This points to the area of strict responsibility which is largely, though not entirely, coextensive with the area of so-called public-welfare offences, to be dealt with later. For this reason, there has been justified criticism of a fairly recent English decision[65] where a company was convicted of making false tax returns *with intent to deceive*, the managers of the company having embezzled the proceeds of sales of the company's stock and then made false returns in respect of purchase tax. Since the managers were acting in the course of their employment, vicarious liability in tort would have been entirely justified in this case, but hardly the criminal responsibility which the court imposed.

Secondly, the nature of criminal sanctions imposes certain obvious limitations on the categories of crimes which may be imputed to a corporation. Corporations cannot be executed or imprisoned. This would seem to exclude certain intensely personal offences, such as murder, rape, and bigamy, and neither practice nor doctrine has hitherto extended the criminal responsibility of corporations to these offences.[66] This leaves as a principal field of offences (other than public-welfare offences) crimes that arise out of economic dealings. Convictions for criminal offences that involve *mens rea* have, both in England and the United States, occurred mainly in the sphere of thefts, fraudulent dealings, and conspiracies (the latter relating for the most part to conspiracies to defraud or to acts in restraint of trade under the anti-trust laws).[67] Further limitations are indicated by the purpose of punishment. In the case of at least the larger corporations, statutory fines are seldom of a magnitude which would act as an effective deterrent through the suffering of serious financial injury. And the shareholders are usually too far removed, both financially and personally, to suffer effective personal detriment. A shareholder of General Motors does not feel personally affected by even a heavy fine imposed upon the corporation. Nor is he financially hit, since his participation is limited to his shareholding.[68] The main effect and usefulness of a criminal conviction imposed upon a corporation cannot be seen either in any personal injury or, in most cases, in the financial detriment, but in the public opprobrium and stigma that attaches to a criminal conviction. Hence, it is particularly important to limit criminal convictions of corporations, for offences other than those which are essentially of an administrative character, to those offences that can properly and fairly expose the corporation to a moral opprobrium.

Third, the rejection of vicarious, as distinct from imputed, liability in the field of criminal law makes it necessary to define the type of relationship which makes it proper to impute the criminal action of an individual to the corporation. The basic criterion for this was laid down many years ago by Viscount Haldane L.C. in a classical passage[69]:

The fault or privity (of the company within the meaning of a statute) is the fault or privity of somebody who is not merely a servant or agent for whom the company is liable upon the footing *respondeat superior*, but somebody for whom the company is liable because his action is the very action of the company itself.

What Lord Haldane has characterized in this way as the *alter ego* of the corporation is essentially described in the definition of the tentative Draft No. 4 (1955) of the Model Penal Code suggested by the American Law Institute, by the term 'high managerial agent'. This is defined as

an officer of a corporation or an unincorporated association, or, in the case of a partnership, a partner, or any other agent of a corporation or association having duties of such responsibility that his conduct may fairly be assumed to represent the policy of the corporation or association.

However precise the definition, a measure of discretion will always have to be left to the individual court in the decision whether a given high officer or group of officers or members of a corporation must, in any individual case, be deemed to have represented the corporation as such.

Special questions arise where the offending body is a government or a government-controlled corporation. Can a government be held capable of a criminal offence? If it is, can it be punished by a fine, which, in a sense, the government pays to itself?

These problems arose directly in an interesting Australian decision.[70]

Under the Australian Commonwealth Re-establishment and Employment Act, 1945, employers are under a duty to reinstate persons who have completed a certain period of war service in their former employment. A further section provides that they shall not without reasonable cause terminate or vary such employment. Offenders are liable to a penalty of £100, to be imposed by a court of summary jurisdiction. Other sections of the Act provide, for certain other offences, imprisonment not exceeding six months, alternatively or in addition to a penalty. The whole Act is specifically declared binding upon the Crown.

The defendant, who was a manager of a Commonwealth munition factory, was prosecuted before a court of petty sessions in Victoria for unlawful termination of the plaintiff's employment. Conviction was possible only under section 5 of the Commonwealth Crimes Act, which provides that 'any person who procures or by any act of commission is in any way directly or indirectly knowingly concerned in or party to any offence against any law of the Commonwealth, shall be deemed to have committed that offence, and shall be punishable accordingly'.

The conviction of the manager, a servant, was dependent upon his being an accessory to an offence committed by the Crown. Although the High Court decided by a bare majority to confirm the order of the magistrate dismissing the information, the majority of the judges did not reject the possibility of the Crown being convicted for a criminal offence.

Only the Chief Justice (Latham c.j.) dismissed the idea that the Crown might commit a criminal offence as unacceptable in principle. His objections were, first, that the fundamental idea of the criminal law is a prosecution of offences against the King's peace; secondly, that the Crown itself would have to be a prosecutor in the case of serious offences; thirdly, that the Commonwealth would have to pay a fine to itself; and fourthly, that where imprisonment was at least an alternative penalty, the Crown could not be included as it could not be imprisoned. The other judges considered the criminal conviction of the Crown at least theoretically possible, though two of them formed a majority with the Chief Justice in rejecting the conviction in the particular case.

At a time when government departments and many independent corporations, directly or indirectly controlled by the government, assume an increasing variety of functions and responsibilities in the social and economic life of nations, the exemption of either government or government corporations from criminal liability generally is neither morally nor technically justified. As we have seen, the main purpose of a fine is not primarily to hurt the defendant financially.

It is to attach a stigma – pronounced by independent law courts – on the breach of legal obligations which have been imposed in the interest of the community. If a modern giant industrial concern is fined for a statutory offence, this does not normally hurt an individual. But an accumulation of such convictions will deservedly impair the standing and reputation of such a concern.

In the case of the British statutory public corporations formed in the process of nationalization of basic industries after the Second World War there is in fact no doubt that they are liable to be fined for statutory offences.

Moreover, private corporations have been quite frequently convicted of offences, for which imprisonment is provided, even though it cannot be inflicted on a corporation.[71]

### STRICT CRIMINAL RESPONSIBILITY
### AND PUBLIC-WELFARE OFFENCES

A whole new area of criminal law has developed out of the steadily increasing responsibilities of the modern State for the maintenance of certain crucial standards demanded by the proper functioning of a modern industrialized and urbanized society. These standards are embodied in a great variety of statutory regulations. They concern safety appliances and sanitary standards in factories and mines, minimum standards in housing accommodation, purity and minimum quality of foodstuffs, drugs, and medical preparations offered to the public, compliance with statutory obligations, unemployment insurance and other forms of social security, registration of professional and trade qualifications, and a multitude of other matters which have become the accepted responsibility of a properly governed contemporary State. Almost invariably, the statutes provide sanctions for the fulfilment of such obligations, mainly in the form of fines. These fines are often imposed by administrative process in the first place, but subject to a trial, if contested by the defendant. Many years ago, a German legal scholar characterized this whole area of criminal law as 'administrative penal law'.[72] Much more recently, common lawyers have directed their attention to this type of criminal offence, and characterized the whole group as 'public-welfare offences'.[73]

It is clear that, as a group, this type of offence, while going under the general label of criminal law, is of an essentially different character from the criminal offences based on individual wrongdoing. Like all law, the conditions under which criminal liability is imposed depend upon a balance of values in a given society. Even the innocent killing of a man harms the society, but the law generally considers that a severe penalty for murder or manslaughter should not be imposed, except on proof of individual guilt. Public-welfare offences are, by contrast, essentially standardized. In the balance of values, it is generally considered more essential that violations of traffic rules or food laws should be strictly punished, in the interests of the public, rather than that the degree of individual guilt should be measured in each case. Moreover, a vast proportion of these offences are nowadays imputable to corporations rather than individuals in such areas as social-insurance obligations, safety and health standards, and the like. It is socially entirely desirable that the corporation, under whose name the business is conducted, should be the carrier of responsibility rather than the individual, although the person immediately responsible may, of course, be subject to a concurrent liability. Given the enormous number of offences falling under these categories, such as violations of traffic regulations, there is also the sheer practical difficulty involved in the limitless number of trials, in which individual guilt would have to be measured. On a balance of social interests, the widespread – though by no means universal – tendency of modern statutes to impose strict liability for violation of public-welfare laws is therefore justifiable. There should also be support for the principle proposed by the draft Model Penal Code of the American Law Institute,[74] that: 'when absolute liability is imposed for the commission of an offence, a legislative purpose to impose liability on a corporation shall be assumed, unless the contrary plainly appears'.

Such a formulation leaves room for contrary interpretations where they must be reasonably inferred from the wording and spirit of a statute.[75] Attacks against the spread of the strict liability principle for this type of offence have often been based on the ground that the imposition of a relatively small fine, e.g. for the operation of dangerous machinery or the sale of injurious drugs, is in any case no adequate sanction.[76] Such criticism seems to misconceive the essentially different character of the sanction imposed in these cases. The purpose is to impose certain standards of conduct in the interest of the community at large, and the maintenance of these standards would be seriously impaired if the individual defence of mistake or blamelessness were generally admitted. This was brought out clearly in a very recent decision of the English Court of Criminal Appeal.[77]

A company whose business comprised the financing of hire-purchase transactions had innocently offended on seven occasions against a statutory order which, to safeguard the currency, had fixed minimum cash payment of 50 per cent for purchases of motor-cars. The finance company had been deceived by the car dealer who had stated an inflated price and also falsely informed the finance company that the purchaser had already paid the required 50 per cent. Yet the finance company was convicted (though the nominal fine took account of its bona fides).

The court pointed out that

...if Parliament enacts that a certain thing shall not be done it is not necessarily an excuse to say: 'I carry on my business in such a way that I may do this thing unwittingly and therefore should suffer no penalty if I transgress.' The answer in some cases is that the importance of not doing what is prohibited is such that the method of business must be rearranged so as to give the necessary knowledge. . . .

The last-quoted sentence points to the real *rationale* of the apparent strictness of this type of offence.

The finance company was guiltless in the sense of the traditional criminal law. But it was not entirely blameless in the sense of managerial standards required by this type of public-welfare order. The fraud of the motor-car dealer was not beyond detection. This was not a case of *force majeure*. The finance company could easily have obtained verified statements, receipts, or affidavits on the relevant aspects of the transaction.

What is emerging in this type of public-welfare offence is a kind of 'negligence without fault'[78] as it has developed in the law of tort within the conceptual framework of fault liability. Its purpose is to compel business to apply stricter standards of inquiry and control to transactions which may endanger public security. This is a logical and sensible development, provided we recognize the importance of public interest in this type of contravention.

There is, however, a strong case for a clearer delimitation of this type of offence from a traditional and graver type of crime. We are, in fact, here dealing with what is essentially a branch of administrative rather than penal law, which should, consequently, be treated as part of the administrative rather than the penal process. Although the courts have sometimes wavered,[79] it is not correct in this writer's opinion to argue that 'the key to understanding the public-welfare offences, . . . is that they are designed to catch the wilful and the negligent; they are not intended to penalize those who were faultless'.[80] The public approach to offences of this kind is, indeed, overwhelmingly different. It makes a clear distinction between the moral impact of a conviction for fraud and conviction for a typical traffic or foodstuffs offence. This distinction is strongly supported by the most authoritative judicial pronouncement on this subject. In *Morissette* v. *U.S.*,[81] the Supreme Court reversed the conviction for theft of one Morissette – who had collected, flattened, and sold spent bomb casings, found on a bombing range, also used for deer hunting. The defendant maintained that he believed the casings to be abandoned, and that he did not intend to steal, but the Court of Appeals had confirmed the conviction on the ground that the relevant statute[82] provides that 'whoever embezzles, steals, purloins, or knowingly converts' property of the United States, is guilty without proof of intent. The opinion of the Supreme Court, delivered by Jackson J., stressed the difference between public-welfare offences, such as conviction under the Narcotic Drugs Act, for which intent is not required,[83] and the offences 'incorporated from the common law', where, in the absence of express statutory language to the contrary, the requirement of intent as evidence of the will to do evil must be presumed.

There is, on the other hand, great force in Hall's argument that specialized courts, investigatory boards, and administrative tribunals should handle public-welfare offences rather than junior criminal courts.[84] If this separation from ordinary criminal procedure were effected, the main criticism of such writers as Stallybrass, Sayre, Hall, or Edwards, that the public-welfare offence undermines the principle of *mens rea*, would lose its force.

A notable attempt to distinguish the whole field of administrative penalties from that of criminal law is made in the Draft Model Penal Code, prepared for the American Law Institute.[85]

It adds to the traditional categories of felony and misdemeanour – not only a 'petty misdemeanour' for minor crimes, but a new offence called 'violation', which is defined as follows:

An offence defined by this Code or by any other statute of this State constitutes a violation if it is so designated in this Code or if no other sentence than a fine, or fine and forfeiture, or other civil penalty is authorized upon conviction. A violation does not constitute a crime and conviction of a violation shall not give rise to any disability or legal disadvantage based on conviction of a criminal offence (Art. 5).

The reasons for this innovation are stated in the following words of comment:

There is, however, need for a public sanction calculated to secure enforcement in situations where it would be impolitic or unjust to condemn the conduct involved as criminal. In our view, the proper way to satisfy that need is to use a category of non-criminal offence, for which the sentence authorized upon conviction does not exceed a fine or fine and forfeiture or other civil penalty, such, for example, as the cancellation or suspension of a licence. This plan, it is believed, will serve the legitimate needs of enforcement, without diluting the concept of crime or authorizing the abusive use of sanctions of imprisonment. It should, moreover, prove of great assistance in dealing with the problem of strict liability, a phenomenon of such pervasive scope in modern regulatory legislation. Abrogation of such liability may be impolitic but authorization of a sentence of imprisonment when the defendant, by hypothesis, has acted without fault seems wholly indefensible. Reducing strict liability offences to the grade of violations may, therefore, be the right solution.[86]

While the Model Penal Code does not go into procedural questions, it would be the logical corollary to its proposal to separate jurisdiction for 'civil' from that for 'criminal' offences.

Whatever the specific solution, we have to recognize that a whole new area of law has developed, as a concomitant to the social responsibilities of the modern State, an area to which the principles and procedures of traditional criminal law are only applicable to a very limited extent. That we have to accept an occasional injustice to the individual is part of the price we have to pay for living in a highly mechanized and closely settled kind of society, in which the health, safety, and well-being of each member of the community depends upon a vast number of other persons and institutions.

Of all the social groups within the State, the family is at once the most closely knit, the smallest, and the most enduring. It has always been recognized by philosophers, jurists, and political scientists that the closeness and intimacy of family ties make the relationship between State and family a problem of special importance. To those who regard unconditional devotion to the State as paramount, the family is an obstacle, to be weakened or even destroyed. There was no place for the family in the life of the rulers of Plato's *Republic*. Plato's prescription for the men and women selected to govern the State – put in the mouth of Socrates – is that 'these women should be all of them wives in common of all these men and that no woman should live with any man privately, and that their children, too, should be common, and the parent should not know his own off-spring nor the child its parent'.[1] This is the complete negation of the concept of the family, based on the privacy of relations between husband and wife, and their children.

Because the intimacy of the personal bonds within the family detracts from single-minded devotion to the State, the integrity of the family is an essential part of any code of 'human rights', or of the groups which, like the various religious communities, wish to preserve personal and ethical values against the omnipotence of government.[2] Any philosophy which sees in the State the highest fulfilment of man must devalue the family.

### BASIC CONCEPTS OF THE WESTERN FAMILY

The analysis attempted here is that of the Western family, a union based on monogamous and – at least in principle – permanent marriage, with a consequently rigid distinction between the status of legitimate and illegitimate children. While this concept of the family is subject to severe strains and changes within Western society itself, it seems to gain ground outside the Western world. This is part of the process by which many Eastern societies, for many centuries subject to static social and economic conditions, attempt to assimilate their life to Western standards. An illustration is the recent Indian statute which has abolished polygamous marriages; even in Moslem States – at least outside the Arab world, as in Pakistan or Indonesia – there is a growing opposition to the exercise of the right to have up to four wives, granted to the husband by the law of the Koran, and to the form of divorce by a simple letter.[3]

## BASIC PRINCIPLES OF THE WESTERN FAMILY

In general terms, the basic principles of the Western family concept can be summed up briefly: husband and wife, through a solemn and officially sanctioned pact[4] – although the sanction outside Catholic states is no longer necessarily religious – enter into a bond for life, which gives them mutual rights and obligations: material support, sexual fidelity, and certain duties in regard to the children's maintenance and education. Sexual or other intimate relations outside marriage not only entail legal sanctions for the responsible party itself, but any children born of an illegitimate union suffer from the consequences in their legal status.

Beneath such deceptively facile generalizations, the Western concept of family law contains fundamental tensions and conflicts, which recent social developments have brought to the surface and intensified. The major problems that have arisen can be summed up in three areas: (1) the husband-wife relationship; (2) the relationships of parents and children; (3) the relationship of the family to the State.

The contemporary crisis of family law results from a variety of factors: changes in social philosophy, which emphasize the freedom of the individual, as against the mainly religiously determined indissolubility of the marriage status; the profound transformation in the economic status of the family in modern urbanized society, and, in particular, in the position of married women; modern scientific and medical developments which make birth control and artificial insemination possible; finally, the growing claims of the modern Welfare State, which makes new demands of, but also assumes far greater responsibilities towards, the family.[5]

## THE INDISSOLUBILITY OF THE MARRIAGE TIE

The principle that still dominates the marriage laws of the Western world is that of the permanency of the marriage union. It is more than a contract, it is a solemn union entered into for life. But behind this broad generalization a deep conflict of philosophies has developed which permeates the controversies about the reform of divorce law.

The basis of the principle of indissolubility is essentially religious; it is the idea of the sacrament of marriage, which is God-made.

The Church admits that the human will enters into marriage.

For each individual marriage, inasmuch as it is a conjugal union of a particular man and woman, arises only from the free consent of each of the spouses . . . This freedom however regards only the question whether the contracting parties really wish to enter upon matrimony or to marry this particular person; but the nature of matrimony is entirely independent from the free will of man . . .[6]

From this premiss follows the remorseless conclusion that any dissolution of marriage, other than by death, is illegitimate, as contrary to the law of God and nature.[7]

The importance of this Catholic doctrine goes far beyond the ecclesiastical sphere. In a considerable number of states it is not only the spiritual, but also the secular law.[8] Implicit in this philosophy is the acceptance of individual unhappiness as part of a status that is ordained by God. 'What therefore God has put together, let not man put asunder.'[9] The shadow of St Augustine still hovers over this concept of marriage. For him all human institutions were essentially sinful, and redeemed only by the grace of God. If men and women have chosen wrongly, let them bear their cross, as a duty owed to God.

The opposite approach, which recognizes marriage as dissoluble under certain circumstances, is compounded of different elements. Perhaps the only common factor in the philosophies which oppose the Augustinian and modern Catholic concept of the indissoluble sacrament of marriage is the recognition of matrimony as a human institution, a bond created by the exercise of a free act of will by a man and a woman who are responsible, but fallible, individuals, who may err and blunder. An individualistic philosophy, which certainly plays a large part in modern reform proposals, postulates the individual right to happiness. People should be able to live out their lives as joyfully as is possible, under conditions which enable them to develop their personal capacities and potentialities. This means the right to correct errors, the right to cast off a burden that has become intolerable and may lead to the sapping of vital energies and the moral fibre of the affected parties.[10] In its extreme version the purely individualistic approach to marriage leads to the consent theory, the interpretation of marriage as a contract based on revocable mutual agreement.[11]

There is, however, an entirely different justification for the rejection of the indissolubility of marriage, based on social rather than individual grounds. This philosophy considers the family as an intimate social unit, a community in miniature, which can be disrupted by an unhappy marriage to the detriment not only of the life and character of the spouses, but of the children. It recognizes that – as has been clearly demonstrated by the social experience of our times – disruption of the marriage may be a prime cause of juvenile delinquency and that, short of criminal actions, it may warp the characters and lives of the children. This philosophy is not, of course, incompatible with that of individual self-fulfilment, but its accent is different. Its central concern is the relation of the marriage bond to the family and, through it, the community.

## The 'Breakdown' Principle

Consideration of the family as a social unit, in which the interests, happiness, and development of the children and other members of the household as well as those of the parents have to be considered, tends to militate against the principle of dissolution of marriage by mutual consent of the spouses. On the one hand, availability of divorce through joint application, i.e. by consent of both parties, offers too great a temptation for hasty and ill-considered actions. A marriage may be dissolved as the result of a momentary quarrel, or a temporary difference of opinion, with irrevocable consequences for the whole family. On the other hand, the requirement of consent may permanently bar the dissolution of a marriage that is disrupted beyond redemption, and the maintenance of which only serves to undermine and poison the relations between the various members of the family, and, particularly, between parents and children. Often, one party, for reasons of convention, social status, or, sometimes, sheer malice, will continue to refuse his consent to the dissolution of a marriage that only survives in name. These social and human considerations demand an objective criterion other than the subjective agreement of the parties.

A substantial number of modern codifications have, in various forms, adopted the principle of 'breakdown' as the decisive criterion, thus departing both from the principle of fault and the principle of consent. First, the Swiss Civil Code of 1907 (Section 142) makes

deterioration of marriage a ground of divorce for either side 'if it
has gone so deep that the spouses must not be expected to cohabit'.
The breakdown principle is, however, blended with the fault theory
in so far as deterioration, predominantly due to the fault of one
spouse, disables that spouse from being the plaintiff in a divorce
action.

A more far-reaching recognition of the breakdown principle is
contained in the West German Marriage Act of 1946[12]:

Where the domestic community of the spouses has ceased to exist for
three years, and where by virtue of a deep-seated and irretrievable disruption of the matrimonial relationship the restitution of a community
of life corresponding to the nature of marriage cannot be expected, either
spouse may apply for divorce.

Where the spouse who makes the application has been wholly or overwhelmingly responsible for the disruption, the other spouse may object
to the divorce. Such objection is to be disregarded where the maintenance of the marriage is not morally justified [*sittlich gerechtfertigt*] considering a proper estimate of the character of marriage and the total
behaviour of both spouses.

The application for divorce is to be refused where the properly
understood interests of one or several minor children of the union
demand the maintenance of the marriage.

In this version, the moral responsibility (fault) of either spouse
is only one factor in a multitude of considerations. The dominant
criterion is the degree to which the marriage ceases to be a relationship which it is worthwhile to maintain. In this estimate, to be made
by the court, the moral guilt of one spouse may be balanced by the
hopelessness of restoration, which may be due to incompatibility,
vast differences of age, or temperament, sexual difficulties, or other
causes, but all these factors may, in turn, be offset by the need to
maintain the marriage for the sake of minor children. While such
a law puts great demands on the wisdom and understanding of a
court, it does clearly see marriage as a complex of human and social
factors, not as a simple equation of guilt and innocence.

Contemporary Soviet law may also be said to have veered from
its original principle of free dissolubility of marriage to an acceptance of the breakdown principle. The Revolutionary Decree of
1917, confirmed in the Family Code of 1926, permitted divorce at
the request of one or both of the parties, without need for any reason.
Differences between registered marriages and *de facto* marriages
were minimized, so much so that in 1929 the Supreme Court regarded two women with whom the deceased had maintained a

relationship of factual marriage as both qualified to inherit his estate.[13] It was an almost inevitable corollary to this attitude to marriage that the legal differences between persons born in or out of wedlock were for all intents and purposes abolished.

A drastic change occurred, however, with the Law of 1944, which abolished *de facto* marriages and declared registered marriages to be the sole legally recognized form of union between man and woman. Above all, the Law of 1944 radically changed the attitude towards divorce. A trial court was directed to attempt reconciliation before granting a divorce. Notice of the proceedings was ordered to be published in the local newspaper, and fees were drastically increased. If all efforts to reconcile the parties failed, the court was authorized to grant the divorce, if it found it necessary to dissolve the marriage. The new law does not spell out the principle on which divorce may be or has to be granted. But the practice of the Soviet courts since the end of the war shows an increasing aversion to the philosophy of easy dissolubility of marriage. Thus the Supreme Court of the U.S.S.R., in an order of 1949, officially criticized the practice of some courts to accept the desire of the parties for divorce as a directing criterion. The court instructed the lower courts to grant divorce only where there were 'deeply considered and well-founded reasons' and where 'continuation of the marriage would conflict with the principles of Communist morals and could not create the conditions necessary to family law and the rearing of children'.[14]

The evolution of Soviet law is in part due to the transformation of a revolutionary society into a firmly established, autocratically governed, and highly disciplined State. In part, however, the abandonment of the theory of free dissolubility of marriage indicates, in this as in other fields of Soviet law, a return to the recognition of a social and legal institution indispensable in any ordered society. It was logical that the Bolshevik revolutionaries should have looked on the existing family as a symbol of the detested society which they wished to destroy. The consolidated Soviet State, which had not 'withered away', needed the family as a stabilizing factor in personal and social relations. Moreover, it wanted children and a high birth rate – partly to offset the enormous losses of the World War – and that meant the restoration of the status and dignity of the family, despite continuing care and concern for illegitimate children. Thus the contemporary Soviet law has come to a position, from one extreme, not far from that to which the laws of a number of Western countries have moved from the other extreme.

A limited form of recognition of the breakdown principle is the power to dissolve a marriage on the ground that the spouses have lived separately for a certain period. Following the law of New Zealand of 1921, nine members of the recent British Royal Commission on Marriage and Divorce recommended that either spouse should be able to obtain a divorce on the ground that they had lived in separation for seven years.[15]

This type of proposal, along with separation, serves as a presumption of breakdown. But the modesty of this reform is apparent not only from the length of the required period of separation, but also from the fact that objection of one spouse is an absolute bar to divorce, even after that period. For this reason, a minority in the Commission wanted to go further and enable a court to dissolve a marriage after seven years' separation, on application by one spouse, even despite objection by the other, 'provided that if the other spouse objects to the dissolution, the applicant must first satisfy the court that the separation was in part due to the unreasonable conduct of the other spouse'. On the other hand, an opposing group rejected even this very cautious departure from the fault principle, with the assertion that any admission of 'breakdown' as a ground for divorce was but a disguised admission of divorce by consent.

Among the contemporary Western systems, the Swedish Marriage Law of 1920 has probably gone farthest in the admission of the breakdown principle. Apart from the already mentioned possibility of joint application by both spouses for a separation decree on the ground of 'profound and lasting disruption', which the court has to accept without examination, a separation decree may also be granted on unilateral application, where the court finds that there has, in fact, been a profound and lasting disruption. Divorce can always be obtained one year after a judicial separation decree, provided the spouses have, in fact, lived separate during that year. Moreover, divorce may be obtained, without forgoing judicial separation, on certain 'breakdown' grounds, most important of which are actual separation for three years or mental insanity for more than three years without hope of recovery.

These grounds for divorce stand side by side with a number of 'fault' grounds, so that the Swedish law combines in a sense the principles of consent, breakdown, and fault.

Despite the impressive advance of the breakdown principle in a number of modern laws, the vast majority of contemporary States still reject it entirely, at least in theory, and adhere to the principle of 'fault'. Although these laws no longer consider the sacrament of marriage as indissoluble in all circumstances, they require a guilty act on the part of one spouse as a condition of divorce. There must be a guilty and an innocent party. Where both parties are guilty, the doctrine of recrimination, almost universally applicable in the American jurisdictions, demands that the divorce action should be dismissed: 'He who comes to equity must come with clean hands.'[16] In England, where both parties are at fault, the court now has a discretion to refuse divorce, 'if it finds that the petitioner has during the marriage been guilty of adultery'. The House of Lords has laid down as guides for the exercise of the discretion: (a) the position and interest of the children; (b) the interest of the party with whom the petitioner has committed adultery, with special regard to their future marriage; (c) the prospects of reconciliation; (d) the interests of the petitioner, particularly his prospects of re-marriage; (e) the interests of the community at large, balancing sanctity of marriage against 'the social considerations which make it contrary to public policy to insist on the maintenance of a union which has utterly broken down'. [17]

In this decision, the highest British court has, within the limited context of a discretion granted by the Act, gone a remarkable distance towards recognition of the breakdown principle and consideration of the family as a social unit.

Most of the contemporary laws still base their law of divorce on a number of enumerated 'faults': adultery, cruelty, desertion, violence, and the like. Some legal systems tend towards general definitions, others prefer the enumeration of a large number of specific offences, such as cruelty to children, gambling, drunkenness, sexual misconduct, etc. Adultery is the backbone of all the legal systems which make 'fault' the basis of their divorce jurisdiction.[18]

The only major open deviation now made in the law of England and Scotland – and all the British Dominions except Canada, in thirty American states, and in nine out of seventeen European countries, sampled in the Report of the Royal Commission[19] – from the principle of 'fault' is the recognition of insanity as a ground for divorce (usually after a specified number of years). Here, divorce is granted because fate – not fault – has made the continuation of the marriage impossible in anything but name.

### Breakdown or Fault: Fact and Fiction

It would, however, be highly unrealistic to judge the present state of marriage and divorce by the enumeration of the grounds of divorce as stated in the various legal systems, by statute of jurisprudence. Judicial interpretations have to a large extent condoned or sanctioned practices designed to satisfy the letter of the law, while violating its spirit. The gaps between theory and practice have deeply alarmed many thoughtful observers. In the words of an English lawyer, 'a valid marriage . . . is the only condition precedent to divorce which cannot be circumvented somehow'.[20] The reasons why the reality of the divorce position, under laws which still rely on fault as the sole or predominant criterion, is so very different from the official theory as laid down in statutes and official policy declarations, have been analysed so often that only a general reference will suffice in this context.[21]

Few areas of legal inquiry point up as dramatically the dangers of letting the tension between legal theory and social reality develop too far.

The strength of the factors undermining the indissolubility of the marriage tie or the strictness of laws which permit divorce only on very few selected grounds, notably adultery of the other party, greatly varies from country to country, and from region to region. On the whole, however, there has been an unquestionable trend towards greater mobility, a trend which is spreading from the Western world to other parts, for example, in the areas of Hindu and Muslim cultures, where women are gradually trying to struggle loose from their traditional status.

In the first place, the strength of religious restraints has weakened, though not everywhere to the same degree. They are still obviously powerful in Catholic countries, and in states with a strong Puritan tradition, such as the New England region of the United States. They are obviously weaker in many of the more recently formed communities, such as many of the western and southern American jurisdictions. Generally, however, religious restraints appear to be weaker in predominantly Protestant countries, not because Protestant Churches encourage divorce, but because the hold of the Churches on the people is no longer as strong a social force (e.g. in England or in the Scandinavian countries) as in Catholic countries.

But even in Catholic or other traditionally religious non-Catholic communities, such as Italy, some of the Latin-American States, or

Quebec, the social facts of modern urbanization, mobility, freedom of movement for women and children, and other social factors are making themselves felt. Above all, the family, outside primitive rural areas, is no longer of necessity held together by physical and economic ties. The livelihood of the family no longer depends predominantly on the common toil of all, and especially of the wife in the house and on the farm. Wives take jobs, exercise professions, conduct business, and are now legally free to dispose of inherited property. Children go to work outside or are subjected to increasingly long periods of school and college education which relieves mothers of daily care and custody, at least for the major part of the working day.

These physical and economic changes go together with a philosophy that in most parts of the world comes to regard the woman – including the married woman – increasingly as equal in her right to move about, develop her faculties, and manage her affairs. While greater facilities for the dissolution of marriages in theory affect both parties equally, in fact it is the greater freedom of movement of the married woman that produces the greater change.[22] Under the formerly predominant social pattern, the husband's freedom of movement was always relatively greater than that of the wife.

With it all goes the spread of a philosophy – praised by some and condemned by others – which stresses individual self-fulfilment and the realization of personal happiness, as against the stern duty imposed by an unalterable status.

Such challenges cannot, in the long run, be ignored by the law. The type of response varies greatly. As we have seen, no major contemporary legal system responds by the free dissolubility of marriage, for even Soviet law, which, in its revolutionary phase, had accepted this principle, has long departed from it. A growing number of jurisdictions accept the challenge by balancing the continuing social requirement of the stability of marriage against the recognition of major factors that will, openly or otherwise, break up many marriages. But in the states in which the fault principle remains exclusive or predominant, the response of the law must be a more devious one. Theories and concepts remain outwardly unchanged, but their meaning is altered. In this way, the moral principle can be saved. The official conscience, expressing itself in legislative bodies, public platform statements, sermons from the pulpit, and many other ways, can protest that it has not departed from the old and stern morality. Even where, under the pressure of social facts, divorce grounds are enlarged from adultery to 'cruelty', 'violence', 'desertion', and the like, it is still possible to proclaim that the principle of fault, i.e. the exclusive dependence of divorce on the proof of guilt on the part of the other side, has been preserved.

In fact, however, the reality of the law is transformed, either by processes of elastic interpretation, or by downright fictions reminiscent of the earlier history of the common law.

The first major technique permitting an expansion of divorce is the judicial interpretation of such comprehensive statutory divorce causes as 'cruelty', 'desertion', and 'violence'.

The extent to which general formulas will be used to facilitate and extend the causes of divorce does, of course, to a considerable extent depend on the elasticity of the term, on the prevailing climate in the jurisdiction in which it is interpreted, and on the individual approach of the court. But it is clear that, in such different jurisdictions as most of the American states, England, or France, the use of such formulas as 'extreme, intolerable, or mental cruelty' or 'constructive desertion' (England) or of *'excès, sévices, ou injures graves'* (France) has facilitated a steady increase in the rate of divorces.[23] This enormous expansion of divorce by judicial construction has occurred largely within the theoretical limits of the 'fault' philosophy. 'Cruelty', 'desertion', 'violence', and 'fraud' denote guilt, an act of wrongdoing by one spouse against the other. Judicial construction, under the pressure of social habits, has been able to expand drastically the rate of divorce, without departing from the fault theory, and without having to rely on such tests as 'incompatibility of temper' (New Mexico law) which come close to the 'breakdown of marriage' theory.

The second, probably the most important and certainly the most ominous, technique is acceptance of the practice of faked evidence. The result, that parties sufficiently wealthy to afford the cost of litigation, and of the various agreements outside and inside the court, which are necessary for the procedure to be brought to a successful conclusion, can, in effect, obtain divorce by consent, discredits the law. It is reached by fraud, and not infrequently perjury, no less objectionable for having become settled practice. It is hypocrisy, inertia, and the interest of some in the maintenance of the existing state of affairs, which stand in the way of a reform of the law that most serious commentators have long recommended. The façade of a semi-puritan ethics is preserved at the cost of sacrificing the integrity of the law and often creating one law for the rich, another for the poor.

Two other reasons of a somewhat different order may be mentioned as adding, at least in some jurisdictions, to the facilitation of divorce without abandonment of the 'fault' theory. The first, welcome as diminishing the gap between the law prevailing for the rich and the poor, is the extension of legal aid in some countries. Among them is, since the Legal Aid and Advice Act of 1948, the United Kingdom. It is quite clear that where legal aid is generally available for people without means, as a matter of right rather than of charity, a vast number of unhappy marriages will be brought before the courts and end in divorce which formerly remained concealed from the public eye, preserved by necessity and poverty.[24]

Finally, in certain federal jurisdictions, particularly in the United States, the divergence of divorce requirements in the different jurisdictions, coupled with the 'full faith and credit' clause of the Constitution, widens the availability of divorce, especially in the age of air transport, in so far as people can evade the law of their home state, and avail themselves of the easier divorce conditions of another state, provided only the divorce thus granted will be recognized.

## *The Remedy : Severity or Relaxation?*

There is some difference of opinion as to the extent to which collusion and other forms of deception have actually undermined the whole edifice of divorce law in the jurisdictions that maintain a theory of restricted divorce grounds based on fault. Obviously, the size of the gulf between theory and practice varies considerably from one jurisdiction to another. In those jurisdictions, for example, where 'mental cruelty' or 'incompatibility of temperament' as divorce grounds are coupled with easy requirements for the establishment of the local jurisdiction, divorce has become more or less a formality for those who can afford it. More interesting is the split of opinion in countries which, like England, are still far from regarding the theory of the divorce law as a mere form. As on so many other matters, the Royal Commission on Marriage and Divorce was almost evenly split on this question. In the view of nine members,[25] cases of 'hotel adultery', while disturbing to the public conscience, are believed to be less frequent than is often supposed. But nine other members went on record with the conviction 'that the law of divorce as it at present exists is indeed weighted in favour of the least scrupulous, the least honourable, and the least sensitive;

and that nobody who is ready to provide a ground of divorce, who is careful to avoid any suggestion of connivance or collusion and who has a cooperative spouse has any difficulty in securing a dissolution of the marriage.[26]

The Report of the Commission – dominated by lawyers – has been severely criticized for its almost total neglect of social facts and statistics. One of the critics[27] shortly afterwards analysed the available English statistics. Some of his most important conclusions are:

(a) that the percentage of marriages terminated by divorce rose from 1·6 per cent in 1937 to 7·1 per cent in 1950, but declined to 6·7 per cent in 1954 (when the post-war rush in divorces had subsided);

(b) that, as pointed out in the Registrar-General's Statistical Review of England and Wales for 1952, 'the bulk of divorce proceedings are instituted with a definite intention of subsequent, immediate remarriage' and that out of 29,000 couples divorced in 1954, only some 8,000 will be permanently lost to the estate of matrimony [with no figures available on the incidence of divorce among subsequent marriages][28];

(c) that 50 per cent of all divorces occur amongst marriages which have lasted more than ten years, and a high proportion of divorces occurs amongst childless couples or those whose children have grown up;

(d) that a great proportion of the increase in contemporary divorces is due to the availability of legal assistance, since 1950, for the poorer classes, which until then, unable to afford divorce, were left to the poor men's device of obtaining separation and maintenance orders from the magistrates' courts, 'a class, as it were, of homeless spirits, neither married nor unmarried, but suspended between the chance of heaven in a happy marriage with a new partner and the certainty of hell with the old one'.[29]

From the admittedly far less than complete data, Mr McGregor deduces that major social changes in the structure of the family and the position of women largely account for the increase in divorce since 1900, but that the distribution of divorce by duration of marriage and the number of children has remained remarkably stable and that enthusiasm for marriage has not diminished. This analysis reinforces the doubts voiced recently by an American student of the problem of marriage stability about the 'widely, if not generally, held opinion that the number of cases of marriage breakdown has greatly increased in recent times and that correspondingly the stability of marriages has seriously declined'.[30]

Such careful investigations show many of the lamentations voiced by the majority of the Commission – as by many others – to be based on prejudices or popular misconceptions rather than on facts.

But granted that disagreement is possible on the extent to which the stability of marriage has decreased, there is no serious doubt that deception and fiction have penetrated the divorce law of every country that maintains a theory of strict divorce to such a degree that any complacency with the existing state of affairs is utterly unjustifiable. The question is what conclusions should be drawn from this state of affairs. Is the answer continued or even increased severity of the law? Should the laws of England, Scotland, or the United States maintain the stern principles of religion and morality which the Puritan forebears imported into the law, trusting that they will educate a laxer generation in the responsibilities of marriage? Or should the law take note of a basic social change, which has reached proportions too great and too universal to be ignored, and adapt the law to the realities of social life by at least reducing, if not eliminating, the tension between fact and theory?

There is, first, the question of values. No conflict arises for the Catholic philosophy, which regards marriage as a sacrament ordained by God, and regards the claim of the individual to full satisfaction of his personal needs as subordinate.[31] There is a grandeur in the rigidity of this philosophy which commands respect, even by those who disagree.

But for all other philosophies, including at least some of the Protestant approaches, which recognize the claim of individual judgement and conscience to a far greater degree than the Catholic philosophy, there is a conflict of value. Sanctity of marriage must be balanced against the often disastrous results of an unhappy marriage for the mental state of the parties, the happiness of the children, and, ultimately, the community.

Overwhelmingly, the Western world, even today, rejects the conception of marriage as analogous to an ordinary contract. With it, it will probably also reject the theory of divorce by mere consent. There is, indeed, considerable justification for the view that the availability of divorce by consent would tempt married couples to magnify temporary disagreement, discomfort, or other difficulties into basic failure. There is much experience to show that patience, continuous effort, and growing maturity can remedy many situations which, in the agony of the moment, appear beyond repair. It will also often, though certainly not always, be true that the interest of the children will be better served by maintenance of the marriage than by the shock of separation. But the demoralizing effect of daily contact with estranged and embittered parents, who will often embroil the children in their conflicts, may be far more damaging. In any case, the contrast between legal theory and social fact is, today, in many states dangerously wide. The law of divorce has, to a greater or lesser extent, become a mockery throughout the modern Western world. Nor is there the slightest evidence in the social or economic moral state of contemporary Western society to assume that the maintenance of a strict law would lead to a change in social facts.

One possible compromise between these conflicting considerations would appear to be a right for either spouse to be able to obtain a divorce on the ground that she or he had lived apart from the other spouse for a specific period.[32] After several years of continuous separation, it may fairly be surmised that the matrimonial community is beyond repair. The alternative to the legal dissolution of marriage after a separation for a number of years is not a restoration of the marriage bond, but maintenance of the fiction of a marriage by a legal tie, which will drive one or the other or both spouses to sexual and other relations with outsiders, clandestinely or under a social stigma, rather than openly. The law in such cases does not serve the sanctity of the marriage, but it preserves sanctimonious righteousness which will, in fact, increase adultery, fornication, and personal bitterness.

The main objection of the nine members of the British Royal Commission who rejected this widening of divorce grounds was, in fact, the very assumption which has been questioned earlier in this chapter: that it would give a husband or wife 'the right to divorce a spouse who, *ex hypothesi*, had committed no recognized matrimonial offence. ...'[33] For those who maintain that the principle of 'matrimonial offence', i.e. of fault, must remain not the major, but the exclusive, basis of the law of divorce, there can, indeed, be no acceptance of this additional ground for divorce. The price to be paid for this view is the continuation or aggravation of the state of affairs as it has been described earlier in this chapter. Quoting a recent American analysis:

the most serious defects in divorce law and administration stem from predicating dissolution on fault of one party, freedom from fault of the other, and the concept of fault having been satisfied, in not requiring any objective assurance of irreparable disruption.[34]

## *Guilt and the Duty of Maintenance*

There is, perhaps, more justification for making the guilt of a spouse in divorce proceedings a relevant factor in the other spouse's obligation of maintenance. After the dissolution of the marriage, the preservation of the family is no longer a consideration, and the refusal of maintenance for the guilty spouse would – as distinct from maintenance for the children – only affect the individual involved. However, such differentiation presupposes that 'guilt' is a meaningful, and not, as in so many cases, a purely fictitious, concept.[35] In such circumstances, a discretionary power for the court would seem to be the best solution. A great majority of the British Royal Commission on Marriage and Divorce thought that the existing law of England, under which the High Court, in proceedings for judicial separation and divorce, had a discretion to order the husband to pay maintenance to his guilty wife – a power exercised 'sparingly and in cases where the wife would have suffered great hardship if the order had not been made'[36] – should be preserved. The same majority considered with obvious logic that the principle of equality of husband and spouse should make that right reciprocal; in other words, a guilty husband, in circumstances of hardship, should be enabled to apply for maintenance against the wife who has obtained the divorce, where the latter is in a position to grant maintenance. Given the dubiousness of the concept of guilt as applied to family law, this would seem to be the wiser as well as a more humane solution than a rigid refusal to grant any maintenance to a guilty spouse.[37]

### CHANGING FOUNDATIONS FOR THE COHESION OF THE FAMILY

Today, the family is to a far lesser extent than in earlier times held together by economic necessity or social subservience. In modern Western society, women can and do operate a business, exercise a profession, or seek industrial employment.[38] In times of depression or in marriages entered into by very young people, the wife is sometimes the main breadwinner, at least temporarily. Children, subject to certain social legislation, go out and earn wages long before they have attained full legal capacity.

It is by no means a bad thing that the bonds of a family, including those between husband and wife, should no longer repose essentially on a stern religious doctrine or on the economic necessity of hanging together as a family, or on the social and legal supremacy of the husband and father. It may be a sign of maturity that, as it has been said[39] 'of the earlier bonds of family, only mutual affection and responsibility for the raising of children are today important, at least in modern Western society'. This change in the foundations of family cohesion does, however, compel a reassessment of the legal remedies for the enforcement of its cohesion or, where necessary, dissolution.

## Preventive Care and Public Policy

By far the most important factor – entirely neglected in the doctrine of the matrimonial offence, but emerging clearly from the data of modern social statistics: juvenile delinquency, psychological, sociological, and ecological studies – is that the relations between husband and wife are not their own exclusive concern, but deeply affect the children. The cost of an unhappy marriage, forcibly maintained by unavailability of legal divorce grounds, or, more frequently, by lack of resources to circumvent the law, may be an increase in juvenile delinquency or lesser forms of social maladjustment. Yet, as has recently been observed with some bitterness,[40] 'in all the laws concerning matrimonial litigation in England and Scotland, there is only one minor reference to the interests of the children', and orders for the custody of children in matrimonial causes are customarily labelled as 'ancillary relief'. It is, therefore, greatly to be welcomed that the Matrimonial Proceedings (Children) Act, 1958, following the Royal Commission, lays greater emphasis on the custody of children in divorce proceedings. No decree nisi (or the corresponding relief in Scotland) is to be made absolute until the court is satisfied, after investigation and report by the court welfare officer, that the arrangements proposed for the care and upbringing of any children under sixteen are the best that can be devised under the circumstances. The court is given wide power to make orders for the future care and upbringing of children under its jurisdiction, e.g. by the designation of probation officers.[41]

One important corollary to this change of emphasis – yet to be translated into statute law – from the exclusive consideration of the husband–wife relation, and of divorce in particular as a matter of bilateral relation, to the consideration of the family as a social unit, should be a shift from the adversary to the inquisitorial function of the public authority dealing with divorce – be this in an ordinary court, a special family or domestic relations court, or an administrative board which would take the place of a litigation procedure altogether.[42] No longer can it be maintained that divorce proceedings are analogous to an action for breach of contract, damages in tort, or the recovery of property. A judge, a conciliation board, or any other public official entrusted with an equitable arrangement for the care of children cannot possibly rest content with the allegations – contested or uncontested – of the parties in regard to the conduct of the other spouse. If consideration for the welfare of the children has to be a major factor in divorce proceedings, the theory of matrimonial offence is at most one of a number of factors to be considered by the competent public authority. No legislator can ultimately evade the choice between the alternatives: of judging the dissolution of marriage by 'fault' or 'quasi-fault' principles as a bilateral matter between husband and wife, with the interests of the children being at most ancillary; or of taking the marriage relationship as a vital component of the family as a social unit. If the latter is the overriding value, then the doctrines of recrimination and comparative rectitude are contrary to public policy. If husband and wife have deceived, abused, or otherwise cruelly treated each other, maintenance of the marriage may be even more harmful to the physical and mental welfare of the children than the fault of one party. The analogy of comparative negligence or of 'coming with clean hands' is faulty, because more than two parties are involved. All these factors point to the need for a procedure – less formal, more inquisitorial, and less modelled upon adversary litigation than the present divorce procedure. But proposals for a 'Family Court', made before the Royal Commission, were curtly rejected by the Commission, on the ground that more, not less, solemnity was required in divorce proceedings (sec. 747).

The principle of an integrated family court, which would deal with the many-sided aspects of family disruption by non-adversary procedures, has, however, been the subject of most intensive study and experimentation in the United States. There are a number of reasons for this difference in approach. The federal structure of the United States, which puts family matters, education, and the administration of justice in the hands of fifty different jurisdictions, encourages diversity and experimentation, although it also leads frequently to a bewildering and confusing variety of institutions. The sociological study of legal institutions is taken far more seriously in the United States than in England. Above all, the United

States, and especially many of its major cities, in their mixture of nationalities, races, religions, and social classes, create social problems of disturbing complexity, which are reflected in family life. The need for an integrated treatment by one institution of such matters as juvenile delinquency, support claims between husband and wife or unmarried couples, divorce and other forms of marriage dissolution, custody of children and adoption has been increasingly recognized by all serious students and practitioners to be an urgent necessity. A number of cities, in Ohio and Oregon, have had integrated family courts for a number of years, and in the testimony of one of the outstanding authorities in the field,[43] in these cities 'complaints about overlapping, defective, and conflicting jurisdiction, of lack of cooperation, of one court either wilfully or unwittingly undoing what another court has striven to do . . . are almost unheard of'.

More typical is the situation in the City of New York,[44] whose population exceeds that of many states. Here, children's neglect and delinquency are handled by the Children's Court, a branch of the Domestic Relations Court. Offences by people over sixteen are dealt with by a variety of other courts. Support claims are handled by the Family Court, unless they arise in connexion with matrimonial proceedings, which are under the jurisdiction of the Supreme Court. The latter also adjudicates disputes concerning custody of children if incidental to a matrimonial action or as presented by a habeas corpus proceeding. But outside such proceedings, these disputes are handled by the Domestic Relations Court.

The proposal of the above-named Committee to substitute for this proliferation of jurisdictions an integrated family court[45] has been substantially incorporated in pending reform proposals for the administration of justice in the State of New York.[46] These unfortunately are retarded by the immense complexity of constitutional reforms in the United States. Yet there is no doubt that the idea is steadily gaining ground that divorce and separation proceedings are not just another form of litigation, but one aspect of a precious and complex social institution, the family, and that they have to be dealt with as a social and therapeutic problem rather than in terms of the success or failure of a legal action.[47]

This approach also leads to the increasing recognition of preventive or curative methods, as an alternative to divorce. Marriage counselling is becoming increasingly recognized and organized on both the public and the private level as a way of ensuring that marriages are concluded with a proper mutual appreciation of the problems and responsibilities. Reconciliation systems have been incorporated in court procedure in a number of states, e.g. in New Jersey, where reconciliation efforts are mandatory whenever there are minor children of the parties. They consist in a pre-trial conference before a reconciliation master designed to make every reasonable effort at reconciliation.[48]

There are dangers that these procedures might be pushed too far in the direction of 'remaking' of personalities, a temptation in a country strongly addicted to psychoanalysis. At the end of the road, there would be premonitions of a Huxleyan or Orwellian society. But there is almost unanimous agreement on the beneficial effect of these devices in the preparation for marriage and the prevention of unnecessary divorces. The main difficulties are not ones of principle, but of organization. An integrated family court, marriage counselling, and reconciliation procedures demand far more well-trained staff than is at present available and legislators are generally willing to provide for. They also require intensive collaboration between lawyers, social workers, psychiatrists, and others. But the need for such collaboration, not only in the field of family law, is one of the challenges put to law and the legal profession in contemporary society. And the provision of the necessary public and private finance is a question of education: of the understanding that the cost of such services is infinitesimal as compared with the material and moral cost to society of juvenile delinquency, broken marriages, and uprooted children.

### PROCREATION OF LIFE AS THE SUPREME GOAL OF MARRIAGE

Although methods of birth control have been known for thousands of years,[49] and were certainly practised on an extensive scale by the sophisticated and decaying Roman society of the imperial days, for mankind at large it has only in recent years become a practicable means of controlling the procreation of children. Progress in the science and techniques of birth control have been stimulated not only by the increasing study of the human body and the genetic process; the application, on a large scale, of biological and mechanical contraceptives has been, above all, stimulated by the revolutionary change in the social conditions of life. Large-scale diseases and famines – until recently more even than wars the brutal controllers of huge population increases – have been mastered to such an extent that, in countries like India, Pakistan, China, and most of the Latin-American States, a net increase of several million births a year swells their already big populations.

In these countries, the spread of birth control on a wide scale, with official encouragement, is likely to become increasingly a matter of life and death, of national survival. The already very depressed standard of living of the masses is likely to decline further, unless some alternative is found for the brutal remedies of famine and disease.[50]

In the Western world, the techniques of birth control are now almost universally known and available, and the philosophy of family planning is widely accepted, over strong religious opposition, especially from the Catholic Church.[51]

Like the move for an extension of divorce grounds, the acceptance of birth control is not solely, or even predominantly, due to individualism or materialism. Unquestionably, the vastly increased opportunities for the modern married woman to move about, physically and professionally, account in large part for a desire to be freed from the bondage of constant childbearing. But the interest of the children, and the happiness of the family as a whole, is at least as powerful a factor in modern family planning. Modern facilities for education and development have increased the desire to give fewer children better opportunities. And no longer is the necessity to produce as many children as actual desire and fertility permit a dictate of nature. The attempt to control the number of births by contraceptives is part of man's constant advance in his mastery over nature. In this sense, it is on a par with other advances of medicine and, indeed, of industrial technique.

The problem of birth control raises, however, deep religious and ethical problems. Next to the problem of total extermination by nuclear weapons, there is perhaps no other question of as fateful an impact on the future of humanity.

The Catholic Church, whose influence upon some 400 million practising Catholics throughout the world is enormous, remains the most uncompromising and outspoken foe of any form of deliberate birth control, other than by the use of the so-called 'rhythm' cycles, i.e. the use by married couples of non-fertile periods for the avoidance of procreation. Even this concession is not unconditional, as we shall see. The reason for this uncompromising attitude has been restated recently in the discourse given by Pope Pius XII in October, 1951, to the Congress of the Italian Catholic Union of Midwives[52]:

Every human being, even the infant in the maternal womb, has the right to life *immediately* from God, not from the parents or any human society or authority. Therefore, there is no man, no human authority, no science, no medical, eugenic, social, economic, or moral 'indication', which can show or give a valid juridical title for *direct* deliberate disposition concerning an innocent human life. . . .

From this premiss follows the absolute condemnation of sterilization, and a halfhearted condonation of the use of the sterile period for the control of conception. The gist of the papal doctrine is that deliberate use of sterile periods by the married couple for the prevention of conception is permissible, provided it is not made a condition of marriage, and provided there are serious motives, of an ethical, eugenic, economic, or social character that justify the observation of non-fertile periods for a long time.

But if, according to a rational and just judgement, there are no similar grave reasons of a personal nature or deriving from external circumstances, then the determination to avoid habitually the fecundity of the union while at the same time to continue fully satisfying their sensuality, can be derived only from a false appreciation of life and from reasons having nothing to do with proper ethical laws.[53]

The distinction thus made is fine and somewhat forced. From an ethical point of view, the deliberate use of the calendar can hardly be judged differently from the use of mechanical contraceptives. If it is immoral to interfere with the God-willed act of sexual union designed to ensure the procreation of children and the conservation of the human race, then any deliberate interference with the natural satisfaction of the sexual impulse between husband and wife must be ethically reprehensible.

The House of Lords, in 1948, expressed a diametrically opposite philosophy when it affirmed the dismissal of a petition for nullity on the ground of a wife's alleged refusal to consummate the marriage, because of insistence on the use by the husband of a contraceptive sheath. The husband petitioner claimed that 'consummation' in the Matrimonial Causes Act of 1937 meant the procreation of children. But the House of Lords rejected this view and preferred an interpretation of a contemporary statute, in accordance with contemporary social conditions. Lord Jowitt L.C. adverted to the 'common knowledge' that birth control clinics existed and that many young people agreed to take contraceptive precautions. 'I take the view that in this legislation Parliament used the word "consummate" as that word is understood in common parlance and in the light of social conditions known to exist. . . .'[54] Later cases[55] have, however, held that refusal by one spouse to have a child where the other desires one may amount to cruelty. The Report of the Royal Commission declined to recommend the addition of refusal to have a child as another ground for divorce, granted wilful for this reason apparently only in Austria.[56]

It follows from the general premisses of the Church that sterilization is unconditionally condemned under any circumstances.[57] More surprisingly, the Catholic Church also condemns unconditionally artificial insemination between husband and wife.

To reduce cohabitation and the conjugal act to a pure organic function for the transmission of seed would be converting the home, the sanctuary of the family, into a mere biological laboratory. In Our address of 29 September 1949, to the International Congress of Catholic Doctors, We formally excluded artificial insemination from marriage. In its natural structure, the conjugal act is a personal action, a simultaneous and immediate cooperation on the part of the husband and wife which by the very nature of the agents and the propriety of the act is the expression of the mutual gift which according to Holy Scripture brings about union 'in one flesh only'.[58]

None of the non-Catholic Churches follow the Catholic Church in this condemnation of artificial insemination between husband and wife, though most of them reject insemination by a donor.[59]

As no possible question of adultery, or any of the many other legal problems created by insemination with the seed of a third donor[60] is involved in cases of artificial insemination between husband and wife, the only justification for its unconditional condemnation by the Catholic Church is the assumption that the natural consummation of the sexual act is more important in the scale of values of the Church than the procreation of children. There seems to be here a strange confusion between nature in the elementary biological sense and nature as an order of reason in which two human beings, endowed with a sense of purpose and conscious love, seek to seal their union by the procreation of a child through artificial insemination, as they cannot achieve it in the usual way. There is surely in such a decision a nobleness of purpose, a deliberate subordination of sexual lust to the desire to fulfil the marriage, which should command respect rather than condemnation. While there may be many other objections to the practice of artificial insemination, it seems inconsistent to condemn it – as between husband and wife – on moral grounds.

### LEGITIMACY OF ABORTION

An even deeper problem is posed by the legitimacy of abortion. Interference with a life created and developing – however remote from a complete human being that lives and acts as a person – is, psychologically and legally, different from acts preventing the creation of life. Again, the Catholic Church has a simple and absolute solution. Its theory is that every human being, including the embryo immediately after the union of the male sperm and the female ovum, has received its right to life immediately from God, not from the parents or any human society or authority, and that, therefore, any interference with this life is a crime against the law of God and nature.[61]

This dogma is based on the conviction that any human being (including the embryo in the womb) which dies unbaptized is incapable of being rescued from sin. With remorseless logic, the Church has deduced from this premiss that the killing of the child in the womb is not even justified in order to save the life of the mother. '. . . the state of grace at the moment of death is absolutely necessary for salvation; without it, no one can attain to supernatural happiness, the beatific vision of God.'[62] Consequently, the life of the infant in the womb must be saved, even if it means certain death for the mother. While the physicians must do everything that modern medicine provides in order to avoid the terrible choice, they have to give preference to the preservation of the innocent life of the unborn infant if there is no other choice. Some slight concession is made by a subtle distinction of intentions which it is extremely difficult to observe in practice: the killing of the embryo may be permitted where it is not the 'direct' consequence of an operation intended to bring about this very result, but only the indirect result of an operation primarily made for other reasons. Thus, an operation upon a tubal pregnancy is now apparently permissible, because the killing of the foetus is not direct, but indirect.[63]

As with the distinction made between the use of the calendar and the use of contraceptives, so the permission to use modern medical science to the utmost to avoid the terrible dilemma, seems to undermine the logic of the acceptance of the 'order of nature'. At what point does human interference with the biological processes become 'unnatural'?

There is, between this and the opposing theory – which, in such a situation, gives preference to the life of the mother – a deep conflict of philosophy. The Catholic philosophy accepts the inescapable consequences of an order of things willed by God, and compelling even the greatest human sacrifices for the sake of a higher order of things which demands the saving of the unborn infant, even if the price is the sacrifice of the mother of a large family that will be left unprotected and bereft.

For the opposing philosophy the family is deeply important, but a human and social institution which human wisdom, helped by modern science, can protect. Where there is an inescapable choice between the life of the mother and that of the infant, the difficulty is to find the proper balance between the protection of a growing life and the considerations which may outweigh that interest.

Most countries now recognize therapeutic abortion. Unlike the Catholic Church, they justify the destruction of the growing life in the womb for the sake of the preservation of the life of the mother. As the preservation of one person's life is not *generally* recognized in these same systems as justification for the taking of another's,[64] this implies a hierarchy of values opposite to that of the Catholic Church, a recognition that the mother is the centre of the family, a full human being with its responsibilities, rights, and burdens, while the embryo is a human being only in a biological but not in an intellectual or ethical sense.

The legitimacy of therapeutic abortion is now recognized by legislation in most of the United States.[65] The position is universally taken to be the same in England, at least since the decision in *Bourne*'s case,[66] where a famous gynaecologist performed an abortion upon a girl of fourteen who had been raped by a number of soldiers and, consequently, had become pregnant. The operating surgeon informed the Attorney-General and thereby invited prosecution. The judge's direction to the jury, which resulted in Mr Bourne's acquittal, clearly legitimates the destruction of the child 'for the purpose of preserving the yet more precious life of the mother'. It is less clear how far this defence of necessity goes, both in contemporary English law and under the statutes of the majority of the American states, which recognize abortion in order to 'save' or 'preserve' the life of the mother. In *Bourne*'s case, it would seem that the danger to the girl consisted not so much in an immediate threat to her life as in the threat to her mental health. The decision was also influenced by the unusually shocking circumstances of the pregnancy. Given the growing range of modern psychiatry, the possible effect of an unwanted pregnancy on mental health can be extended far. While it seems likely that many contemporary courts, at least outside predominantly Catholic influence, may regard serious danger to physical health as equivalent to a danger to life, a judicial recognition of an extension to the threat to mental health is far less certain, especially as it opens the way towards 'social' as distinct from 'medical' indication.[67]

As long as the legitimation of abortion is as strictly and narrowly defined as it still is in the contemporary common-law jurisdictions – in so far as they do not preclude it altogether – interpretation in a concrete case will always remain somewhat uncertain, dependent on the sympathies of judge and jury in the concrete circumstances. Such a state of law is likely to increase, if possible, the fantastic discrepancy between prosecutions for abortion and the number of abortions actually performed.[68] Moreover, because of the grave uncertainties of the legal position and the threat to their professional status, or even to their personal liberty in case of an error of interpretation, a very large number of qualified medical practitioners will abstain from performing abortions which they consider necessary and desirable, thus leaving the field to the thousands of unqualified practitioners. These, in order to compensate for the dangers of their clandestine occupation, charge very high fees. The discrepancy between social facts and the present state of the law in the majority of countries is far more serious than the problem of artificial insemination, which only affects a relatively small number of people.

Two of the world's most populous states have adopted the radically different solution of permitting abortion virtually without limitation. The Soviet Union, together with its many other radical departures in family relations, legalized abortion after the Revolution, until 1936, when the practice was prohibited except for medical and eugenic reasons. At the end of 1955, the legality of abortion – without any restriction, except that the operation has to be performed by qualified persons in hospitals or other health institutions – was restored. It is likely that the legislation of 1936, apparently in the face of strong popular opposition,[69] was connected with a drive to increase the birth-rate, in response to the growing military threat from Germany and Japan.

In Japan, where sterilization and abortion were legalized for medical, economic, and eugenic reasons in 1948, with the result that well over one million abortions were recorded in 1954, the main reason is unquestionably the desperate threat to Japan's economic existence stemming from the rapid population increase on a small, very densely populated and fully developed island which no longer sees conquest as a means of expansion.

Deserving of more serious consideration in other Western countries are the more limited reforms introduced, first, in Sweden in 1938, and later followed by Denmark and Finland. Apart from medical indication, i.e. serious danger to the life or health of the mother – the ground of abortion recognized in most Western countries – and of 'humanitarian' abortion, where the woman has become pregnant through a criminal act such as rape – again a situation in which probably most of the common-law jurisdictions would come to a justification of the abortion by roundabout ways, as in *Bourne*'s case – the Scandinavian laws also permit abortion on account of 'weakness' of the prospective mother, and on certain eugenic grounds (danger of transmission to the offspring through hereditary channels of insanity, mental deficiency, or serious physical disease). More far-reaching proposals for abortion on grounds of 'social indication', i.e. where the advent of the child might inflict upon the mother lasting misery or distress, have so far been rejected. The administration of these acts is entrusted to medical boards, and it is only on their authorization that pregnancy may be terminated on one of the grounds stated in the law. It is perhaps equally significant that, simultaneously with this statutory reform, the Scandinavian states have encouraged the setting up of contraceptive clinics, together with their far-reaching social welfare legislation, which includes maternal welfare centres, subsidized housing, far-reaching tax relief for families with children, and other measures designed to increase the well-being of families. Although in Sweden, where the experience is longest, the new laws have brought about a very substantial increase in the number of official abortions, there is some controversy as to its effect on illegal abortions.[70]

Unless we accept the absolute condemnation of abortion on any ground – a philosophy unacceptable to this writer on ethical grounds as well as because of its contempt for the social facts – we will always be faced with a difficult problem of adjustment. A modern Western legislator must recognize that abortion is a very major social phenomenon in any country, and that the alternative is between giving it some legal outlet or driving it entirely underground. As for the limits of legalization, the recognition of the legality of abortion in the case of serious threat to life or health of the mother should be far more clearly and definitely recognized than it is at present so that numerous medical practitioners will no longer have to refrain from perfectly justified abortions because of the possible threat to their position. The necessity for such verification is all the greater as a substantial number of medical practitioners will continue to refuse any abortion on religious grounds. It is as desirable that they should be legally and morally protected in their personal faith, as it is undesirable that the religious views of any group should tyrannize the whole medical profession and community.

Beyond danger to life and health, an open recognition of the defence on the grounds given in the Scandinavian laws, for humanitarian or eugenic reasons, should raise no serious problem. Threatened with many other disasters, mankind has no interest in the multiplication of defective children who will be a burden to themselves and to others, nor is there moral justification to compel mothers to have children in the circumstances of *Bourne*'s case.

Abortion for 'social indication' proper will remain a more controversial matter. To this writer it seems that, where a board composed of public officials, social workers, and experienced doctors should decide that the continuation of a pregnancy would gravely affect the life of a family, abortion should be permitted. The legitimation of such carefully controlled grounds for abortion, following the pattern of recent Scandinavian legislation, would be likely at least to narrow the glaring discrepancy between the letter of the law and the social reality in every modern country. The law of abortion, as it now stands in the great majority of countries, is not, like the law punishing murder or theft, a generally effective deterrent against the commission of the offence. Its most important effect has been to deter qualified practitioners from performing abortion in cases in which they would feel medically and morally justified to do so, and thereby to put a great majority of abortions into the hands of quacks who exercise a profitable, dangerous, and clandestine profession. The present law of abortion, as it prevails in the common-law countries and many other States, has not proved to be an effective instrument of social control. It remains as it is largely because of the adamant position of an influential religious and political minority, which, in turn, makes it politically inexpedient for many who hold different convictions to press their own point of view.

The state of the law has induced some critics[71] to reject the criminal sanction as altogether fallacious, since it has involved 'social evils greater than the alleged evil of abortion itself, without, in fact, preventing abortions'. That such is the case, it would be difficult to deny. The only reason for advocating the more limited extension of the legitimacy of abortion as described earlier is that public opinion, in most countries of the Western world, would not presently support the radical jump from a narrowly confined legalization of abortion to the complete abolition of criminal sanction. Hence, the more cautious and controlled extension of the Scandinavian pattern seems to be a more realistic approach to the problem.

## EQUALITY OF HUSBAND AND WIFE IN THE MARRIAGE COMMUNITY

In the present century, the social and economic position of the married woman has changed more drastically than in any previous period of Western history. In the predominantly agrarian economy of earlier centuries, the wife played the part of the manager, though not the head, of the household, guarding the children, preparing meals, supervising the staff in the wealthier families, and generally managing the internal economy of the household.[72] In the increasingly industrialized and urbanized society of the nineteenth century, these conditions changed drastically. But the social and legal concepts, framed in earlier centuries, of the supremacy of the husband were preserved and, indeed, to some extent magnified in the Victorian middle-class conception of the patriarchal father, majestically and often pompously ruling the family in his wisdom.

### MATRIMONIAL PROPERTY LAW

The matrimonial law – both of the civil-law codifications of the nineteenth and early twentieth centuries, and of the common-law jurisdictions – reflects this social supremacy of the husband. In the civil-law world – except for the recent statutory reforms in Scandinavia and West Germany – community property systems predominate. Until well into the present century, and to some extent even today, community property means largely that 'husband and wife are one, and the husband is the one'. Throughout the nineteenth century, and in some legislations such as that of the Province of Quebec even at the present time, the married woman remains severely limited in her freedom of movement and in the right to dispose of her own property. Community property systems, whether of the full community variety or of the more limited type such as the community of acquests, embody the principle of the supremacy of the husband.[73]

In the common-law jurisdictions, the common law proper, classically exposed in Blackstone's *Commentaries on the Laws of England*,[74] enshrines the superiority of the husband. The married woman was incapable of owning, acquiring, or disposing of tangible or intangible movable property, as well as of disposing of immovable property (without her husband's consent). A similar position prevailed in Scotland through the *jus mariti*, which made all the wife's movable estate, acquired before or after marriage, the husband's property and gave him the right of administration over her entire estate. Being incapable of acquiring or disposing of property, the married woman was also considered incapable of assuming responsibility for any debts which the law might have imposed upon her. It was only through equity that a gradual change occurred. Originally, it was for the protection of family fortunes against the depredations of extravagant husbands that equity developed the concept of the 'separate property' of the married woman, over which she, herself, was considered capable of disposing, without the concurrence of the husband. Simultaneously, however, equity admitted the 'restraint upon anticipation' by which the family of the wife was enabled to shield the property settled upon a married woman from disposal by her under the influence of her husband. But the equity concept of 'separate property' paved the way in England and, through the adoption of the English common law in the majority of the American common-law jurisdictions, also in the United States for the gradual introduction of the new public policy of equality of husband and wife. In England, a statute of 1882 created a statutory separate estate (all the wife's real and personal property acquired before or after marriage) over which any married woman had free control. The restraint on anticipation was abolished in several stages and, finally, in English legislation of 1949.[75] By a parallel process, the common-law jurisdictions of the United States[76] have enlarged the equity concept of separate property into a general system of separate ownership and administration, on a basis of equality of the assets of husband and wife.[77] Thus the modern common-law jurisdictions – in England, the majority of the American states, the common-law provinces of Canada, and in the other British Dominions which share the common-law tradition – have coupled the notions of equality and separateness. Together with the legal supremacy of the husband, they have abandoned the legal concept of community in the management of the marriage. They have recognized the claim to free mobility and responsibility of the modern married woman by constituting her an equal but separate partner in the marriage household.

At the same time, the civilian systems – responding, though in very unequal measure, to the same social pressures, namely, the gradual transformation of the position of the married woman from domestic inferiority to equal partnership – have attempted to modify the systems of community property so as to give greater legal freedom to the married woman. This process is, however, far from complete. Vestiges of inequality between husband and wife remain in all the legal systems which preserve a community property régime – be it the full community or the community of acquests, or another of the four or five variants of community régimes. It is only in Soviet law, which, in the Family Code of 1926, introduced the community of acquests,[78] that – consistent with the recognition of the full legal equality of the woman – the legal status and capacity of the married woman is in no way different from that of the husband or from that of an unmarried woman.[79] 'Marriage creates no limitations upon the capacity of a wife as a legal person.'[80] But in France which, in the Code Civil, introduced the era of modern statutory community régimes, the disabilities of the married woman remain considerable, despite recent extension of the wife's capacity to contract. The Code itself gave to the husband the most extensive power of administration and disposal over the assets of the community. Though this did not extend to the wife's immovables, the change of emphasis in industrialized society from land to other assets served, if anything, to increase this predominance of the husband. Reforms in the present century have empowered the married woman to deal freely with her own salary and her own savings, and to act for the community in cases where the husband is unable to exercise his normal power of administration. But major inequalities remain. In Quebec, which has modelled its law upon the Code Civil, but is socially a long way behind the mother country, the position of the married woman remains inferior. 'The husband . . . is the lord and master of the community property as well as of the revenues of the separate property of each of the consorts, since these revenues belong to the community'.[81]

The German Civil Code of 1900 similarly provided for a statutory community of all except certain reserved assets of the wife. The husband had the sole administration as well as the usufruct of all the properties falling into the community. In the eight states of the United States in which community régimes apply, under the influence of French or Spanish antecedents, the prevalent régime is that of the community of acquests, i.e. of property acquired by either spouse after marriage, unless it is specifically reserved by a donor from such a community. But in these systems, too, it is the husband who alone has the power of administration over the community property,[82] except that, in some states, the wife may dispose freely over her own earnings, and that, in some cases, husband and wife must join in real-property transactions.[83] It is, of course, possible, under any of these legal systems, to exclude the statutory community by marriage contract or to provide for alternative methods of management. However, in family law, the proportion of such arrangements is insignificant. It is on the whole confined to the marriages of propertied people, into which the wife brings a considerable property of her own, or where she runs a separate business. The great majority of family households are run, without settlements or marriage contracts, according to the statutory principles laid down in the law of the land. It is, therefore, the statutory or common-law régime that is of overwhelming practical significance. Except for the U.S.S.R., those countries which have introduced full equality of the spouses have done so by abandoning or drastically modifying the traditional community-property system altogether. The basic principle of reform – introduced by the model Swedish Marriage Code of 1920 – which is substantially identical with the laws of Denmark, Finland, Iceland, and Norway and whose concepts have, to a large extent, been incorporated in the West German Matrimonial Property Law of 1957 – is that the property of both spouses remains entirely separate during marriage, with full independence and equality on the part of both to administer their property, while, on the dissolution of the marriage, the 'matrimonial property', i.e. all property of both spouses other than certain gifts or other property declared separate, is equally divided between the spouses. Thus the community idea applies not during marriage, but only upon its dissolution for the purpose of an equitable settlement.[84] This means, in effect, separation of property during marriage. The community idea is preserved only as an accounting procedure on the dissolution of marriage, not as a partnership during marriage.

An extremely complicated process of accounting is necessary to determine how the matrimonial property is to be equitably divided on the dissolution of the marriage.[85] Even if one ignores the apparently successful experience of the new Soviet family law in introducing the community of acquests coupled with full equality of the spouses, because of the relatively limited proportion of privately owned assets,[86] there remains the testimony of an eminent contemporary French jurist:[87]

The community of acquests presents practical advantages which explain its very widespread application. Of the statutory community, it maintains the essential element of participation by two spouses in the gains realized during marriage; the conjugal association is applied to an effective and equitable merger of pecuniary interests. But at the same time the personal patrimony of the spouses remains intact, whatever its composition. The adoption of the community is reconciled with the traditional idea of the conservation of assets inside the family.

The importance of the community idea in the management of family affairs is tellingly illustrated in certain recent developments within the common-law jurisdiction, especially in England. As stated before, the emancipation of the married woman in the common-law world has been affected by a coupling of the idea of liberty with absolute separation of goods. In some common-law jurisdictions, notably in the Western Provinces of Canada and some American states in the United States, a certain recognition of the community element is found in the legal acknowledgement of the matrimonial homestead, over which the husband has no power to dispose without the concurrence of his wife, regardless of the formal property rights.[88] Apart from this exception, significant mainly in rural areas,[89] and the introduction of the joint income and property concept into Federal Tax declarations by husband and wife in the United States,[90] the common-law jurisdictions seem to have been content, until recently, with the principle of full separation. But recent judicial developments in England indicate that a factual community of work and property, which controls the overwhelming majority of working family households, cannot be altogether ignored by the law. The most significant of a number of remarkable decisions by the English Court of Appeal is the judicial creation of a 'new equity' in favour of the deserted wife, a partial substitute for the homestead. In *Bendall* v. *McWhirter*[91] and a number of other cases, it was laid down that the right of the wife to occupancy of the matrimonial home survives the consortium. The deserted wife has been held entitled to continue to occupy the matrimonial home, although legal title is vested in the deserting husband, by a right analogous to an irrevocable contractual licence.[92] In other decisions,[93] it has been held that where husband and wife have both contributed during marriage to certain acquisitions, such as the purchase of a house, 'and where it is not possible or right to assume some more precise calculation of their shares', the division should be on a fifty-fifty basis, irrespective of the fact that unequal amounts may have been contributed. Here again, the idea of partnership prevails. The wife contributes through her work to the education of her children and the management of the household as much as the husband who goes out and earns. The same, of course, applies where both spouses go out and work in a business, profession, or for wages. In the latter case, however, it is generally easier to establish the identity of the separate contributions.[94]

The impact of these ideas of equality and partnership is illustrated by the *Report of the Royal Commission*. Seven of the nineteen members of the Commission actually advocated the introduction of a measure of community property into the law of England and Scotland – a revolutionary reversal of a long tradition.[95] The majority recoiled from such 'a striking departure from the traditional law' (only a little less alien to Scottish than to English law).

But, with only one dissent, the Commission supported introduction of the homestead principle into English and Scottish law, in advocating that, in cases of desertion, neither spouse should be able to turn out the other spouse or take away any of the essential contents of the home without an order of the court, which, on application by the other spouse, should also be empowered to restrain (by an order capable of registration as a land charge) that spouse from disposing of the house or its essential contents, or surrendering the tenancy.

In cases of divorce, nullity, or judicial separation, the husband or wife who has obtained the decree should be able to secure a court order providing for residence and/or substitution as tenant, and/or an equitable division between husband and wife of the contents of the matrimonial home.

The legal developments here described tend to bring the law closer to the facts of life in the great majority of marriages, where husband and wife pool their earnings and capital and, more and more frequently, achieve a partial community of property through joint tenure of land and joint bank accounts.

Basically, the same kind of social transformation has operated in the civilian and common-law jurisdictions of the Western world. In the civilian systems, the entrenched power of the husband as 'lord and master', with unilateral powers of management and disposal over the wife's property, is fighting a rearguard battle. The solution has been in part to give both spouses equal powers of management. But in other cases, such as those of Scandinavia and West Germany, it has been found preferable to keep them separate and equal in the actual management of the marriage and reserve the community idea to equitable apportionment. Conversely, the common-law jurisdictions are coming to recognize the *de facto* community of marriage by actual or proposed restrictions on the unilateral power of either spouse to dispose freely of certain matters of joint concern, by protecting the deserted wife in the possession of the matrimonial home against the deserting husband, by protecting the wife, like other dependants, against arbitrary wills by means of a minimum portion. The systematic – and the actual – gap between the two systems is thus diminishing to the extent that they recognize the transformation in the position of the modern married woman.

## PARENTS AND CHILDREN

Inevitably, the transformation in the economic and social condition of the modern family has profoundly affected the legal relationships between parents and children. It is naturally least pronounced, or totally absent, in societies which have not yet felt any substantial change in the traditional status of the family, such as many of the contemporary Muslim societies. It is most pronounced in the societies which have most strongly felt the impact of the change in the position of modern women and children, and which are most exposed to the influence of economic, physical, and social mobility that characterizes urbanization and industrialization. In the common-law jurisdictions, which have been subjected to gradual evolution, the adaptation is also a gradual and continuing one. In some other legal systems, where there has been a radical social and constitutional change, the transformation is more abrupt.[96]

The transformation of the relationship between parents and children can be summed up under three major headings: (1) the replacement of the more or less absolute powers of the father, based on property rights, by broader moral and legal responsibility towards his children; (2) the translation of the social and legal emancipation of the married woman into a corresponding equality of rights and duties towards the children; (3) the increasing responsibilities of the State and other public authorities for the welfare of children.

In the common-law jurisdictions, a lingering survival of the earlier emphasis on property rights has generally made it necessary to express changes in the legal relationships between parents and children by statutes regulating the functions of the Chancery Courts or their modern successors.[97] In the most recent of the Continental statutory reforms, however, the West German *Gleichberechtigungsgesetz* of 1957, amending the Civil Code of 1900, the duty of care is formulated as part of the general nexus of relationship between parents and children:

The child stays, as long as it has not come of age, under the parental power of his father and mother.

The father and the mother have . . . by virtue of their parental power the right and the duty to look after the person and the property of the child; the care for his person and property comprises the power of legal representation.[98]

The care for the person of the child specifically comprises the right and the duty 'to educate, to supervise, and to determine his residence'.[99]

In this modern formulation, the accent is properly shifted from the supervisory functions of guardian courts to the normal relationships of parents and children.

A principal aspect of the duty of care is the duty to support the child. Here again, the common law has only gradually, and by no means unanimously, developed a legal, as distinct from a moral, duty of the parents, 'regardless of any statute, to maintain their legitimate minor children, the obligation being sometimes spoken of as one under the common law, and sometimes as a matter of natural right and justice, and often accepted as a matter of course without the assignment of any reason'.[100] In some American jurisdictions, the obligation of parents to support their minor children is still regarded as a moral, and not a legal, one under the common law.[101] Similarly, it has recently been stated to be the English position that 'the liability of a parent to maintain his or her child arises, not under the common law, but under various statutory provisions'.[102]

Such duty now exists under a variety of statutes.[103] Again, the duty of maintenance is stated comprehensively in the amendment of the German Civil Code by the Statute of 1957:

The spouses 'are mutually obliged to maintain the family adequately through their work and their assets. . . . The adequate maintenance of the family comprises everything that, considering the circumstances of the spouses, is necessary to meet the costs of the household and to satisfy the personal wants of the spouses and the needs of their common children entitled to maintenance.'[104]

Correspondingly, the parent of a minor child is not only empowered to administer his assets, but he is also legally entitled to the services and earnings of the child, until the latter is 'emancipated'.[105] The occurrence of 'emancipation', and the practical significance of this control over property and earnings of the child is, of course, greatly affected by the vastly increased habits and possibilities of minor children of working age – long customary in the working classes, but increasingly practised among the middle classes of the Western countries – to take employment, or training, coupled with earnings outside the family. In this they are legally supported by the right, long recognized by the common law, to contract for 'necessaries'. It has been held that 'where . . . the parent in authority permits the child to contract for himself, emancipation in respect of earnings may be implied.'[106] In some cases, the condition under which the parental control over the proceeds of the labour of the child is lost has been formulated by statute. Thus, the Georgia Code provides that the parental power shall be lost by:

1. Voluntary contract, releasing the right to a third person. 2. Consenting to the adoption of the child by a third person. 3. Failure of the father to provide necessaries for his child, or his abandonment. 4. Consent of the father to the child's receiving the proceeds of his own labour, which consent shall be revocable at any time. 5. Consent to the marriage of the child, who thus assumes inconsistent responsibilities. 6. Cruel treatment of the child.[107]

The restriction and regulation of the once unconditional paternal power over the child has been accompanied by the increasing recognition of the mother's rights and obligations. This is a necessary corollary to the modern emancipation of the married woman, of her recognition as a person equal in status to her husband and contributing fully to the maintenance of the family, whether she goes out to work, in employment, the exercise of a profession, or the conduct of a business, or whether she contributes her share through responsibility for the household. The German Act of 1957 recognizes this evolution by emphasizing the right of every married woman to earn, while emphasizing her primary sphere in the family.[108] Both spouses are under an obligation to collaborate in the professional business of the other spouse in so far as this is usual in the conditions under which the spouses live.[109]

The wife complies with her obligation to contribute to the maintenance of the family by her own work normally through the conduct of the household; she is obliged to engage in gainful work only in so far as the working capacity of the husband and the revenues of the spouses are not sufficient for the maintenance of the family, and in so far as it is not in accordance with the financial circumstances of the spouses that she should use her own capital assets.[110]

While, in the common-law jurisdictions, the primary obligation for maintenance still generally rests with the father,[111] the trend is clearly in the same direction. This finds expression in the generally rather conservative Report of the British Royal Commission –

that in England and Scotland the principle that husband and wife are jointly liable for the maintenance of the children should be followed in any matrimonial proceedings in which the question of maintenance of children arises.[112]

Again, this only expresses the reality of contemporary conditions in the Western world, where –

while husband and wife are living together it usually happens that both help to support the children in proportion to their respective means.[113]

Where, as in Soviet Russia, the right and the practice of married women to work outside the family is widespread and officially recognized, it is logical that the law should stipulate the duty of mutual support of parents and children.[114] The practice of the Soviet courts and public authorities has emphasized this duty of mutual maintenance.[115]

## *The Status of the Illegitimate Child*

The unfortunate, and often tragic, status of the illegitimate child in the great majority of modern Western family laws is an outcome of the Christian conception of the monogamous marriage. In polygamous societies, 'children are the *desideratum*; not too great an emphasis is placed on their source'.[116] But it is only the philosophy of original sin and the fall from grace that can justify the continuing discrimination against the illegitimate child. It can hold that to be born out of wedlock is a curse visited on the bastard by a destiny that he must accept, as part of the immutable order of nature, which ordains the monogamous Christian family. As we have seen, this philosophy no longer dominates modern family law outside the strictly Catholic domain. To the consideration that an individual is entitled to be protected in the attainment of his possibilities, as a human being potentially equal to all others, must be added the particular iniquity of punishing the innocent product of a non-marital union. Yet the principle of moral responsibility as a regulator of rights and duties in family law is still abandoned by its upholders when it comes to the illegitimate child. Penalized in social and public life, it is still regarded by all too many as outside the normal fabric of society.

Admittedly, a satisfactory alternative to this morally indefensible attitude is not easy to find. To equate an illegitimate child for all and every purpose with legitimate children is clearly not possible without undermining the legal principles of the monogamous family. This is quite apart from the practical difficulty of discovering the father in the large number of cases where the illegitimate child is the unwanted product of chance encounter. The very least the law can do is to minimize the misfortunes of children born out of wedlock. In the first place, it can, and should, encourage the legitimation of children by subsequent marriage. Legitimation is now recognized in a large number of laws. But this is subject to considerable limitations. Under Scottish law, for instance, a child is not legitimated by the subsequent marriage of its parents, unless they were free to marry at the time of its conception. In England, the position is the same except that the relevant date is that of the birth of the child. In the recent Report of the Royal Commission on Marriage and Divorce, a minority of seven argued persuasively that this differentiation stigmatized children for the shortcomings of their parents. Socially, there is everything to be said for making any children, born at any time to a man and woman who subsequently become husband and wife, legitimate, and full members of the family. Yet, a majority of the Commission held that

so long as marriage is held to be the voluntary union for life of one man with one woman, that conception is wholly incompatible with the provision that one or other of the parties can, during the subsistence of the marriage, beget by some other person children who may later be legitimated. . . . Any departure from that conception can only be made by ignoring the essential moral principle that a man cannot, during the subsistence of his marriage, beget lawful children by another woman. It is unthinkable that the State should lend its sanction to such a step, for it could not fail to result in a blurring of moral values in the public mind. A powerful deterrent to illicit relationships would be removed, with disastrous results for the status of marriage as at present understood.[117]

For the contention that the possible subsequent legitimation of an adulterous child may be an incentive to adulterous relations, there is, of course, no evidence, and it seems patently contrary to common experience. And what the majority considered as 'unthinkable,' was regarded as highly desirable by seven other greatly respected members of the same community as well as by most other civilized communities.[118] To many – among them the present writer – it seems equally 'unthinkable' that men and women with a sense of moral responsibility as it permeates Western law, should condemn innocent persons to a permanent status of legal and social inferiority even where their own parents want to provide a home for them.

A second modest reform, advocated by the Report, is the extension of the law as it obtains in many Continental countries and in Scotland, which holds children of a void marriage to be legitimate, and entitled to the ordinary rights of succession, where, at the time of the marriage, one or both of the parties to the marriage was (or were) ignorant of the impediment (putative marriage).

The vast majority of the illegitimate children will remain unaffected by such modest reforms, controversial though they still are. Far more important to the majority is the – as yet exceptional – recognition of a family relationship between the child and the unmarried father. Under the Norwegian law of 1915, for example, the illegitimate child has the same relationship to the father as to the mother. It is entitled to bear the father's or the mother's name, and it also has a claim to maintenance and education by both, the economic situation of the more favourably placed parent determining the type of education. Moreover, both parents qualify for custody of the child. What is perhaps important is that the search of paternity is a duty put upon the State rather than on the mother. Generally, the illegitimate child under such a law is equally related to both his parents – as it should be, provided, of course, paternity can be established. It still lacks equality with the legitimate child living under the protection and the permanent bond of the family. But this is probably as far as the law can go in a society where the Western monogamous family is recognized as the basic institution of union between man and woman.[119]

### THE STATE AND THE FAMILY

Every modern State is taking an active and, often, a commanding part in the regulation of family life. Many of these functions are of a judicial or quasi-judicial nature and go back to the traditional role of the courts as guardians of the weak and unprotected. In the history of the common law, these functions originated with the equity jurisdiction of the Chancellor, who became the guardian of persons and properties of infants. Today, the supervisory and protective functions of the Chancery are exercised not only by Chancery divisions or equity courts proper, but also by a multitude of specialized tribunals, such as juvenile courts, family courts, domestic relations courts, and the like, as well as by county courts and magistrates' courts.[120] Although adjudication arises, in the form of maintenance or custody actions or disputes about property settlements, overwhelmingly this jurisdiction is of a supervisory and administrative character.[121] It is in that capacity that a court may make 'such order with respect to the property in dispute . . . as he thinks fit'[122] or authorize a deserted wife to continue to reside in the matrimonial home; decide on the custody of children in the case of divorce, give its consent or assistance to the parents in the education of the children,[123] approve or reject an application for an adoption order, appoint tutors or executors, and exercise a multitude of other supervisory activities. The extent of these judicial, quasi-judicial, and administrative functions of State courts is an indication of the social importance of the family, and of the responsibility which the State has traditionally felt for the children. But the care which was once concentrated on the protection of property, has now been greatly enlarged, and partly changed in character, in line with the extension of the social-welfare functions of the modern State. In regard to economic subsistence, the primitive beginnings of earlier poor law legislation have been broadened into general schemes of public assistance, such as the British National Assistance Legislation of 1948. It is in regard to the social welfare of the neglected child as a person that the most significant developments have taken place.

The greatly increased role of the State in the life of the family arises from the general pattern of modern State organization.

On the one hand, the number of obligations imposed upon the members of the family has drastically increased compared with even a century ago. Compulsory school education, often including higher education, compulsory health tests, and military service are now standard law in many countries. By establishing the appropriate institutions, the State assumes a large responsibility for the material and spiritual development of the growing child, a responsibility that formerly resided entirely in the parents. Correspondingly, through the provision of public-school education and the maintenance, at the expense of the State, of those serving in the Armed Forces, the State takes over some of the financial responsibilities of the parents. Some countries have, in recent years, gone further by establishing a State-financed national health service.[124] In these countries, the State regards it as a duty to provide for the health of its citizens, and it thereby takes a great financial burden from the individual family, which it redistributes among the general taxpayers of the nation.[125]

Every contemporary State, to a greater or lesser extent, further distributes the burdens of the family by comprehensive social-insurance schemes. Basic pillars of social insurance are unemployment insurance, health insurance, old age and retirement pensions, and death benefits in the case of the demise of the insured, usually the breadwinner. While they greatly differ from each other in detail, all these schemes are generally financed by a combination of compulsory contributions by employees and employers, and a contribution from the State out of the general budget (i.e. by the taxpayer). A growing number of States – among them France, Germany, Great Britain, and Canada – now grant family allowances as a public contribution to the cost of bringing up children. The alternative method of tax exemptions for dependants is, of course, less beneficial to low-income families which pay little or no tax.

To these State supports for the family must be added various forms of workmen's compensation, which give the employed – at least the industrial worker – a minimum compensation for accident suffered in the course of employment, regardless of the fault of the employer. At times, workmen's compensation is merged in a national insurance scheme, as in the contemporary legislation of Great Britain. In any case, the statutory compulsion, and the usual administration of these schemes by a State authority, such as the Workmen's Compensation Board, also serve to take over some of the burden otherwise imposed upon the family.

For the purposes of our discussion of the relation between family and the State, the most interesting aspect of these manifold schemes of social security, public pensions, or public assistance is that they are gradually developing a family law that, in many respects, differs from that developed in civil codes or case law. Thus, under the National Assistance Act, a woman is as much liable to maintain a husband and her children as the man is liable to maintain his wife and children. Yet, the private family law of England and most other common-law jurisdictions still discriminate between the obligations of husband and wife.[126] Again, the tribunals instituted for the purpose of determination of claims under the British National Insurance legislation have held that, for the purpose of calculating the extent to which one member of the family is maintained by any other member, the earnings of all members of a household must be considered as a common family fund, to which some contribute more and others less than the cost of maintaining them.[127] To take another discrepancy between the common law and the public law of family relations, during the last World War, the military authorities regarded a '*de facto* wife' in Great Britain as entitled to dependents' allowance to the same extent as a properly married wife. That this frequent discrepancy between the 'private' family law and the family law of the modern welfare state is not an isolated or national phenomenon, is shown by the following observation made about developments in the United States:

> The notable point about this congeries of federal pension plans making payments to surviving spouses is that in administering them the Federal Government does not consider itself bound by the various state rules of law, whether of domestic relations or of matrimonial property. There is thus growing up a vast body of federal family law, largely in the form of administrative rulings, which is independent for the most part of the state rules governing other legal incidents of the lives of the persons concerned. This body of law has not been adequately described or investigated by legal scholars up to this time.[128]

Does this growth of an 'administrative' family law, arising from a vast and complex network of modern social-welfare obligations, indicate an undermining of the whole concept of the family? Does it mean that an impersonal bureaucratic machine is gradually replacing the personal responsibility which members of a family, and, in particular a husband and wife, have towards each other?

There are, of course, those who maintain that any social-security scheme undermines the personal sense of responsibility of the husband as provider. This argument is on the same plane as that which regards unemployment insurance as an improper interference of the State in the natural vicissitudes of life. It ignores the fact that the structure of modern industrial society, with the shadow of all-destructive wars hanging over it, has undermined the stability of conditions of employment and the sense of personal security. In no country does social security go so far as to eliminate or even substantially reduce the incentive for the various members of the family, and for the main breadwinner in particular, to improve the standard of living of the family by his work. But in so far as modern social-security provisions ban, for millions of families, the spectre of total misery, in cases of death or disability of the breadwinner, they surely do not loosen or weaken family ties, but, on the contrary, they provide the conditions for a fuller and happier family life by removing at least the worst aspects of total insecurity. This has been amply demonstrated by the remarkable rise of birthrates in most Western countries after the last World War, in conditions of stable employment and increased social security.

Contrary to many dire predictions, millions of modern families, to whom contraceptives are known and easily accessible, have preferred the joys and responsibilities of parenthood to the greater material comfort and freedom of movement of childlessness.

The social-security schemes of the modern State recognize the family as an essential unit in it. They seek to strengthen the family, although, in the process, the growing public family law may modify a great deal of the traditional private law of the family. Here, as in other fields, only a combination of public and private responsibilities can create conditions that are in accordance with contemporary social needs.

# Part Three

# Society and the Individual

### THE IDEAL OF FREEDOM OF TRADE: SOME BASIC ANTINOMIES

Of all the basic ideals of modern liberal democracy, that of freedom of trade is perhaps the most ambiguous, and the most elusive. To some it means mainly the expression of a social philosophy: freedom of private trade and business from all government interference.[1] To others, it has essentially an international connotation: removal of restrictions from the free flow of trade among nations, as symbolized by tariffs, import quotas, currency restrictions, bilateral treaties, and other instruments of modern economic nationalism. The partly successful endeavours to establish a common market and free trade between the nations of Western Europe, through the European Coal and Steel Community and the more recent European Economic Community, illustrate this aspect of freedom of trade as much as the recurrent struggles in the United States, between the high tariff forces and those favouring a relatively more liberal international trade policy, through participation of the United States in the General Agreement on Tariffs and Trade (G.A.T.T.) and the proposed Organization for Trade Cooperation (O.T.C.).

Our main concern, however, in this chapter will be with the difficulties and contradictions inherent in the Benthamite idea of free trade as commonly accepted by liberal economic philosophers: that all citizens within a legal community should be given an equal start, an opportunity to trade freely which, through the pursuit by each trader of his economic advantage, would work out to the common good.

Like a field of runners who start but do not finish together, the field of initially equal free traders soon thins out: favoured by resources, ability, ruthlessness, or luck, some competitors will outdistance others. They will accumulate economic power, which will enable them to push others against the wall, devise restrictive schemes which underpin their own stronger position, or, in extreme cases, establish a complete monopoly which extinguishes competition. For the strong or lucky, freedom of trade just means freedom to expand; it means the survival of the fittest and the eventual destruction of the weak. To the others, however, it means the opposite:

a duty of the community to restore, as far as possible, conditions of freedom of competition. This means restraint by legislative intervention and, at least to some extent, a denial of the very idea of freedom of trade. For inevitably, any legislature which seeks to establish legal rules preventing the consequences of uninhibited competition, by which the strong may destroy the weak, must establish an administrative apparatus, often of great complexity. This is the dilemma of all anti-trust legislation. Every industrial society needs some competition; but none can afford to let it develop without any interference, lest a surfeit of competition should lead to the destruction of all competition. Nor have attempts to apply the Socialist postulate of socialization of industrial enterprise eliminated the problem. The Soviet Union, which has transferred all industrial production of any significance to the State, has, since 1923, attempted to restore conditions of competition by giving relative autonomy to industrial units and stimulating competition between them.[2] Those countries which, like Great Britain and France, have created an economic society mixed of public and private enterprise, attempt to approximate the public enterprise as far as possible to commercial companies operating in comparable competitive conditions.[3]

Leaving aside the problem of total or partial socialization, the different countries have gone different ways to solve the dilemma. And the sharpest contrast is, perhaps, between the major representatives of the common-law world, Great Britain and the United States. Spurred by the more ruthless methods of a new and vigorously expanding competitive society, both Canada and the United States began to enact fairly radical anti-trust legislation at the end of the nineteenth century (Canada in 1889, the U.S. in 1890). Some salient features of this approach to the problem of freedom of trade will be analysed later in this chapter. Great Britain and, with it, most of the British Commonwealth,[4] until a few years ago, rested content with judicial interpretations of the common law of restraint of trade, while anti-trust legislation in the United States and Canada pushed the common law on restraint of trade into the background. The contrast is dramatic. Although the Monopolies Act, 1948, and the Restrictive Trade Practices Act, 1956, are likely to reduce drastically the importance of the English courts in the adjudication of restrictive trade practices, in favour of the investigatory, administrative, and special judicial agencies created by these two statutes, the role of the courts in the development of the common law of restraint of trade remains important.

### JUDICIAL IMPASSE AND STATUTORY INTERVENTION

By eliminating the tort of conspiracy as an effective legal weapon in the struggle between conflicting social groups – capital and labour, rival unions, or rival trade associations – the House of Lords restored a kind of rough equality between them. Except for pathological cases of 'disinterested malevolence', the decision permitted organized economic or social groups within the State to fight it out with each other, without legal restraint, except always for the use of specifically illegal means, such as physical coercion or blackmail. The tort of conspiracy no longer serves, as it once did, as a means of preventing or restricting the organization of labour while failing similarly to constrain collective pressures in business.

But the far more influential and vital spheres of coercion by corporate group pressure were left in an unsatisfactory and unrealistic state by the escapist approach of the courts. The presumption that restrictive agreements, if reasonable between the parties, were not against the public interest, left the field free for the many types of restrictive agreements, recently classified by a learned writer,[5] in five categories:

(1) simple contracts between two or more parties, limiting competition *inter se*, or limiting the competitive scope of trade rivals of a party to the contract;

(2) contracts creating a relatively permanent relationship amounting sometimes to a trade combination;

(3) unincorporated trade associations;

(4) cooperative marketing agencies or incorporated trading societies;

(5) monopolies organized as companies.

The British courts had failed to impose any effective restraint on such favourite economic weapons as price fixing, typing clauses, production quotas, collective boycotts, monopolistic exploitations, and other forms of restraint. On the other hand, the courts remained, until very recently, equally passive in regard to the growing quasi-public power enjoyed by organizations capable of making or breaking the livelihood of a vast proportion of the citizens of a country.

## British Anti-trust Legislation

Meanwhile, many factors tended to accelerate the concentration of economic resources and power. Competition as a basic principle of economic life has never been as vigorously supported in England and other parts of Europe as in the United States. In the absence of legal controls by the courts restrictive practices continue to prosper. They were encouraged in part by such factors as defence needs in two world wars, the concentration of research and technological resources in many fields of modern industry, and the general trend towards standardization of production. More than anything else, it was perhaps the challenge of the post-war economic crisis, which threatened to leave an impoverished Britain too far behind in the race for exports, that produced a remarkable change of attitude expressed in the two important statutes of 1948 and 1956. Monopoly and restrictive trade practices were at last seen to be a major public problem, too great to be left to the haphazard and, on the whole, ineffectual treatment of the courts. The Monopolies Act, 1948, as amended in 1953, did not follow the model of the American and Canadian legislation, which condemns in principle all restrictive agreements. It provides for the establishment of a Monopolies and Restrictive Practices Commission charged with the duty of making inquiries into industries and trades. But the Act does not condemn monopoly or restrictive practices as such. The Monopolies Commission is charged with the duty of reporting on individual situations.[6]

Under the 1948 Act, it is for the Government to act or otherwise on the Reports of the Commission. The main significance of the Act, and of the work of the Commission, is that it has, for the first time in generations, directed the attention of the British public to restrictive trade practices as a general problem.

But the Monopolies Commission – and following most though not all of its recommendations, the British Government – has hitherto dealt with the situations on an *ad hoc* basis. The Commission has, for example, recommended the termination of certain exclusionary practices, including the revision of the rules of some traders' associations. It has recommended official price control to prevent the use of monopoly power, whether by groups of firms acting together or by individual firms. It has not condemned simple price-fixing agreements in all cases, although it has condemned the collective enforcement of exclusive dealing arrangements, resale price maintenance, and other widely prevalent collectively enforced restrictive practices. On the other hand, the Commission has not recommended any action which would alter the structure of an industry. In the case of the match industry, it has conceded that a monopolistic structure was more or less inevitable. In that case, the Commission did, however, recommend official controls of various types to prevent an abuse of monopoly power.

The Act of 1956 goes one step farther in the direction of the condemnation in principle of monopolies and other restrictive practices. Certain classes of restrictive agreements and arrangements, as specified from time to time, have to be registered.[7] Any registered agreement may be challenged by an independent registrar before a Restrictive Trade Practices Court, consisting of five judges and up to nine lay members.[8] A challenged agreement is presumed to be against the public interest, unless the court is satisfied that it does not unreasonably operate to the detriment of the public. Collective enforcement of resale price stipulations, but not price-fixing as such, is prohibited unconditionally.

The new British legislation, which is similar to that of some other European countries, notably Norway, Sweden, the Netherlands, and more recently South Africa, stands half-way between the former 'do nothing' approach of the common-law courts and the *per se* prohibition of the Sherman Act and of the Canadian legislation. The completely untenable maxim that a restrictive agreement reasonable between the parties must be presumed to be in the public interest has at last been thrown overboard, and the opposite presumption established. An independent judicial agency has the last word, but it is not a pure law court. The majority of the members of this new court are not lawyers, but persons 'appearing to the Lord Chancellor to be qualified by virtue of . . . knowledge of or experience in industry, or public affairs'.

The first few decisions of the new court indicate that the change is likely to be more than one of form or legal theory. In its first major decision, the court invalidated the restrictions imposed by a federation of manufacturers, wholesalers, and retailers of medical and pharmaceutical products, under which the proprietary medicines made by its manufacturer members could be sold to the public only under the control of registered pharmacists. These restrictions affected about one-third of the total manufacturers, and an equal proportion of the sale of all proprietary medicines. Partly because a majority of the products could reach the public without these restrictions, and partly because the public was sufficiently protected by existing legislation, the court held these restrictions not justified as 'reasonably necessary to protect the public' and therefore as against public policy under section 21 of the Act.[9] Of even greater economic importance was the invalidation, by the court, of the Lancashire Yarn Spinners' Agreement, which had protected the weaker members of this ailing industry – suffering from increased competition by cheaper Asian cotton exports – by a minimum-price scheme. Having weighed carefully the dangers of increased unemployment and the closing down of marginal concerns, which would result from the invalidation of the scheme, against the benefits of open competition, the court held that the public detriment from excess capacity in the industry and (to a lesser degree) the maintenance of high prices and the loss of export trade prevailed, and the restrictions were not, therefore, in the public interest.[10] This decision is likely to result in a far-reaching reorganization of the Lancashire cotton industry.

The indirect effects of this new legislation and its interpretation far outweigh the recorded decisions. Already numerous agreements have been revised or terminated in the light of the Act.[11] This is an important illustration of the effect which modern legislation can have on established economic and social practices.[12]

Thus one more important field has been taken from the sphere of case law and the jurisdiction of the common-law courts, and been subjected to judicial statutory regulation and procedures. But it would be hard to deny that this was anything more than a long overdue response to the failure of the common-law courts to cope with a task which was entrusted to them for so long.


### AMERICAN ANTI-TRUST LEGISLATION

In the United States and Canada – whose legislation is similar in principle though not in detail – the ordinary courts have played a decisive role within a statutory framework. It has been for them to interpret the sweeping scope of clauses such as sections 1 and 2 of the Sherman Act:

Every contract, combination in the form of trust or otherwise, or conspiracy, in restraint of trade or commerce among the several States, or with foreign nations, is hereby declared to be illegal . . .
Every person who shall monopolize, or attempt to monopolize, or combine or conspire with any other person or persons, to monopolize any part of the trade or commerce among the several States, or with foreign nations, shall be deemed guilty of a misdemeanor . . .

Section 411 of the Canadian Criminal Code is more detailed, but similarly comprehensive.[13]

Both the United States and Canada have important supplementary anti-trust legislation. In the United States, the Clayton Act of 1914, as amended in 1950, added a number of specific illegal practices and situations, among them, tie-in sales or leases and mergers. By another Act of 1914, the Federal Trade Commission was established as a quasi-legislative agency, to conduct investigations and make reports to Congress. It was also given authority to proceed against 'unfair methods of competition'.[14] The Canadian Combines Investigation Act, 1910–52, requires investigations into 'combinations, mergers, trusts, or monopolies', which have 'operated or . . . are likely to operate to the detriment or against the interest of the public, whether consumers, producers, or others'. Two investigating authorities, namely a Director of Investigation and Research, and the Restrictive Trade Practices Commission are established to investigate these practices, which may or may not lead to prosecution. While the emphasis in Canadian law is on criminal prosecution – there are no civil remedies and the power to order structural changes in the industries concerned would at least be constitutionally questionable in view of the reservation of legislative power in matters of 'property and civil rights' to the provinces – the United States legislation knows criminal prosecution as well as civil suits and administrative or judicial orders that may involve far-reaching structural changes in ownership and management including the divestiture of holdings. Another apparent difference between the United States and the Canadian legislation, namely, the emphasis of the latter on the 'public interest' as a criterion, which is absent in the text of the Sherman Act, has not in practice led to any significant difference of approach.[15]

The courts in both countries have generally shied away from an investigation of the complex economic facts which would be necessary for an evaluation of restrictive practices from the standpoint of the public interest. The Canadian courts have, despite the apparent contrary legislative injunction, evaded this task more definitely than the United States Courts, which have, in the nearly seventy years of the history of the Sherman Act, vacillated between unconditional condemnation of restrictive practices, and a discriminating appraisal of the factors that might or might not make certain practices excusable. Considering the sweeping character of the statutory prohibitions, and the complexity of the economic and administrative problems involved, it is not surprising that the courts should have vacillated between what is commonly described as the *per se* rule and the rule of reason.[16] The battle has been more open and articulate in the United States, where the whole problem of anti-trust has, since the inception of the Sherman Act, played an outstanding role in the legal and general public life of the country. Similarly sweeping Canadian legislation began to affect industry and business in a major way only after the Second World War. Broadly speaking, the American judicial interpretations have veered from an at first literal application of section 1 – which knows no defence of reasonableness – to the establishment of the rule of reason in the first *Standard Oil* case of 1911,[17] which set forth as the economic objectives of anti-trust policy the avoidance of arbitrary and unreasonable prices, of limitation of production, and of deterioration of commodities. Under this guidance, the legal threat to industry and business remained fairly weak until the New Deal in the late 1930s initiated a new period of vigorous enforcement of anti-trust law, an approach which celebrated its judicial triumph in the famous *Alcoa* decision rendered in 1945 by the Second Circuit Court of Appeal through Judge Learned Hand.[18] That case went far in establishing the *per se* rule, by holding that the then near-monopoly of the Aluminium Company of America was condemned by section 2 of the Sherman Act regardless of intent, reasonableness of prices, or other economic or moral factors. On the whole, this has remained the basic approach of the United States as of the Canadian courts. Both have repeatedly, though by no means unanimously, stressed the principle of free competition as an unconditional objective of the legislation. It may be that the American and Canadian courts in following the *per se* rule and thus refusing, though not consistently, the examination of such economic factors as the reasonableness of prices and profits, have avoided the fallacies of the English courts in their somewhat naïve interpretation of the 'public interest' in regard to restrictive covenants. But they have, at the same time, evaded problems that remain open. As Justice Brandeis, himself an ardent critic of 'big business', said in a famous dissenting judgement:

The refusal to permit a multitude of small rivals to cooperate, as they have done here, in order to protect themselves and the public from the chaos and havoc wrought in their trade by ignorance, may result in suppressing competition in the hardwood industry. These keen business rivals, who sought through cooperative exchange of trade information to create conditions under which alone rational competition is possible, produce in the aggregate about one-third of the hardwood lumber of the country. This court held in *United States* v. *United States Steel Corporation*, 251 U.S. 417, that it was not unlawful to vest in a single corporation control of practically the whole shoe-machinery industry. May not these hardwood lumber concerns, frustrated in their efforts to rationalize competition, be led to enter the inviting field of consolidation? And if they do, may not another huge trust with highly centralized control over vast resources, natural, manufacturing, and financial, become so powerful as to dominate competitors, wholesalers, retailers, consumers, employees, and, in large measure, the community?[19]

These observations illustrate once again the danger of over-simplification, of the 'all or nothing' approach to complex social and economic situations. Clearly, cooperation between rivals is often beneficial and in some cases even necessary for survival. It may be the only answer to extermination by more powerful competitors. On the other hand, cooperation may reach dimensions at which it stultifies all competition and impedes technical and economic progress. No general formula can answer in advance or lay down infallible tests for infinitely various situations. It may well be that the 'ordinary' law courts do not feel sufficiently equipped to handle the intricate economic or technical investigations inherent in an appraisal of 'reasonableness' of certain restrictive practices. Certainly, the answer cannot be found in the simple equation of public and private interests applied by the British courts in their interpretation of restrictive trade covenants.[20] If that attitude is correct, then the task of a discriminating appraisal of trade practices must be entrusted to certain other official agencies, either an investigatory body such as the British Monopolies Commission or the Canadian Restrictive Trade Practices Commission, or mixed tribunals such as have been introduced in recent British, Scandinavian, and South African legislation. It may be that a combination of all these methods will best cope with the problem: investigatory bodies for research and analysis; special tribunals with expertise on economic and technical matters to deal with specific restrictive practices and their relation to the public interest; and the ordinary law courts to deal with damage actions and criminal prosecutions.

To translate this problem into terms of an age-old controversy of legal philosophy: a basic philosophy of values must underlie any legal approach to the problem of excessive concentration of economic power and other restrictive practices and situations. But the answer to a problem which is as complex as modern industrial society as a whole cannot be sought in dogmatic deductions from 'natural-law' premises. It is, as in so many other fields, a matter of conflicting interests and values: the interest in reasonable cooperation against the interest in vigorous competition; the interest in technological development and pooling of research against the interest in competitive endeavour in the improvement of production; the interest of the producer and trader against those of the consumer; the interest in international cooperation in the development of resources, or for other reasons (e.g. in the case of the Iranian Oil Consortium) against the danger of private international cartels, which would arrogate to themselves an international power that pertains to the public, not to the private sphere. This list could be indefinitely extended.

At least, it seems that in recent years a new interest taken in the subject in so many countries that left it formerly neglected, may lead to a gradual approximation of the 'radical' approach of Canada and the United States on the one hand, and the more discriminatory and casuistic approach of the other countries, including Great Britain. It is a field in which an intelligent comparative study might help to deepen the understanding of a problem whose interest and importance reaches far beyond that of the sphere of the lawyer.

The area of controversy can at least be limited, if not eliminated, by the remarkable measure of agreement that exists in the contemporary legislation of the United States and Canada on the one hand, and of Great Britain, Germany, Norway, Sweden, the Netherlands, on the other hand, as to restrictive practices which must be presumed to be objectionable. These would seem to comprise any collective measures of repression or exclusion of entries or discrimination; strict market allocations through production quotas or other measures; fraudulent and collusive tenders; prevention of the use of patented or unpatented inventions; price cutting by 'fighting brands', i.e. products specifically designed to drive a competitor out of business through the use of superior economic resources; tying arrangements; and clearly monopolistic situations. The new British legislation regards such practices as prima facie objectionable and North American jurisprudence has long concentrated on similar practices as the most essential instances of restrictive practices under the Sherman Act and the Canadian Criminal Code. That more and more matters are beyond the scope of a lawyer untrained in economic science or other non-legal branches of knowledge, is not surprising. It is a reflection of the complexity of our society. We should therefore come more and more to regard specialized courts or other quasi-judicial agencies, which are not exclusively staffed with lawyers, not as 'extraordinary' courts, but as a new form of tribunal demanded by the social conditions of our time.

### CONCLUSIONS

The conclusions to be drawn may be thus summarized:

1. Individual freedom of economic movement, in all spheres, has increasingly been displaced in the industrially developed countries of the West by the self-organization of the different economic interests. It has led both to a predominance of collective action against opposing interests, and to a rigid policy of disciplinary control and, if necessary, ostracizing of outsiders or rebels within a particular group by the predominant organization.

2. The courts have gradually come to recognize as legitimate, within very wide limits, the power of group organization to replace the individual in the economic struggle. The recognition, at first halting in the case of collective labour action, is now extended to all types of labour, trade, and professional organizations, and the checks imposed by the test of reasonableness (in regard to conspiracy, restrictive covenants, and blackmail) would operate only in very exceptional cases.

3. In dealing with restraint of trade, conspiracy, and similar problems, the courts have conspicuously failed to develop the notion of 'public interest' to any real significance.

4. The common law of restraint of trade is gradually being displaced by extra-judicial and statutory developments. This has long been the case in the United States and Canada which, since the end of the nineteenth century, have looked to anti-trust legislation for the restoration of a modicum of fair conditions of competition and a market economy regulated by competition.

The new British legislation follows a somewhat different pattern. Unlike the Canadian and the United States legislation, it combines investigation by a public commission with publicity by registration and adjudication by a tribunal composed of a minority of lawyers and a majority of non-lawyers.

5. The problem of excessive economic power used for restrictive practices and the elimination of weaker competitors is thus coming to be recognized more and more universally as a major problem of public policy. There are, however, still differences in the approach to the problem, as between recent British, German, or Scandinavian legislation on the one hand, and that of the United States and Canada on the other hand.

6. While these and other legislative and administrative measures have proved an indispensable brake on the steady progress towards a greater concentration of power in corporate and quasi-corporate groups, they have not been able to arrest, let alone reverse, the process.[21]

Corporate Power, the Law, and
            the State

In this chapter we shall be concerned with some significant aspects
of the growth of corporate power and their effect on the legal foundations of modern democracy. The growing aggregate power of the
industrial giants, of the labour unions, of the charitable foundations,
and of certain other organized groups, compels a reassessment of
the relation between group power and the modern State, on the one
hand, and the freedom of the individual, on the other. An appreciation of the major problems involved requires an analysis of the
legal factors which have, until recently, excluded them from a
juristic discussion commensurate with their social significance.

### LEGAL CLOAKS OF CORPORATE
### POWER

Ironically enough, the immense sociological and juristic aspects of
the problem of group power within the State have largely remained
hidden behind accidents of legal form, especially in the Anglo-
American system. Here, four legal factors have combined to shield
the growth of group power from legal control: first, the ability and
the custom of powerful organizations – which do not engage in
commercial operations themselves – to remain unincorporated and,
therefore, to escape many of the liabilities of the corporate person;
second, the versatility of the trust device which mitigates to a large
extent the clumsiness of the unincorporated society; third, the
limitations of equitable remedies which have, to a large extent, prevented the courts from remedying abuses of power by organizations
in regard to their members unless 'property' interests were involved;
last, an excessive liberality in the interpretation of the 'charitable
trust' which has permitted many business undertakings to be
clothed in the form of charitable foundations.

To understand the extent to which major social evolutions have
been hidden by the combination of a number of technical devices,
we must turn back to the brilliant analysis given by Maitland well
over half a century ago. In several striking passages he has characterized the social function of the English trust as that of supplying a

personalized substitute for the far more comprehensive use of corporate devices in German law.

But there are two achievements of the trust which in social importance and juristic interest seem to eclipse all the rest. The trust has given us a liberal substitute for a law about personified institutions. The trust has given us a liberal supplement for a necessarily meagre law of corporations.[1]

[M]any reformers of our 'charities' have deliberately preferred that 'charitable trusts' should be confided, not to corporations, but to 'natural persons'. It is said – and appeal is made to long experience – that men are more conscientious when they are doing acts in their own names than when they are using the name of a corporation.[2]

But apparently there is a widespread, though not very definite belief, that by placing itself under an incorporating *Gesetz*, however liberal and elastic that *Gesetz* may be, a *Verein* would forfeit some of its liberty, some of its autonomy, and would not be so completely the mistress of its own destiny as it is when it has asked nothing and obtained nothing from the State.[3]

Maitland's theme is the contrast between the personalized English concept of trust and the impersonal, 'collectivized', German concept of an association (*Verein*), an incorporated public institution (*Anstalt*), or a private charity (*Stiftung*). The trust has enabled hundreds of important corporate institutions to remain unincorporated because 'the hedge of the trust' made possible a continuity of legal relationships and a stability of property rights which Continental law could not provide without a corporate form. The combination of trust and contract relations has enabled institutions of immense social and economic significance, such as the Stock Exchange and the Inns of Court, to remain unincorporated.

None of Maitland's brilliant generalizations would appear to remain unimpaired in the mid twentieth century. In the first place, the contrast between Continental and Anglo-American legal devices in the field of unincorporated associations and endowments seems to have narrowed considerably; in the second place, unincorporated associations have acquired so many attributes of legal personality that the difference between incorporated and unincorporated bodies, though still important, is no longer fundamental; in the third place, the reluctance of charities and other institutions to incorporate has greatly lessened. The advantages of incorporation are increasingly outweighing the snobbism of aloofness, while in the United States and Canada the heavy taxation demands of the modern welfare state and the tax privileges accorded to all charitable foundations have led to a veritable flood of charities, most of which are incorporated.[4]

But perhaps the greatest problem suggested by Maitland's thesis – a problem infinitely more acute today than at the beginning of the century – is the social and political danger of the assumption that an association, corporate or unincorporated, merely by being in form private rather than public, should still enjoy the far-reaching immunity from judicial or other official control which the courts have accorded it. In this field above all, economic and social developments of the last half-century make a re-examination necessary.

### THE AMERICAN FOUNDATION – SOCIAL AND LEGAL IMPACTS

Perhaps the most important modern institution in the field of group power – and it contrasts dramatically with Maitland's picture of clubs, religious associations, and charities preferring the hedge of the trust and the anonymity of unincorporated status – is the 'foundation' which flourishes in contemporary America.

The foundation is largely an American creation. No doubt the accumulation of vast wealth was one reason for its rise; another – at least in the days when Carnegie, Rockefeller, and others perpetuated their names through their now world-famous bequests – was unquestionably a desire of wealthy and successful men to purge their consciences before God and man, and to justify the acquisitive society which had enabled them to accumulate enormous riches by leaving a vast proportion of their wealth for the benefit of mankind.[5] But in recent years these reasons for the earlier foundations have become less important, and the incorporated foundation or trust has become predominantly a business device, a paramount instrument in the struggle between the demands of the modern welfare state and the wish of the individual entrepreneur to perpetuate his fortune and his name. The greatest and most influential of the foundations (Ford, Rockefeller, Carnegie) are the creations of individuals or families, but the large foundations of the future will increasingly be the creations of corporations. The desires to give and to perpetuate the name of the individual or corporate donor are undoubtedly still important motivations, but the immense growth in the number and size of foundations in recent years[6] suggests that business considerations play an increasing role. By either bequeathing or giving during his lifetime a proportion of his estate to a permanent institution established for officially recognized charitable purposes, the donor, usually the controller of an industrial or business empire,[7] achieves a number of purposes.[8] In the United States gifts to such organizations are exempt from gift taxes, and bequests to them are deductible for estate-tax purposes. The organizations themselves are normally exempt from income tax, property tax, and other taxes. A charitable gift *inter vivos* is an allowable deduction from the taxable income of the donor.[9] The absence of the latter privilege in English law may be one reason why incorporated charities are not so widespread in Britain (apart, of course, from the vastly greater capital wealth of United States business). Otherwise, motivations for the establishment of charitable companies are very similar.[10] The arithmetics of these benefits vary from year to year and are, of course, subject to legislative changes. Unless, however, there were to be a fundamental change in legislation in regard to charitable gifts,[11] the advantages of transferring both capital and annual income away from the personal estate of a taxpayer in the high-income brackets or away from a corporation are very considerable.[12] But in the age of the managerial revolution and the welfare state, a motive at least equal to that of providing a suitable mechanism for philanthropy and a tax-free reservoir for an otherwise highly taxable income is the power which the foundation gives to the controller of a business or industry to perpetuate his control.[13]

The recently established Ford Foundation, for example, by far the wealthiest of all, with assets estimated in excess of two billion dollars (at current market values), has undoubtedly greatly increased the scope of educational and other charitable activities to which foundations have contributed so much in the United States, but it also preserves the bulk of the Ford enterprise in the hands of the family. Originally all its stock in the Ford Motor Company was non-voting stock, and the Ford family retained all the voting stock. This voting stock constituted a very small proportion of the total shares issued, however, and so the foundation received the bulk of the income of the company. In December, 1955, a new scheme was devised which enabled the foundation to convert part of its stock into voting shares and to offer these for sale to the public.

The common voting shares sold to the public represent 60 per cent of the total number of votes, with certain restrictions on the right of any one person to hold more than a certain number of shares. The Ford family exchanged its old shares for a new class of non-transferable voting shares representing 40 per cent of the voting power. This arrangement assures continued control of the enterprise to the Ford family, while it enables the Ford Foundation to diversify its holdings.

A detailed analysis of the many methods and purposes for which the modern American foundation is used would greatly exceed the scope of this inquiry. It clearly represents a development strikingly different from the state of affairs which Maitland portrayed. As many modern jurists and sociologists have pointed out,[14] the modern industrial enterprise has become a corporate empire within the State in which control of management is more important than nominal ownership of shares. Modern government attempts to counter the accumulation of private wealth and power partly by supervisory regulation and partly by heavy taxation. The controllers of enterprises counter by divesting themselves of assets which they would otherwise pay to the State as income tax. At the same time they sanctify their name and give public proof of their sense of social responsibility through the establishment of charitable institutions. Examples are known of large business concerns vesting their entire real-property assets in a controlled charitable foundation and renting them back from that foundation.[15] As long as charities retain the legal benefits and advantages which they have traditionally enjoyed – and it would be difficult for any legislature to take them away[16] – the modern business corporation gains by diminishing its assets and its income. By this device persons and corporations not only reduce their liabilities without losing control but also make their name a household word in philanthropy.

The very complexity and size of the enterprises involved makes it necessary to establish these foundations as permanent and, almost invariably, incorporated institutions. They are mostly incorporated as membership or non-profit-making charitable corporations.[17] While they have no capital stock and may not distribute dividends or profits, and while they must hold their funds in trust for the charitable objects defined in the charter, their organization is very much like that of the ordinary business corporation. The charter is the empowering instrument; a board of directors, managers, or trustees administers it; and the larger foundations have vast staffs of executive officers, many of them highly paid. Provided its income is destined for charitable purposes, a corporation does not lose its charitable character by conducting a business enterprise.[18]

### THE SOCIAL IMPACT OF
### INSTITUTIONALIZED GIVING

Growing out of the ancient legal device of charitable trust – devised in a pre-industrial age for an infinitely less organized society when the social functions and responsibilities of the State were relatively negligible – the modern corporate foundation is rapidly becoming a major power in modern industrial democracy. Although the influence of the charitable foundation on the public and social life of the nation is today very much more advanced in the United States than anywhere else, the reasons which foster its growth apply to a large extent everywhere, at least outside the Communist world. The institutionalization of large-scale giving is a necessary concomitant of the growth of corporate power. The major reasons for the continued growth of the charitable foundation are likely to endure in our time, for they are partly inherent in the structure of modern industrial organization in all but completely socialized States. In the first place, the incidence of taxation, both income and succession, although fluctuating somewhat with varying economic conditions and government policies, is likely to remain sufficiently heavy to induce both wealthy individuals and corporations to divert as large a proportion of their disposable resources as possible away from the State as revenue collector to channels which they are in a better position to control themselves.[19] Second, in the case of the relatively few but important major industrial enterprises which are still substantially under family control, the foundation is, as already mentioned, the best device to perpetuate the donors' control over the business.[20] At the same time, such a giant family foundation is akin to the older foundations of the Carnegie and Rockefeller type in identifying the name of the donor forever with the educational and social improvement of the nation. In the eyes of the average person, the name of Ford today stands not only for a famous automobile but also for an institution that raises university salaries and improves education in India.

But most of the major industrial enterprises have long been converted into depersonalized permanent institutions in which boards of directors, managing chairmen, and presidents, the symbols of the managerial revolution, have taken the place of the individual lords of business and industry of the nineteenth century. Such giant concerns as General Motors, General Electric, United States Steel, and Standard Oil of New Jersey – and most of the two hundred corporations that are said to dominate the tempo and direction of economic life in the United States – are permanent institutions in which certain individuals hold great power for the time being, but come and go, while the institution survives. Correspondingly, a state of mind which Adolf Berle has described as 'corporate conscience',[21] but which can, perhaps, more cautiously be called 'corporate self-consciousness', is developing. Whether we attribute it to an increased sense of social responsibility, to a good sense of public relations, or even just to an enlightened consideration of the future needs of the corporations themselves,[22] the fact is that the giant industrial corporations of today can no longer afford to pour their profits entirely into dividends or increased salaries. It is not tax reasons alone that compel an increasing number of them to give visible evidence of the kind of attitude that impelled Rockefeller, Carnegie, and others to leave their fortunes for the advancement of education.

Nor can these big corporations, whose names and affairs are the subject of frequent public discussion, afford to set up foundations that do not genuinely pursue the objectives for which they have been established.[23] Fortunately, a high standard of integrity and genuine achievement, especially in the fields of higher education and medical research, was established by the older foundations, notably the Rockefeller Foundation and the various Carnegie institutions, which were, from their inception, detached from any industrial empire. While some of the lesser foundations of recent years appear to identify educational advancement with political propaganda (e.g. for 'free enterprise'), the major foundations have scrupulously adhered to the objectives for which they were established. They function as public rather than private institutions, and they have so far survived without much injury the many, often grotesque, accusations of sponsorship of 'subversive' causes of individuals, of 'internationalism', and the like.[24]

Inevitably these foundations are becoming one of the major institutional forces of the modern State. In particular, their influence is of increasing importance in the determination of educational policy, the goals of research in all spheres, and the direction of thinking in international affairs. The definition of charitable objectives directs the foundations not only towards educational objectives and scientific research, but also towards the promotion of international understanding and the furtherance of peace.[25] In June 1956, the presidents of eight major private universities issued a statement laying down for their own guidance certain directives in regard to corporate giving.[26] So far it is fair to say that the major foundations have maintained the tradition, established by the Rockefeller and Carnegie foundations, of regarding themselves as trustees of education in a free society and have avoided interference with university policy or the attachment of strings to the vast gifts which they make. Senior officers of these foundations are men of integrity and high standards, often coming themselves from an academic background and behaving like civil servants rather than company executives. The great foundations have generally furthered objectives of universal acclaim, such as medical research or the increase of certain university salaries, but present conditions may change.

In any event, general pressures of public opinion cannot but have a certain influence on the choice of objectives by foundations which are faced with floods of applications, while their decisions frequently incur congressional or press criticisms in an excitable society preoccupied with the dangers of subversion. When a foundation bears the name of an operative enterprise, any adverse publicity may affect the competitive position of the 'parent' corporation.[27] Even where such direct implications are absent, most foundations will prefer to finance uncontroversial rather than politically controversial fields of education and research. The universities, in turn, may prefer to encourage applications for grants that are likely to produce funds rather than those that might stir up controversy. The result may, in due course, be a very gradual though indirect restriction of the freedom of research that is, in any case, threatened by the disciplined society of our time. Such restrictions are likely to operate less through direct censure than through the narrowing down of the scope of research.

### CORPORATE POWER AND THE STATE

Organized industry and organized labour have, in modern democratic society, become giant and powerful social forces. It is only exceptionally, as in the case of the aluminium industry where until a few years ago one company controlled 90 per cent of the national production,[28] that power is concentrated in a single corporation. More frequently, a small group of major concerns exercises joint dominion over the industry. The nation awaits with bated breath the result of negotiations between the 'Big Three' of the automobile industry – General Motors, Ford, and Chrysler – and the United Automobile Workers, a major member of the A.F.L.–C.I.O. Similarly, negotiations between the major steel firms and the United Steel workers set a pattern not only for industrial organization, labour relations, and the cost of steel production, but also for the economic life of the nation for years to come. The result of such negotiations has a decisive influence on the volume of production and the price level not only in the industry affected but also in the many ancillary and subsidiary industries; and it has profound effects as well on the general level of wages and national income. A nation-wide social trend is established when General Motors or United States Steel conclude a long-term contract with the appropriate labour union.[29]

To these two great types of organized corporate power in modern industrial democracy must be added other forces that differ in importance from country to country. In the United States, as mentioned, the charitable foundation, a by-product of corporate power, exercises an increasing influence of its own. In a number of European countries, on the other hand, such as Great Britain, Germany, or in the Scandinavian States, the consumer exercises a considerable influence through the consumers' cooperatives, organizations which have grown from relatively small non-profit-making cooperative ventures into powerful movements. Like the big industrial corporations, they have become institutionalized; and, in some countries like Great Britain, they exercise a considerable political influence, usually through one of the major political parties.

So decisive is the combined influence of these powerful and tightly organized social groups within the State, that their relationship to the legal and political power of the modern State requires some re-evaluation. During the last few centuries the modern national State has had an increasing tendency to become the Leviathan of which Hobbes wrote, not only the repository of physical and legal restraining power and the protector of the nation against an external enemy, but also the main directive force in the shaping of the economic and social life of the nation. It has gradually absorbed, unified, and come to control most of the functions previously exercised by social groups – merchants, landowners, craftsmen's guilds, churches. Are we in the process of another dialectic reversal?

Only a generation ago advocates of 'pluralism', such as Figgis or Laski, pleaded for more recognition of the social groups within the State – trade unions, churches, and others – in mitigation of the legal and ideological glorification of the State. A generation later, the question must be raised in all seriousness whether the 'over-mighty subjects' of our time – the giant corporations, both of a commercial and non-commercial character, the labour unions, the trade associations, farmers' organizations, veterans' legions, and some other highly organized groups – have taken over the substance of sovereignty. Has the balance of pressures and counter-pressures between these groups left the legal power of the State as a mere shell? If this is a correct interpretation of the social change of our time, we are witnessing another dialectic process in history: the national sovereign State – having taken over effective legal and political power from the social groups of the previous age – surrenders its power to the new massive social groups of the industrial age.

Before attempting even a tentative assessment of such a generalization, we ought to clarify the much used, but also much confused, concepts of 'State' and 'sovereignty'. To what extent has the State ever been more than a symbol, more than the machinery developed by the social and economic groupings struggling for supremacy behind the symbols of political sovereignty? On the one side, Marxist theory asserts that the State is no more than the structure erected by the dominant class which moulds the State and its institutions according to its own interests and power. On the other side, Hegelian and Neo-Hegelian doctrine elevate the State into the positive embodiment of the 'absolute spirit', the highest development of human society, the integration of all the human and social forces which have, both logically and historically, developed in the processes of world history.[30] There is no other aspect of Marxist theory which has been as fully refuted in history as the belief in the withering of the State and its coercive machinery. The country which has gone furthest in applying the Marxist theory of the socialization of means of production, Soviet Russia, has politically and legally not only retained the trappings of sovereignty, but reached new heights of concentrated State power. Indeed, there is perhaps no other type of modern State in which the effective power of social groups within the State – industry, organized labour, cultural groups – has been so completely absorbed into State authority. For in the totalitarian States of Fascist persuasion – Nazi Germany, Mussolini's Italy, Franco's Spain – the real power of the State was – or is – not nearly so concentrated as it would appear. The Nazi State based itself on the integrated cooperation of certain groups which supported its purposes, in particular, the military and the industrialists.[31] The organized labour movement, believed to be hostile, had been destroyed. For a while, the organized political power of the State and the most powerful social groups in the State – the military and organized industry[32] – directed it together towards its doom in the common pursuit of conquest. But it was certainly not a question of one-sided domination. Hegelian ideology, in its nefarious identification of 'the State' with *any* State as the ideal integration of all human and social forces in society, mainly served as a convenient ideological cloak for the unrestrained glorification of absolute State power. It was put in the service of Nazi philosophy as a justification for the destruction of all institutional obstacles, such as a free labour movement or an independent judiciary.

In democratic societies, which permit and, indeed, depend on a certain play and balance of social forces within the framework of the institutional organizations of State, the picture is less clear. It would be as misleading to regard the modern democratic 'State' merely as a skeleton without flesh, a mere apparatus manipulated by various groups, as it would be to identify the institutional framework of the State and the legal coercive powers which it exercises with the real social power and its distribution in the society. In the normal functioning of a democracy there is a perpetual struggle between various organized social forces striving to translate their particular interests and aims into legislative and administrative action. Clearly, the influence of any particular group is largely dependent on the weight behind it. Such weight can be measured not only in terms of numbers of members, but also in terms of financial resources, discipline, and organization. In our highly articulate society, public relations have become immensely important. The availability of mass media of communication, such as radio, television, and the press, has greatly increased the gap between the influence of the organized articulate pressure group and the mass of unorganized individuals.

There are clearly dangers in this state of affairs. The most powerful, wealthy, and highly organized group may succeed in identifying the 'public interest' with its own interests. There are, however, two important counterbalancing and mitigating factors. The first lies, in any normally functioning democracy, in the balance of forces, or, as it has recently been put by an American economist, in 'countervailing power'.[33] A highly organized manufacturers' association may be faced by an equally well-organized association of wholesalers or retailers. The once overwhelming power of the owner of the means of production to dictate terms of employment, under the guise of contract, is today checked by the power of the labour unions. Farmers' or consumers' cooperatives may check the power of the traders. However, the degree of organization and the power of these various interest groups are grossly unequal, both inside one particular country and between different countries. At the same time, there is an increasing tendency to consolidate small sectional groups into vast monolithic organizations. Bargaining between individual manufacturers and local unions is, at least in the major industries, increasingly replaced by nation-wide bargaining between an entire industry and a monolithic union, usually part of a national trade union or labour union organization.

If the legal sovereignty of the modern State were indeed nothing more than the product of the pulls exercised by various social power groups, the 'public interest' or 'national interest' would dissolve itself into an uneasy balance between conflicting pulls. Marxism, at least, in its original dogmatic form, accepted this hypothesis and preached the necessity of displacing the identification of the interests of the dominant property-owning middle classes with those of the State by means of a revolution that would identify the interests of the proletariat with those of the State (followed by the Utopia in which the State would eventually wither away because exploitation would no longer occur). Hegelianism, on the other hand, while preaching that 'the State' was the integration and the sublimation of all forces within society, inevitably substituted, in practice, an intensely nationalist and socially conservative State for the abstract and universal ideal. For Hegel the perfect State, the culmination of world history, was, in effect, the autocratic Prussian monarchy of the eighteen-twenties. For the Neo-Hegelians it was the Nazi State.

Modern democratic society does not correspond to either of these extremes. We should think of the State not in the Hegelian sense, but as something more than a mere computing machine of conflicting social forces, a 'cash register, ringing up the additions and withdrawals of strength, a mindless balance pointing and marking the weight and distribution of power among the contending groups'.[34] Clearly, there is a 'reserve function' in the State.[35] Acting through the main branches of government – legislative, executive, judicial – it expresses and articulates, especially in times of crisis, national policies and sentiments which do not normally express themselves in organized pressure groups. Sometimes, this reserve power of the State as expressing the general interest is all but completely paralysed, because of the particular distribution of group pressures within the State. An interesting illustration of this state of affairs is the contemporary situation of the Republic of Austria, as documented by an Austrian jurist, in a discussion of 'The Protection of the General Interest Against Particular Interests' at the

Chicago Colloquium of the Rule of Law of September, 1957. As Professor Spanner pointed out, the coalition of the two major political parties which form the Government, and the corresponding absence of any Opposition, has led to the result that Parliament has no more than formal functions. Not only must there be agreement between the two political parties on any major question, with almost arithmetical apportionment of appointments to public posts in proportion to the votes cast, but also groups such as the trade unions and the Chambers of Commerce have extended their influence into all spheres of economic and political life. According to this analysis, agreements are reached between these groups on such matters as wages and prices which almost automatically pass into law. Parliament, the voice of the State, has no more than a formal 'rubber stamp' function, sanctioning arrangements reached between the two almost equally balanced dominant political and economic forces of the country. It is regrettable that the direct impact of the unorganized public on State action should seldom occur except under the pressure or threat of war. Faced with the threat of physical extinction, public opinion may impel legislation prohibiting commercially profitable transactions with potential enemies.[36] It may, and normally does, produce legislation against profiteering in times of scarcity. It tolerates or even demands official price controls. It puts a severe brake on strikes of more than local importance. In times of emergency the 'national interest' may suddenly assume concrete importance in judicial condemnation of the tax dodger[37] who, in times of less stress, is regarded with leniency or even sympathy.[38]

But it is not only the occasional spurt that makes the State something more than the point of balance between contending social forces. The modern State is expected to assume responsibility for an irreducible minimum of welfare functions far exceeding the traditional spheres of State activity: defence, foreign affairs, police, and a machinery of justice.[39] In the United States no less than in Great Britain, France, Scandinavia, India, or the Soviet Union, the State is expected to give minimum insurance against such national vicissitudes as unemployment, sickness, and accidents suffered in the course of employment. The most conservative Republican Administration in the United States would not be permitted to watch passively – as it still could a generation ago – a major depression. It would be compelled by public opinion to enact a programme of public works and other relief measures designed to stimulate employment. Such a minimum programme entails continuous heavy taxation. The cost of social insurance, whether borne by the taxpayer (as in the case of the British National Health Service) or by a combination of government, employers, and employees (as in the case of most other forms of social insurance), burdens the productive machinery of the State. Again, defence expenditure is a major and continuous financial charge on every major democracy. Clearly, each organized group, manufacturers, labourers, retailers, consumers, would improve its own position by having the one or the other of these burdens reduced. But it is not only balance of forces, it is an irreducible minimum of articulated demands of public opinion at a given time that makes it impossible to reduce basically the minimum responsibilities of the modern State.[40]

### RECENT ANALYSES OF THE FUNCTION OF THE LARGE CORPORATION

The emergence of the large industrial corporation – depersonalized and institutionalized – as a major social phenomenon and its impact on the legal, economic, and social structure of society have, not surprisingly, occupied the attention of American thinkers more than those of any other country. Since the end of the Second World War, several eminent American lawyers, sociologists, and economists have attempted to analyse some of the long-term impacts of this new development. They have, again not surprisingly, arrived at very different conclusions. They agree only on one fact: that the big corporation can neither be legislated nor wished out of the fabric of modern industrial society; that it is an inevitable product of modern industrial technique, the organization of modern industrial society and the minimum demands for mass production, which a world constantly geared for possible war must make on the productive resources of the country. In 1946 Mr Peter Drucker published a study based on an analysis of the General Motors Corporation.[41] Its central theme was that in contemporary American society the large corporation was 'the institution which sets the standard for the way of life and the mode of living of our citizens; which leads, moulds and directs; which determines our perspective on our own society; around which crystallize our social problems and to which we look for their solution'.[42] In 1952 two challenging studies were published, one by a lawyer-administrator and the other by an economist. Both studies accepted the permanence and inevitability of 'big business', but arrived at different assessments of the legal and social policy which the community should adopt towards it. Mr David Lilienthal, one-time chairman of the publicly owned Tennessee Valley Authority and later of the Atomic Energy Commission, emphatically came out in defence of big business as the agent of technical as well as social progress.[43] He roundly condemned the whole elaborate and cherished edifice of anti-trust legislation as a reactionary curb on the dynamic progress of society, which depended on big business, i.e. the large corporation. The real stimulus to competition he saw not in any artificial attempt to curb bigness or to forbid this or that practice, but in the constant challenge of better and more efficient technological and production processes, stimulated by the increasing competition between different industries and materials, such as wool and synthetic fibres, metal and timber, electricity, coal, natural gas, and – eventually – atomic power.[44] Abuses could, if necessary, be remedied by public administrative controls.

At the same time a Harvard economist, Kenneth Galbraith, surveying the structure of contemporary American capitalism, noticed, like Lilienthal, the curious antinomy between the constant drive towards bigness in industrial organization – reflected in the worship of the big executive, not only in the economic but also in the social scale of values – and the strong, almost axiomatic distrust of bigness in the political life of the nation.[45] Unlike Lilienthal, however, Galbraith did recognize the need for some check on the unmitigated power of bigness. But he saw the check in 'countervailing power', the emergence of powerful, organized economic and social groups, whose respective pulls and interests held those of the other groups in check. The great nation-wide retailers can check price policy abuses on the part of manufacturers. Organized labour counterbalances the massed power of organized business. None of the powerful economic groups within the State could get away with too much without being checked by one of the countervailing forces. On the whole, this analysis not only confirmed that contemporary American democracy was dominated by powerful social and economic groups rather than by an omnipotent State or a large number of free individuals, it also implied that the state of affairs was not nearly so dangerous as was often supposed.

Shortly afterwards another – qualified – apologia for the present role of the big corporation was offered by Professor Berle.[46] Accepting the fact that the two hundred or so largest corporations in the United States had a decisive impact on the economic and social development of the nation, Berle sees the principal restraining factor in the gradual growth of the 'corporate conscience', the increasing transformation of the large corporation from the ruthless and essentially individualistic profit-seeking entrepreneur of the nineteenth century to a social organism conscious of its public functions, its social responsibilities, and of the force of public opinion. These factors compel the large corporations of the present day, for example, to refrain from pushing prices of their products as high as any scarcity might economically allow them (as in the case of the post-war automobile shortage).[47] They also compel the management of the large corporations to refrain from pursuing their own personal advantage in the exercise of their administrative powers.[48] At the same time the large corporations with international interests are often called upon to exercise quasi-diplomatic functions in delicate international situations, as in the case of the Iranian Oil Agreement of 1954. Berle acknowledges, however, that this process of transformation, especially in regard to employment contracts and employment policy, is far from complete.[49] His concluding chapter on 'Corporate Capitalism and the City of God' gives a semi-theological flavour to his thesis that the large corporation is the principal organizational force of modern industrial society, not only in a purely economic or business sense, but as a political institution.[50]

## THE QUASI-PUBLIC POWER OF THE LARGE CORPORATION AND THE PROBLEM OF LEGAL CONTROL

One paramount conclusion emerges from the various representative analyses that have been sketched out above – and they apply to all industrialized democracies of our time, with differences only of degree rather than substance. The corporate organizations of business and labour have long ceased to be a private phenomena. That they have a direct and decisive impact on the social, economic, and political life of the nation is no longer a matter of argument. It is an undeniable fact of daily experience. The challenge to the contemporary lawyer is to translate the social transformation of these organizations from private associations to public organisms into legal terms. In attempting to do so, we have to recognize that both business and labour currently exercise vast powers. First, they have power over the millions of men and women whose lives they largely control as employees or as members. Second, they exercise power more indirectly, though not less powerfully, over the unorganized citizens whose lives they largely control through standardized terms of contract, through price policy, through the tempo of production and the terms and conditions of labour. Last, they exercise control over the organized community, represented by the organs of State, in a multitude of ways: direct lobby pressures, control over the election and policies of the elected representatives of the people, control over the appointment of the judiciary in many States, and far reaching control over the mass media of communication. In this sense 'government' or 'law making' by private groups[51] is today an irreversible fact. But if our previous analysis of the 'reserve function' of the State as the organized expression and instrument of national public opinion, as distinct from a mere parallelogram of group pressures, is correct, a survey of the legal checks, of the 'countervailing power', which is or ought to be at the disposal of the organized community, is a paramount task of modern jurisprudence.

Although both big business and big labour currently exercise much quasi-public authority, a 'delegated power of command',[52] they do not do so in identical ways. The power of big business over public life operates essentially in three directions: in the first place, the concentration of disposable capital resources[53] largely determines the direction and tempo of industrial production, technological research, price policy, and the standard of consumption (in this, big business is, however, counterchecked by a number of forces, notably collective bargaining with organized labour, the partial dependence on government contracts, and, to some extent, mutual competition); in the second place, the large corporations control the conditions of employment for millions of employees, and they set the tone for the rest of the nation[54] (in this they are largely counterchecked by the organized bargaining power of labour and by social legislation of various kinds); third, in so far as the large-scale charitable foundation with educational and social purposes is increasingly becoming a by-product of the large business corporation, the latter can, to a significant extent, influence educational and cultural policy.

Organized labour, on the other hand, has hitherto exercised its influence in two major ways. First, it is steadily increasing its share in the determination of the terms of production, since wages and other terms of collective labour agreements are a major component of the price of products. Second, unions exercise disciplinary control over the vast majority of the nation's industrial workers, organized in their ranks and generally dependent for their livelihood on their union membership (whether or not there is, legally, a 'closed shop' agreement). Big-scale labour organizations have not hitherto been an important source of investment capital, although there is no reason why they should not become more influential in this field.[55] Nor have the labour unions hitherto exercised a major influence on educational and social policy. Here again, the role played by the trade union movement in some Continental countries, notably Germany and the Scandinavian countries, through workers' colleges and other labour-sponsored educational institutions, has been far more conspicuous. In the United Kingdom, the main direct cultural association of organized labour has been with the Workers' Educational Association, whose influence on the cultural and educational life of the country is limited. Trade unions also exercise a considerable influence on educational policy in a large number of Labour-controlled local government authorities. The very small influence which, by comparison, organized labour has hitherto had in the United States in educational matters is due to several factors. The major reason is probably the almost complete absence – until recently – of ideological motivations in the American labour movement. The older A.F.L. developed from craft unions, devoid of political ideology,[56] and the American labour movement is still dominated by the down-to-earth objective of securing better terms for the members. Under the influence of the newer C.I.O. – now amalgamated with the A.F.L. – political issues are beginning to play a larger part, although it is difficult to imagine a unified policy.[57] By contrast, the European trade unions are closely associated with political movements, notably Marxist and Christian Socialism. This has often led to direct associations with political parties.[58] Another contributing factor is the fact that public education, including college education, is used by a far greater proportion of the population in the United States than in Europe. In England and other parts of the British Commonwealth, publicly or privately financed scholarship, the establishment of the new 'Red Brick' universities, and other developments are gradually increasing the proportion of university students coming from the working class. On the Continent, with the possible exception of Scandinavia and, of course, the Communist countries, the almost exclusive domination of universities by the middle classes is still a marked phenomenon, though changes are gradually occurring.

The problem of public law controls over the large corporate groups therefore arises essentially in three fields: (1) excessive concentration and abuse of economic power; (2) excessive group power over the individual as employee; (3) excessive control over the cultural and educational policy of the nation. The major problem posed by the disciplinary power of organized labour over its members is the degree to which public law can control the actions of legally 'private' organizations.

### LEGAL REMEDIES FOR ABUSES OF GROUP POWER

#### *Total Socialization*

That the trend towards corporate bigness was an inevitable and continuing one was on the whole correctly foreseen by Marxist theory. Marxism also devised a theoretically complete solution: the transfer of all means of production into the hands of the community (i.e. the State until it 'withered away'). In application of this doctrine, substantially all industrial assets in the Soviet Union and other Communist States have been transferred from private ownership to that of the State. Soviet legal theory has attempted to counter the danger of excessive concentration and bureaucratization of economic life by constituting the major industries as semi-autonomous State trusts with regional divisions and by giving the managements considerable, though precarious, autonomy. The cost-accounting principle has taken the place of the private-profit principle as a yardstick by which to measure the efficiency of the State units. Far-reaching political and disciplinary penalties have been added whips, though it is doubtful to what extent they have helped efficiency.[59]

It is, however, difficult to assess the effectiveness of a total socialization of industrial production unaccompanied by political totalitarianism. Whether it would be possible to maintain a political democracy together with complete socialization of all major assets and economic activities is an open question. In theory, of course, political democracy could be maintained; in practice, the concentration of *all* economic power in the hands of a managerial public bureaucracy might lead to the undermining of political democracy and freedom. Be that as it may, the democracies both of the common-law and the civil-law worlds have hitherto rejected this solution to the problem of big business, and they show no intention of attempting it in the future.

#### *Mixed Public and Private Enterprise*

On the other hand, public enterprises, managed through semi-autonomous public corporations in a mixed economy where they operate side by side with private enterprise, are today a fairly universal phenomenon in modern industrial democracy. In such a mixed system public enterprise can be used for various purposes. It can be used to respond to nationally felt needs which private enterprise fails or is financially unable to satisfy. This motivation for the creation of public corporations naturally plays a much larger part in underdeveloped and capital-poor countries than in industrially more highly developed countries. It accounts for the early emergence of the public corporation in Australia in the 1880s and for the present significance of public enterprise in such countries as India.[60] In the more highly developed countries public enterprise plays only a limited role in the field of manufacture except in wartime. It is of considerably greater importance in the field of certain basic services and public utilities. Thus, in the anti-socialist United States, the Tennessee Valley Authority was created on the initiative of President Roosevelt in 1933 to cope with the problem of a chronically flooded, eroded, and backward area which badly needed electric power that private enterprise had failed to supply. The result of this eminently successful enterprise, which in the course of a decade revitalized an entire region and produced abundant inexpensive electric power, was, among others, to stimulate private enterprise into a new effort and more competitive prices. This can, at best, be one of the constructive functions of public enterprise. Equally successful have been certain public transport enterprises like Trans-Canada Airlines, which has a near-monopoly over air transport in Canada.[61]

The more far-reaching use of the public enterprise in post-war Britain and France is due to a mixture of political and technical motivations. Necessity to save a backward and declining industry of national importance was the predominant motivation for the nationalization of the British coal industry through the National Coal Board. While this agency has not succeeded in turning the coal industry into a profitable enterprise, it has at least slowed down its decline and effected urgently needed modernization. The nationalization of the electricity and transport utilities in Britain and France, on the other hand, is due in part at least to the political philosophy of the governments which legislated these programmes after the Second World War. The concentration of responsibility for the development of nuclear energy in the hands of the Atomic Energy Authority in Britain is due both to technical reasons and the overwhelming public importance of this matter. In the field of public utilities of national importance, which require nation-wide develop-

ment and a national policy, there has been little public opposition
to such transformation of private into public enterprise. Legally,
some of the public enterprises like the nationalized coal and electricity industries in Great Britain and France operate as statutory
monopolies. In other cases, as in that of the Canadian railways,
public and private enterprise operate side by side, although competition is usually limited through publicly controlled rates and a
considerable number of joint services (as in Canada).[62]

## Cooperatives

An alternative method of countering the power of private corporations to produce or not to produce is the creation, with public
assistance, of cooperatives. This was done in the case of the Rural
Electrification Authority, also of the New Deal period, under whose
auspices numerous farmers' cooperatives were set up in regions
which private enterprise had failed to supply with power. Once
again, the result was not only the rapid electrification of the relevant
regions, but also a new-found readiness of private enterprise to
develop power at competitive prices.[63]

## Mixed Companies

An alternative way of mitigating the unchecked power of the private
corporation is a partnership between public and private interests
operating through mixed companies. This has occurred on a large
scale in a number of European countries, such as Germany, France,
and, in particular, Italy, since the First World War. It is also a form
of enterprise that is sometimes favoured by industrially under-
developed countries for development schemes that require foreign
participation.[64] Where the government or a government-controlled
corporation holds the majority interest in such a company, it can
control economic policy. In Italy, the numerous State holdings of
this kind, especially in the field of minerals and shipping, have been
coordinated in State holding companies which, in this way, control
a major share of national production.[65] On the whole, however, this
form of combination of public and private enterprise is the result
of chance or emergency rather than of design. Thus, in Germany
after the First World War the Government had to acquire share
packets of numerous enterprises which were on the verge of bankruptcy to alleviate the threat of widespread unemployment. Where
the government holds a minority interest, it can usually exercise

little influence on policy, unless the majority holdings are scattered. In any case, the holding by the State of widely dispersed share packets of various importance in a number of different industries does not seem to be a desirable way of exercising the necessary public checks on private economic power. Except in the case of joint international ventures between capital-exporting and under-developed countries, it is not likely to develop further.

## *Partnership of Capital and Labour*

A very different form of partnership, though also designed to break the excessive predominance of capital ownership and private con-trol over the nation's economic life, is the participation of workers' representatives in the management of corporations. This so-called principle of 'co-determination' (*Mitbestimmungsrecht*) was intro-duced into the coal and steel industries of West Germany in the course of industrial reconstruction after the Second World War.[66] The whole principle and its extension to other industries is spon-sored by the West German trade-union movement. The underlying idea is that the right of control over enterprises should be shared between the owners of capital, who bear only limited financial risk and otherwise contribute nothing to production, and labour, which contributes the major share of the product. As a result, the supervisory boards (*Aufsichtsrat*) of the firms in the coal and steel industries in West Germany are now composed in equal parts of representatives of the shareholders and of the employees (the workers' representation is divided between direct nominees from the workers concerned and nominees from the central trade-union organization). In the larger corporations each side nominates seven members. There is also a fifteenth member, the 'odd man', who sometimes, but not always, serves as chairman. He is supposed to be 'neutral' and is chosen by agreement of the two groups or, in default of agreement, by the shareholders. While this cooperation seems, generally, to have worked harmoniously, especially in the time of reconstruction of the German economy, it has already become apparent that such partial alteration in the composition of the organs of company control will not produce any basic change in the pattern of industrial management. Workers' nominees soon come to regard themselves as mainly concerned in the progress and efficiency of the enterprise, which is usually dictated by sober realistic and competitive economic conditions. The 'national' or 'workers'' interests as a matter of general and distinct policy soon recede, and little remains but the fact that some of the members of the companies' boards are not elected in the traditional way by the shareholders but come from a different background.[67] On the other hand, the unions tend to become more 'management-minded'. Perhaps the real test of the value of this experiment will come in times of economic depression and threat of unemployment. It is in such situations, rather than in times of prosperity and over-employment, that the interests of employers and workers tend to clash most sharply.

## Regulatory Public Authorities

In economic systems which, in general, reject public enterprise and other forms of economic management by the government on ideological grounds and accept them, at most, in restricted fields such as soil conservation or electric power development or in situations of great emergency, the major check on the excessive power in the hands of private business lies in the use of the supervisory public authority as a regulatory, not as a managing, body. In various vital fields of economic life, federal public authorities such as the Interstate Commerce Commission, the Federal Trade Commission, or the Securities and Exchange Commission, exercise such functions. Thus, the Federal Trade Commission uses such legal means as 'cease and desist orders' to curb all manner of 'unfair competition' which includes the entire field of anti-trust legislation.

## Anti-trust Law

Anti-trust law, as administered by a combination of legislative, administrative, and judicial efforts, remains the cornerstone of 'anti-bigness' policy in a country dedicated to free enterprise like the United States. This is not, of course, the place to give yet another analysis of this immensely complex and controversial part of the law, but merely to note its place in the arsenal of legal counters to excessive corporate power. The gradual spread of more effective anti-trust legislation to countries which have ignored this legal curb until the present[68] shows that it is an indispensable means of controlling private economic power. On the other hand, it is not in itself an effective counter to the growth of the big corporation.[69] American anti-trust legislation goes farther than that of any other country in allowing among the available legal remedies the compulsory 'divorcement, dissolution, and divestiture' of assets, i.e. the break-up of existing concentrations. Yet the remedy is seldom applied.[70]

## Social Restraints

Short of the dogmatic remedy of transferring the entire machinery and means of production of the nation into the hands of the State – a remedy that, even if politically acceptable, would at best substitute for the power of a small number of giant private corporations the power of an *élite* bureaucracy – it seems clear that in modern industrial democratic society no single remedy can cope with the problem of private corporate power. There are, on the other hand, as we have seen, a number of various remedies which, singly or in combinations, have modified or can modify the extent as well as the possible abuses of such power. Public enterprise can always be used – and it has been used – to care for vital national developments which are not adequately covered by or cannot safely be entrusted to private enterprise. It can also be used to stimulate private enterprise into greater activity, as in the case of rural electrification in the United States. Anti-trust legislation, coupled with some administrative supervision, can remedy the more serious abuses of excessive concentration of economic power, though it can only slow down rather than arrest the continuing process of concentration of industrial production in a relatively small number of big corporations. Social-security legislation and the countervailing process of collective bargaining as well as, more vaguely, the pressure of public opinion on the 'corporate conscience' help to protect those who would otherwise be – and who formerly were – at the mercy of vastly greater economic power than they themselves possessed.

## CORPORATE POWER AND THE INDIVIDUAL

The impact of group power on the freedom of the individual has dramatically changed, in substance and emphasis, during the present century. Before the turn of the century, the United States and Canada had begun to take the first legislative measures to cope with the rapidly proceeding concentration of monopolistic power, with its double threat to the smaller manufacturer and businessman, who faced extinction or subjection to conditions vitally impairing his freedom of movement, and to the consumer who was inadequately protected against exploitation. The result was a combination of legislative, administrative, and judicial measures outlawing some of the most injurious practices in this field, such as price-fixing, tie-in sales, boycotts of newcomers, and other restrictions limiting freedom of entry into business.

At the same time, labour unions were still at the beginning of their struggle to restore a modicum of equality of economic power between employers and employees, capital and labour. Today, in most of the industrial democracies of the Western world, there is no longer any serious problem of *legal* recognition of the trade unions as the acknowledged spokesman of organized labour, although the degree of their actual power varies. The struggle of organized labour for recognition has been displaced by another problem: the protection of the individual member of the union against arbitrary penalties, including expulsion, by uncontrollable decisions of the union. This leads us back to the problem raised by Maitland's analysis of the unincorporated association.[1] Is it socially bearable, and jurisprudentially tenable, to withhold legal review from the entire sphere of relationships between associations exercising almost complete control over the working life of their members, and these members, simply on the ground that the majority of these associations are in form 'clubs', mostly unincorporated, and, in regard to their disciplinary powers, classed as 'domestic tribunals' in whose affairs the courts of the State traditionally are reluctant to intervene?[2]

### Legal Controls over Union Discipline

There are three aspects to the problem, all of which have in recent years occupied both British and American legislators, and, more particularly, the courts.

In the first place, it is possible to judge the activities of labour unions from the standpoint of monopolistic, exclusionary, or otherwise restrictive practices, applying, in other words, the standards of anti-monopoly and anti-trust legislation to the practices of collective labour organizations. Despite some pressures in that direction, the direct application of anti-trust or anti-monopoly legislation to labour has hitherto been excluded not only in the more moderate British and similar types of legislation, but in the far more radical and comprehensive American anti-trust law structure.[3] The major reason for this attitude is an obvious one of principle: labour, despite its far-reaching share in the prices of products and the conditions of trade, is not a 'commodity'. The regulation of labour conditions is still predominantly and rightly regarded as a problem of human and social relationships. Within the framework of labour law, recent legislative trends indicate, however, a tendency to restrict or exclude the abuse of monopolistic positions by labour unions in the process of collective bargaining. The basic principle, long established in British and American practice without statutory regulation, and specifically recognized in the United States Wagner Act of 1936, that a labour union representing the majority of the employees in the trade bargains for the unit concerned, remains unimpaired.[4] United States and Canadian legislation has established special public Labour Relations Boards, whose functions include, among others, the certification of a specific union as representing in fact a majority of the employees, and the decision of disputes between rival unions on this question. The United States Labour Management Relations Act of 1947 (commonly known as the Taft-Hartley Act) has, however, imposed certain further restrictions on union practices, prohibiting 'closed-shop' agreements, and permitting a majority of the employees to vote to rescind the authority of a labour organization to conclude a 'union-shop' agreement.[5] Such provisions have not substantially affected the increasingly monolithic character of trade-union organization, which corresponds to the growth of industrial corporate power, and which is based on social realities rather than on legal authorization. It has, however, to some extent weakened the power of unions to use the threat of expulsion and consequent loss of employment as a deterrent against the formation of rival unions or the exercise of any other dissentient activities.[6] There are no legislative provisions in Great Britain regulating or outlawing the 'closed-shop' agreement.[7] It is possible, however, that the law courts might, in certain circumstances, regard a 'closed-shop' agreement as against public policy in regard to an employee thereby deprived of his livelihood.[8] In a sense, such tendencies may be regarded as an equivalent in labour law to the attempts made by anti-trust law to nullify certain exclusionary business practices enforcing collective boycotts, or restricting otherwise the freedom of entry for a newcomer or dissident. In regard to compulsory unionism, Continental labour law presents a dramatic contrast to the common-law countries. Despite the social and – in contrast to the United States and Canada – articulate political strength of trade unionism in the European democracies, not one of them favours the 'closed shop' or any compulsory unionism. In such strongly unionized countries as Belgium, France, the Netherlands, Norway, Sweden, and West Germany, constitutional and other legislative provisions combine with judicial interpretation and the overwhelming opinion of legal writers in the rejection of any legal compulsion to join a particular – or indeed any union – by collective agreement or otherwise. Nor – as Professor Lenhoff has recently pointed out[9] – is this due mainly to religious and political differences between the unions which, in Scandinavia, for example, are in no way ideologically divided. One explanation may be that in most of these countries collective agreements may, by administrative order, be extended beyond the parties to an entire industry and thus become official law. A more convincing explanation is, perhaps, that in at least some parts of Europe, unionism has developed social and political strength gradually, and over a longer period than in North America. Finally, it may be that the overwhelming emphasis is, in North America, on tough bargaining between strong employers' and labour organizations and the still powerful distrust by both of State regulations affords a psychological explanation of this contrast between the American and the Continental approach. In West Germany, the rejection of compulsory unionism is probably part of a constitutional and emotional reaction against the totalitarianism of the Nazi period.[10] There are, of course, equally strong provisions against discrimination by employers based on union membership. The European approach is endorsed in a Report by a Committee of Experts to the 31st Session of the International Labour Organization.

A second, related, approach is the constitutional or statutory protection of the 'right to work' of the individual against any attempts of a group, in particular, of a trade union, to make exclusion of unorganized workers a term of a collective agreement. Not only in Great Britain, which has no written constitution and no formal 'Bill of Rights', except in certain procedural respects (such as *habeas corpus*), but also in other British Commonwealth countries like Australia and Canada which have written constitutions, but no code of individual rights, this question does not easily arise. The problem has, however, become acute in the United States, where both the Federal and the forty-eight State Constitutions have many explicit provisions on fundamental human rights. Until the advent of the Wagner Act of the 'New Deal' period and other federal and state legislation, giving recognition to the labour unions, and creating statutory obligations for the employer to bargain collectively with representative unions, a constitutional protection of the individual 'right to work' would, in most cases, have been an empty and ironic gesture, despite the 'open-shop' campaign of 1900–10 and the American Plan campaign of 1920–30. The vast majority of workers were still struggling for a minimum of economic and social protection through the strengthening of the labour unions, even though in some trades (e.g. printing) unions and collective bargaining had long enjoyed a respected position. But the dramatic advance of the social and legal power of the unions is producing a political reaction against their growing power, particularly in the more conservative states of the South. A series of constitutional and statutory provisions have been enacted purporting to protect the diffident individual against compulsory unionism and collective agreements directly or indirectly making union membership a condition of employment. A representative provision is that of the Nebraska Constitution:

No person shall be denied employment because of membership in or affiliation with, or resignation or expulsion from a labor organization or because of refusal to join or affiliate with a labor organization; nor shall any individual or corporation or association of any kind enter into any contract, written or oral, to exclude persons from employment because of membership in or nonmembership in a labor organization.[11]

Here one of the acute conflicts of public policy and competing social interests, inevitable in a complex democratic society, arises. Since 1936, the United States Congress has made collective bargaining by appropriate employers and labour organizations the cornerstone of its legislative policy. While the Taft-Hartley Act of 1947 has somewhat restricted the coercive powers of the predominant unions, and, correspondingly, strengthened dissenting groups, it has not basically impaired the principle, by which the labour unions – within the procedures laid down in the National Labor Relations Act – are empowered to bargain on behalf of the employees in the unit which they represent, and bargaining with such unions is a statutory duty incumbent on the employers. The philosophy underlying this legislation is that labour unions have been by far the most powerful single instrument in the improvement of the social status and the economic lot of the worker, that the organization of modern industrial society recognizes the power, and requires the legal recognition, of groups capable of speaking authoritatively on behalf of employers and employees respectively, whether on a local or nationwide basis, and that the interests of the occasional dissenter – who participates in any case, willingly or otherwise, in the benefits conferred on workers in collective agreements – must be subordinated to this principle of collective bargaining. That this philosophy is a constitutionally admissible Congressional policy not impairing freedom of association as protected by the First Amendment was confirmed by the Supreme Court of the United States, when in a recent judgement[12] it considered the above-quoted provision of the Nebraska Constitution to be incompatible with the (Federal) Railway Labor Act, which permits 'union-shop' agreements between a carrier and a labour organization, requiring payment of union dues. The court reversed the decision of the Nebraska Supreme Court, which had dismissed the suit brought by organized employees to enjoin the application and enforcement of a 'union-shop' agreement.

The importance of this decision can be assessed only against the social background. It took many decades of bitter struggle to attain the status which labour unions have reached today. Despite some abuses, they have conferred incalculable social and economic benefits on many millions of American workers previously disorganized and underprivileged. Any substantial loophole might reopen the door to company unions or 'yellow-dog' contracts and gradually weaken the position of labour, especially in many states of the south where labour organization is more recent and relatively weaker than in the north east.[13]

Yet, the problem of threats to individual freedom by union tyranny remains.[14] It leads us to the third and, in recent developments, most important of the attempts made to impose legal checks on the activities of 'private' associations, in particular of labour unions, *vis-à-vis* their members.

We have discussed earlier the increasing anomaly of the characterization as 'private', of associations which exercise an increasingly exclusive – and, to a large extent, legally recognized – control over the livelihood of millions of people. A theory – or a habit – developed for clubs, membership in which confers at most social privileges, come to be applied to associations, membership in which is a condition for earning one's livelihood. The theory has a twofold root: one ideological, one technical. The ideological motive is respect for freedom of association, and a long-standing disinclination of the courts to interfere in domestic quarrels. An American commentator has summarized this attitude as follows:

> This reluctance is a product of long judicial experience in attempting to settle family fights in religious and fraternal associations. The courts have recognized that they have no workable standards for refereeing disputes based on obscure doctrines within a church, or for judging the virtues of cliquish factions within a lodge. Any order which the court may issue will not heal the schism, but will only embitter the fight. The dispute seldom involves anything but wounded dignity, and the award serves only to soothe the feelings of one of the parties. This policy of non-intervention which the courts developed in cases involving churches and lodges was early applied with equal strictness to labour unions.[15]

By default rather than by detention the theory was applied to the emergent labour unions.

> The Elks may expel an errant Elk with fair trial for any constitutional violation. The Baptist church can expel a member for opposing union policy. This is the contract theory – the theory that the constitution is a contract, and if the prospective union member accepts membership, he accepts these terms.[16]

The above-quoted statements are perhaps today a more accurate summary of the British rather than the American legal approach. The technical obstacles to legal control of 'private' associations stem from the fetters put on the courts by the 'property' basis of equitable remedies, and the 'contractual' character of membership in an unincorporated association.

British courts still generally adhere to the view that the activities of what are often called 'domestic tribunals' are, with rare exceptions, beyond the control of the courts. A certain amount of supervision is exercised over those bodies which, by law, exercise a statutory jurisdiction over a profession. By controlling the admission, conduct, and expulsion of doctors, lawyers, pharmacists, nurses, and others, the relevant bodies enjoy a judicial power directly delegated to them by act of State. Consequently, in such cases a prerogative writ will lie to a court, and such writ will occasionally be granted.[17] But a graver and more intractable problem is presented by those bodies which, like churches, employers' organizations, trade associations, or labour unions, exercise a *de facto* compulsory control over vast sections of the population while still enjoying the legal privileges of private organizations. Maitland drew attention[18] to the celebrated case[19] which showed the limitations of the trust concept as a controlling device for a living religious organization. The effect of the decision was overcome by Act of Parliament. The control of courts over private associations is still limited by two principles: on the one hand such associations enjoy complete autonomy in their internal dealings, including the admission and expulsion of members and other disciplinary measures. This is limited only by the so-called principles of natural justice which, in practice, are reduced to the two modest propositions that a fair hearing must be granted and that nobody must be judge in his own cause. Yet in practice even these modest principles are hardly applied to private associations. In *Weinberger* v. *Inglis*[20] the House of Lords refused to review the action of the Stock Exchange, which, during the First World War, had expelled a naturalized British subject of German birth. The deed of settlement should admit members 'as they think proper'. The House unanimously thought that there had been no improper exercise of the discretion. In *MacLean* v. *Workers' Union*[21] Maugham J. similarly refused to scrutinize the resolution of a union which had expelled the plaintiff. Although the learned judge mentioned the rules of natural justice, he specifically stated that even an unfair or an unjust decision made by a domestic tribunal of this type could not be reviewed, provided it was given 'honestly and in good faith'.

The Privy Council reaffirmed this approach when in *White* v. *Kuzych*[22] it dismissed the action of a welder expelled by his Canadian union for having opposed the 'closed-shop' policy. It avoided the direct issue of public policy by putting its decision on the procedural ground that the plaintiff had failed to use his right of appeal to the Shipyard Workers' Federation as provided in his contract with the union. In the circumstances, as in many other cases, this proved a very theoretical remedy.[23]

The *Kuzych* case is one of many which, in recent years, have directed the attention of British, Canadian, and American courts to the facts of union organization.[24] Any labour union of significance has a considerable code of offences and penalties, including the gravest penalty of all, expulsion from the union.[25] Offences cover all kinds of activities deemed injurious to the union, among them opposition to union policies, agitation for rival unions, membership of certain political organizations, and, in some cases, personal moral conduct. It is not so much the nature of the offences that challenges criticism – although the concept and interpretation of, e.g. 'anti-union' activities alters in significance when union membership is a *de facto* condition of obtaining employment in one's trade – as the procedures by which these offences are determined.[26] The executive officers of the union normally decide whether an offence has been committed, and it is usually the same officers who sit as a disciplinary 'tribunal' on complaints from the members. There is very little, if any, distinction between prosecutor and judge. Appeal procedure is lengthy, difficult, and often quite fictitious, a fact which underlines the lack of realism of the Privy Council decision in the *Kuzych* case.

## Some Recent Judicial Advances

In recent years the English Court of Appeal and the House of Lords have attempted, with more than customary boldness, to dispose of the limitation imposed by the law of contract, the historical restrictions of equitable relief, and the unincorporated status of trade unions. In order to do this they have adopted some ingenious constructions, but they have above all relied upon elementary considerations of public policy, justice, and common sense, and they have incidentally demonstrated that the alleged chains of strict obedience to precedent can be cast off with relative ease, where the will to do so exists.

The House of Lords granted damages for breach of contract to a wrongfully expelled member of a union. In *Bonsor* v. *Musicians' Union*[27] the plaintiff, a musician, had for many years been a member of the defendant union. In 1949, when the plaintiff was fifty-two weekly payments of his weekly contributions in arrear, a branch secretary of the union purported to exclude him from membership by virtue of union rules. A few months later the plaintiff asked to be reinstated so as to enable him to obtain employment as a musician. This the branch secretary refused, except on payment of a fine and all arrears. He rejected the plaintiff's offer to pay the sum out of his first week's wages. The plaintiff was therefore unable to obtain employment as a musician. He claimed a declaration that he was wrongfully expelled, that he was entitled to be reinstated as a member, as well as an injunction restraining the union and its officers from treating him as an expelled member, and finally damages or other relief. The majority of the Court of Appeal held that the expulsion of the plaintiff was ineffective, because the union rules gave that power only to a branch committee, and not to an individual officer. In accordance with *Kelly*'s case, the declarations and the injunction were granted, but the claim for damages was denied.

In a surprisingly unorthodox decision the House of Lords upheld the dissenting judgement of Denning L.J., which would have granted damages. The significance of a unanimous judgement of Britain's highest court awarding damages for breach of contract to a wrongfully expelled member of a union despite its lack of legal personality is probably more important than the technical arguments by which this result was reached. It is, indeed, difficult to find the common line of reasoning in the judgements of the House.[28] Some judgements sought support mainly in the older decision of the *Taff Vale* case,[29] which had treated an unincorporated but registered union as a *de facto* legal person, capable of being sued in tort. Others preferred to consider an unincorporated trade union as a hybrid, which had certain aspects of a legal person, though not all of them. An unincorporated, but registered, union was capable of being sued in its registered name, despite shifting membership. In this it differed from an unincorporated association without these qualities. The House of Lords also disposed of the agency problem. While the membership nexus could, in a sense, be regarded as a contract with the trade union, the latter, in expelling the plaintiff, represented all the members except the plaintiff, who, for this purpose, faced the union as an entity. The many nuances of the different judgements are all dominated by the desire of the House of Lords to overcome the technical obstacles created by lack of legal personality.[30] A few years later an engineer, who had quarrelled with his district union committee for not having joined a strike, and who, though not expelled by the central executive council, had been hounded out of every job by the District Committee, obtained damages.[31] But there was, in this case, an unusual element of vindictiveness.

An American student of this problem has expressed the view that, in three major areas, the present law is in serious need of change.[32]

First, increased protection must be given to members engaging in political activities within the union.

Second, greater protection must be given to insure a full and fair hearing.

Third, the legal remedies need to be substantially strengthened. The disciplined member must be protected during the time required for an appeal within the union.

Professor Summers is of the opinion that, in the first two areas, most of the necessary protection can be provided by the courts under existing principles, or by a closer judicial scrutiny of procedures followed in the unions. As regards the protection of the disciplined member during the time required for an appeal, he considers, however, that legislation is needed which will aid the expelled member to bear the burden of obtaining legal relief. Finally, Professor Summers somewhat vaguely suggests legislation or 'administrative machinery' providing for the naming of independent arbitrators in cases of union discipline.[33]

Another authority on American labour law[34] is of the opinion that the Bonsor-type problem is no longer a serious one in the United States, but that action is required to protect the individual (member or non-member) against exclusive dependence on union action.

I believe administrative action is needed to protect the member who is too inarticulate to get into court.

The problem of union discipline is really a comparatively minor one in this country today because

(1) Expulsion has no effect on job security, except in cases of non-payment of dues.

(2) The courts are handling most cases perfectly adequately and have been for many years.

(3) The only people who ordinarily get expelled are those who are vigorous and articulate enough to cause hostility, and they usually have enough stake in the matter to get the courts to reinstate them (*with* damages).

In this country we have got far beyond the problem of union dicipline to a much more serious problem, that of the duty of the union to provide fair and adequate representation in collective bargaining and grievance procedures.

The above-mentioned American and English judgements have gone a long way towards (*a*) strengthening the remedies of the individual member, in particular by giving him an action for damages in breach of contract[35]; (*b*) widening the scope of judicial review over arbitrary and obviously unfair interpretations of union rules; (*c*) strengthening the requirements for minimum standards of procedural justice. These are, on the whole, welcome developments, designed to restore a balance which the progressive increase of union discipline over the individual has disturbed. It is doubtful, however, whether any supervisory public body, or any other institutional official intervention, could be established without seriously interfering with the essential autonomy of union organization.

It must be emphasized that any strengthening of judicial supervision should not be confined to labour union procedures, but should equally apply to any other unincorporated associations (such as trade associations) whose power over the individual is comparable. This would include institutions like the English Jockey Club, which has the monopoly of issuing trainers' licences. But it should probably exclude a golf club. The borderline is not always easy to draw. All the judicial and theoretical discussions have emphasized the 'monopoly' or 'quasi-public' power of certain associations as the reason for the necessity of greater public control. The inference is that those 'private' associations which do not affect a person's livelihood or freedom of movement, but his pleasures, relaxations, or proclivities for 'conspicuous waste', should continue to function behind the 'hedges' of trust, contract, and lack of incorporation.[36] There is certainly a strong element of artificiality in the continuation of the privileges of non-incorporation for groups which act and function as powerful corporate bodies. The courts have mitigated some of these consequences by robustly blurring analytical distinctions. The ultimate classification of the legal status of trade unions and other bodies with quasi-public functions must, however, like all regulation of status problems, remain a matter for the legislator.

### Big Business and the Individual

Before the general incidence and legal recognition of collective bargaining between employers and unions had restored a rough equality, the overwhelming power of employers, especially of the large corporations, over the individual worker had, of course, lain in their economic superiority rather than in their formal legal power to terminate any individual labour contract at short notice. While this condition lasted, the legal equality of modern contract, giving in theory both parties equal rights and obligations, was the fiction disguising the power of one party to deal with the other more or less at will.

The drastic change of this state of affairs in modern industrial democracy, one of the major social revolutions of our time, has largely abolished this unilateral power. While the freedom to hire and fire remains in law – subject to the terms of collective labour contracts – the exercise of this power by the employer, including the largest corporations, or perhaps particularly the largest corporations, is restrained by countervailing economic power as well as by certain social considerations (impact on public opinion, etc.). The freedom to dismiss or to lock out is countered by the freedom to strike. And where, as in some countries, the State intervenes to a greater extent than in the United States in the determination of labour disputes, it does so as an arbiter, representing the 'national interests' in the sense discussed in this article, rather than reinforcing the power of the one or other side.

But there remain spheres in which the collective power of the union *vis-à-vis* the employer does not protect the individual. Two types of relationships have to be briefly considered. One is the relationship between the big corporation and a nominally independent party, which is, however, in a relation of economic dependency. Among them are the many smaller contractors, manufacturing parts for the big manufacturers, or licensed dealers obtaining strictly conditioned 'franchises' from the big makers. Some of these relationships come within the purview of anti-trust law. In so far as tie-in clauses, black-lists, or other measures clearly impeding freedom of trade by exclusionary conditions – either tying an individual to a particular company or excluding entry for newcomers – unduly impair freedom of trade, the law provides certain remedies.[37] But the scope of these remedies is strictly limited. The granting of a franchise by a large automobile manufacturer to a dealer is, in fact, an exclusive association. Only in so far as a large corporation would make such a franchise contract openly dependent upon abstention from, or termination of, any other business associations, anti-trust might be applicable. But the real dependence is not expressed in legal formulas. Where manufacturers exercise a preponderant power, like the 'Big Three' in the automobile industry, or International Business Machines in the field of automation machines, it is economic rather than legal conditions, minimum requirements rather than exclusionary terms of the contract, that create an unequal relationship. Anti-trust law cannot cope with the imposition of minimum capital requirements or the fulfilment of certain minimum quotas of sales as a condition of the continuation of the franchise. To some extent, of course, individual dealers can counter this state of affairs by acting collectively as a group, in the way in which workers act through unions. In certain fields such a rough restoration of equality has occurred.[38] But it would appear, for example, from the Congressional investigations made in 1956, that nothing like equality of bargaining exists as yet as between the major corporations and their dealers.[39]

Another, possibly more critical, aspect of the intrusion of public law into private legal relationships concerns the employer-employee contract. It arises from the fact that a considerable proportion of industry, and, in particular, of the large corporations nowadays work to a very large extent under Government contracts. These contracts overwhelmingly relate, directly or indirectly, to defence requirements. Most of these contracts involve secret scientific and technological processes with a high security risk. This applies, for example, to all phases of aviation equipment, an industry in which the links between the Government and a nominally private industry are particularly strong. It will also increasingly apply to the manufacturers of atomic reactors and all aspects of utilization of nuclear energy, except in so far as the 'peaceful-use' aspects can be clearly separated out from defence uses – apparently a very difficult matter. In so far as all these corporations enter into contracts with the Defence Department – and hardly one of the large manufacturers today would not – they come under the security regulations of the Department of Defence, which are incorporated in the terms of the contract.[40] To that extent the private corporations are in fact, though not in name, agents of the Government.[41] The security officers of the Defence Department or, in certain situations, the Congressional Committee, may investigate the personnel of any of these plants. The officers may demand the dismissal of certain employees as bad security risks. While these employees are in this respect 'public' employees, they do not enjoy any of the modest safeguards of public employees against arbitrary dismissal. There is, in fact, no 'arbitrary' dismissal, except in so far as exceptionally an individual contract with a higher employee or a collective labour agreement for an entire group may have given a limited security. The large private corporations engaged in defence work are today in a legal twilight, somewhere between the spheres of public law and private law. As far as the individual employee is concerned, he might conceivably find protection in the terms of a collective labour agreement. But they do not normally touch these matters. A joint arbitration machinery in cases of security dismissals disputed by a member might afford some relief. Generally, the unions show little inclination to intervene in the protection of the individual who is, rightly or wrongly, suspected of Communist affiliations. While no official stigma attaches to the determination of a private relationship, it may affect the individual's employability as severely as the loss of union membership (which it may, incidentally, entail). As shown in official statutes, employers sometimes anticipate public inquiry by terminating an employment that may conceivably come under questioning. Although the effect of unemployability is graver than punishment for all but grave criminal offences, dismissal is not, of course, in any sense classified as criminal law so that the protection of criminal procedure is absent. The 'right to work' may be destroyed without any legal process or remedy.

## CONCLUSIONS

The broad general conclusion which emerges from an examination of the various spheres in which the legal classification of a relationship as 'private' conceals a different social reality – be it the membership of a club, a trade union, a trade association, or a private employment contract – is the increasing interpenetration of public and private law elements. The totalitarian State can solve this problem by transforming almost the entire body of private law into public law.[42] In the mixed economic systems of modern industrial democracy this is not a possible solution. Democracies must, instead, use a blend of the eight types of legal restraint on private economic and social power which have been briefly surveyed in the preceding chapter.[43] It is all the more important that the law should respond to social change by giving recognition to the public-law aspects of a legal relationship. The most important aspect is a more than formal safeguarding of 'due process' in the personal, political, and social life of the individual. It will be necessary to make a distinction between the affairs of private associations which affect the basic freedoms (opinion, movement, business, work) and those which do not (social clubs of various kinds). In regard to the former, the response of the law can largely be in terms of judicial interpretation. Just as the Supreme Court of the United States has denied enforceability to racial covenant clauses,[44] so the courts can extend the reviewability of unfair practices and lack of procedural safeguards in the affairs of associations. Such trends are indicated by recent judicial developments, both in Great Britain and the United States. On the other hand, any system of continuous administrative supervision over private institutions – trade unions, trade associations, or foundations – would jeopardize that minimum of freedom of association without which democracies can slide to the brink of totalitarianism.

As regards the public-law protection of private employment relationships, it seems that the State will have to interfere by the legislative or administrative establishment of procedural safeguards. This is no new principle. It is the continuation of a process which, for many decades, has imposed social-security obligations of many kinds on private contracts, and has, in such fields as workmen's compensation, substituted public minimum standards, administered by public authorities, for private standards.

Part Four

Public Law

# 11

# The Growth of Administration and the Evolution of Public Law

## THE GROWTH OF THE ADMINISTRATIVE FUNCTION

The growth of the administrative process has been a universal phenomenon of contemporary society, although both speed and manner of its development have varied greatly from country to country. A minimum of administration is, of course, inherent in the very notion of government. The most ardent advocates of *laissez-faire* policy concede to government the minimum functions of defence, administration of justice and police. But, regardless of political philosophy, the needs of an increasingly complex society have forced upon one country after another a multiplicity of additional functions: to the protection of elementary standards of health and safety, both for the public in general and employees – which accounted for the first major growth of public services in nineteenth-century England – were rapidly added a vast number of additional social services, from elementary measures of public assistance to the highly diversified social-security systems of the mid twentieth century; the supervision of public utilities, labour relations, and many other economic and social processes intimately affecting the public interest. In times of war or emergency, a multitude of controls over supply and distribution of essential commodities and products further enlarges the functions of government.

Beyond the irreducible minimum imposed by external conditions, the type and direction of the administrative function is influenced by the political and economic system of the country. In socialized States – as shown by the Soviet Union and its affiliated systems – the State takes over the managerial as well as the regulatory function. The conduct of major economic enterprises becomes an administrative function: contracts of supply between the State-owned corporations producing commodities and manufactured goods are at once civil and administrative transactions. Managers and other personnel are not only in the civil relationship of servants to masters, but also in the disciplinary relationship of public officials to their superiors.

At the next level, the mixed economies which today characterize the political and economic systems of many States – such as France, Great Britain, Italy, India, Japan, as well as many of the smaller states, both of Western Europe and Asia – have a combination of managerial and regulatory administrative functions. Certain industries and public utilities are operated by the State itself – either through government departments[1] or with increasing frequency through semi-autonomous public corporations, responsible to government, but equipped with more or less far-reaching managerial autonomy.[2] At the same time, the bulk of industry and business, which remains in private ownership, is subject to varying degrees of public supervision and regulations, while another set of public authorities administers the various social services.

In the United States, too, the managerial aspect of the administrative process is not unknown, although, perhaps due to ideological inhibitions, astonishingly little attention is paid by the highly developed science of administrative law to this aspect of public activity. The main emphasis, however, has been on the regulative function of administration. The establishment of a series of permanent regulatory federal agencies[3] testifies to the fact that even the most strongly private-enterprise and capitalist-minded contemporary State cannot leave its economic system to the free play of economic forces. It cannot afford to look passively at the 'free' play of forces, with strong enterprises squeezing out the weak, with the consumer being helpless against exploitation by monopolies and unregulated public utilities. Under such conditions, 'the general statutory or common law which administers itself through the moral conscience of the citizen is no longer enough to deal with the vast machinery of power and abuses which economic control can become if unfettered from the ties of public interest'. On the other hand, public ownership, adopted, wholly or in part, in so many other countries, is overwhelmingly rejected by American public opinion 'as the complete pattern of our economy and final destiny of our whole lives'.[4] Between the Scylla of unregulated economic enterprise and the Charybdis of public ownership lies public regulation, 'the answer to the challenge which public ownership and operation of all economic enterprise presents.'[5]

In a highly industrialized and dynamic society like that of the United States, which is complicated by the existence of fifty state governments, side by side with the Federal Government, such regulation means, however, a vast and complicated mechanism of administration. In a sense, the contemporary United States is the administrative State *par excellence*, if administration is taken in the traditional sense of the public supervision and control of private and official activities.

## THE NEED FOR A SYSTEM OF PUBLIC LAW

In an absolutist State, whether of the feudal, the monarchical, the Communist, or the Fascist pattern, the dichotomy of public and private law makes no sense, even though, in modern systems of this kind, it may be maintained as a matter of form. Ultimately, all law dissolves into administrative discretion. Such was the conclusion drawn for Communist society by the once influential Soviet legal philosopher Pashukanis, who maintained that in a Communist State there was no room for law at all, since all law became administration directed by the demands of public utility.[6] The same thought was expressed in more conventional terms by Lenin when he wrote that 'for us everything in the field of economy bears the character of public law and not of private law. . . . Hence we should broaden the application of State intervention into "private-law" relationships.'[7]

From very different premisses, the idea of a dichotomy of public and private law, with the former representing a system of norms regulating the legal relations between public authority and the individual, has been opposed by three major legal thinkers of the Western world, vastly though they differ from each other in background and philosophy.

The French legal philosopher and constitutional lawyer, Léon Duguit, opposed the dualism of public and private law in the name of 'social solidarity', which demanded that all, governors and governed alike, were subject to the same principle of service to the community. From the standpoint of a hierarchy of legal norms in a system of 'pure science of law', the Austrian, Hans Kelsen, opposes the division of public and private law, as being contrary to the 'step by step' unfolding of legal norms from the ultimate *Grundnorm* to the individual decisions of administrative authorities and private parties alike. Coupled with this, however, is a consideration of political theory, which sees in the development of administrative law an entrenchment of public authority in a position of superiority and arbitrariness as against the private citizen.

Neither of these two influential legal theorists has prevented the continuous growth of highly developed systems of administrative law in the civil-law jurisdictions, buttressed by a complete hierarchy

of administrative courts.[8] Far more influential has been the opposition of the English jurist Dicey to any system of *droit administratif* in
England, as being contrary to the spirit and tradition of the common
law.

For Dicey,[9] the 'rule of law' has three aspects: first, no man is
punishable except for 'a distinct breach of law established in the
ordinary legal manner before the ordinary courts of the land', and
therefore the rule of law is not consistent with arbitrary 'or even
wide discretionary authority on the part of the government'. In the
second place, the rule of law means equal subjection of all classes to
the ordinary law of the land as administered by the ordinary law
courts, and therefore a rejection of so-called administrative justice
applied by special tribunals on the Continental model. The third
aspect of Dicey's rule of law means in essence a historic generalization: in English law, private individual rights derive from court
precedents rather than from constitutional codes. This quite clearly
applies only to Britain itself and would have no application to a
State which, like Australia, is governed by a written constitution,
let alone to the United States, whose constitution embodies a comprehensive catalogue of individual rights.

It is no exaggeration to say that the views of this eminent, influential jurist played a considerable part in delaying the growth, not
of administration, but of administrative law in the common-law
world, for several decades. Yet, almost simultaneously with the
publication of the first edition of Dicey's *Law of the Constitution*, in
1885, his great contemporary, Maitland, clearly saw the growth of
administrative law in England, the growing importance of 'the
subordinate Government of England'.[10]

That Dicey ignored the then prominent privileges and immunities
of the Crown, that he completely misunderstood the French *droit
administratif* which, far from protecting governmental arbitrariness,
had already gone far – and has since gone further – in the legal protection of the citizen against such arbitrariness, has been pointed out
by many contemporary critics of Dicey's theory.[11] For an understanding of the essential conditions of a system of administrative
law, it is perhaps more important to point out the basic fallacy in
Dicey's juxtaposition of two principles: one expresses the need for
restraint of the arbitrary power of government; the other says that
there must be 'equal subjection of all classes' to 'the ordinary
courts'. Even within the formulation of these two principles, Dicey
makes some questionable assumptions. The equation of 'arbitrary'
with 'wide discretionary' power of government is one that few

students of the modern administrative process would accept without severe reservations. Again, the identification of 'ordinary' courts with the courts developed in the common-law tradition assumes *a priori* that no differently constituted courts, including courts of the eminence, expertise, and judicial independence of the French Conseil d'État, can be considered as genuine courts.[12]

The deeper fallacy of Dicey's assumptions lies in his contention that the rule of law demands full equality in every respect between government and subjects or citizens. But it is inherent in the very notion of government that it cannot in all respects be equal to the governed, because it has to govern. In a multitude of ways, government must be left to interfere, without legal sanctions, in the lives and interests of citizens, where private persons could not be allowed to do so with impunity. To some extent, the range of these immunities is expressed in the 'prerogatives' of the Crown, or in the equivalent French concept of '*actes de Gouvernement*'. Declarations of war, or other military interventions, diplomatic relations including the recognition of governments, may or may not be subject to legislative control, but they cannot form the subject of individual actions, even though incalculable damage may be inflicted on millions of individuals as a result of irresponsible action by the executive. No action may be brought for loss of life, limb, or property, as the result of foreign policy decisions, although most States, in and after the last World War, enacted certain legislation compensating citizens for war damage. The refusal of Anglo-American courts to examine or question the recognition of foreign States or governments is another indication of this basic distinction between government and citizens. It goes, however, beyond the international sphere. The refusal of the courts to make planning or policy decisions of government the subject of legal action,[13] also shows that the inequality of government and governed in certain respects is an indispensable fact of organized political life. Where the borderline between governmental freedom and legal responsibility has to be drawn, is, indeed, a very difficult problem. It may be described as the key problem of administrative law. But we can only begin to understand it after having accepted, unlike Dicey, that inequalities between government and citizens are inherent in the very nature of political society.

Although the struggle against a system of administrative justice had its counterparts on the Continent,[14] Continental jurisprudence, following the French model, has long established full-fledged systems of administrative justice, which have come to be recognized as bulwarks against arbitrary administrative power, and not, as contended by Dicey or Kelsen, as legitimized oppressions of the individual.[15]

In the common-law world, there has been a belated and hesitant but now increasingly accepted development of a system and science of administrative law.[16] The definition of the sphere of administrative law has, however, especially in the United States, tended to remain narrowly confined to procedural methods and safeguards.[17] This distinguishes the American science and doctrine of administrative law – and to a far lesser extent, that of English administrative law – from the Continental conception of administrative law. As even a cursory survey of any of the leading texts[18] will show, the discussion of remedies and procedures against administrative authorities, and the system of administrative justice, occupies only one, and not the major, part of administrative law. For the greater part, Continental administrative law is concerned with such matters of substance as public-law contracts, domains and principles of public ownership, principles of legal responsibility on the part of government and other public authorities.[19] By contrast, the almost total failure, in the common-law science of administrative law, to regard such matters as the status and powers of public enterprises, the development of public-law contracts within the general field of contract, or the borderlines between legal duty and discretion in the conduct of public authorities, still greatly limits the understanding of administrative law in the common-law world. Many of the vital problems of public law have to be culled from scattered decisions, standard conditions of government contracts, and other materials found in the case-books and textbooks on contract, tort, or property, which, in turn, largely fail to analyse the public-law problems as such. Because such limitations greatly impede the understanding of the essential characteristics of public law, a – necessarily cursory – survey of some of the substantial as well as of the procedural problems of administrative law will be attempted, on a comparative basis, in this chapter.

## SEPARATION OF POWERS AND ADMINISTRATIVE LAW

In 1881 the Supreme Court declared in *Kilbourn* v. *Thompson*[20] that all powers of government are divided into executive, legislative, and judicial, and that it is 'essential to the successful working of this system that the persons entrusted with power in any one of these branches shall not be permitted to encroach upon the powers confided to the others, but that each shall by the law of its creation be limited to the exercise of the powers appropriate to its own department and no other . . .'

The antithesis to this deceptively simple conception of government[21] was stated by Woodrow Wilson in 1908[22].

The trouble with the theory is that government is not a machine, but a living thing. . . . No living thing can have its organs offset against each other as checks, and live. On the contrary, its life is dependent upon their quick cooperation, their ready response to the commands of instinct or intelligence, their amicable community of purpose. Government is not a body of blind forces; it is a body of men, with highly differentiated functions no doubt, in our modern day of specialization, but with a common task and purpose. Their cooperation is indispensable, their warfare fatal. . . .

In the mid twentieth century, it is commonplace that a strict doctrine of separation of powers is not only a theoretical absurdity and a practical impossibility, but that it has not been embodied, in anything like the strictness presumed by the Supreme Court in the above-quoted decision, in any contemporary constitution. The constitutional system of the United States has been recently characterized by one American scholar as one of checks and balances rather than separation of powers,[23] while another has stressed that not separation of powers, but judicial supremacy is a characteristic feature of the American Constitution.[24] Yet another recent analysis[25] detects, on the contrary, a decline of the relative power of both judiciary and legislature, 'accompanied by a corresponding growth of relative power in the executive . . . branch of government'. Clearly, all these analyses emphasize different aspects of a complex and constantly shifting system of checks and balances.[26] Whichever aspect is emphasized, it is evident that separation of powers can be only relative, not absolute. The executive must appoint judges, unless the legislature or the electorate do so. Executive and legislature must cooperate in the enactment of laws, although the forms of doing so differ in various democracies. In Great Britain, which formed the model for Montesquieu's theory of the separation of powers, the principle has never been even theoretically enshrined. The executive is formed by the majority party in the House of Commons, which thus both controls the Government and is, in turn, under its direction. The Lord Chancellor combines the functions of the highest judge, a member of the Cabinet, and the presiding officer of the Upper Legislative Chamber. The vitality and importance of the doctrine of the separation of powers lies not in any rigid separation of functions, but in a working hypothesis, i.e. in the basic differentiation of the three functions of law-making, administration, and adjudication. By far the most important aspect of separation of powers is judicial independence from administrative direction, and that is perhaps the only aspect of the doctrine on which all democracies concur.

As we have seen, the process of law-finding is a constant and painful adjustment of conflicting values. So is the problem of adjustment between private economic power and public interest. Nor are public and private interests always clearly distinct. The regulatory authority sometimes becomes too closely identified with the interest and outlook of the regulated industry.[27] The exercise of public functions may, deliberately or by stealth, slide into the hands of private groups, such as employers' associations or trade unions.

The problem of the relations between public authority and the citizen (private or corporate) cannot be solved in terms of conceptual absolutes. Nor can it be solved simply by the elaboration of procedural safeguards. Whether and to what extent such safeguards have to be provided, must in large measure depend on the fundamental adjustment of the relations between public power and private rights.

### THE LIMITS OF ADMINISTRATIVE DISCRETION

Once we have conceded that government must govern, and that it cannot, therefore, be in all respects on a footing of equality with the citizen, the formula stated by Dicey that government must not have 'arbitrary' or even 'wide discretionary' powers becomes mere question begging, as do the limitless variations of this formula used in Bar association speeches, on public platforms, and the like. For what is 'arbitrary' and where, consequently, the limits of the discretion have to be drawn, depends on the scale of human values as it is enshrined in the contemporary legal system. It should be evident that this has, in many respects, greatly altered during the present century. As the basis, there remains, in all civilized systems, the protection – though not unqualified and subject to due process – of life, liberty, and property. Administrative processes are seldom concerned with the protection of life, except in connexion with the execution of capital sentences. But they are deeply and seriously concerned with the protection of liberty and property. However, instead of devoting all our attention to the minute details of safe-guards, we should, perhaps, do a little rethinking on the meaning of such basic values as liberty and property in the legal and social context of contemporary society. At a time of international tensions and apprehensions about Communist subversion, the very same people who, a generation ago, condemned the growth of the administrative process as an intolerable encroachment on separation of functions and the rule of law are today disposed to leave almost unlimited powers to administrative discretion in the domain of national security, deportation, immigration, and other matters vitally concerning the liberty, freedom of movement, and employability of the citizen at large, of aliens, or of more limited groups of the population. Conversely, those who favoured wide administrative discretion in the era of economic and social reform, now condemn administrative latitude, especially in the area of human rights. Professor Gellhorn has recently drawn up an impressive catalogue of administrative powers which have been allowed to grow with little or no legal check.[28] These include press and book censorship, the various 'loyalty' procedures, the issue of passports, and others. Again, if liberty is a value to be protected, unless there is a clear statutory command to the contrary, such decisions as *Liversidge* v. *Anderson*,[29] where the power of the Home Secretary to detain aliens where he 'has reasonable cause to believe' was interpreted by the majority of the House of Lords as equivalent to: 'where the Home Secretary thinks that he has . . . cause to believe', are open to serious objections.

The right to earn a living, according to one's capabilities and training, may be regarded either as an aspect of liberty (to develop one's personality) or as an aspect of property, if property, as it must, is no longer defined as a compound of tangible, real, and personal assets, but the totality of all rights and interests capable of legal protection which have an economic value. Whatever its characterization, the right to earn a living has barely been articulated as an essential value to be protected in the administrative process, although its protection is for the ordinary citizen, the 'common man', perhaps a matter of greater practical importance than any of the traditionally articulated values. If this is a value worthy of protection in contemporary democracy, the unchecked power of Congressional committees, government departments, or even private employers,[30] to deprive persons of their livelihood and employability in the field of their training and skill, is truly 'arbitrary' power. So is the delegation, by indirection, of the power to deprive a person of employment in his trade to labour unions which effectively control employment in a particular industry.[31]

From the same angle, the steady – and largely unnoticed because scattered – growth of licensing powers over a multitude of professional and commercial activities, not by public authority, but by interested groups, is a serious interference with the right to earn a living[32] unless checked by constitutional tests or public supervision.

While liberty and property should thus be interpreted not in the light of conditions and ideas prevalent a century ago, but of those of the mid twentieth century, the right of property is subject to reinterpretation in other respects. In the light of official legal policy, as embodied not only in the Sherman Antitrust Act, the statutory power of the Federal Trade Commission, and ancillary legislation in the United States, but also more recently in the anti-trust laws of England, Germany, and other States,[33] the protection of property certainly must find its limitation in the concentration of excessive economic power. Again, the statutory acknowledgement of legal values, such as soil conservation or the husbanding of agricultural resources or of water resources, does mean a different adjustment of values, and, therefore, a different conception of 'arbitrary' than would have been the case a century ago.

Continental textbooks on administrative law, while hardly sufficiently elaborate on the subject, stress certain elementary *Rechtsgrundsätze*[34] or *principes généraux du droit*[35] which must guide administrative decision. First among these basic principles stands that of equality. This, of course, is general, not without ambiguity and subject to many qualifications. Yet, it is of great practical significance, often insufficiently appreciated in the decision of problems of administrative law. Procedurally, the principle of equality means non-discrimination in the treatment of persons or groups entitled to equal consideration, e.g. in the awarding of building licences, trading permits, or admission to educational establishments.[36] It must be based on comparable standards; there must be no discrimination between equals, whether based on personal vindictiveness, pecuniary interests, or political prejudices not sanctioned by the law. All such actions are aspects of abuse of power (*détournement de pouvoir*).

A consideration of basic principles governing administrative law would not, of course, by itself, solve a multitude of problems which, as stated before, depend on a delicate balance of conflicting interests and values. It would, however, give a firmer background, and a greater sense of direction to many decisions of administrative agencies, administrative tribunals, and ordinary courts, which, today, seem to vacillate all too often between general platitudes and pure empiricism.

But even if we attain such sense of direction in the basic principles of administrative law, in the great majority of cases an administrative body exercises powers given to it by statute in good faith, without discrimination, for a public purpose. It is in these cases that the problem of the limits of administrative discretion emerges in all its complexity.

Despite the vast differences in the organization of administrative services, and in the structure and scope of legal remedies against administrative action, this problem presents itself, basically in similar terms, to any system – civil law or common law – which attempts to balance the necessary freedom of governmental decision-making with the protection of basic individual rights.

The general common-law approach was put tersely in a recent lecture by an eminent British judge[37]:

Broadly speaking, the courts will investigate and give relief in respect of acts of the executive which are shown to be bad in law or to have been done without or in excess of authority, or in bad faith, or because of irrelevant or extraneous considerations; but they will not revise decisions lawfully taken or interfere by substituting one view of the merits for another.

In the United States, where the main emphasis is on the scope of review from a multitude of administrative agencies constituted by statute, a similar principle is expressed with a different emphasis in a judgement of the Supreme Court[38]:

Our duty is at an end when we find that the action of the Commission was based on findings supported by evidence, and was made pursuant to authority granted by Congress.

After a much longer preoccupation with organized administrative justice and in the light of many hundreds of authoritative decisions on the problem, contemporary Continental authorities on administrative law have given up any attempts to define the limit of administrative discretion in more than a very few broad formulas. While the leading modern French textbook[39] enumerates five major limits of discretionary power (lack of competence, fault of form, violation of the law, incorrect motivation, and, most important and vaguest of all, failure to act 'in the public interest'), modern German doctrine is content with three[40]: first, error about the existence or limits of the exercise of discretion, or their conscious

violation; second, error about legitimate motives, or their deliberate neglect; third, faults in the appreciation of the relevant facts.

From these broad formulations we gain little more than the insight that there are certain limits to the freedom of administrative
action. But under what circumstances a particular administrative
action has been 'improperly motivated', or neglected to be guided
by the 'public interest', cannot be ascertained from general formulas. To be sure, the multiplicity of administrative contacts with
individual interests is infinite, and it increases steadily as the activities of governments and other public authorities spread out,
horizontally and vertically. Regulatory and supervisory activities
range from the control of sanitary standards, in houses and factories,
of the uses of land, the control of floods, dikes, forests, to the public
supervision, by way of arbitration or active regulation, of labour
conditions. On the other hand, governments, municipal authorities,
and public corporations make long-term contracts for supplies and
services, and they operate a large number of public utilities and, in
some cases, industries. With the multiplicity of functions, the
possibilities of friction between public and private interests increase.
It is not surprising that the growing flood of decisions on the proper
limits of administrative discretion, by semi-judicial agencies,
ordinary courts, or administrative tribunals, should be full of contradictions and inconsistencies, that more and more we have to
look to the courts' experience and good sense in the delicate adjustment of conflicting values and interests in the individual case at
hand.

Yet it is not necessary to lose sight of the wood for the trees. It is
possible to provide general guides, beyond the vague formulations
of the above-mentioned authorities, without ignoring that there is
always an element of choice, and therefore of creative law-making,
in each individual decision that applies general criteria.

First, it is accepted in the theory and practice of all States that
certain major policy functions of government, especially in the
international sphere, cannot be subject to judicial control. The
most articulate discussion of the scope of this immunity has been in
French law, around the concept of '*actes de gouvernement*'.[41] The scope
of this once wide exemption has been greatly curtailed in recent
times, but it still includes *actes diplomatiques*. While there is some
controversy on the exact scope of this immunity of governmental
action in international affairs,[42] it would seem to correspond to the
scope of governmental prerogative conceded by the common-law
courts to the actions of government in international affairs. A well-

known English illustration is the *Amphitrite* case,[43] where, during the First World War, a Swedish ship was seized by the British Government, despite an undertaking given by the British Legation at Stockholm that, by carrying a cargo of at least 60 per cent approved goods, the ship would be released. In rejecting the claim for damages Rowlatt J. held that an 'intention to act in a particular way in a certain event' could not be made binding on the government. The rationalization of this freedom of action has been formulated as 'the inability of a person to whom a discretion is entrusted to bind himself as to any future exercise of it'.[44]

To the exemptions concerning government actions essentially in the sphere of international relations French practice and doctrine add a certain, not very precisely defined, category of actions concerning 'public security'.[45] This has been steadily narrowed down from its formerly very wide scope, and now appears to be confined to actions dealing with very major disturbances, such as war, states of siege, but probably no longer anti-flood or anti-epidemic measures. There is less and less disposition to grant the executive a blank cheque, in the form of emergency powers, unless they are clearly defined by statute. In recent United States practice a certain parallel to this development may be seen in the *Steel Seizure* cases,[46] where the Supreme Court refused to legalize a presidential executive order directing the Secretary of Commerce to seize the steel industry on behalf of the Government (during a prolonged strike), alleged to be inherent in the functions of the President as the Supreme Executive. In Great Britain the last World War showed a far-reaching substitution of statutory emergency legislation for common-law prerogative powers,[47] where the majority of the House of Lords, over the vigorous dissent of Lord Atkin, construed the Home Secretary's emergency power to detain aliens 'which he had reasonable cause to suspect . . .' as being a decision to be taken in his own discretion, and not therefore reviewable.

The second category of governmental exemptions from legal responsibility is far more important in the everyday practice of administration. It concerns what is variously called the 'planning' or 'policy-making' decisions of governments and other public authorities. In its law-making, planning, or policy decisions, government must not be hampered by contractual or tort liabilities. In the former sphere this means that either a commitment given to a private individual cannot be construed as contractual or that the contract will be superseded by superior considerations of public policy.

It has long been held by the Court of Claims that the United States when sued as a contractor cannot be held liable for an obstruction to the performance of the particular contract resulting from its public and general acts as a sovereign.[48]

The problem is well illustrated by some recent English decisions. In *Ransom and Luck* v. *Surbiton B. C.*[49] a local authority had, under the then effective Town and Country Planning Act, given permission for interim development to land owners, subject to certain conditions laid down in agreements between the owners and the local authority. After the war, acting under a new Town and Country Planning Act, the Minister included the area in the so-called Greater London Plan and withheld permission for further development, although the plaintiffs had already laid out some money for the construction of sewers. The Court of Appeal held that the Planning Authority could not bargain away its statutory powers of planning conferred on it by a statute in the public interest. Consequently, the agreements into which the authority had entered were not construed as being contractual and, in any case, subject to the overriding purpose of the statute as a whole. Similarly, another decision of the Court of Appeal, a few years later,[50] held that the City of London Corporation could not impair its powers of regulation as a health authority by a private contract, and that, therefore, the exercise of these powers rendered the further performance of the contract impossible, without attaching to the public authority any liability for breach of contract.

In the sphere of tort the problem has become acute in the interpretation of the 'discretionary' exemption from tort liability in the United States Federal Torts Claims Act[51] by a confusing trilogy of decisions. The Supreme Court held the U.S. Government not liable for a disastrous explosion in Texas City caused by the negligence of various government agencies and officials in planning, manufacturing, storing, and fighting the explosion of fertilizer-grade ammonium nitrate used as part of a foreign-aid programme.[52] Some years later the Court held the Government liable for damages resulting from failure of a lighthouse light, due to negligent maintenance of the light by the coast-guard.[53] More recently, the Court again held the Government liable for negligence in the fighting of a forest fire by the U.S. Forest Service.[54]

One aspect of the reasoning in the *Dalehite* decision is of basic importance to the present discussion. The Supreme Court refused to hold the Government liable for negligence in the manufacture of the explosive materials on the ground that 'the decisions held culpable were all responsibly made at a planning rather than operational level and involved considerations more or less important to the practicability of the Government's fertilizer programme'.[55]

In the view of a leading American authority on administrative law,[56] 'the concept of "a planning rather than operational level" is important and may be destined to become a landmark in law development'.

From this antithesis of 'planning' and 'operational' activities we can draw certain conclusions which should help to clarify the often extremely confusing interpretations by both British and American courts.

The sound kernel of the 'planning' exemption not only for federal and state governments but also for other public authorities, such as municipal corporations, catchment boards, and others, is that they must have freedom to exercise a choice entrusted to them for the execution of their functions, and not be hampered by subsequent court judgements on the wisdom of such decision. Without such freedom of movement any effective administration would be paralysed. If, for example, a public authority, limited in its budget and personnel, has been given a discretion to repair breaches in dykes,[57] to undertake a lighthouse service,[58] or to fix wages of municipal employees 'as they think fit',[59] it is certainly not for any court to substitute its own judgement *ex post* on the policy considerations governing the exercise of this discretion. Against this principle English courts appear to have sinned more frequently than American courts. The high-water mark is still the decision of the House of Lords in *Roberts* v. *Hopwood*, where a London local authority had exercised its statutory power 'to fix wages as they think fit' by granting a minimum wage to all employees, without distinction of sex. The House of Lords confirmed the surcharge imposed by the District Auditor on the councillors. It rejected the very conception of a basic minimum wage for all employees as not being a reward for labour.[60] It also considered the weekly minimum wage of £4 as grossly extravagant. Lord Atkinson said that the council 'allowed themselves to be guided in preference by some eccentric principles of Socialist philanthropy, or by a feminist ambition to secure the equality of the sexes in the matter of wages in the world of labour'.[61] In order to translate this outburst of political prejudice into legal reasoning the House had to interpolate the word 'reasonably' into the text of the statute, contrary to all canons of statutory construction.[62]

There was reason to hope that the *Roberts* v. *Hopwood* approach

had given way to a wider conception of the relations between administrative discretion and judicial supervision.[63] Unfortunately, a
more recent decision of the Court of Appeal[64] is reminiscent of the
*Roberts* attitude. The Birmingham Corporation was authorized by
statute to maintain and operate its transport undertaking and to
'charge such fares as it thought fit', subject to certain conditions
with which the corporation had complied. With the consent of the
licensing authority, it decided to provide free travelling facilities at
certain hours for a limited class of aged men and women, to be
financed out of the general rate fund. The Court of Appeal held this
action to be *ultra vires*, with the following reasoning:

> We think it is clearly implicit in the legislation, that while it was left
> to the defendants to decide what fares should be charged within any
> prescribed statutory maxima for the time being in force, the undertaking
> was to be run as a business venture, or, in other words, that fares fixed
> by the defendants at their discretion, in accordance with ordinary
> business principles, were to be charged.

Just as the House of Lords in the earlier case had read the word
'reasonably' into the unqualified discretion granted by statute, so
the Court of Appeal in the later case read 'ordinary business principles' into the statutory power to charge fares as the local authority,
with the consent of the licensing authority thought fit. It would be
difficult to find any guidance in the court's judgement on the meaning of 'ordinary business principles' and, in particular, on the point
at which differential fares would cease to be permissible as 'giving
away rights of free travel'.[65] It may, of course, be that the recent
decision of the Court of Appeal, like many other judgements, was an
indirect way to grant something like a regular appeal against
decisions of administrative authorities.[66] But it is both against the
tradition of the courts and detrimental to the development of a
healthy relationship between administrative authorities and supervisory courts to distort clear statutory language so as to substitute
half-baked policy advice by the court for the decisions of the elected
body – on a national or local level. The distinction drawn in *Dalehite*,
though difficult to apply with precision in individual cases, is a sound
one. The choices between alternative policies, provided they remain within the clear framework of administrative powers, are not
a matter for review by courts which are not responsible either to the
elector or to the superior administrative authorities for the policy
principles that they enunciate.

If the courts have thus, on more than one occasion, confused administrative action and discretion by policy interferences, they have on the other hand, been often remarkably, though confusedly, liberal in the protection of public authorities from legal liability, where no such immunity should or needed to be granted.

The principle of equality which, as we have seen, is a cornerstone of administrative justice, demands that public authorities be held liable for interference with legitimate interests of citizens, unless such liability would impede the overriding needs of public service. Where, in other words, public authorities engage in transactions with private citizens through contractual commitments, or where they interfere with their interests through tortious conduct, they should be held liable unless principles of superior validity prevent it. Such a view does emphatically not mean an acceptance of the dichotomy of 'governmental' and 'proprietary' or 'non-governmental' functions. That such a distinction is both bad in principle and incapable of practical application will be shown later in this chapter.[67] It is the above-mentioned distinction between the 'planning' and the 'operational' level which furnishes a guide. Many decisions, both in the British and the American jurisdictions, have entirely failed to make a distinction between: (*a*) the exercise of an administrative discretion as such which, as discussed earlier, should not be reviewable, and (*b*) the manner of carrying out an administrative decision after the discretion has been exercised. The latter should be subject to general principles of legal liability. For this reason the argument of the Supreme Court in the *Dalehite* opinion was unsound, in so far as it denied liability for negligence in firefighting by public employees. The phrase that the Federal Torts Claims Act 'did not change the normal rule that an alleged failure or carelessness of public firemen does not create private actionable rights' begs the question.[68] This reasoning was entirely, and rightly, abandoned in the two later decisions of the Court, which held the coast-guard liable for negligent maintenance of a lighthouse service which they need or need not have undertaken in the first place, and held the United States Forest Service liable for negligence in the fighting of fires once they had undertaken the responsibility of doing so.

The correct test was formulated by Lord Greene M.R., in a judgement by the English Court of Appeal, which cleared up the confusions of a large number of wartime decisions on the question whether local authorities, absolved during the last war from their normal duty to light streets and simultaneously equipped with power to build air-raid shelters, were absolved from legal responsibility for accidents happening in the blackout to pedestrians, cyclists, and motorists[69]:

The question, therefore, in any given case appears to resolve itself into this – does the statute, on its true construction, in authorizing the act in question, exclude the duty of taking care in its performance?

The true view, in my opinion, is that the date of the erection of an obstruction and the purposes for which it is intended to be used are (apart from some special circumstances or some special language in the statute) both immaterial; that the duty to take reasonable care to prevent danger to the public is present throughout: that so long as the streets are properly lit the duty is *ipso facto* performed: but that when the street lighting is suspended, either as the result of lighting restrictions or (in cases where street lighting is optional) as the result of the local authority's decision to extinguish the street lamps or as the result of a break-down in the lighting system it becomes the duty of the local authority to take such steps to safeguard the public by special danger lights or otherwise, as in the circumstances of the case are reasonably possible.[70]

This decision makes a clear distinction between the planning or policy level – where discretion must be unhampered, unless the statute imposes a clear public or private duty to act – and the operational level – where the duties of care and the standards to be demanded of public authority must, in the public interest, be equal to those demanded of private citizens.

The consistent application of this distinction would eliminate many unjust decisions based on a wrong theory: it would obviate the need to resort to spurious distinctions such as that between 'governmental' and 'non-governmental' activities; it would, at the same time, preserve the inequalities between government and governed, where they are justified by the necessities of public service.

# 12

# Government Liability, Administrative Discretion, and the Individual

## SOME LESSONS FROM THE CONTINENT

In the major countries of continental Europe the progress of the *Rechtsstaat* idea, combined with the all but universal recognition of a separate system of administrative law and jurisdiction, promoted the principle of governmental legal responsibility at a time when the common-law jurisdictions were still firmly caught in the web of feudal government immunities. On the one hand, the *Rechtsstaat* principle demanded that governments and other public authorities should, as far as possible, be held liable on a basis comparable with that of private law. On the other hand, the gradual elaboration of the distinctive principles of administrative law led to the early recognition of inherent differences in the position of public authorities and private individuals, especially through the development of the *contrat administratif* in French jurisprudence, but also through the development of distinctive principles of governmental liability outside contract.

## Liability in Contract

The famous *Blanco* case of 1873,[1] which held that damages against the central administration were within the exclusive jurisdiction of the administrative courts, set the Conseil d'État free to develop its own judge-made body of rules of administrative liability. One of its most important creations was the development of legal characteristics of administrative transactions. Public authorities are now held in French law to be able to engage in transactions, either on a private-law basis (*gestions privées*) – in which case they are subject to civil jurisdiction and the principles of private law – or by way of a public-law contract, a *contrat administratif*, which is compounded of elements of contract and inequalities held to be inherent in the concept of public service. A public authority may, for example, contract for the services of radio performers or the supply of uniforms, or the purchase of paving stones in the form of a civil or an administrative contract. Normally, but not necessarily, the contracting for the execution of typical public-service functions, such as water supply or electricity grids, or sanitary services will indicate an administrative contract. In the summary formulation of a recent English comparative study on the subject:

What is necessary is, it seems, to contemplate the whole surroundings, the parties, the nature of the administrative organization with which the contract is made, the nature of the service, and the terms of the contract itself and the conditions on which it is made. In the last resort it seems that it is the terms of the contract which will decide the issue, provided that they are operative terms. The test may sound uncertain but probably the appearance is more uncertain than the reality, and in the ordinary cases there will be little doubt. In borderline cases doubt will remain whatever test is chosen. [2]

It may suffice to add to this summary a reference to the two most recent decisions of the Conseil d'État on this subject. [3] Where the administration had contracted with a private individual for the food supplies to a repatriation centre for foreign refugees the contract was held to be an administrative one – whether or not it contained terms specifically derogating from the provisions of civil law, [4] since the contract had, for its direct object, the execution of a public service, namely, the repatriation of foreign refugees. On the other hand, a contract between the State and a transport company for the handling of customs, transit, and transport of certain merchandise was held not to be a *marché de fourniture*, and therefore a *contrat administratif*, but a contract of private law. The reasoning was, first, that the contract did not contain any *clause exorbitante du droit*, i.e. that it was formulated in the manner of a private contract, and, second, that, although concluded for the purpose of a public service, the object of the contract was not the very execution by a private party of the public service. The fundamental characteristic of a *contrat administratif* is the recognition of certain unilateral powers of control by the administration in the public interest. The demands of the public service empower the administrative authority to carry out continuous supervision over the execution of the contract. To ensure this continuity of execution the administration has certain unilateral powers: to suspend, vary, or rescind the contract, to transfer it to another party, or to take it over itself (*mise en régie*). [5] Not only does the administrative authority have the right to interfere unilaterally in the contract; it has the duty to do so, because it is responsible for the public service. Hence, consumers or other interested parties may bring an action to compel the administration to exercise its powers and sue for damages for its refusal to do so (a kind of mandamus). [6] Moreover, the contract is always subject to the changing needs of the public service, '*suivant les besoins sociaux, économiques du moment*'.[7] Thus, a long-term concession for street lighting by gas may be converted into a demand for lighting by electricity if this is required by modern technical developments and public needs.[8] If the contractor is unable to fulfil the changed conditions the contract may be terminated or transferred to another contractor. However, the contractor is entitled to a full indemnity in any case of variation. The private party has '*ce que l'on appelle l'équilibre financier de son contrat*'.[9] This means not only an indemnity for the interference other than for fault on the part of the contractor, with the contract by the administrative authority; it means also – by one of the most famous pieces of judicial law-making evolved in any modern system – an equitable adjustment of the remuneration contractually agreed upon, if the equilibrium of the contract has been upset by economic causes beyond the control of the parties, and the increasing burden on the contractor, caused thereby, was not foreseeable at the time of the conclusion of the contract. This is the theory of *imprévision* first established by the Conseil d'État in the *Gaz de Bordeaux* case in 1916,[10] and since then steadily developed through the vicissitudes of inflation, war, shortages of materials, and the other major economic disturbances that have characterized European history since the First World War.[11]

The elasticity of the contract, the restrictions on *pacta sunt servanda*, are not, therefore, entirely a unilateral matter. If the public authority has many prerogatives and unilateral powers which would be improper in a private contract, the private contractor enjoys, on the other hand, the recognition of variability of terms in his favour, where the circumstances so demand.[12]

The *contrat administratif* is, in fact, dominated by the principles of the continuity of the public service, from which flows the concept of the relation between authority and contractor as one of cooperation. The contractor is an instrumentality for the execution of public services and functions. As such, he may incur graver risks than the private contractor, because in undertaking the supply of a long-term service or commodity he subjects himself to the above-mentioned variations or vicissitudes demanded by the public interest. On the other hand, it is in the interest of the public that the contractor should be enabled to supply the contracted goods or services satisfactorily; that he should not go bankrupt; that he should be able to pay his workmen adequately; and that he should be in a position to purchase the essential raw materials. Hence, the theory of *imprévision* – now usually replaced by specific terms of adjustment in the conditions which form the basis of the contracts – and the concept of the administrative contract as basically different from the civil-law contract, not indeed in all respects – for in the absence of a public code of contract there is, of course, reference to many provisions of the civil law – but in some essential respects.

While the concept of a distinctive public-law contract is also well developed in Belgium, Italy,[13] and some Latin-American countries influenced by French law, it is far less developed in Germany, where the emphasis is still on the unilateral character of the '*Verwaltungsakt*'. Thus, the granting of concessions and licences – a typical illustration of the *contrat administratif* – is generally regarded as a unilateral administrative act. However, arrangements for the use of public utilities (such as electricity or telephones) may be concluded in the form of a '*Vertrag*', an agreement between the public authority and the individual. The main field of application of the public-law contract in the German system is the regulation of relations between the numerous persons of public law, such as regional, municipal, or functional authorities which abound in the German administrative system, contrasting with the centralization of French administration.[14] The *öffentlichrechtliche Vertrag* does not, like the *contrat administratif*, blend administrative and contractual elements in the relations between public authority and the citizen. It is characterized by the coordination of the parties, which are administrative authorities.[15]

It has been rightly observed[16] that there is far more similarity to the French conception in modern Anglo-American legal developments, although the disinclination to recognize the dualism of private and public law still prevents, especially in England, clear recognition and elaboration of the concept of public or administrative contract.[17]

In American law there is growing recognition of the 'government contract' as a distinct category.[18] Now that liability and actionability of governments in contract have at last been widely recognized in the major common-law jurisdictions,[19] the legal analysis of government contracts is a matter of growing importance.

The admission that English legal practice and theory is hardly yet aware of government contracts as in any way distinct from private contracts does not, of course, mean that there is not, in fact, such a category. But this branch of the law is hidden in standard conditions of governments, where the real 'living law' of today is to be found.[20] From these standard conditions, the individual contractor is no more able to depart in his bid for government contracts than an individual insurer can modify the standard terms of insurance contracts, or the passenger of an ocean liner or an aeroplane can modify the conditions of transportation. Much of the law of the *droit administratif* will be found in these standard terms: the continuing power of the government officer to give directions as to the carrying out of the work; the unilateral power of the government authority to require alterations in the work done under the contract, subject to adjustment of the contract price; repayment of liquidated damages in the event of default; and, most important of all, the liberty of the Government to terminate the contract at any time by notice in writing, subject to compensation for work done.[21] In fact, the terms of compensation for the contract in the event of termination by the Government are more favourable to the Government than those elaborated by the French courts. The default clause of the Standard Building Contract, used by local authorities in Britain, provides that, given certain stated conditions of default, the public employer may determine the employment of the contractor by registered notice.

Although it has frequently been said that government contracts are governed by general principles of contract law,[22] recent students of the subject have pointed out the distinctive features of the government contract in terms that show the similarity of problems and solutions imposed by the functions of modern government on systems as fundamentally different as French and American law.

To begin with, a government contract is a contract of adhesion, that is to say, a contract with standard terms and conditions, prepared by one party and offered to the other on a take-it-or-leave-it basis. The consensual element is reduced to a minimum. . . . Obviously, principles of general contract law, based on theories of freedom of contract, can have little application to such a clause.

Also, a government contract is apt to differ markedly from a private contract in the very feature which lies at the heart of the traditional contract relationship: the concept of a voluntary assumption of risk, agreed to by parties dealing at arm's length. Many government contracts are nothing of the sort. Between the two extremes of the simple purchase order and the cost-reimbursement-no-fee research contract is every variety of pricing and risk-taking arrangement. . . . Hanging over all government contracts and sub-contractors is the prospect of renegotiation to recapture excessive profits. In short, while the risk element is still present (the Government does not insure contractors against loss), the simple bargain-exchange of the typical private contract has been transformed into something much more complicated. Risk of loss and prospect of profit have become interwoven into a whole complex of tangled relationships, which only the lawyer and cost-accountant can fully understand.[23]

Federal contracts in the United States used to contain provisions that the decision of the federal contracting agent would be final as to disputes over questions of fact,[24] or, in some cases, as to questions of law as well.[25] Such clauses have recently been outlawed by statute which provides that final decisions by the administrative authority to the contract on questions of law are no longer permitted, and that findings of fact can be set aside whenever 'fraudulent or capricious or arbitrary or so grossly erroneous as necessarily to imply bad faith, or . . . not supported by substantial evidence'.[26] Apart from the outlawing of this particularly obnoxious form of inequality, there is no doubt that, despite a general statement that the contractual relations between the United States and contractors are governed by rules of law applicable to contracts between individuals,[27] 'there are so many exceptions to this generalization . . . that government-contract law is often treated as a special field of its own'.[28] This applies, for example, to the necessarily different and stricter rules about agency and authority to contract on behalf of the government; or to the problems created by governmental action which causes impossibility of performance. Here, the dual capacity of one of the contracting parties, as a government taking action binding on all its citizens, and as a party to an individual contract between itself and a private person, becomes relevant. Such problems, known in French jurisprudence as *'le fait du prince'*, are no less relevant in common-law jurisdictions, for the dual position of public authority is the same. Nor is the answer to the problem any different. In the United States the general rule is that the Government is said to act in its sovereign capacity whenever its acts are public and general in their application, so that they are not considered as directed against the other contracting party alone, and therefore entail no sanction for breach of contract. But it has, rightly, been suggested that, where the Government, for reasons of general public policy, creates conditions that make the performance of the contract impossible, it should be held liable to pay the fair value of the benefits received in quasi contract[29]; this does not affect the basic fact that government contracts are not just another species of private contracts.

The fact that the common law recognizes in theory only one type of contract has, however, another consequence: in the legal systems that know both private and public-law contracts a commitment given by a public authority to a private party, under conditions which make it justifiable to assume a legal commitment, can be allocated to the sphere of either private or public-law contract. The remedies for the other party are, as we have seen, not identical, but they are substantial in either case, and, in some respects, the position of the private party in the *contrat administratif* is more favourable than that of a party to a private contract.

In the common law, however, the alternative is between contract according to the common law or no legal tie at all. Hence, common-law courts often find themselves in the difficult position of having to hold public authorities, especially State governments or municipal authorities, in circumstances where no standard conditions apply, either liable for contract under common-law rules, or not held by any contractual commitment at all.

Reference has already been made to the *Amphitrite* case, which may, however, be justified as dealing with the freedom of government in matters of international policy, especially in wartime. A contrary tendency, to make governments liable for promises made by the authorized officers to individuals, was encouraged by the decision of Denning J. (as he then was) in *Robertson* v. *Minister of Pensions*.[30] The Minister of Pensions attempted to revoke the acceptance by the War Office of liability to pay a disability pension to an officer injured in the war, partly on the ground that it amounted to a fetter on the future executive action of the Crown. In his judgement, Denning J. sought to liken the formal promise of a government authority to an individual to a contractual commitment not revocable by unilateral Crown action. Reference has also been made to the decision of the Court of Appeal, which found that the Minister of Town and Country Planning could not be hampered in the exercise of his planning functions by the existence of a previous contractual commitment of a local authority, although, alternatively, the court suggested that that commitment had not been of a contractual nature at all. On the other hand, in another post-war case,[31] a local education authority which, on the outbreak of the last war, had promised employees joining the forces certain pay increments which they would have received in the ordinary way, were held by the Court of Appeal to have 'entered into a contract voluntarily, and when they made payments under such a contract, they did so in pursuance of the contract, and not in the execution of any public duty'. However, another decision of the same court denied that a local authority could be hampered in the exercise of its public-health functions by contractual ties.[32] Unquestionably, many of these decisions were prompted by individual considerations of equity and fairness. Nevertheless, the situation remains confused, and the state of the authorities most uncertain.[33] While the *contrat administratif*, as developed by the Conseil d'État, has many features which cannot be easily detached from the peculiar structure and traditions of the French legal system, the case for open recognition, and appropriate regulation, of the contract between government and other public authorities on the one part, and private individuals on the other, is overwhelming.[34] The Renegotiation Acts in the United States, which were the reaction to situations created by wartime contracts of the *Bethlehem Steel* case type,[35] underline the necessity to regard the contracts made between government and private parties in a mixed economy, often in fields of defence and other matters of vital public interest, as cooperative efforts subject to certain legal rules – like partnerships and other social compacts – rather than as contracts subject to rules shaped centuries ago for entirely different conditions and social systems.

Some of the constitutional and other legal problems of contracts to which governments are parties (such as authorization by Congress or the necessity of parliamentary approval for expenditure[36]) can probably be avoided where a semi-autonomous government corporation can take the place of government departments.[37]

## The Legal Status of the Public Servant

Brief reference should be made to the complex problem of the legal status of the public servant. In this field, too, the insufficient elaboration of public-law relationships as being distinctly legal in character, but different from civil-law relationships, has created, and still continues to cause, in the common-law jurisdictions, an unsatisfactory mixture of lingering feudal concepts, public law concepts, and civil law concepts.[38]

Generally, it may be a fair summary of many conflicting and uncertain decisions to say that, both in Britain and the United States, a civil servant, well below the level of policy-making or other senior officers, may be dismissed at pleasure, as an exercise of what, in Britain, is still the prerogative of the Crown, and in the United States, the general executive power of the President.[39] The relatively few subsequent decisions dealing with this point seem to be inconclusive in both systems.[40] Much uncertainty prevails on the point to what extent central governments as well as other public authorities may exclude the power of arbitrary dismissal by contract, although in Britain at least, statutory authorites (i.e. in particular local authorities) do not share the privileged position of the

Crown.[41] On the other hand, it appears to be established in the U.S., but not in Britain, that a public servant may sue for accrued pay, a question obviously different in principle from the question of dismissibility.[42]

It should be added that the actual position of public servants, especially in regard to pay, pensions, etc., is now largely regulated by statute, and in practice more secure than would appear from the general legal rules governing civil servants in the common-law systems.[43] The problem of dismissibility at will remains, however, one of great significance, not only in theory, but also of practical importance in times of public nervousness and preoccupation with security and loyalty considerations.[44] Again, the position is dramatically different in the Continental jurisdictions, long schooled in the dichotomy of civil and administrative law. It may be that the very elaborate structure of *Beamtenrecht*, characteristic of the German legal system,[45] is to some extent due to the high status of the *Beamte* in that country. But the principle of statutory regulation of the status, rights, and duties of the civil servant is also implemented in France.[46] The statutory regulations in both countries amount to a complete code defining the obligations and rights of the public servant.

## Governmental Liability and Tort

For Dicey, the principle that the government servant was personally liable for wrongs committed in the exercise of his public functions – coupled with the then prevailing immunity of the Crown from any corresponding liability – was a vindication of the principle of equality before the law.

> With us every official, from the Prime Minister down to a constable or a collector of taxes, is under the same responsibility for every act done without legal justification as any citizen.[47]

Today, the very opposite philosophy may be said to predominate among the students of this problem.[48] The scope, as well as the delicacy of the multitudinous functions of public service that affect private interests, is seen to be demanding freedom of action unhampered by fears of personal liability, which could, in many cases, ruin the individual officer concerned, and thus would lead to a general attitude of excessive caution and passivity, detrimental to the public interest. In fact, the whole doctrine of the common law has long ceased to have much vitality, mainly by the exemption, either through traditional 'prerogatives' of the Crown, or, more frequently in recent times, through the scope of discretionary powers granted to public officials by the relevant statutes.[49] A case like *Miller* v. *Horton*,[50] where a public-health officer vested with statutory authority to destroy diseased animals was held liable for the destruction of the plaintiff's horse which he wrongly believed to be infected with the disease, is difficult to imagine today. But, of course, the extension of the personal immunity of public officers makes all the more urgent the problem of the corresponding extension of governmental responsibility.

Again, the problem of State liability for tortious actions – and, to a considerable extent, for interferences with private interests beyond the realm not only of fault, but of tort altogether – has long ceased to be a major juristic problem in Continental jurisdictions, although a number of new problems has arisen through the very recognition of State liability. Contemporary French law is based on the distinction between *faute de service* and *faute personnelle*. The public official is personally liable for a wrong committed by him *hors de l'exercice de ses fonctions*.[51] This is construed fairly widely, for personal fault includes not only such action clearly 'outside the scope of employment' as the use of a government motor-car for personal business,[52] but also any act characterized as malicious or grossly negligent, e.g. commitment, in error, of persons to a mental instead of an ordinary hospital, or a hospital for prostitutes.[53] The public official is thus not personally immune from liability, even for acts which might be construed by Anglo-American courts as being, however objectionably, committed in the exercise of public functions. Personal liability is, in French jurisprudence, in a sense a penalty for such actions as are so clearly unworthy of public office as not to be properly attributable.[54] But in the overwhelming majority of cases, including even most cases of excess of statutory power,[55] the personal liability of the individual official – before the ordinary civil courts – is replaced by the liability of the State before the administrative courts.[56]

The development in German law has been somewhat similar, under parallel and partly overlapping provisions of the German Civil Code[57] and of both the Weimar Constitution and the Bonn *Grundgesetz* of 1949 (art. 34). Under these provisions, the State is liable to a third party for any delictual conduct of a public official in the exercise of a public function, and in violation of an official duty owed to a third party. In the case of negligent conduct, State liability is, in principle, subsidiary, although this direct liability of the official plays no greater part in modern conditions than it does in the Anglo-American jurisdictions by virtue of the discretionary statutory exemptions. Contrary to French law, however, all actions against the State, arising from liability for violation of duty to a private party, must be brought before the civil, not the administrative, courts.[58]

The precise delimitation between acts committed in exercise of a public function for service, and those not connected with such service, with an intermediate category, in French law, of 'service-connected' torts, have, of course, been the subject of innumerable decisions and controversies. This, however, is not a criticism against the principle and the distinction as such – which only illustrates the basic difficulty of applying any general definition to concrete cases.[59] The principle that responsibility for illegal interference with the protected interests of the citizen is primarily a responsibility of the public authority in whose service the officer stands rather than of the individual concerned, is firmly and irrevocably established in the Continental jurisdictions, even though they differ on the allocation of these matters to civil or administrative courts.

The recognition of State liability has, in fact, gone far beyond the traditional fault liability. This is, in part, due to the evolution of the law of tort itself, which, particularly in France, by a creative interpretation of articles 1384 C.C., has adapted the principles prevalent at the beginning of the nineteenth century to the vastly more complex conditions of the industrialized society of the mid-twenties.

However, it is still the prevalent view that, in the sphere of the private law of tort, fault should remain the rule, since it is concerned with the problem of adjustment of a burden between two private parties and that it is still generally a proper principle that, as between two innocent parties, the burden should lie where it falls.[60] But in the field of public-law responsibility, the position is different. As it has been stated in a leading French treatise,[61] damage to private persons arises often from actions taken in the public interest, deliberately. The prejudice caused to the private party is, in such cases, a kind of public charge, which, in accordance with the principle of equality, should not accidentally rest with the one or small number of persons affected by the public measure, but be redistributed among the members of the community, through the responsibility for compensation attached to the public authority.[62] Accordingly, State responsibility under French law has been extended not only to *responsabilité du fait des choses*, i.e. to responsibility for damages arising from dangerous operations,[63] or to movable and immovable objects for which the State ought to assume responsibility, because they are under its control (notably motor-cars) – for these are extensions parallel to those of the civil law by the jurisprudence of the civil courts – or for *risques professionels* – a kind of workmen's compensation principle in public law – but also for what is called the *risque social*,[64] i.e. for public disorders of varying magnitude. In a similar vein, the principle of liability for dangerous activities has, in the field of public law, been extended to the consequences of general measures justified by public necessity – such as ammunition depots[65] – but apt by their very existence to cause damage to various sections of the public field.

Since the Second World War, the jurisdictions of the British Commonwealth[66] have, at last, abolished the privileges which had originated in feudal English doctrine of the immunity of the sovereign. Such doctrine rested basically on an identification of the person of the sovereign with the State; this has never been explicitly abandoned in Britain, where the Government is still exercising its functions in the name of His or Her Majesty. The King as a person is today entirely different from the King as the nominal head of government. The theory of the immunity of the sovereign had, in fact, become a theory that 'government can do no wrong'. The British Crown Proceedings Act of 1947 states: 'the Crown shall be subject to all those liabilities in tort to which, if it were a private person of full age and capacity, it would be subject in respect of torts committed by its servants or agents.'[67] It is furthermore liable for breach of duties of an employer to an employee and for breach of the duties attaching at common law to the ownership, occupation, possession, or control of property. While some difficulties have arisen from the definition of 'agent or servant',[68] the British Act, and those modelled on it in the Commonwealth, can be fairly said to have established government liability in tort on a basis of equality between governors and governed, in so far as the position of government is not inherently different (as, for example, in the substitution of an authorizing order for a writ of execution against the Crown). In particular, the British Act is free from the qualifications which, as will be seen, greatly restrict the scope of the liability of government in the U.S. Federal Tort Claims Act. In so far, for example, as tort liability is, in contemporary English law, strict and not fault liability, government liability will be the same.

However, as an eminent British judge has recently pointed out,[69] the very fact that government liability in tort has been hitched on to private-tort liability, has prevented the courts from 'settling the general nature of the duties owed by the executive to the subject outside the realm of contract'. A subsection provides that no action shall lie against the Crown in respect of torts committed by its servants or agents, 'unless the act or omission would apart from the provisions of this Act, have given rise to this cause of action in tort against that servant or agent or his estate'. This means, according to Lord MacDermott, 'that a plaintiff has to show that, apart from the Act, his loss was due to the negligence of some official of a Ministry who would have been *personally* liable if he had been sued'. There may, however, be cases in which the government should be held responsible to a private person, even though the official acting for it, would not have been so liable, e.g. where a Ministry negligently delays the issue of a trading licence.[70] In other words, there may be public-law duties which find no parallel in the private law of tort. This underlines again the need for the common law to develop a public law, of tort as of contract, not as mere appendix to the private law.

It is one of the great ironies of legal history that British immigrants who left the country in protest against autocracy and oppression, took with them, not only the great principles of the common law, but also those aspects of the common law which were expressions of absolutism and feudalism. After early hesitations,[71] United States courts wholeheartedly embraced the doctrine of sovereign immunity during the nineteenth century, and this doctrine survives to the present day in a great majority of the state jurisdictions, while it has been curtailed, though not abolished, in the federal sphere. Meanwhile, England, whence the doctrine came, has quietly, but firmly, abolished it.

Not only did the American courts introduce the doctrine of sovereign immunity into the republican setting of the United States, but they extended it to municipal corporations, as subdivisions of states, at a time when the decision of Blackburn J. in *Mersey Docks and Harbour Board Trustees* v. *Gibbs*[72] denied its application to statutory authorities. In this manner, public authorities other than organs of the general government of the country were subjected to the ordinary liabilities of the common law. But not so in the United States.

Today, the Federal Tort Claims Act of 1946 recognizes government liability in principle, but subject to certain exceptions of which the exception for claims arising out of wilful torts,[73] for acts or omissions 'based upon the exercise or performance or the failure to exercise or perform a discretionary function or duty on the part of a federal agency or an employee of the Government',[74] and the limitation of liability to claims based on 'negligent or wrongful' acts or omissions, which follows from the limitation of the clause conferring jurisdiction upon the district courts for claims against the United States,[75] are the most important. Of these exceptions, the one limiting tort liability to 'fault' seems unreasonable, in view of the extension of general liability in tort far beyond the fault principle. It is in contrast to the above-mentioned Continental trends towards State liability for dangerous operations and, beyond that, for risk situations created by State action. Nor has this limitation of federal tort liability any parallel in the British corresponding legislation. Without it, the action in *Dalehite*[76] would probably have succeeded. The main difficulty of the 'discretionary' exception is its vagueness, and the consequent uncertainties and vacillations in judicial interpretation, which we have discussed earlier. If, however, as has been suggested here in accordance with the views of Professor Davis,[77] it is interpreted as separating the planning from the operational level, it is a good and, indeed, an inevitable limitation which must be accepted in every legal system.

The position in forty-eight state jurisdictions has been analysed in an exhaustive and informative article.[78] This survey shows that only one state, New York, has all but completely abolished immunity in tort, thus going far beyond the federal legislation. Twelve other states are classed as undertaking responsibility in most cases. In the remaining states – the great majority – tort claims are granted only occasionally, seldom, or not at all.

Finally, the courts have attempted to mitigate the severity of the extension of government immunity to municipal corporations, by introducing a distinction between 'governmental' and 'proprietary' functions, and limiting immunity to the former. This distinction has been the source of unending confusion.[79]

It is hardly necessary to add to the many criticisms of the logical fallacy and practical absurdity of the distinction between 'governmental' and 'non-governmental' functions. Such justification as there exists for it derives from extra-legal considerations: the desire to protect the impecunious small authority from liability.[80] But, as has been stated before, the remedy for such a state of affairs should be administrative and budgetary reorganization, not the shifting of the burden to the helpless victims of particular accidents. In 1955, a majority of the Supreme Court justices described the distinction as a 'quagmire that has long plagued the law of municipal corporations'.[81] The quagmire is well illustrated by one of hundreds of decisions,[82] where the plaintiff had been injured when her hand struck a barbed wire fence while in a swimming pool owned and operated by the City of Richmond. After a careful survey of the cases which have, for example, held the operation of hospitals or the regulation of streets, maintenance of police forces, and the removal of garbage to be governmental functions, while the operation of a wharf and the conducting of public utilities, such as gaslight and sewage systems, is 'proprietary', the court finally held the swimming-pool operation to be 'proprietary', because it could best be compared to the furnishing of water for domestic purposes. Yet, the municipal swimming pool is obviously designed for the promotion of public health.

The distinction is misconceived, and other than arbitrary answers to the question whether a particular activity belongs to the one or the other category are impossible, because the test artificially divides and truncates the ubiquitous functions of public authority which, today, extend to a multitude of businesslike operations that are nevertheless conducted for the general welfare.

Meanwhile, the situation is mitigated by a number of practical devices.[83] The most important ways by which the theoretical severity of government immunity is mitigated in practice are the following: (1) In many cases – such as the Texas City explosion, which was the subject of the *Dalehite* case – private laws are passed granting compensation and assuming liability, often irrespective of fault[84]; (2) a vast number of claims sounding in tort are settled by administrative machinery, through government departments, such as the departments for the Army, the Interior, and the Postmaster-General; (3) employees who are held personally liable, are frequently indemnified by the authority in whose service they are; (4) it is sometimes possible to bring a claim for wrongful injury not under the heading of tort, but under that of 'taking of property', which is subject to just compensation[85]; (5) many of the public authorities take out liability insurance, the terms of which often specifically exclude the defence of sovereign immunity.[86]

Granted all these concessions and mitigations of the harshness of an antiquated principle, the legal situation remains unsatisfactory. The various exceptions depend upon legislative or administrative action, by a multitude of federal, State, and municipal authorities. Compensation is not a matter of law, but of concession. Moreover, a bad legal theory is perpetuated, obscuring an understanding of the greatly changed functions and methods of modern government and entailing the retention of basically misconceived legal criteria, such as the distinction between 'governmental' and 'proprietary' functions.

## Function and Status of the Public Corporation

The steady multiplication of government functions of all kinds, as well as the increasing complexity of carrying out such modern government functions as the operation of vast public utilities, and, in some cases, industries, the provision of hospital and many other social services, or the administration of government loans to business, has, during the present century, led to the development of a new type of public institution, designed to overcome the antithesis of government and business, as it still survives in the judicial distinction between 'governmental' and 'proprietary' or 'business' activities of public authorities. Hence, the public corporation,[87] an institution 'clothed with the power of governments but possessed of the flexibility and initiative of a private enterprise',[88] has, since the end of the First World War, become a familiar device for the organization of public enterprises and services, in many different countries and legal systems.[89]

Both its value and its elasticity can be gauged from the fact that it has been adopted in the Socialist and entirely State-controlled economic system of Soviet Russia as well as in the non-Socialist system of the United States.

The Soviet Union proceeded, only a few years after the Revolution, to develop the institution of the State trusts for the running of major industrial State enterprises. These trusts are constituted as autonomous legal units; they receive their charter from the Supreme Council of National Economy, which also appoints the members of the board; they have two types of capital assets which roughly correspond to the distinction between fixed and floating assets of British company law. The fixed assets belong to the State, the floating assets belong to the trusts. That is to say, they are State property at one remove and can be freely disposed of. The trusts enter into contractual and other legal transactions, and legal disputes between them are settled by special courts which appear to have developed principles of mixed contract and administrative law.

In Germany, France, Italy, and other Continental countries the public corporation appears in two forms. One makes the State or other public authorities a shareholder in a company. The undertaking is organized in the form of a joint-stock company and governed by company law, with the State or other public authorities holding a controlling or substantial interest as shareholders.[90] A more genuine form of public corporation is the West German *Bundesbahn*, now organized as an autonomous public enterprise, or the French *établissements publics*, such as the *Électricité de France* or *les Charbonnages de France*.

In the United States, the development of the public (government) corporation was mainly spurred, first by the necessities of the First World War, and, second, by the economic crisis as well as the new economic philosophy of the 'New Deal' era. The first produced such bodies as the Emergency Fleet Corporation or the Grain Corporation, all of which were liquidated in the course of time. The second produced a considerable variety of agencies, such as the Reconstruction Finance Corporation, the Commodity Credit Corporation, and the U.S. Housing Authority. The most celebrated as well as the most successful of the managerial enterprises is the Tennessee Valley Authority. Since the end of the Second World War, however, renewed political hostility to public enterprise, and, in particular, Congressional jealousy of the success of the T.V.A. – nursed by powerful lobbying from the private power industry – has greatly hindered any further development of public corporations in the United States. It has also led to drastic changes in their legal status, to which reference will be made later. Public corporations are of great importance in the different states. At least one of them, New York, which has over one hundred of them, representing operations of many billions of dollars, has recently produced a systematic study of their status, functions, organization, responsibilities, and financial administration.[91]

It is in Britain and the British Dominions that the public corporation has achieved particular significance. A multitude of enterprises of all kinds are organized in this form: from the British Broadcasting Corporation to the National Coal Board, and the other recently nationalized basic industries; from the Regional Hospital Boards and Management Committees administering the National Health Service to the Australian Forest and Housing Commissions; from the Trans-Australian Airlines, operating in competition with private air services, to the Canadian Hydro-Power Commissions and the Canadian National Railways; from the British Development Corporations, set up under the New Towns Act, to the Australian Repatriation Commission, in charge of the civilian rehabilitation of ex-servicemen. The development of atomic energy for governmental and industrial purposes – in which Britain is far ahead of any other Western country – is in the hands of the Atomic

Energy Authority, another public corporation. In Britain and the British Dominions, which, despite many differences and changes of government, broadly concur in the blending of an extensive social-service State with the preservation of a large degree of private enterprise, the public corporation is regarded as the best way in which to combine the principle of public service and ownership with those of managerial responsibility and financial accountability.

Lastly, the legal form of the public corporation has been adopted by the constitutions of the many functional international agencies created in conjunction with the United Nations Organization. Such institutions as the Food and Agriculture Organization, the World Health Organization, Unesco, the International Monetary Fund, and others may conveniently be termed international public corporations.[92] The six nations of the European Community have formed the European Atomic Authority (Euratom), charged with the development of atomic energy on behalf of this supra-national community. Their constitutions and functions naturally differ somewhat from those of the national corporations, as they are institutions of international law. They share with the national public corporations, however, the essential characteristics of a separate legal personality, and relative autonomy of management (represented by the Director-General and his permanent staff), coupled with responsibility to a political body (the delegates of the member nations) and financial accountability.

Where administrative justice is recognized as an equal and autonomous branch of judicial administration, designed to regulate the
legal relations between public authority and citizen, the problem
of remedies against administrative authorities is relatively simple.

In France the general administrative remedy is a petition filed by
the person seeking review with the appropriate administrative
court, and containing a summary statement of the facts, the grounds
on which relief is sought, and the nature of the relief that is sought.
This remedy is characterized by the utmost absence of technicali-
ties.[1] Although the Conseil d'État requires an individual interest for
any petitioner to have *locus standi*, this has been construed very
liberally, so that, for example, any consumer of a product affected
by administrative action is entitled to petition for review. Delays
and complexities arise mainly from the difficulty, in some cases, of
deciding whether the civil or the administrative tribunals are
competent, a matter over which the *Tribunal des Conflits* has
ultimate jurisdiction, and on which delays may be protracted.

Perhaps even more significant are recent developments in
Germany, where administrative law has been, and to a lesser extent
still is, within the competence of the individual *Länder*. In most of
these, notably in Prussia, administrative remedies were enumer-
ative. Under the impact of Allied Military Government, which, in
this field at least, wisely saw the value of the system of administrative justice and did not attempt to substitute common-law principles, the availability of the remedy has been greatly strengthened,
so that now the so-called *Generalklausel* applies throughout Western
Germany. The *Generalklausel* gives anyone who claims to be injured in his rights by public power a right to legal redress.[2] The
challenge is by petition, either for nullification (*Anfechtungsklage*),
declaration (*Feststellungsklage*), or – and this is a significant innovation – for performance of an administrative act (*Vornahmeklage*).[3]

Like France, Germany has no *actio popularis*, but any injury to a
legitimate interest suffices, and the remedy is widely available.

There is thus no doubt that in the leading Continental systems
there are, at the disposal of the aggrieved individual, simple and

comprehensive remedies which may lead to the annulment of the challenged act, to a declaration of rights, to compensation,[4] or, under the post-war German reform, to a kind of equivalent of mandamus.[5]

By contrast, the development of administrative-law remedies in the common-law sphere proceeded piecemeal from a variety of historical antecedents and, until well into the present century, without any recognition of the character and needs of administrative justice as a separate legal discipline.

An eminent American authority[6] has both characterized and castigated the prevailing common-law system in no uncertain terms:

> For no practical reason, the remedies are plural. A cardinal principle, now and then erratically ignored, denies one method of review when another is adequate. The lines are moved about through discussions of such concepts as judicial, non-judicial, discretionary, and ministerial. These concepts are acutely unfortunate not only because they defy definition but because of the complete folly of using any concepts whatever to divide one remedy from another.
>
> The cure is easy. Establish a single, simple form of proceeding for all review of administrative action. Call it 'petition for review'. Get rid of extraordinary remedies as means of review. Focus attention then on the problems having significance – whether, when, and how much to review.

The cure prayed for by the learned author is, in fact, the law in Continental jurisdictions, such as those of France and Germany. While there is little sign of any response, in either the British or the American jurisdictions, to a simple uniform review procedure as a substitute for the multiplicity of present remedies, there are signs of tendencies to widen the scope of the administrative appeal.

Whether the revocation of a cab-driver's licence by a police commissioner,[7] or the exercise of disciplinary authority by a chief fire officer over a fireman,[8] or the granting of a licence for the Sunday opening of a cinema,[9] or the approval of a limited-dividend housing project by a state agency,[10] or the granting, modification, reversal, or revocation of countless other licences, is 'administrative', 'judicial', or 'quasi-judicial' in character remains deeply uncertain and controversial.[11]

The considerable but uncertain stretching of prerogative remedies, originally designed to cure excesses of jurisdiction, into some kind of appeal against decisions of administrative bodies has been aided by the use of various concepts designed to review the substance of the challenged decision.

First, the courts, in the examination of 'excess of power', have often gone into the so-called 'jurisdictional facts'. Following the lead given by Lord Esher M.R. in *R.* v. *Commissioners for Special Purposes of the Income Tax*,[12] the action of an inferior 'court or tribunal or body' which has wrongly interpreted the facts constituting its jurisdiction (such as the definition of a 'park', 'an employee', or 'fitness for human habitation') has acted in excess of jurisdiction, so that the superior court can reconstrue these concepts.[13]

Second, the courts review so-called 'procedural defects', i.e. proceedings before the lower body alleged to constitute a 'denial of justice', e.g. by insufficient opportunity for the aggrieved to be heard, failure to give due notice of an impending decision, etc.

Third, there is the so-called 'error of law on the face of the record' which, in an English leading case, has been extended to bodies that are not courts of record.[14] Where, upon the face of the record, it appears that the determination of the inferior tribunal is wrong in law, certiorari will be granted. Apart from documents which record the determination, documents which initiate the proceeding and the pleadings are also now included.[15]

Fourth, in the United States the so-called 'substantial-evidence' rule enables a superior court to review findings of administrative bodies if they are not supported by 'such relevant evidence as a reasonable mind might accept as adequate to support a conclusion. . . .'[16] But, on the whole, this review power has been exercised with considerable restraint.[17]

Lastly, there is the power of the superior courts to review administrative decisions for 'abuse of discretion' or for being 'unreasonable'. This is the corner-stone of judicial review of administrative decisions, even in Continental systems (*détournement de pouvoir*). But this test can be and has been used at times to substitute the reviewing courts' own opinions and prejudices for those of the administrative body.[18]

In recent years two more 'ordinary' remedies have been added to this array of 'extraordinary' remedies: the injunction and the declaratory judgement. In the United States the injunction has, at least in the federal sphere, taken the place of certiorari, which was declared to be inapplicable to the review of administrative orders[19] but remains the main appellate remedy in the state jurisdictions.[20] In England it is still uncertain in what cases the Attorney-General must be joined as the party applying for an injunction to the motion of a private individual.[21] But the remedy has become increasingly popular, for example, in judgements restraining trade unions and other 'domestic tribunals' from unlawfully expelling members.[22]

The declaratory judgement is the most ubiquitous, but perhaps the most generally useful, of the remedies now available in proceedings against administrative authorities. A good example is a recent decision of the English Court of Appeal.[23] The plaintiffs, a number of registered dock-workers, had been dismissed by the board manager, to whom the London Dock Labour Board had purported to delegate certain statutory disciplinary functions. They asked for a declaratory judgement that the delegation of power had been *ultra vires* and invalid. The Court of Appeal granted the declaratory judgement to the effect that there was no such power, and it also pointed out that certiorari could not have been obtained in this case because the plaintiffs did not know the facts. 'In certiorari there is no discovery, whereas in an action for a declaration it can be had.'[24]

In the United States it has recently been stated that 'at best this new remedy has served to fill in several gaps where, for one reason or another, the existing remedies appeared to be unsatisfactory'.[25] It has, for example, been used to review deportation and exclusion orders. But it has also been used in a number of cases where it was important for the petitioner to have a doubtful legal situation clarified, such as the obligation to obtain certain licences.

Finally, there are a considerable number of statutory appeals, usually on points of law or on a case stated from certain administrative bodies to a court of law.[26] These, of course, bring administrative remedies much nearer to the ordinary appeal procedure, and they are steadily gaining in importance as legislative regulation of administrative procedures increases.

While the details of this immensely complex subject-matter must be studied in the voluminous literature on this subject, the brief survey attempted here shows clearly that the pressure towards a widening scope of review against administrative decisions has been irresistible in the common-law jurisdictions, but that the methods of accomplishing it in part have led to an immensely complicated and confusing structure, still falling far short of a simple general remedy against wrongful administrative decisions.

The systematization and unification of the principles governing the review of administrative actions can be attempted either by the granting of a general right of reviewability of administrative decisions to the 'aggrieved' party; or by a reform of the machinery of justice, e.g. by the establishment of a general appeal court from administrative decisions; or by a combination of these two methods.

To some extent the United States Federal Procedure Act of 1946 chooses the first of these alternative methods, while the recent Report of the British Committee on Administrative Tribunals and Inquiries[27] concentrates on the second problem.

However, the reservation of statutory exceptions from the right of review as well as of discretionary decisions, coupled with the uncertainty of the meaning of 'affected' or 'aggrieved', makes the scope of this apparent reform very uncertain.[28] It seems that the Act in no way disposes of the exceedingly complex problem of 'standing' and 'ripeness' to secure judicial review, on which there is a multitude of decisions interpreting a multitude of statutes in a manner which the same learned critic has described as 'unsteady and fluctuating, and at times even erratic'.[29] The uncertainty of the present state of the law is tellingly illustrated by a number of recent decisions arising from the dismissal of public employees on 'loyalty' grounds. In a strong criticism of observations on standing made by Frankfurter J. in *Adler* v. *Board of Education*,[30] where the action by a group of parents, teachers, and taxpayers, alleging the unconstitutionality of a New York statute authorizing the dismissal of teachers suspected of 'advocating the overthrow of government' by virtue of membership of certain listed organizations, was dismissed, Professor Davis has formulated the following general principle of standing in matters of reviewability:

One whose interests are *in fact* subjected to or imminently threatened with substantial injury from governmental action satisfies the requirements of standing and ripeness to challenge the legality of that action unless for reasons of substantive policy the interests are undeserving of legal protection.[31]

This brings us finally to the problem of the structural organization of administrative justice.

## THE ORGANIZATION OF ADMINISTRATIVE JUSTICE

In the Continental systems, built upon a dichotomy of civil and administrative law, full-fledged hierarchies of administrative courts, equal in status to the 'ordinary' courts, but staffed with judges who combine legal qualifications with administrative experience, provide a separate and – subject to occasional conflicts of jurisdiction, to be settled by a Conflicts Tribunal – self-contained structure of administrative justice. Post-war reforms in both countries have made the French and West German systems rather similar in this respect. In France, the reform of 1953 has relieved the Conseil d'État of the increasingly unmanageable burden of being, in all major matters, a court of first, as well as of last, instance, and has instituted, as courts of first instance, twenty-four '*tribunaux administratifs*', staffed with a president and from three to four counsellors. Their competence extends to the overwhelming majority of administrative litigation. The Conseil d'État, principal architect of the French *droit administratif*, since the reforms of 1953 generally acts as appeal court against the decisions of the administrative tribunals.[32]

Similarly, in West Germany, since the post-war reforms, administrative disputes are in first instance decided by administrative tribunals, now – though not formerly – completely separate from the administrative authorities whose decisions are challenged. An appeal (on facts and law) lies to the administrative appeal courts (*Verwaltungsgerichtshöfe*) of the different States, from which, in certain matters of fundamental importance, a revision (on points of law) lies to the newly established federal administrative court (*Bundesverwaltungsgericht*).[33] The administrative courts of first instance are usually staffed by a combination of professional judges and lay assessors, while the appeal courts and the supreme administrative court are entirely staffed with professional judges.[34]

It should be added that, particularly in Germany, there has been a tendency to create separate court structures for an increasing number of special subjects: such as tax law, labour law, and cartel law, while constitutional disputes also go to a special court, the Supreme Constitutional Court for the Federal Republic. But in all these cases hierarchies of courts have been established, which are equal in status and prestige to the ordinary courts.

In the common-law world a proliferation of administrative tribunals of all kinds has resulted from the prolonged delay in recognizing the need for a discipline and system of administrative justice, although the multiplication of the administrative functions is shared by the common-law world with the civil-law world. Neither American nor British reforms have attempted to substitute for the multiplicity of specialized administrative tribunals any uniform structure of administrative courts of first instance. Instead, attempts have been made to introduce minimum standards applicable to all administrative actions and agencies. In this respect the principal provisions of the Federal Administrative Procedure Act, 1946, prescribe: (*a*) minimum standards of public information, on the organization, procedure, and rule-making by administrative agencies; (*b*) minimum standards on hearings in every case of administrative adjudication; (*c*) separation of functions of hearing officers and reviewing bodies.[35]

In a similar vein the British Committee on Administrative Tribunals and Inquiries (1957) recommends, as basic in all administrative proceedings, the principles of 'fairness, openness, impartiality'. To that end the Committee makes various recommendations to ensure fair procedure before, at, and after the hearing before an administrative tribunal. This includes requirements of publicity, fair notice, the issue of reasoned decisions, and other matters which may fairly be compared to the standards of the U.S. legislation.

The Committee's recommendations go some way towards the systematization of judicial procedure in administrative matters and even the recognition of a separate hierarchy of administrative tribunals.

Having acknowledged that, despite various criticisms, the 'method of decision by tribunals' has worked 'on the whole reasonably well',[36] the Committee recommends that there should be an appeal on fact, law, and merits from an administrative tribunal of first instance to an appellate administrative tribunal, except in three specified cases, where the tribunal of first instance was considered as exceptionally strong and well qualified.[37] In many cases such an appeal would take the place of the present appeal to the competent Minister, i.e. the superior departmental authority, a procedure which the Committee firmly rejects.

On the question of a further appeal, the Committee's recommendation that, in addition to the prerogative remedies, a statutory right of appeal on points of law or on a case stated by the tribunal, to the High Court (more specifically the Divisional Court of the Queen's Bench Division) should be created, has been substantially accepted by the Tribunals and Inquiries Act, 1958.[38] This, for the present, disposes of the question of a general administrative appeal tribunal, to which the Committee gave some consideration but which it rejected, reasoning, first that 'appeals would thus lie from an expert tribunal to a comparatively inexpert body', and second, 'that the establishment of a general appellate body would seem inevitably to involve a departure from the principle whereby all adjudicating bodies in this country, whether designated as inferior courts or as tribunals, are in matters of jurisdiction subject to the control of the superior courts. This unifying control has been so long established and is of such fundamental importance in our legal system that the onus of proof must lie clearly upon the advocates of change.'

Third, the Committee deprecates the likely evolution of 'two systems of law . . . with all the evils attendant on this dichotomy'.[39]

Two common-law scholars who have recently studied the working of the French administrative-law system, and who, in most respects, regard it as providing better protection for the citizen than present-day common law, nevertheless agree with the rejection of a separate administrative appeal court. Professor Schwartz[40] rejects the duality mainly because of the possibility of conflicts of jurisdiction between administrative and civil courts, and the consequent prolongation of a dispute which, in certain cases, might take many years. Considering his previous praise of the standing, quality, and spirit of independence of the Conseil d'État, this seems a remarkably narrow ground to choose. Professor Hamson concludes an admiring account of the role and working of the Conseil d'État, and of its highly beneficial work in the restraint of administrative arbitrariness, due in large part to the administrative expertise of its members, with a rather curt rejection of the dual structure for the common-law world. 'A tribunal independent of and parallel to the high court would introduce a duality into our jurisdiction which we could not easily tolerate.'[41]

This reasoning is no more convincing than that of the Franks Committee. It appears to be based on several fallacies.

First, there is in all these arguments a total absence of doubt in the expertise and ability of the 'ordinary' judges to deal with matters of administrative law, and to pave the way for its further development – as the highest administrative courts on the Continent have done. This assumption is all the more surprising as the multitude of present-day administrative tribunals have sprung from the very absence of such ability. Unless there is a drastic change in the training and experience of lawyers from whom the judges are recruited, it is a matter of sheer accident if some of them, through wartime government service, or some other public mission, have acquired experience of the administrative process.[42] Nor is it an answer that the High Court should function as the highest appeal court only on 'points of law'. The whole discussion of this chapter has shown how deeply, though indirectly, even the present-day prerogative jurisdiction of the ordinary courts in matters of administrative law goes into questions of fact. It seems contradictory to praise the achievements of the Conseil d'État and of similar bodies in other countries, largely because of their combination of full judicial independence with intimate acquaintance of the processes of administration, and then to reject any similar system for the common-law jurisdictions, although the administrative and social problems with which they are faced are basically the same as in the civil-law jurisdictions. And why, in the light of the experience of the Continental highest administrative appeal courts, such a court in England – or the United States – should be a 'relatively inexpert' body is difficult to grasp. What is needed is experience in, and understanding of, the nature of the administrative process and of the basic problems of the relation between governors and governed. Whether such a highest administrative court should be constituted inside or outside the organization of the superior courts of the common law is a relatively subordinate question. The latter solution would preserve something of the mystical 'unity' of the common law, but such a special division with the High Court would certainly make sense only if it were staffed with judges trained in the processes of administration and more than casually acquainted with the problems of administrative law.

This leads us to the final and probably the most basic fallacy in the reasoning of the Committee (as of many others). As the discussion of this chapter has shown on almost every page, there *are*, in fact, two systems of law in existence, and the dichotomy, 'evil' or otherwise, has been with us for some time. The only difference between the civil-law and the common-law jurisdictions is that the former openly recognize administrative law as a discipline of its own, with its characteristic problems and solutions, whereas the latter continue to live with the fiction that there is only one system of law, the common law, with administrative sideshoots sprouting from the stem here and there. The result is, as we have seen, that there is a wide-spread lack of proper appreciation of characteristic public-law problems and institutions, such as the nature of government contracts, the status of the public corporation, the statutory immunities of public authorities, and many more. The recognition of the duality of the legal system as an inevitable corollary to the development of modern government – is a basis problem which the common-law world can continue to ignore or belittle only at the cost of failing to develop a healthy balance between the needs of administration in the modern welfare state and the essential rights of the citizen.

Part Five

# Law Between Nations

# 14

# Social Organization and International Law

Since the end of the First World War, the predominant concern of international lawyers, as of statesmen and politicians, has been the horizontal widening of universal international law in a limited but vital sphere: the establishment and strengthening of inter-State covenants and international organizations which would eliminate, or at least greatly reduce, the danger of increasingly destructive wars among the nations, by substituting for the traditional privileges of national sovereignty, i.e. war, reprisals, and other acts of force applied at the discretion of the national States, covenants of restraint and methods of peaceful settlement.

The development of the law of nations cannot, however, be found solely on the *horizontal* plane. There have also been far-reaching *vertical* changes in the law of nations which still lack comprehensive analysis. This chapter will attempt to give a general survey of the different ways in which these changes affect the structure and direction of international law in our time.[1]

In the present century, and particularly since the end of the First World War, scope and purposes of law inside the States that form the family of nations have widened greatly and become much more diversified. These changes are also affecting profoundly the scope and objectives of international law. On the one hand, the traditional system of legal inter-State relations is, to some extent, modified by the disappearance of certain commonly held, though seldom explicit, assumptions on the respective spheres of State and individual in the regulation of human and social affairs. On the other hand, international law, like municipal law, is increasingly concerned with the development and regulation of international collaboration in spheres formerly outside the field of international law. While textbooks and casebooks on international law still predominantly emphasize the traditional fields of inter-State relations, i.e. the various aspects of international diplomacy conducted on a more or less formal level between governments, the vital concern of international law, as of international politics, has in recent years been increasingly with international economic and social organization, and with problems of human welfare. The municipal law of all civilized nations, as reflected in statute books, administrative orders, and court decisions, deals today increasingly with such matters as the redistribution of wealth, social security and insurance, the development and regulation of economic, resources, education, and other vital fields of social activity. This is increasingly true of international law as well, whether we look at the efforts of the International Labour Organization or of other functional United Nations agencies, at the European Coal and Steel Community, at the various forms of organizing in a permanent or semi-permanent way assistance to underdeveloped countries, or at the transactions of such international financial institutions as the International Bank for Reconstruction and Development.

But as the rate as well as the direction of the advance of law into a widening field of social and human relationships varies from State to State, universality becomes more difficult to attain. The chief makers of international law in the nineteenth century were broadly agreed on the scope of law, and with it, on the function of the State. Governments were generally held entitled and assumed to be responsible for what was then conceived to be the scope of external affairs: the control of armed forces and of diplomatic relations. They were furthermore assumed to be responsible for the administration of justice and the maintenance of internal order. From this followed certain rules of international State responsibility predicated on the assumption of certain general minimum standards of justice, i.e. a reasonably independent judiciary, and a certain minimum of protection of the individual against arbitrary State action. There were only the most modest beginnings of internal responsibility for social welfare and the redistribution of wealth. Taxation was not thought of as a major instrument of economic policy, but as a means of enabling governments to maintain the above-mentioned minimum functions. The sphere of international law corresponded broadly to this implicit assumption of the scope of government functions held among the chief makers and exponents of international law. International law, concerned as it was with the regulation of a minimum of diplomatic inter-State relations, did not often have to refer explicitly to these matters at all. Where it did, it assumed that States, the subjects of international law, did not normally engage in economic and social activities. [2]

The relatively few international agreements or conventions on matters outside the sphere of traditional diplomacy were concerned with certain services and communications on which little more than technical agreement had to be obtained, and in regard to which differences of State organization did not occur or were not relevant (as in the field of postal services or copyright protection).

Both in volume and scope, the area of international institutions and agreements has greatly widened. International law is today actively and continuously concerned with such divergent and vital matters as human rights and crimes against peace and humanity, the labour international control of nuclear energy, trade organization, conventions, transport control, or health regulation. This is not to say that in all or any of these fields international law prevails. But there is no doubt today that they are its legitimate concern.

As international law moves today on so many levels, it would be surprising indeed if the traditional principles of inter-State relations developed in previous centuries were adequate to cope with the vastly more divergent subject-matters of international law of the present day. Quantitatively, international law is still dominated by the established principles concerned with the formalization of inter-State relations of a diplomatic character. For this type of international legal relations it is sufficient that two major assumptions should continue to be correct: first, an international society composed of sovereign States whose internal structure or political system is irrelevant to the international legal rules involved; second, general agreement that the subject-matter in question is within the competence of governments. The basic structure of international society, as one composed of legally – though not always politically – sovereign States with widely differing political and economic systems, seems to be as firmly established as ever.

International legal rules remain basically unimpaired in so far as the second basic assumption applies; namely, general international agreement on the extent of government responsibility for the subject-matter in question. Such matters as the position of States in international relations (personality, rank, dignity, independence, self-preservation, intervention, and the limits of jurisdiction over foreigners); legal rules relating to State territory, and the many contentious problems deriving from it in regard to the limits of territorial sovereignty on land, sea, and air; the problems relating to the freedom of the seas; and the numerous more specifically formal diplomatic rules relating to State representation, diplomatic immunities, etc., are not greatly affected by the social change of which we have spoken. They relate either to the elements of statehood or to the universally acknowledged responsibilities of the State in matters of defence and foreign affairs.[3]

There are, however, a number of international legal principles

which cannot remain unaffected by changes in the internal structure of States. These changes affect, on the one hand, certain privileges traditionally enjoyed as attributes of sovereignty, and, on the
other hand, certain duties of abstention. In both areas, the changes
which we are about to analyse stem from a shift in the practice of
modern States regarding the traditional distribution of functions
between governments and private citizens. Additional problems
arise from the fact that these shifts and changes have not occurred
everywhere with the same intensity so that, even granted the obsolescence of certain customary rules of international law, it may not
be easy to formulate a substitute.

### PRIVILEGES OF SOVEREIGNTY AND L'ÉTAT COMMERÇANT

The degree to which States, directly or through the instrumentality
of public corporations,[4] have engaged or are engaging in commercial activities differs considerably from country to country. It is,
however, a fair generalization to say that in no country today could
the pursuit of economic activities by the State be regarded as a non-
governmental function. This goes without saying in the case of
countries that have nationalized all or part of their industries, or
assume in other ways direct responsibility for the economic development of the country. Among such countries are, despite the many
divergences of their economic systems, the U.S.S.R., China, Great
Britain, India, and Mexico.[5] But it is significant that the United
States, probably less given to the adoption of socialistic doctrines
than any other modern State, has specifically rejected the theory
expressed, for example, in *Ohio* v. *Helvering*,[6] that the State, when
engaging in commercial activities, forfeits its sovereign position.[7]
How far the State should engage in economic activities of different
kinds, how far it should confine itself to regulatory rather than
managerial functions, how far it should enter into partnerships with
private enterprise, these and similar questions are a matter of continuing controversy. But the assumption that governments do not
engage in such activities no longer rules. Hence the question, by
what criterion the truly sovereign and therefore non-justiciable
activities of the State should be distinguished from those for which
it should be held accountable, has become important in international – as in municipal – law. It has assumed particular importance in regard to the legal status of State-owned merchant vessels.
It is, however, no less relevant in the classification of international

commercial transactions. The voluminous discussion on this problem may be briefly summarized as follows:

There are three major approaches to the question whether the traditional immunity of State-owned property from foreign jurisdiction as well as execution should be modified. The first and simplest proposition is that the absolute immunity should not be tampered with. That the English courts, despite many openly expressed doubts,[8] still rigidly adhere to this doctrine was confirmed in the case of *Krajina* v. *Tass Agency*,[9] where an action brought against the wholly government-controlled Soviet Tass Agency for alleged libel was dismissed for want of jurisdiction, and again in *Rahimtoola* v. *Nizam of Hyderabad*[10] where the immunity was extended to the agent of a foreign sovereign State in regard to a debt situate in England. The United States courts, on the other hand, which until recently supported the doctrine of absolute State immunity, are now likely to be in a state of uncertainty since the official abandonment of this doctrine in the letter published in 1952 by the Department of State and the apparent qualification of that abandonment in 1955.[11]

The second major approach, now adopted by most Continental countries, substitutes for the doctrine of absolute State immunity that of qualified immunity. Foreign States, under this doctrine, may or may not be immune from jurisdiction, according to the kind of activity in which they are engaged. Following the leadership of the Belgian and Italian courts which have since been followed by the courts of France and many other Continental countries, a distinction, familiar in Continental administrative law,[12] between acts *jure imperii* and acts *jure gestionis* has been applied to this branch of international law.[13] The difficulty is how to find a reasonably precise distinction between acts of the one and the other kind, in view of the many diverse ways in which governments may engage in economic and commercial activities. For this reason neither the functional test (Does the State act in its sovereign capacity?) nor the test of the forms of the transaction is satisfactory. Any government activity may fulfil 'sovereign' purposes.[14]

And while, on the one hand, the standard contract (or contract of adhesion) that nowadays dominates in private commercial transactions (transport, insurance, leases, etc.) has many quasi-public normative elements imposed by the stronger on the weaker party, on the other hand, most government departments obtained their purchases and supplies in the form of standard contracts that are not very different from administrative regulations.[15]

The third approach, which makes the nature of the transaction the test, was adopted in the Brussels Convention of 1926 in regard to seagoing vessels owned or operated by States. Under the convention, ships (with their cargoes) operated or owned by governments for commercial purposes are in time of peace subject to the same rules as those applicable to private vessels, cargoes, and equipment, and do not enjoy the immunities of government property.[16]

While this pragmatic distinction between commercial and non-commercial activities avoids the fallacious criterion of sovereignty, it leaves other doubts and difficulties unsolved. It is implicit in the doctrine that the States will continue to enjoy the traditional immunities in regard to such activities as have traditionally been held to be their proper sphere. This is not because commercial activities should be regarded as 'non-sovereign', but because any distinction between privileged and non-privileged government activities must separate out the hard core of an *irreducible minimum of government activities*. While economic activities may, in contemporary society, be undertaken by private enterprise, governments, or mixed undertakings, certain activities are universally recognized to be necessarily governmental in the practice of nations. These minimum spheres include, undoubtedly, military and foreign affairs, the administration of justice, and the activities inevitably related to them. Here the difficulties of the other tests recur, at least, to a limited extent. Military operations may include purchases, service contracts, and licence agreements. The conduct of foreign affairs may include broadcasting contracts or the purchase of land. These problems are parallel to the difficulties of distinguishing between *gestion publique* and *gestion privée*, in the administrative law of France and other countries, as a criterion for the allocation of jurisdiction to either the administrative or the civil courts.[17] But modern jurisprudence has abandoned the illusion, prevalent in earlier analytical positivism, that any theoretical test or principle can avoid the agonies and complexities of the concrete decision. The distinction between *gestion publique* and *gestion privée*, or between commercial and non-commercial activities of a State is, in contemporary conditions, a sound and necessary one, even if it is difficult to apply in certain individual cases. This is no less true of such standard formulas of the common law as 'the conduct of the reasonable man', or the distinction, in an individual case, between contractees, invitees, and licensees, in regard to the liabilities of the occupier of the land on which they suffer injuries. No theoretical distinction can provide certainty. It can only provide guidance for individual decisions.

### THE LEGAL CHARACTER OF
### INTERNATIONAL STATE TRANSACTIONS

The widening and diversification of State activities is no less important for the legal characterization of international State transactions.
The traditional doctrine is that governments entering into international commercial transactions and, in particular, governments
seeking foreign loans, can never be deemed to have submitted to a
law other than their own, because to hold otherwise would derogate
from their sovereignty. This doctrine, which, in its most radical
form, sponsored by Latin America, regards State loans as diplomatic acts rather than legal transactions, received a rather fatal
blow from the decision of the House of Lords in the *Bondholders'*
case[18] and in simultaneous decisions of the Supreme Courts of
Sweden and Norway. All these cases arose in connexion with the
Joint Resolution of the United States Congress (1933) which had
declared any provision requiring payment in gold or in a particular
kind of coin or currency to be contrary to public policy. The above-
mentioned judgements all denied that the fact that a State was a
party to a transaction precluded it from submitting to a foreign law,
in this case, the law of the United States:

> It cannot be disputed that a government may expressly agree to be
> bound by a foreign law. It seems to me equally indisputable that without
> any expressed intention the inference that a government so intended
> may be necessarily inferred from the circumstances; as where a govern-
> ment enters into a contract in a foreign country for the purchase of land
> situate in that country in the terms appropriate only to the law of that
> country; or enters into a contract of affreightment with the owners of a
> foreign ship on the terms expressed in a foreign bill of lading; or employs
> in a foreign country labour in circumstances to which labour laws would
> apply.[19]

The significance of the admission that sovereign States entering
into financial or commercial transactions may drop the mantle of
sovereignty and participate in agreements either governed by the
private law of another State, or by some specially drawn-up provisions that may contain elements blended of public and private
law, will survive the occasion that caused the new departure. Again
we should avoid the fallacy of concluding that this type of
transaction is 'non-sovereign' or 'non-governmental'. The basic
social fact, of which international, like municipal, law must take
account, is that:

> The lines of demarcation between the political and economic activities

of the State have become blurred and it is in this borderland that State trading flourishes.[20]

Governments may borrow money from foreign private institutions, as in the above-mentioned cases; or they may subscribe shares in international public institutions which, in turn, make loans to other governments or private enterprises. Such loans may have to be backed by government guarantees (as in the case of loans made by the International Bank for Reconstruction and Development), or they may be given on a commercial basis (as in the case of the newly constituted International Finance Corporation). The public lender may acquire bonds (portfolio investment) or equity shares. Governments that need the investment of capital and skill from abroad may go into partnership with foreign private enterprises through joint companies in which they retain a majority, and the foreign interest acquire a minority holding (as in the case of the reconstituted Burma Oil Company); or through a concession agreement between the government and a group of foreign companies (as in the case of the Iranian Oil Consortium of 1954); or a government may make a loan to an international public entity for a mixture of economic and political reasons (e.g. the recent loan of $100,000,000 by the U.S. Government to the European Coal and Steel Community). Public international institutions and governments may engage in a joint loan to another government (as in the case of the loan given to India in 1958 by the International Bank in association with the Governments of Britain, U.S., West Germany, and Japan). Governments have become, and will increasingly become, engaged in international economic transactions and enterprises in a variety of ways. Neither politically nor technically has the ancient assumption that a government, when consenting to borrow money from abroad, does so with the condescending gesture of a sovereign, kept much of its validity. At present, most of the relevant transactions are *sui generis*. Certain standard forms are developing very much like the standard contracts of private law. Arbitration clauses often avoid the awkward problem of the submission of the borrowing State to a foreign municipal law and jurisdiction. In the absence of specific provisions, the usual tests of private international law will decide the proper law and competent jurisdiction, and the above-mentioned difficulties of deciding by the form of transaction or by the status of the parties recur in this connexion. In a basic article on the subject, Dr Mann has not only suggested that the intention of the parties should be the guiding test for the ascertainment of the 'proper law' of the transaction, but also that these international contracts should be internationalized, in the sense that generally acknowledged international contract rules, perhaps the specific application of the general principles of law recognized among civilized nations in this sphere, should be applied.[21] The obvious difficulty in this suggestion is that at present supra-national rules of contract or other branches of law are too uncertain and contradictory to permit any reliable application of an international law of contract.[22] However, in years to come, the crystallization of standard practices developed by bilateral or multilateral transactions of the kind mentioned earlier may well develop such a law.

### THE GOVERNMENT CORPORATION IN INTERNATIONAL LEGAL TRANSACTIONS

We have discussed earlier in this book the growing importance of the public corporation in many countries and the duality of its status as government organ and commercial enterprise. Just as, in the discussion of the problem of government immunities, courts and writers have frequently confused the problem of the proper extent of government liability for commercial State activities – a problem of practical expediency and equity – with the theoretical problem of sovereignty, so they have all too often failed to recognize that the substitution of a public corporation for the government itself in international transactions offered an opportunity to avoid the obstacle of government immunities or of other traditional privileges attached to government activities in international law. Thus, a recent American decision[23] granted immunity to the Anglo-Iranian Oil Company on the ground that Anglo-Iranian was indistinguishable from the British Government, which owned the greater proportion of the voting stock (though only 35 per cent of the capital). A far sounder approach was taken in the earlier decision of *U.S.* v. *Deutsches Kalisyndikat Gesellschaft*,[24] where an agency for the sale of potash controlled by the French Government was held to be a commercial concern.[25] Unless we can free ourselves from the fallacy that the undeniably public purposes of corporations, that are to a greater or lesser extent established and controlled by governments, impair their character as autonomous entities designed to be legally separate and distinct in status and structure from the government, much of the usefulness and flexibility of this device of the public corporation – as valuable in international as it is in national municipal law – will be lost. The above-mentioned decision of the English Court of Appeal in the *Tass Agency* case[26] does not help much, for it rests primarily on the ground that the status of the Tass Agency as a separate legal entity rather than a government department had not been established. Once such legally separate identity is established, there is no justification for denying it the status of a private corporation simply on the ground that it fulfils government purposes.

Such an approach – which is both technically simple and desirable on grounds of policy – also avoids another difficulty that has greatly bedevilled the court decisions of many countries in these matters. Whereas some countries, notably Great Britain and the other major Dominions of the British Commonwealth, prefer the form of the public corporation proper, i.e. an enterprise not constituted in the form of a commercial company under the Companies Act, others, notably many Continental countries, prefer the form of the commercial company in which the State has an exclusive or controlling interest. Some countries, like France, combine both forms.[27] The reason why so many wholly or partly government-controlled enterprises in France, Germany, Italy, and other countries are constituted as commercial companies is largely historical. After the First World War, governments in Europe, in order to maintain employment or the production of vital commodities, were often compelled to rescue from bankruptcy industries that had greatly developed under wartime conditions. To make the foreign status, privileges, and liabilities of publicly controlled corporations dependent on the purely formal test whether they have been established as joint-stock companies or as public corporations of the British pattern (or the equivalent institution of *établissements publics* in France) would only increase the complexities and artificialities that have dominated this problem for so long.[28]

## NEW SUBJECTS OF INTERNATIONAL LAW

Not only has the scope of international law widened from the traditional fields of inter-State diplomatic relations to a variety of international economic and social transactions; there is also an increasing multiplicity of agents of international law. Governments as such appear in different capacities and functions – not only as 'sovereign', but also as lenders, borrowers, and partners in international business enterprises and suppliers of goods.

But, as we have seen, governments often act internationally through public corporations, which have certain private-law aspects and should legally be clearly distinguished from the government, or through private-law companies in which they hold a controlling or substantial interest.[29]

Increasingly, private corporations are parties to international transactions in which public and private-law aspects are intermingled, and which sometimes are international treaties in disguise. An outstanding illustration of the latter is the Iranian Oil Agreement of 1954.

That the contemporary study of international law must include not only the nation-State, but also international government organizations, transnational political parties, pressure groups, private associations, and the individual human being, has been suggested by Professor M. S. McDougal.[30] More recently, Professor Jessup has emphasized the increasing fluidity of the traditional distinction between public and private international law, and pleaded for a 'transnational law', which 'would not start with sovereignty or power but from the premiss that jurisdiction is essentially a matter of procedure which could be amicably arranged among the nations of the world'.[31]

Since none of these organizations other than States have formal standing in international law – e.g. as parties before the International Court of Justice – the gap is, in part, being filled by arbitration agreements which institute some form of settlement machinery and sometimes refer[32] to the principles of law common to the parties as the law governing the transaction.

Clearly, such public and private bodies are, in fact, becoming subjects of international law, and their transactions and associations form an increasingly important part of the contemporary law of nations, which, in the process, absorbs or adapts many categories and concepts of the private law of contract, tort, and property.[33] But while States remain, for most purposes, the sole subject of international law, the gap between the theory and the reality of contemporary international law remains serious.

### THE IMPACT OF STATE TRADING ON INTERNATIONAL LEGAL OBLIGATIONS

If the transition from the 'night-watchman' State to one actively moulding the economic and social life of the nation proceeded everywhere to the same degree and at the same pace, the equilibrium of international law would not be greatly disturbed. While the substance of mutual obligations might be affected, it would be essentially the same for all States, and the reciprocity of international obligations, which is essential to the functioning of international law in a society of sovereign States, would not be impaired. However, the change in the functions and philosophies of government is not universal. At the very least there are vital differences of emphasis and tempo. This is most marked in the sphere of international trade. Such legal rules and standards as have developed in this field presuppose that trade is conducted by private enterprise, while the State exercises at most certain police functions, notably in the regulation of exports and imports, through customs, tariffs, quotas, quality tests, and the like.

While, in the course of the present century, this presumption of a family of nations trading freely, through private enterprise, guided only by economic considerations of cost price and profit, has been increasingly eroded under the impact of nationalist policies, the forms of private trade have been retained in a majority of States. The political scientist or the economist may well hold that, for example, the apostle of free enterprise, the United States, has, through a powerful arsenal of legislative and administrative measures, greatly departed from the concept of free international trade.[34] In this arsenal are tariffs or quotas, the direction of trade in certain goods to certain countries, the granting of subsidies to agricultural products, the compulsory use of American shipping for waterborne trade or bilateral deals in surplus commodities. But in legal theory international trade in the United States remains private. In many States, on the other hand, notably in the whole of the Communist bloc, the State as such is, either directly or through a wholly government-controlled corporation, the actual manager and operator of trading corporations. International trading organizations and mechanisms in such States are instruments of economic planning. They are also, to a far larger extent than in the more or less liberal economic systems that survive, agents of State policy. For example, the granting of long-term credits, at very low rates of interest, by State-owned Soviet credit institutions to the governments of underdeveloped countries may or may not be justified in the long run by economic considerations. Certainly, the terms of the loans made are determined by considerations of State policy. The relatively liberal States may counter – and they may, indeed, be compelled to do so by the exigencies of international politics – by using their own State instrumentalities, such as government-owned export-import banks, for the corresponding granting of low-interest loans at deliberately uneconomic rates. But they can do so only at the expense of their free-trade philosophy, and by the sacrifice of the principles of commercial and economic philosophy which their private industries and commercial financial institutions wish to maintain.[35]

For an international economy which is at least basically directed by private enterprise and free-trade ideals, the most important single instrument of legal support for an expansion of international trade has been the 'most-favoured-nation' clause. As formulated in the General Agreement on Tariffs and Trade (Art. I), this means that 'any advantage, privilege, or immunity granted by a contracting party to a product originating in or destined for any other country . . . should be immediately and unconditionally accorded to similar products originating in or destined for the territories of all other contracting parties.'[36]

The 'most-favoured-nation' clause does not as such lead to a direct increase of trade between two or more States. But, by guaranteeing equality of treatment to rival commercial States in the markets of a third State, and by thus eliminating discriminatory measures, especially through tariffs and customs duties, the clause serves to expand international trade under free market conditions. Any concession, any advantage granted, under free enterprise conditions by one State to another would open the doors to the enterprises able to compete commercially of any other State benefiting from the clause.

The duty of the Government under the clause is, in free trade conditions, essentially one of abstention. The obligation is not to put obstacles in the way of trade flowing between private parties. But a State which conducts its own trade, through the Government itself or through State-controlled corporations, buys and sells, lends or borrows, supplies or hires services, as part of an official economic policy. It tends to operate by way of specific agreements, which implement this policy: by barter deals, by special loan or technical assistance agreements, by bulk purchases or sales. Hence, the 'most-favoured-nation' clause cannot have the same meaning for a State-trading State as it has for a differently organized State. Thus the first commercial agreement between the U.S.S.R. and the U.S.A. of 11 July 1935, accorded most-favoured-nation treatment (except for purchase of coal) to the U.S.S.R. in the American markets, but the U.S.S.R., instead of a reciprocal obligation, was asked to commit

itself to purchase in the United States commodities of a specified
value within a given period.[37] The British-Soviet Commercial
Agreement of April 1930 attempted to restore a measure of meaning
to the most-favoured-nation treatment of a State-trading partner
by a protocol, by which the parties undertook to eliminate from
their mutual economic relations all forms of discrimination and to
be 'guided in regard to the purchase and sale of goods, in regard to
the employment of shipping, and in regard to all similar matters by
commercial and financial considerations only . . .' The subsequent
denunciation of the Agreement was explained by a British Cabinet
member in the following words:

It is impossible to work a normal most-favoured-nation clause as an
automatic piece of commercial policy, when, on one side, you have a
private individual acting as a trader, merchant, broker, shipowner, and
so on, and on the other side a State which can control the whole of the
commercial transactions into and out of a country.[38]

In the words of a recent commentator:

The clause cannot operate to encourage expansion of trade by opening
markets on a non-discriminatory basis to low-cost producers because
factors other than cost and tariffs influence the decisions of state-trading
buyers. In short, the most-favoured-nation clause has proved itself to be
no longer a sufficient desideratum for private-enterprise states in their
commercial relations with state-trading states to constitute a *quid pro quo*
for important tariff concessions by private-enterprise states.[39]

Yet, the State-trading nations of the Soviet bloc have been
insistent on the use of the most-favoured-nation clause, for example,
in a recent Soviet proposal to include an unconditional most-
favoured-nation clause in an all-European Agreement of Economic
Cooperation.[40] They have explained this desire as an expression of
the principle of sovereign equality in the relations of nations, as a
symbol of the principle of non-discrimination rather than an instrument of active expansion of trade.[41] But after the unsuccessful
experiments of the inter-war period it is unlikely that a general
agreement on these lines, between State-trading nations and the
others, will be possible. General trade agreements, such as G.A.T.T.,
based on the most-favoured-nation clause are likely to remain
limited to States that share at least a minimum of common organization and principles in the conduct of trade. Even in the relations
between these States serious rifts have already occurred, because
some of the parties depart more heavily than others from the principle of free trade and equality of opportunity (for example, through
the granting of special subsidies to agriculture). In an insecure and

tense world, preoccupied with cold-war strategy and defence considerations, the tendency is, in many ways, more strongly towards the Soviet principle than towards free trade. As for the relations between 'private traders' and 'State traders' – at least those State-trading nations that are politically divided from the private-trade nations – international economic relations are likely to develop, if at all, on the basis of *quid pro quo*.[42] In fact, only one State-trading nation (Czechoslovakia) is an (inactive) party to G.A.T.T., and 'no one as yet has been able to envisage a way in which to extend the specific commitment system of purchases to the multilateral level'.[43] Any retention of the most-favoured-nation clause in relations between State-trading nations and others has political rather than economic significance. It emphasizes the principle of equality of opportunity.[44] But the actual trade relations between such States will be governed by specific agreements for the purchase and sale of fixed quantities of goods.[45] Such agreements, however, mean inevitably, for the purposes of the bilateral agreement, a departure of the private trading States from their professed standard. To the extent that a State commits itself to the purchase or sale of certain quantities of goods, it abandons the principle of free trade – and of private enterprise – even though it may fulfil the agreement through sub-contracting. In so far as it is possible to restore at all the equilibrium of international obligations in the trading relations between State-trading and other States, it can happen only by the acceptance of obligations incompatible with the principles of free enterprise.

The difficulties of maintaining an equilibrium of rights and obligations, or even a comparable meaning of concepts, such as 'commercial and financial considerations'[46] or 'most-favoured-nation treatment' between States of basically different economic organization are likely to lead to an increasing disintegration of universal trading agreements, and a corresponding intensification of trade relations between more compact groups of States linked by common interests and principles. The counterpart to the Communist trading bloc, whose members all regard trade as an adjunct of State policy, is not so much G.A.T.T. as the evolving European Economic Communities. In the first of these the E.C.S.C., a joint supra-national authority, controls and supervises the conditions under which trade in coal and steel flows between the participating industries, although certain strains have resulted from the fact that some of them are publicly and others privately owned. In the second, the European Atomic Energy Community (Euratom), the

Commission exercises managerial and operating as well as regulatory functions.

In the third and most ambitious, the Economic Community, the Commission supervises above all the implementation of the free-trade and investment provisions. In all of them a strong community of political purpose and economic organization is the indispensable prerequisite.

### INTERNATIONAL STATE RESPONSIBILITIES AND THE PROBLEM OF COMMON STANDARDS

Customary and treaty law have mitigated the principle of territorial sovereignty, which permits a State to deal in peace as in war with its territory and with the people subject to its sovereignty (including, in almost all respects, persons of foreign nationality permanently resident in the territory), by certain principles of international State responsibility for injuries caused to nationals of other States.

This section will survey briefly how far recent developments, of more than temporary significance, have either added to the sphere of universally recognized minimum responsibilities of States, or have, on the other hand, created divergences between groups of States that affect the customary rules of international law, because formerly held assumptions on the division of powers between State and citizens no longer apply generally. It seems that there are at least three major areas to which this inquiry is relevant. There is, first, the question to what extent significant shifts in the relation of the State authorities to privileged political parties, labour organizations, and other social groups, and, in some cases, far tighter control over the activities of individuals, have affected traditional assumptions about the limitation of State responsibility for acts of groups and individuals that have international consequences. There is, second, the question how far the tremendous expansion of international political propaganda as a weapon of both 'hot' and 'cold' warfare has added to the minimum responsibilities of States in this field. There is, third, the question of the reassessment of international minimum standards in the fields in which some measure of international State responsibility has come to be universally recognized: denial of justice to aliens through inadequate legal protection; and, in particular, interference with economic rights and interests of aliens through legislative or administrative measures taken inside any one State.

### International Responsibility for State-Controlled Groups

The first question has become acute since the rise of a number of totalitarian régimes which have, in varying degrees and forms, abolished freedom of political association and usually made one 'party' the privileged and exclusive organ of State policy and public opinion. Such identification was not only achieved in practice, but emphasized in theory in Nazi Germany and Fascist Italy.[47] A similar factual and constitutional identification of State and party exists today in the Soviet Union and Communist China as well as in all the satellite Communist States. It also exists in present-day Spain, and indeed in any country where the predominance of one party is constitutionally assured. On the other hand, such States as India, where the Congress Party dominates parliamentary processes and constitutional decisions *de facto*, but not by virtue of any constitutional provision, do not fall in the same category.[48] Invariably the States which have abolished freedom of political organization and have made one party the mouthpiece and spearhead of the policy and official opinion have not stopped at the suppression of freedom of opinion in the purely political field. They have applied the same process to all significant group organizations. The abolition of all freedom of association has been an inevitable corollary to the abolition of freedom in the formation and activities of the political parties. Where one political party or one officially sponsored industrial or labour organization enjoys a monopoly, it is irrelevant whether some appearances of free choice are maintained by a process of sham elections. The traditional doctrine of international law, which restricts State responsibility to persons officially connected with government, as distinct from private persons,[49] is predicated on the assumption that the latter are free from government direction or control in their actions affecting foreign States. Only in so far as this assumption applies is the statement correct that 'international society cannot be regarded as an institution for the mutual assurance of established governments'.[50]

The degree to which identity between the State and organizations within the State can be legally articulated is important in at least four kinds of activities that directly affect foreign States or international organizations: first, terrorist activities; second, hostile propaganda designed to undermine a foreign government; third, boycott of goods of specified foreign origin by groups within the State; fourth, membership of international organizations whose constitutions provide for representation of member States not, or not only, by their governments, but by specified group organizations within the State.

## Terrorist and Subversive Activities

From the many forms of organized terrorist activities in other States, we might single out such activities as assume the form of commonly recognized crimes in international law. There is strong support for the view that the encouragement and support by a government of armed hostile expeditions, as well as of attempts against life or property in foreign countries, are international delinquencies. The extension of this principle to the activities of individuals is more difficult because it touches the extremely controversial problem of extradition for crimes that are essentially 'political' but contain elements of common crime. However, where it can be shown that an individual committed an act of terrorism on the instructions and with the direct support of a foreign government, the latter should clearly be held responsible.

Such organizations as the *Bund für Auslanddeutsche* – which attempted to undermine the allegiance of foreign nationals of German descent – were clearly emanations of the German Nazi Party and, therefore, of the German Government. The character and organization of the Nazi movement created an irrebuttable presumption that the activities of these organizations were directed by the German National Socialist Government.

The legal relationship of the many national Communist Parties in the different countries to the Communist governments of such countries as the Soviet Union or Communist China is far more complex. In its theoretical premisses as well as in its practical effects, Communism is an international political movement which has recruited large numbers of spontaneous adherents and organizations in many countries. Although most of them take their inspirations and policy directives from the Soviet Union or Communist China, it would be incorrect to regard, for example, the powerful Communist Parties of France or Italy as subsidiary organizations of the Soviet Union. They are national parties, however much they may be mentally subservient to a foreign Power.

## Boycott

While, in the case of organized attempts on life, installations, or other property of a foreign State, there is little doubt about the criminal character of these actions – all of which can be classed as internationally recognized crimes – and the main difficulty lies often in tracing the responsibility to a foreign government, the problem of interference with foreign trade as an international delinquency meets with the principal difficulty of defining the limits of legality. Only brief reference need be made to this problem, which received a considerable amount of discussion before the last war,[51] but is unlikely to be of great practical significance in contemporary conditions. The extent to which, short of contract or treaty, the right to free trade is legally protected is extremely doubtful even in municipal law. The common-law doctrine of conspiracy – which has no parallel in civilian systems – is probably a dying action. Since the decision of the House of Lords in the *Crofter* case,[52] it is clear that in England, at least, an action for conspiracy will never lie when the organized attempt to interfere with the trade of another can be attributed to some legitimate economic or social interest, however much it may be combined with the desire to do injury to the other party. In the United States, the situation is uncertain,[53] but again it seems clear that combinations to refuse to deal with another party are not unlawful, and that some additional element which in itself is illegal, e.g. physical violence or coercion, is needed to render the group action unlawful. In analogy to this position, one of the writers on the international aspects of boycott has argued that the element of coercion, through the combined action of other compatriots forcing him to withdraw his trade from the victim of the boycott, creates an international delinquency.[54] The courts of many countries have experienced great difficulties in fixing for purposes of municipal law the borderlines between organized group pressure, including peaceful picketing and similar measures of restraint, and the additional elements that turn legitimate into unlawful collective action. This is one, though not the only, reason for the fact that the common-law doctrine in this field is increasingly replaced by statutory regulations.[55]

Lauterpacht argued in 1933 that governments could in no circumstances have a responsibility for acts other than those of State organs because rules of international law in the matter of State responsibility were based on the separation of the State from the individuals and associations of which it is composed,[56] some other writers[57] argued that a State must bear the measure of international responsibility which corresponds to its real control, and that in totalitarian States the private organizations had no freedom of movement but could only act by direction or specific authority of the State. The result seemed to be that divergences of State organization led to differential degrees of State responsibility and a consequent threat to the universality of any legal standards in this field. On reconsideration, it seems to the present writer that in the field of international trade this is a somewhat theoretical controversy. Where there is a minimum of genuine group autonomy, where trade associations, labour unions, religious or political associations or racial groups can operate in freedom, subject only to the general security laws of the country, it is obvious that the State cannot be held responsible for their actions organizing a boycott on trade from a foreign State, even if one could otherwise assume that such an action might be an international delinquency. Undoubtedly such independent action did not exist in Nazi Germany or similarly organized Fascist countries. It would have been unthinkable, for example, for the German Labour Front, the compulsory State labour organization, to take any such action other than by direction of the government. Nor is the position any different for present-day trade union organizations of the Soviet Union or similarly organized countries. However, whenever the status and activities of any such organization are sufficiently closely associated with the government to justify identification, they must be classified as, in effect, actions of a foreign State. It is difficult to see how any such action of a State interfering with the flow of foreign trade could lead to legal responsibility, short of bilateral or multilateral treaty obligations (such as those undertaken by the parties to the General Agreement on Tariffs and Trade). As, in the absence of such specific obligations, any State is free to impose such restrictions on imports and exports as it chooses, by a vast variety of means, its obligation can hardly be increased by vicarious action on the part of organizations that are closely identified with the government. This is probably the main reason why the problem of group interference with foreign trade is likely to remain a theoretical one, outside the sphere of international agreements.

## Hostile Propaganda

The possibilities of inciting disaffection against a foreign government, short of terrorist attacks upon the life or property of persons or institutions within that State, have been immensely increased by the progress of radio telecommunication. Contrary to organized attempts to boycott foreign goods, the physical effect of broadcasting mainly occurs in the foreign territory, while its source is in the state that may be held responsible. It is in that respect far closer to the physical attacks upon lives or properties within the foreign State. It is also more akin to the latter in so far as the emission of radio waves interferes with the sovereignty over the airspace, a principle that the various international conventions concluded between 1927 and 1948 on this subject[58] have not impaired.

For our purposes – an investigation of the extent to which changes in internal social organization affect international legal responsibilities – the main problem is to what extent in times of peace a government must be held responsible for broadcasts hostile to a foreign government, even though it has not itself organized the emission. It is relevant here to note the immense extension of psychological warfare – with radio as its chief instrument – in the last twenty years, and particularly since the last World War. In all the major armed forces of the belligerent nations psychological warfare, i.e. the organized dissemination of propaganda as a means of undermining the will to resistance and inciting disaffection against the hostile government, became a major and integral part of military organization. Its relative significance has, if anything, increased in the period of 'cold war' which precludes direct armed action, but intensifies manoeuvring for political gains in foreign areas.

As this is a new field of international activity – on which customary rules have not developed – there are no more generally recognized international legal rules in this area than, for example, in regard to air warfare which developed after The Hague Conventions on Land and Sea Warfare. Various international conventions on matters of radio communications have been concerned with technical arrangements, except for the Convention of 23 September 1936, concerning the Use of Broadcasting in the Cause of Peace.[59] In that convention, which was signed, among others, by Great Britain, France, the Soviet Union, and the British Dominions, but not ratified by the Soviet Union, the signatories undertook to prohibit the broadcasting within their territories of any transmission calculated by reason of its inaccuracy or otherwise to disturb international understanding or to incite the population of any territory to acts incompatible with the internal order or the security of a territory of a contracting party. It is not unfair to say that this prohibition defines precisely the very activities in which the major parties in the 'cold war' have been engaged since the end of the last war.

What before the war was more or less the monopoly of totalitarian governments has since become a recognized weapon of international political warfare. It is only a logical corollary to the addition of a new arm of warfare to the traditional arsenal of weapons that the sphere of government responsibility should be correspondingly expanded. Nor could or should it make any difference whether the offending broadcasting station is directly government-controlled or operates only by permission of the government. The situation is analogous to that discussed earlier of the export of arms, for which governments now generally assume responsibility by the granting or withholding of export licences. As long as the United States Government exercised sovereignty over West German territory, it could fairly be held responsible for the activities of the privately financed Radio Free Europe. Now such responsibility rests on the West German Government. This corresponds to the quite obvious responsibilities of governments organized as those of the U.S.S.R., Yugoslavia, the United Arab Republic, or Spain. The main difficulty will normally be the proof of any legal connexion between the offending broadcast and any subsequent injury. The degree to which foreign propaganda could be held legally causative of an unsuccessful rebellion will hardly ever be ascertainable, while a successful revolution would turn wrong into right. There remain, of course, political remedies such as diplomatic protests or complaints to the United Nations. For all these purposes, the degree of State responsibility for private propaganda activities is legally relevant. And direct damage may be caused where physical objects, such as balloons with propaganda material, cause damage to aircraft or installations. It is clear, however, that only specific international agreements, either through the United Nations or between a number of States directly concerned, could lead to any definable commitments in this critically important but elusive field.

## International Minimum Standards of Justice

Generally speaking, the citizens of any country residing abroad are subject to the laws of their State of residence. They are thus, in most respects, subject to the combination of legislative, administrative, and judicial standards of the country of residence. But international law has long imposed certain limitations upon the absoluteness of that territorial sovereignty of the national State. The State of the nationality of the alien, claiming on his behalf, has been held entitled to assert a certain minimum of rights in the name of international law. The type of claim that arises in this field – damages for injury to life, liberty, or property caused by legislative, administrative, or judicial actions of the defendant State – is, more than most parts of international law, a matter for litigation. Hence it is not surprising that in this branch of international law international courts and arbitral tribunals have been responsible for the main development of such principles as exist. Despite the voluminous number of judicial precedents, and the extraordinarily large number of monographs and articles written on the subject, much uncertainty remains.[60] This is not surprising, for the question of what may be regarded as a 'minimum standard' of international justice as reflected in the treatment of aliens[61] is intimately connected with the prevailing political philosophy and practice of States. It is not the general subject of State responsibility for international delinquencies, but only the question to what extent major shifts in political and social philosophy may have affected the international minimum standards that will occupy us here.

The problem of minimum standards of protection for individuals is not, of course, confined to international law. It arises in any municipal legal system, either articulately through the embodiment of certain basic rights in a constitution – as in the United States Constitution – or implicitly in standards evolved over the centuries by the courts – as in English law. But international minimum standards are obviously more difficult to ascertain, and more liable to modifications, because only such standards as are prevalent and firmly adhered to among the majority of States that form the family of nations can be deemed to be incorporated in international law.[62]

The most sensitive aspects of 'international minimum standards of justice' crystallize around two major areas: On the one hand, there is the problem of 'due process', a complex of procedural safeguards designed to protect the individual against arbitrariness in the dealings of a foreign State with his life, liberty, or property. On the other hand, there is the question whether there are any limits that international law may properly impose – or can, at least, in the present state of international society, be deemed to have imposed – upon the liberty of any one State to interfere with the life, liberty, and property of an alien in the course of a general legislative change.

To some extent the approach to both these questions depends upon one's basic legal philosophy. Those who believe in a minimum of inalienable natural rights will be more disposed to regard the departure from such rights by any one State as a violation of basic legal principles. Those who, like the present writer, believe that there are no transcendental and immutable natural-law principles detached from specific political and ethical beliefs – however widely these may be accepted among nations – will reject this approach.[63] However, the practical differences between these two approaches should not be exaggerated, at least in the realm of international law. Even the most enthusiastic supporters of natural-law philosophy must concede wide liberty of action to the 'sovereign' States which, with all the variety of their political philosophies, administrative standards, and degrees of development, compose the family of over one hundred and twenty nations. On the other hand, the most determined positivists will not deny that 'general principles of law recognized by civilized nations' constitute a proper source of law, not only for the International Court of Justice,[64] but for the ascertainment of international minimum standards at any given time. It is only on this question, how far, at a time of great turbulence of clashes of political philosophies, and of much social experimentation, such international minimum standards still exist, that some observations will be offered.

*Nationalization and Expropriation.* The basic position is concisely formulated in a statement made by Elihu Root in 1910:

There is a standard of justice, very simple, very fundamental, and of such general acceptance by all civilized countries as to form a part of the international law of the world. The condition upon which any country is entitled to measure the justice due from it to an alien by the justice which it accords to its own citizens is that its system of law and administration shall conform to this general standard. If any country's system of law and administration does not conform to that standard, although the people of the country may be content or compelled to live under it, no other country can be compelled to accept it as furnishing a satisfactory measure of treatment to its citizens. . . .[65]

But the contention that a State may be held legally responsible for any discrepancy between its own legal standards, if applied to nationals and foreigners alike, and any international minimum standards for the benefit of any aliens resident within its jurisdiction, is challenged in the Convention on Rights and Duties of States adopted by the Seventh Pan American Conference at Montevideo in 1933:

The jurisdiction of States within the limits of national territory applies to all the inhabitants.

Nationals and foreigners are under the same protection of the law and the national authorities and the foreigners may not claim rights other or more extensive than those of the nationals.[66]

The controversy between the States that maintain an international minimum standard for aliens, even if this means preferred treatment over nationals, and those States that do not go beyond the acknowledgement of equality between nationals and aliens, is unlikely ever to be resolved. The first group will generally consist of the capital-exporting States, interested in the protection of their foreign investments and the commercial activities of their citizens abroad. The latter will consist of the capital-importing States in a relatively primitive stage of economic development. The number of these States – formerly concentrated in Latin America – has, in the last generation, vastly increased, not only with a series of social revolutions that have swept over Eastern Europe, but through the political emancipation of a number of Asian and African countries which wish to be unimpeded in the manner of their economic and social planning. These countries are to a large extent the same that are still emotionally influenced by resentment against former political and economic domination by certain Western Powers. In practice, however, this attitude is mitigated by their growing realization of the need to give some reasonable protection to foreign capital and enterprise, whose participation, though not domination, the under-developed countries need. On the other hand, even the Communist countries seek increased commercial relations with the West.

It is believed that a solution must be sought on the basis of certain principles 'generally recognized by civilized nations'.

The first of these principles is that generally international law – as distinct from specific regional or bilateral arrangements – cannot interfere with the freedom of political and social experimentation – a legitimate and cherished aspect of national sovereignty on which present-day international law is based. No State or individual can therefore challenge any legal measures of another State that interfere with property, however sweepingly, provided only such legal measures are of general application in the country and do not single out aliens for discriminatory treatment. A necessary proviso is that such seemingly general measures do not disguise a deliberate discrimination against aliens. This can be ascertained only against the specific circumstances of the case. A State is therefore under an obligation to pay compensation for the taking of individual properties of aliens when nationals are not similarly treated.[67] On the other hand, the liberty of a State to expropriate the property of aliens in the course of a general measure affecting nationals and aliens alike is no longer seriously challenged by most authors. Indeed, it is specifically acknowledged by the United States Government in its discussion with Mexico of 1938. There is not a single State today which, by means of an entire or partial nationalization of industries, by police-power or 'eminent domain', restrictions on the acquisition and use of property, or by taxation and a multitude of other instruments of the modern welfare state, does not, to a larger or smaller extent, interfere with private property.

On the second and consequent question whether, in the case of a general expropriation, international law can demand compensation for foreigners, even if it means preferred treatment of aliens, opinions are deeply divided.[68]

It has already been pointed out that on the general principle the 'have' and the 'have-not' nations are bound to remain divided. At the very least, it must be admitted that the assumption that nationalization without compensation is generally held to be a violation of international law is no longer valid. Here, as in so many other fields, beliefs once universally held now deeply divide the nations according to political development and economic circumstances. Nor does the International Declaration of Human Rights of 1948, which may be said to be representative of universally held opinions, take us any further. Article 17, paragraph 2, says that 'No one shall be arbitrarily deprived of his property'. But the word 'arbitrarily' is, of course, subject to different interpretations, and the States claiming the right to expropriate without compensation in the course of a general legislative reform affecting nationals and foreigners alike will claim with strong reason that this is not an 'arbitrary' measure.

It seems more profitable to single out certain situations in which general principles of law recognized among civilized nations clearly demand compensation for the taking of alien property.[69]

The first category derives from the principle of *pacta sunt servanda*. Where a State, by international treaty, or by special contractual arrangements or concessions with foreign individuals or companies, has undertaken to protect them against expropriation or other forms of interference with property, a breach of such undertaking will be clearly an international delinquency. This is so regardless of the international constitutional position of the offending State. A distinction must be drawn between municipal power and international obligation.[70] A national parliament may have power to amend legislation that has incorporated promises in regard to the sanctity of foreign property. The enactment of such amending legislation in breach of an international commitment nevertheless constitutes an international delinquency.

Secondly, the principle of unjust enrichment should now be held to be a general principle of law recognized by civilized nations.[71] Where, as for example in the *Lena Goldfields* case,[72] a foreign company at the specific request of a foreign government has invested capital, work, and technical skill in the development of mines, the expropriation of such property without compensation constitutes an unjust enrichment by the expropriating government at the expense of the alien. The acknowledgement of such a principle will undoubtedly be an important safeguard in the many cases where foreign, e.g. American or British, companies participate at the request of another government in the development of its industries.

Thirdly, there is the principle of estoppel.[73] The borderline between foreign investment undertaken without specific encouragement as a commercial venture and similar actions prompted by specific reliance on the undertakings of another government will not be easy to draw. Nevertheless, such distinctions are real. Where, for example, a State invites, by prospectus or general advertisement, foreign capital to invest in the development of certain utilities or industries, and foreign entrepreneurs have responded to this invitation, an expropriation without compensation clearly justifies the application of the principles of estoppel or *venire contra factum proprium*. The government must be held estopped from acting contrary to reasonable expectations that it has itself created.

If to these categories is added the above-mentioned case of discriminatory treatment of aliens, a large number of situations in which compensation can fairly be expected can be met consistently with general principles of international law and equity, and without adopting the conflicting philosophies and interests of either the 'have' or the 'have-not' countries.

Considerable progress towards workable compromises between the conflicting interests and viewpoints of creditor and debtor States has, in fact, been made in recent years.

Some of the under-developed countries, such as Burma, India, Iran, anxious to attract foreign capital and skill, have either enacted special investment laws or used periodic investment-policy statements laying down the conditions for the admission of foreign enterprises.[74] These usually contain promises of protection of lawfully made investments the violation of which would undoubtedly be subject to estoppel.

Sometimes special agreements are concluded, as the parallel agreements made in 1953 between the Indian Government and three foreign oil companies for the construction of oil refineries, which contain promises of non-expropriation for twenty-five years, and of reasonable compensation for any expropriation undertaken thereafter.

Such agreements are not, of course, treaties, since one of the parties is not a government, nor can they affect the power of the other party to use its sovereign legislative power so as to supersede the promises. This may happen as the result of drastic changes of government or policy, and in the absence of any supra-national authority the value of such promises is limited. However, the solemn public affirmation of certain principles of conduct has a moral as well as a practical sanction, and it is on these that international law mainly rests. Even the most powerful and aggressive State hesitates to be branded as a law-breaker, at a time when the collective impact of world opinion, while far from decisive, plays an increasingly important part in the delicate balance of world power.

Moreover, any State that wishes to keep in good standing with international credit institutions such as the World Bank, will hesitate long before showing contempt for promises given to foreign investors.

A legally somewhat stronger instrument of protection is the bilateral or multilateral treaty, which binds States as such.

In recent years, the United States has concluded a series of bilateral Treaties of Friendship and Commerce, which contain the following typical clause:

Property of nationals and companies of either Party shall not be taken within the territories of the other Party except for a public purpose, nor shall it be taken without the prompt payment of just compensation. Such compensation shall be in an effectively realizable form and shall represent the full equivalent of the property taken; and adequate provision shall have been made at or prior to the time of taking for the determination and payment thereof.[75]

Further typical clauses provide against discrimination in the matter of expropriations and sequestrations and beyond expropriation proper, and include a general injunction against 'unreasonable or discriminatory' impairments of vested interests.

Such treaties are no protection against bad faith or revolutionary upheavals, which may sweep the arbitration clauses overboard, together with the substance of the treaty. But neither do internal constitutions offer absolute protection against revolution or disobedience, as the struggle over desegregation in the United States, or the suspension of the Weimar Constitution by the Hitler government show.

But they do represent express and articulate commitments which impose restraints on the parties as long as observance of international standards does not cease altogether.

There is far less prospect at the present stage for a multilateral convention for the protection of foreign property and investment as it has been recently proposed by a German group.[76] Such a convention must either comprise a majority of capital-importing as well as of capital-exporting States, or it is worthless. But while States of the former group, such as India or Mexico, may enter into *ad hoc* arrangements departing from their general principles, the gap between the interests as well as the political systems and social philosophies of the two groups of States is too fundamental to permit formal agreement on the sacrosanctity of private property. The price of any multilateral convention would be vagueness, and a host of reservations in cases of 'national interest', public emergencies, 'economic necessity', and the like. Such a convention would be likely to share the fate of the 'Optional Clause', which has been effectively submerged under the weight of national reservations.

The less spectacular methods described earlier are likely to be more effective in the slow and painful evolution of principles of international law commensurate with the economic interdependence of nations.

*Due Process.* A far more absolute stand can be taken on the 'due-process' problem. It is true that there are considerable divergences in the civil and criminal procedure as between the common-law and the civil-law countries. It is also true that totalitarian countries, of both the Fascist and the Communist persuasion, have often deviated drastically from standards of administration of justice commonly assumed among civilized nations. Judges selected by political standards, arrest without judicial safeguards, conviction without proper trial, unlimited powers of a secret police responsible to no one except the government, extrajudicial methods of deprivation of personal liberty, procedures of the modern police State – these and a host of other matters are only too familiar. But this is not comparable to the movement for greater legal freedom in regard to interference with property and economic interests – a reflection of general developments in the structure of modern industrial society. With the partial exception of Nazi Germany, totalitarian States have not openly acknowledged or defended arbitrary procedures. They often conflict with their own professed protestations, and international law can clearly take them at their word. The Soviet Constitution of 1936 proclaims the independence of justice,[77] the inviolability of the person,[78] and the inviolability of the homes of citizens.[79] The Universal Declaration of Human Rights – from which the five Communist members abstained, but did not dissent – specifically states (in Articles 9–11) that no one shall be subjected to arbitrary arrest or detention, that everyone is entitled to fair and public hearings by an independent and impartial tribunal, and that everyone charged with a penal offence has the right to be presumed innocent until proved guilty in a public trial provided with proper safeguards for the defence.

From all this it follows that we can still regard a minimum set of safeguards of proper procedure as a general principle of law recognized among civilized nations, and as one which any State can claim on behalf of its nationals abroad.[80]

## SUMMARY OF CONCLUSIONS

1. The increase of direct or indirect State control over economic activities does not affect the traditional field of inter-State relations, except where the rule of law is based on the assumption of private control of economic activities. This is so in the case of jurisdictional State immunities, where the universal adoption of the principles of the Brussels Convention of 1926 is clearly justified. Government corporations formed for the purpose of carrying out commercial or other economic activities should clearly be presumed to be outside the sphere of State immunities.

2. International trade agreements cannot have the same meaning and impose equivalent obligations on State-trading and private-trading States, as trade in the former is essentially an instrument of economic planning and international policy, which alters, for example, the meaning of the most-favoured-nation clause. Trade agreements will tend more and more to be concluded and effective among States of comparable organization.

3. The neutrality rules, which are based on the assumption of private control over trade between neutrals and belligerents, can no longer effectively operate because of the imbalance of obligations between States whose trade is openly State-controlled, and those whose trade is still essentially private. Responsibility can, however, be clearly attached to governments for all those activities over which they have actual or potential legal control powers (e.g. licensing of exports of arms). In regard to neutral trade in general,

the most equitable solution would be to permit neutral governments that openly control their trade to engage in the same activities as the private citizen of other neutral States, and to subject them
to the same penalties. But such a solution, like any other change of
the former rules of neutrality, is unlikely to be acceptable, and it
would greatly increase the risk of direct clashes between belligerent
and neutral governments. In the circumstances effective customary
rules on the subject no longer appear to exist, and the only remedy
lies in *ad hoc* agreements.

4. International State transactions of an economic character,
such as international loans, have elements of both public and private
law breaking across the traditional distinctions between State acts
and private acts.

5. Government responsibility must now be presumed to exist for
activities that are, in effect, an extension of political warfare, even
though they are financed and managed privately. Any State must
be presumed to have the means of stopping activities that are intimately connected with the conduct of foreign relations.

6. State responsibility for international delinquencies extends to
the activities of all those groups and individuals who, by the structure of the State, must be presumed to act by authority of the government.

7. As international law cannot interfere with national freedom of
social and economic experimentation, measures of nationalization
or other interference with private property cannot be considered as
international delinquencies *per se*, unless they are applied arbitrarily
against aliens as such. Where general measures are applied equally
to nationals and foreigners alike, it is doubtful how far a principle of
international law that would justify a claim for compensation is still
recognized among the nations.

Compensation should, however, always be payable as a matter of
law in cases of: (*a*) specific commitments by treaty or contract;
(*b*) unjust enrichment through appropriation of the benefits of
foreign enterprise; (*c*) estoppel, i.e. action contrary to reasonable
expectations created by the action of the offending State itself. Such
compensation will normally be for losses incurred rather than injury
to the expectation of future profits.

8. International law still demands strict adherence to the principles of due process developed by jurisprudence and legal writers
over the years. Even though the administration of justice differs
greatly as between the totalitarian and the non-totalitarian countries, all agree, at least in their professions, on minimum standards

of procedural justice. This is also reflected in the International Declaration on Human Rights.

9. In international cooperative law, the degree of conformity in political and social structure depends on the type of cooperation. Generally, technical agreements and organizations are independent of social structure and therefore still possible on a universal scale. Where such cooperation demands a broad similarity of economic and social organization or principles, it will be essentially confined to States that agree on these matters.

# 15

National Sovereignty and
World Order in the
Nuclear Age

Behind the many discrepancies of social and political structure that
tend to undermine the equilibrium of general international law, and
to intensify legal relations between like-minded States and groups,
there lies the deeper problem of the general trend of international
law and the pattern of international order. The alternative is no
longer simply between, on the one hand, an international society
based on national sovereignty, and, on the other hand, an international society based on the supremacy of a universal international
law and authority. A third alternative, spurred by social developments and international tensions of the post-war period, is the
emergence of several international orders, overcoming the age of
national sovereignty, but dividing the world into several legal
systems, governed by different principles, and linked with each
other at best by loose rules of mutual tolerance, at worst by deep
antagonisms which only the mutual fear of destruction keeps from
bursting out into open war.

### THE PRESENT POSITION OF
### NATIONAL SOVEREIGNTY

After the disasters of the First World War – which shook the physical
and moral foundations of the prosperous and relatively pacific
Western-dominated world of pre-1914 – there was a widespread
belief that the destructiveness of modern war and the growing prox-
imity and interdependence of nations was bound to lead the world
out of the age of national sovereignty and of the national State as
the ultimate repository of legal and political power. The alternative
vision of universal world order began to take practical shape in the
Covenant of the League of Nations. But this was widely seen only as
the beginning of further developments, which would ultimately
produce a world federation or even a world State. The inter-war
period witnessed dozens of blueprints, setting forth in detail the
constitution of such supra-national bodies. Meanwhile, the League
of Nations, cautiously constructed on the principle of unanimity
of decisions of national sovereignty, struggled to work out the

procedures which would turn it into an effective organization for the outlawing and suppression of aggressive war, by a combination of the processes of peaceful settlement and – economic or military – sanctions provided in Articles 11, 15, and 16 of the Covenant. After many years of doubt and failure, these efforts very nearly triumphed when Mussolini's Italy committed an act of unprovoked and naked aggression against Abyssinia, challenging, without adequate military and economic resources, the combined economic and military power of the League members, who had then the sympathy of the United States, not itself a member of the League. It was not the constitutional weaknesses of the League that led to its tragic failure at that historic moment – for the procedures of condemning an act of aggression and imposing the necessary sanctions were developed quickly, and with amazing smoothness, both in the League Council and in the League Assembly – but the combination of political weakness, lack of leadership, and economic interests, particularly in Great Britain and France. The collapse of the League as an effective instrument of international policing against aggression gave the final push to the new Nazi imperialism, which had visions of world order based on one-sided domination.

After the Second World War, an even more deeply shaken and disorganized world approached the problem of world order, as it seemed, more soberly and realistically. The United Nations Charter made a limited gesture in the direction of world law supremacy over national supremacy, by empowering the General Assembly to make recommendations by simple, or in important matters, by a two-thirds majority. But as the recommendations of the Assembly have, in the theory of the Charter, no binding effect, the concession to the majority principle is a limited one. The executive authority was placed by the U.N. Charter in the hands of the Security Council, whose effectiveness depends, by virtue of the veto power of any one of them, on the collaboration of the five permanent members of the Council in the supervision and enforcement of peace and security throughout the world. Provided that a majority of the members of the Security Council, including the five permanent members, agree on a particular course of action, all the members of the United Nations are bound and, to that extent, they have renounced the sovereignty of national decision. But as the veto principle applies to the enforcement of any decisions against one of the permanent members of the Security Council, the national sovereignty of the 'Big Five' effectively limits the majority principle and thereby the supremacy of international law over national sovereignty.

So much for the theory of the United Nations Charter. In practice, the persistence of the tension between the Soviet Union on the one hand, and the other permanent members on the other hand, has paralysed the Security Council as an effective instrument of world order, while it has, to a limited extent, strengthened the authority of the General Assembly and given its recommendations in some cases a moral force stronger than that of a mere recommendation. The relative strengthening of the authority of the General Assembly has occurred simultaneously with the creation and admission to the United Nations of many new States. As, in the General Assembly, each member has one vote, the collective influence of the small States has risen to unprecedented dimensions – ironically at a time when effective military and economic power has come to be more than ever concentrated in the hands of a very few super-States. Whereas, in the former, less organized, international society, a new State had to make its place in the family of nations slowly, by a gradual process of recognition, diplomatic relations, and its effective role in international affairs, today new States, such as Ghana or Guinea, obtain international status and an equal vote, almost immediately after their creation, through their admission to the United Nations. However weak and poor, the new State must establish the apparatus and symbols of sovereignty – diplomatic representation, a government, a civil service, and at least token armed forces. The irony of the situation is heightened by the fact that two of the world's most important States – Communist China and Germany – are kept outside the United Nations, as a result of the tensions between the Soviet *bloc* and the West. The conception of the U.N. Charter, which was to restrain the theoretical legal principle of the equality of all States by an effective predominance, by rights and responsibilities, of the major Powers, has thus become gravely distorted, at least in so far as the United Nations still effectively reflects the actual balance of forces in the world. The price of this increasing gap between political reality and legal form has been an almost continuous decrease in the effectiveness of the United Nations as an international organization of peace, security, and order. On the last occasion when it made, through the General Assembly, an effective contribution to the solution of a major international problem – the Suez Canal crisis – it could do so because, for entirely different reasons, the two most powerful members of the organization, the U.S.A. and the U.S.S.R., joined in the condemnation of the British-French-Israeli intervention.[1]

The triumph of national sovereignty is thus, to some extent, illusory. A price has to be paid for the increasing divergence between legal and political sovereignty. The United Nations General Assembly as a forum of world opinion is used by the major Powers to the extent that they wish to support their claims and positions in international controversies by an appeal to the organized voice of the smaller nations of the world, and these are usually as are the large Powers, divided into contending *blocs*.

It would, however, be dangerously superficial to dismiss the proliferation of national sovereignties as a mere *fata morgana*, a fictitious application of the principle of equality of nations in international law, hiding the reality of world power and world order. In the voting procedures of the United Nations, the triumph of national sovereignties, measured in numbers, may be largely deceptive. But, inside and outside the United Nations, it is buttressed by the stalemate between the major Powers, which, in their world-wide battle for influence and position, must pay high regard to the individual or collective voice of smaller States, whose inclination, one way or another, may decisively tilt the balance. Disregard of the claims of any Arab or Muslim State, however small by itself, may inflame the entire world of Islam and, incidentally, threaten oil supplies. A cavalier treatment of the territorial waters claims of any one Latin American State may affect the entire group of the Latin American world. Alienation of one of the new States of South-East Asia may swing one or several of them from a pro-Western or a neutral position to increasing alignment with the Communist world.

The tension and continuing manoeuvring for position between the big Powers, has worked in support of claims of national sovereignty, especially of the smaller States, far beyond that of earlier periods, mainly in two respects: first, nationalist tensions and the stalemate in the battle between the major Powers have combined to produce a spate of partitions of States once united. In a few cases, the pressure has come mainly from within, an expression of religious, racial, or other factors tending to create a new State. In the post-war period, this has been the main cause of the partition of British India between the Republic of India and the Republic of Pakistan. In the latter, only the common Muslim religion holds together two almost equal parts, separated from each other geographically, traditionally, and economically. Religious and national sentiment have carved the State of Israel out of Palestine. Piecemeal liberation from colonial control has created a large number of new Arab States, but it is the stalemate of the cold war, and no genuine force of nationalism, that has produced the separate States of West and East Germany, of North and South Korea, of North and South Vietnam. But the longer the stalemate goes on, the more do the originally artificial new landmarks of sovereignty tend to become permanent. The new State creates its symbols, its machinery, and traditions. Divergent political, economic, and educational systems in course of time widen the gulf, and a new act of force is needed to restore former or create new unities.[2]

The new partitions and sovereignties create many problems of international law. The division of the waters of the Indus system between India and Pakistan, and of the River Jordan between Israel and the hostile neighbouring Arab States, has highlighted the unsolved problems of the allocation of water rights between upper and lower riparian States, and the technically quite feasible solution of these principles is made infinitely more difficult by the antagonism between the rival partitioned States.

The second, and in this case world-wide, extension of national legal claims, at the expense of long-established international legal freedoms, is a continuing spread of national territorial claims over the once-free sea. The traditionally prevalent three-mile limit for territorial waters is today defended only, with decreasing conviction and effectiveness, by a few Powers with strong maritime interests and traditions (Great Britain, Japan, the United States). A number of States, big and small, such as the Soviet Union, Communist China, Iceland, claim a 12-mile limit. The effectiveness of this inroad upon the freedom of the seas is considerably increased by the decision of the International Court of Justice, in the *Anglo-Norwegian Fisheries* case[3] – now adopted by Article 4 of the Geneva Convention on the Territorial Sea and the Contiguous Zone, of April 1958 – that 'in localities where the coastline is deeply indented and cut into, or if there is a fringe of islands along the coast in its immediate vicinity, the method of straight base lines joining appropriate points may be employed in drawing the base line from which the breadth of the territorial sea is measured'. This has been exploited, for example, by the Republic of Indonesia to draw the base line along the entire group of the archipelago of islands, thus enclosing a formerly open part of the sea as national waters.

Two large maritime States, Great Britain in 1942 and the United States in 1945, themselves took the initiative in claiming exclusive national rights over the exploitation of the resources of the so-called Continental Shelf. Within a few years, this doctrine has been so widely applied by one State after another as to have become part of the accepted law of nations, a short time after its inception.[4] To compensate for the absence of a Continental Shelf, Chile, Peru, and Ecuador have claimed the fantastic limit of 200 miles of territorial waters, although such a claim has not been internationally accepted. The claim of a 12-mile limit by a small State like Iceland, overwhelmingly dependent on its fishery, has led to a state of near warfare between Great Britain and Iceland, and a similar situation may occur at any time off the coast of China.

To the extension of territorial water limits and the recognition of the Continental Shelf must be added the recognition of the 'contiguous zone', of 'hot pursuit', and the claim for exclusive powers over certain areas adjacent to a 'coastal State' by the latter. It is no exaggeration to speak of a 'crisis in the law of the sea'.[5]

In this clash of conflicting national claims, the Powers, and even the major naval Powers, are divided by their own conflicting interests (e.g. as between Great Britain and the United States on the one hand, and the Soviet Union on the other) or by cold-war strategy, which may, for example, impel Russia to lend support to exaggerated territorial claims of such States as the various parts of Arabia or to Indonesia, in order to deny traditional rights to the Western Powers.

The proliferation, both of the number and the extent of conflicting national claims put forward in the name of sovereignty, greatly increases the need for a world-wide international legal solution. The conflicting national interests in the exploitation of fishing grounds call for an international convention – as universal as possible – on the conservation of fishing resources, and for joint scientific study. But while the Whaling Convention – which is in force – and the as yet unratified International Fishery Conservation Conventions of 1958 are modest beginnings in this direction, the intensity of the national emotions aroused, as well as the strategic conflicts of the various Powers, make a general solution a hope for the future. There is also an urgent need for an international convention on the use of international rivers, applying the principles of equitable distribution and abuse of rights between the various riparian States as a restraint on national power. But in this field, too, national antagonisms have so far prevented even the most desperately needed solutions.

### REGIONAL GROUPINGS AND UNIVERSAL INTERNATIONAL LAW

For all the deep political rivalries and fissures of the post-war world, the legal organization of mankind, on a universal basis, has made some advance. It is, however, significant that real progress has been almost entirely confined to the fields in which the vital interests and standards of nations diverge little. Thus the World Health Organization has been empowered and been able to get certain international sanitary standards and procedures adopted among its near-universal membership; the International Civil Aviation Organization has enacted a navigation code which is used not only by the large number of its Member States, but will almost certainly have to be observed by non-members, such as the Soviet Union, as they come to take a significant part in international commercial aviation. On the other hand, the International Labour Organization has been able to make only very limited progress in the definite adoption, by way of multilateral conventions, of labour standards in all but a few fields, even though its advisory and directive influence has been considerable. For the common regulation of labour standards in matters of wages, working hours, holidays, employment of women and children, and the like, cuts deeply into the field of vastly divergent national, economic, and social standards.

Because a common law in matters affecting the constitutional, social, economic, and personal life demands a degree of common interests and values that, unhappily, does not at present unite the nations at large, some of the most important developments in international law have occurred through regional or functional groupings, some of them antagonistic to each other. Such groupings arise from a variety of motives. The North Atlantic Treaty Organization (N.A.T.O.) and the Warsaw Pact bring together, in a military alliance that entails varying degrees of integration of military command, coordination of defence production, and joint policy bodies, the States that face each other in the European theatre of the cold war. The various European regional organizations which partly supplement and partly overlap each other, such as the three community organizations of six West European States, the wider Organization for Economic Cooperation and Development (O.E.C.D.) and the even wider Council of Europe have arisen, more positively, from the increasing recognition of joint interests and values, which the preservation of old national sovereignties and rivalries would increasingly have imperilled. Significantly, much the most important development in this direction has occurred among mature European States, which have long histories of national sovereignty, and bitter memories of the destructiveness of the exercise of military, political, and economic sovereignty in our time. Much more dimly, similar tendencies begin to take shape among other groups of States, linked by common ties of geography, religion, political aspirations, or economic interests, but as yet too much enmeshed in their recently won political or economic sovereignty to see it in all its limitations. There are efforts to create closer economic links between the States of Latin America, inspired by the incipient Customs Union of the European Economic Community of the Six; there are dim outlines of an emergent regional association of the Arab States, and West Africa, though they may become submerged in a continuing expansion of Nasser's United Arab Republic; but it would seem that far greater emergencies and catastrophes may be needed to produce major developments outside the heart of Europe.

## THE DEVELOPMENT OF INTERNATIONAL LAW ON THREE LEVELS

International law is today developing on three different levels, and it is only by seeing them in perspective that we can hope to ascertain the trend of international society.

On the first level, international law is still based and, in certain respects as shown, continues to expand on the basis of national sovereignty and legal equality of nations.[6] But the growing discrepancy between the extravagant claims based on the national sovereignty of a rapidly increasing number of States, only a small minority of which have the minimum attributes of political, military, economic – as distinct from legal – sovereignty, heightened by the strategic exigencies of the cold war, is leading to a second level of regional or functional groupings of States. Such groupings may well be the most fertile and intensive source of international legal development in the fields reaching below the surface of social and human relationships. Thirdly, universal international law, as represented by the United Nations Organization, its special agencies and international conventions on specific subjects, of a universal or near-universal character, is expanding slowly in those fields where common interests and necessity are not deeply affected by divergent interests and standards. This is particularly the case in the areas of communications and health.

The interrelation of these three levels of international law requires further elaboration.

Much the most definite developments in the direction of closer legal integration between like-minded States are today presented by the Communist *bloc* directed by the Soviet Union, and by the more halting efforts of groups of West European nations to form closer legal units.

Without any need to abandon the formal symbols of national sovereignty – which, indeed, is a vital weapon in the arsenal of the Communist ideology of 'coexistence' – the policies and systems of Communist nations can be easily coordinated because of the similarity of their structure. Their political organization, centred in a strong executive, operating throughout the monolithic party organization which controls all spheres of public and social life, is almost identical in all the Communist States. This facilitates, in inter-State relations, the formation of a trading *bloc*, in inverse proportion to the difficulties of trading between State-trading and free-trading nations.[7] All external trade is centred in national agencies which form part of the national economic plan and can trade with the other Communist States on a basis of barter for specific items guided by economic development plans.

Far more interesting as well as difficult are the corresponding efforts recently made by democratic nations of Western Europe and the North Atlantic region.

The widest of these, N.A.T.O., is also the most loosely organized. It has no separate legal personality; it is essentially still a multilateral military alliance, although one that, contrary to the traditional alliances, has permanent headquarters and coordination at the command level, and, to a limited extent, on the operational level. A permanent Secretariat, headed by a Secretary General, and a permanent Council of Delegates, supplemented periodically by meetings of Foreign Ministers, reinforces this structure, however. In the long run, the fate of N.A.T.O. depends on the success of, so far inconclusive, efforts to coordinate the various national defence organisms and, in particular, the allocation and production of vital defence items. The theoretically most challenging provision of the Treaty is Article 2,[8] which so far has remained an aspiration, and it is doubtful whether it will ever surmount the obstacles presented by national economic policies as well as by other more active regional economic groupings.

The Council of Europe also is a loose organization without separate personality, expressing the common aspirations of Western Europe in the wider sense rather than an integrated organization. It is devoid of executive power and the deliberations of its Assembly often have an air of impotence and futility. Yet, it has to its credit some significant achievements, such as the initiative in the creation

of the European Payments Union. By far its most important achievements in the legal field are the Conventions on Human Rights, concluded in 1949 and 1952. For these Conventions, now ratified by the
required minimum number of members, have established, within
the framework of the Council, both a Commission equipped with
inquiry and quasi-judicial functions, and the European Court of
Human Rights,[9] to which the Member States and, where the particular State has agreed, also groups and individuals within the
State, may appeal for redress against infractions of human rights.[10]
In other words, a supra-national authority is here empowered to
call to justice States for the infringement of rights that are generally
still considered as a cherished preserve of national sovereignty. Such
a partial transfer of national power to a supra-national authority is
possible only among States which, for all differences of tradition
and political philosophy, share a minimum of common standards
and traditions in the relation of State and individual.

Much the most important experiment in the integration of standards, in the transfer of national powers to a supra-national authority, is the progress of the community institutions of the six States of
Western Europe which, in 1952, formed the European Coal and
Steel Community. While the Constitutions of the European Coal
and Steel Community, Euratom, and the Economic Community
differ from each other in significant respects, both as regards the
functions and the scope of the Executive Authority (called High
Authority or Commission), the powers of the Council of Ministers,
which represents the national sovereignty element, and the functions of the Court of Justice and Assembly – both organs serving the
three Communities, but interpreting three different Treaties – they
all represent a decisive advance over the principle of unanimity of
decision, implemented in the universal international organizations.
The decisions validly taken by the Executive Authority – with or
without the concurrence of the Council of Ministers, as the case may
be, and subject to the vote of non-confidence that may be passed by
a two-thirds majority of the Assembly – are majority decisions, and
automatically binding on the members, who are also obliged to
enforce the decisions by their own judicial organs.

The partial integration of national sovereignties, in regional or
functional groupings, presents new problems for a universal international order. The establishment of a Customs Union between the
six West European States, through the Economic Community,
creates tensions with the wider and looser O.E.C.D. Organization,
as well as with the even wider General Agreement on Tariffs and

Trade (G.A.T.T.). Whether the eventual effect of these partial and more closely knit international organizations on universal world order will be beneficial or otherwise is as yet an open question. But it is a situation which cannot be altered by mere technical improvements of organization and coordination. It is quite possible that the international or supra-national associations, now developing monolithically in the Communist world and, more experimentally, in different parts of the Western world, will remain or even grow in mutual antagonism, that they will establish a minimum of mutual contacts, beyond the necessities of diplomatic relations, or that they will even go to war with each other. But the political and social forces in the world today are such that it is these competing orders which are the chief agents in the development of what I have tentatively termed 'cooperative international law', and that some of them may become federal or even unitary States. Certainly, it is not possible to evade this problem by elaborate constitutional blueprints of world organizations, such as has recently been attempted.[11] The proposal, for example, to divide the members of a reformed General Assembly of the United Nations into seven groups, from those over 140 million to those under 0·5 million, with correspondingly staggered representation, as the pre-condition of giving such an Assembly legislative power in matters related to the maintenance of peace, is, of course, more realistic than one which would maintain the equality of vote for all. But it ignores the vital question whether the rapidly increasing number of states will be prepared to entrust legislative powers to such an Assembly, merging all their deep-seated differences and conflicts of values and interests. Creative imagination and scholarship are indeed needed to articulate nascent trends and ideas, to fire the imagination of the indifferent and the hesitant, and to devise legal procedures concretizing new principles and ideas. But to elaborate detailed constitutional procedures unrelated to the basic political realities of a period is an exercise in draftsmanship rather than a contribution to the overwhelming problems of our time.

The only serious justification for any hope that the deeply divided and antagonistic nations and power *blocs* of the world may merge their powers and purposes in a universal organization equipped with more than debating functions, lies in the overwhelming threat of contemporary technological and scientific developments to the security and, indeed, to the survival of mankind. The destructive capacity of the H-bomb, which dwarfs the destructive power even of the early A-bombs; the development of inter-continental missiles which can cross the oceans in fractions of an hour, travelling at tremendous heights; the early prospect of manned rockets landing on the moon or, in years to come, even on planets, coupled with the capacity to set up service stations in outer space, and the fact that all these overwhelmingly destructive devices are now available to the major opposing powers, and not to one side only, are held by some to be an almost irresistible impelling force towards a far more advanced world order than that represented by the present world Organization.[12]

There can be few who would not ardently desire that this prediction comes true, but many who will doubt that fear of untold misery and extinction, even if mutually administered to all the major powers and perhaps all mankind, will, by itself, bring about the surrender of vital sovereign powers to a body in which no one nation can hope to attain control, or even a decisive influence. Perhaps another, unimaginably destructive world war will teach the lesson, though mankind, after such a war, is more likely to find itself reduced to a level of primitive and disorganized existence rather than engaged in the elaboration of world constitutions. Meanwhile, the evidence seems overwhelming that the admittedly unparalleled destructive power of modern weapons will, at best, induce the contending *blocs* to remain at arm's length and to develop for this purpose such legal relations and contacts as are required for the maintenance of a live and let live co-existence. This is a very different thing from the gradual integration of principles and institutions, as it is being attempted by the nations of Western Europe. It is possible that the desire to minimize serious and possibly mortal conflicts between the rival groups of powers will lead to some agreement on partly or wholly neutralized zones of 'disengagement', and to a measure of joint or international control over the maintenance of the state of balance. It is conceivable that the almost fantastic progress of the means of transport and communication will at last bring home to the nations of the world the anachronisms of national sovereignty. In the Antarctic region, some at least of the many different nations that have established outposts and sent scientific expeditions have so far refrained from claiming sovereignty over certain parts of the region, while they are far from agreeing on any form of international ownership or control. National sovereignty over outer space above the air – which latter is universally considered as part of national territory[13] – is a physical impossibility, since the area above the national airspace constantly changes, owing to the rotation of the earth around its own axis and around the sun.[14] Perhaps the rival States which are attempting to be the first to land on the moon will refrain from appropriating all or part of it as national territory. Such agreements, silent or overt, of abstention are as necessary as the multiplicity of contacts which are necessary and increasing, to maintain even the essentially technical level of relations between the different nations of the world. It is extremely important that a universal organization, such as the United Nations, be kept in active operation for the purpose of these universal levels of coexistence and even limited cooperation. It is most desirable that membership of such an organization – as detached as possible from the rivalry of ideologies and political systems – be universal. Hence, it is deeply to be regretted that recent State practice, and particularly that of the United States, has once more deflected the essentially technical instrument of recognition of a State which is effectively in control of a given territory and population, to ideological purposes, and thus made it almost impossible to make international agreements, on surprise attacks, nuclear detection, and the like universal. This seems to be a misconception of the function of recognition in international law, and it appears to be based on the failure to distinguish between the different levels of international law. On the level on which universality is both necessary and possible, recognition is and should be the necessary mechanism of acknowledging the existence of a State, or of a new government of a State, as an effective unit of international society. On the level of cooperative international law, where we deal with the community of economic and social institutions, and of human rights, the world will have to progress through less than universal regional or functional groupings of more closely knit States – often developing in mutual antagonism – hoping for the day when common faith or necessity may bring about a truly universal world order.

Part Six

Conclusions

STATE, GROUP, AND INDIVIDUAL

Each of the foregoing chapters has been concerned with some aspects of the tension between the claims of the individual, the claims of a group with which the individual is linked by ties of choice or necessity, and the claims of the State. Which of these is supreme in contemporary society? Has the State, a modern Leviathan, absorbed the individual in his service, determining not only the conditions of his material existence, but of his thoughts and emotions? Or is he enchained by the group on which he is dependent, by tradition or necessity, such as the Catholic Church – more demanding in its control over the lives and actions of its members than any other religious authority – the industrial corporation by which he is employed; the labour union to which he must belong, in law or in fact, if he wishes to exercise his skill; the semi-official guild which controls the conditions of admission to a skilled profession? Or has the individual, on the contrary, begun to be truly emancipated, free at last from the shackles of status, from the taboos of caste class or race distinctions, freer above all than at any other time in history from the enslaving effects of poverty and ignorance?

It is possible to support any of these contentions with powerful arguments.

That the State today exercises a degree of control over the individual far exceeding, in scope and intensity, that of any other period in history, has been apparent throughout our discussion of the major legal institutions of the contemporary world. It has taken over many responsibilities formerly confined to the family, or it has added new duties which take the individual out of the family nexus: responsibility for education, obligations of national service, family allowances; in the field of personal family relations, the enlargement of divorce and nullity grounds, adoption and other new State-regulated institutions profoundly affect the conditions of family life. The State has taken over vast responsibilities in the field of employment: statutory minimum standards of wages and of conditions of work; unemployment insurance and old-age pensions;

workman's compensation or industrial insurance; and the official protection of collective labour agreements.

The State has everywhere imposed far-reaching restrictions upon the use of private property, culminating in various degrees of power to expropriate for public purposes and, in many cases, the public ownership and operation of basic industries.

In the field of contract, public policy restricts the freedom of the parties by various illegality tests, designed to protect certain basic freedoms: of worship, association, labour, trade, and others, and by shielding, to some extent, the weaker party from the more obvious effects of inequality of bargaining.

Where trade remains in private hands, a complex supervisory apparatus regulates the conditions of fair trade, by a multitude of statutory provisions and institutional controls, from compulsory tariffs of hire-purchase transactions to the elaborate apparatus of anti-trust laws, restrictions on mergers, monopolies, and so forth.

To some extent, similar functions are exercised by the criminal law which, by means of so-called public-welfare offences, assures compliance with certain minimum standards of trade and business.

To many it will appear, however, that, at least in contemporary Western society outside the Communist sphere, the group to which the individual is immediately beholden controls his life more directly, and more powerfully, than the more distant State.

While, on the whole, religious controls have greatly weakened in modern society, the Catholic Church still has a commanding influence over the personal life of its followers, especially in such matters as divorce and birth control. The great majority of people, dependent for their livelihood on gainful employment, are subject to the dual discipline of their employer and of the collective organization – professional body, trade association, or labour union – which in large measure controls the conditions under which they may work, and often enjoys monopolistic power. At the same time, every member of the community is, as citizen and consumer, subject to the conditions imposed by the standardized contract terms of the group in control of the particular activity: transport, insurance, rent, supplies of basic materials.

To a considerable extent, the power of one group is checked by the countervailing power of another: that of the corporation by that of the labour union, that of the big manufacturer by that of the big retailer, that of the dominating producers in one commodity by the competition of other materials. But the consumer is generally unorganized and helpless, except for the minimum protection afforded to him by the State, e.g. through supervision of public utilities or the protection, as yet very halting, of the individual employee or worker against the arbitrary power of the corporation or the union.

Again, certain important activities are controlled in some communities by the State, in others by the private group. This is particularly true of the sensitive and, for the long-term future of humanity, probably decisive, sphere of the activities of the mind: schools, universities, public press, radio, and television. Here, the freedom of the mind and the ability of the individual to develop to his fullest potential are perilously poised between the dangers of total State control over the instrumentalities of modern education and communications and the dangers of private group control, dominated by commercial interests and the political philosophy of big business.

Clearly, the balance between these conflicting claims, pressures, and values is differently struck in different communities. Where either the State – controlled by a small group of policy-makers – or a private group equipped with overwhelming resources is wholly or overwhelmingly in control, the individual is crushed, and freedom is either extinguished or emptied of its meaning. Either the direct thought-control of the totalitarian State – Communist or Fascist – or the deadening glare of commercial television, with its subtle undermining of individual judgement, may lead modern mankind towards 1984.

The law can do much to ensure a fair balance between the conflicting demands and pressures. It can, as we have seen, devise safeguards for the protection of the individual, both against arbitrary executive power and against the unchecked power of private groups, so that it can help to ensure a fair balance between conflicting groups within the State. It can help or hinder a particular trend. But in the strong battle of social forces on which our future depends, the law is but one of many moulding elements. Although, as we have seen in the introductory chapter, the law is today a much more active agent in social evolution than in former times, it is still an instrument of order, bearing the imprint of the forces that shape our society.

## *Freedom and Status*

In legal terms, some of the major issues of our time can be formulated in terms of the antithesis of status and freedom. Maine's celebrated dictum that, in progressive societies, the move has been from status to freedom, has long been modified by events which have surrounded the freedom of modern man with new status conditions. This expresses itself not only in the field of contract – Maine's symbol of the emancipation of the individual – but in many other fields of law. The institutionalization of contract, through compulsory terms, standardized conditions, collective bargaining, and other developments, has been analysed in the contract chapter.[1] The result is a new kind of status, for the worker who must accept the conditions set for him by groups of employers and labour officials, while the consumer must eat, dwell, or travel on terms prescribed for him by standardized contracts. Similar developments can be traced in the field of tort liability and, to some extent, in criminal law. The theory corresponding to Maine's contract dictum would show a movement from liability and responsibility for acts as such, to liability for actions or omissions for which a morally fully responsible individual would answer because he has exercised freedom of choice. Yet, we have seen that tort liability is increasingly moving away from the fault principle – which, itself, has lost the moral connotation of former centuries – and that, to an ever-increasing extent, status-like insurance is substituted for the individual responsibility flowing from the tortious act. In some degree, the growth of the statutory offence – often detached from *mens rea* – shows a parallel development in criminal law. The growth of the new status versus individual freedom means that legal liability again results more and more from a given position – as employer, land owner, consumer, worker – rather than from the exercise of the free will by an independent individual.

Yet this is not the status of medieval law. For the new status, while limiting this often theoretical freedom of decision of the individual – a freedom that led to the degradations, the slums, the miseries of the many, compared with the wealth and power of a very few – has at the same time released new energies and given new opportunities. The worker who is dependent on whatever his employers and union may work out for him between them has, at the same time, far greater opportunities of education and intellectual development. The law ensures for him minimum standards of work, housing, and compensation, which free him from the incessant toil of the feudal peasant and the early industrial worker. In modern democracies the law has gradually, though often against tremendous obstacles, diminished or removed the status barriers that kept people relentlessly within their class, race, or religion. In particular – and here we see the main principle still working itself out in a kind of delayed action effect – the married woman now enjoys a legal freedom of movement never enjoyed before in the history of Western civilization.

And where modern industrial and urbanized man has surrendered his legal freedom – as he has largely in labour relations, as a member of the armed forces or civil service, or as a consumer – he has done so not by a necessity inherited by tradition from generation to generation, but by choice, for in a world where the average person is perilously poised between an abundant life and total destruction, the craving for security has largely displaced the craving for freedom. It is not only the worker who increasingly prefers a civil-service-like security to the individual freedom to come and go as he likes, but in the days of the large corporation, of the salaried executive replacing the old-style entrepreneur, the desire for security and stability of employment has largely displaced the adventurousness and uncertainties of early capitalism. The mythology of 'free enterprise' survives, especially in the annual speeches of the presidents of manufacturers' and employers' associations. The ideology of 'free enterprise' is usually more articulate when it is a question of opposing taxation or union demands than when it comes to a call for State action for higher protective tariffs against competitive imports. It is not from higher taxes – which may, or at least should, in part finance better schools – but from the dulling of the minds through mass-produced slogans and entertainment that the danger of a new 'status' society arises, a society more enslaved than feudal Europe, because it has the memory and the techniques of freedom, because it is articulate in a way that an inner élite of skilful and ruthless manipulators can exploit to consolidate their own dominion, while keeping the masses in a state of dumb passivity, hovering between contentment and the threat of annihilation.

## The Welfare State and the Rule of Law

The scientific significance of the vast volume of discussion – learned and otherwise – about the meaning of the 'rule of law' is of modest proportions.

In a purely formal sense, the rule of law means no more than organized public power. In that sense, any system of norms based on a hierarchy of orders, even the organized mass murders of the Nazi régime, qualify as law.[2] As the 'science of law' is understood by positivist theories – the rule of law means the rule of organization. Such a concept is as unassailable as it is empty.

It is on the rule of law in its ideological sense, as implying the yardstick by which to measure 'good' against 'bad' law that the discussion has centred.[3] The difficulty, however, is that to give to the 'rule of law' concept a universally acceptable ideological content is as difficult as to achieve the same for 'natural law'. In fact, the two concepts converge. Just as natural-law philosophy covers the whole spectrum from revolutionary to ultra-conservative ideologies, so the 'rule of law' means to one the absolute integrity of private property, to another the maintenance of private enterprise, free from State control and official regulation, and to another the preservation of the 'right to work' against the power of the unions to determine conditions of labour. To some, the rule of law means a minimum of administrative power, even if it entails the sacrifice of good government, whereas to others it means, on the contrary, assurance of the State to all of minimum standards of living and security.

Is it possible to extract, from the welter of extravagant and conflicting claims, any minimum content that is generally acceptable? Such an attempt must, of course, base itself on values and standards acceptable to contemporary society, not on conditions of the past. For this reason, as we already noted in an earlier chapter,[4] Dicey's formulation of the rule of law is no longer acceptable, since it equates the rule of law with the absence not only of arbitrary, but even of 'wide discretionary' power.[5]

The weaknesses of Dicey's conception are magnified in the modern reformulation of the rule of law by Hayek, which: (a) identifies the rule of law with the economic and political philosophy of *laissez faire*, and (b) is predicated on the fixity of legal rules, and the corresponding absence of judicial discretion.[6]

Other than in a purely formal sense, we cannot formulate any content for the 'rule of law' which would be equally applicable to Democratic, Fascist, Communist, Socialist, and Catholic States. The problem is narrowed down if we seek to establish a meaning for the rule of law in modern democratic society, but even here we shall have to differentiate between various types of democracies. Thus, the common-law tradition emphasizes the need for a unitary system of judicial control as an essential safeguard of individual liberties against administrative arbitrariness, while the Continental systems regard the full-fledged hierarchy of administrative courts as a more secure safeguard against abuse of public power.

But the differences within the common-law family are no less important, especially as between the British and the American model of a 'government under law'. Any attempt to formulate a concept of the rule of law acceptable to modern democratic ideas must seek to find a common denominator.[7]

A democratic ideal of justice must rest on the three foundations of equality, liberty, and ultimate control of government by the people. It is, however, far from easy to give these concepts a specific content. Democracy is certainly based on the ideal of equality, but no democratic State has seriously attempted to translate this ideal into the absolute equality of all. There are numerous inevitable inequalities of function and status, between adults and infants, between sane persons and insane, between civilians and military, between private citizens and officials. We can still not formulate the principle of equality in more specific terms than Aristotle who said that justice meant the equal treatment of those who are equal before the law. We can give to this apparent tautology a more concrete meaning by saying that a democratic ideal of justice demands that inequalities shall be inequalities of function and service but shall not be derived from distinctions based on race, religion, or other personal attributes. In a society governed by international law we should add that inequalities must not be based on nationality. But in a society still dominated by national sovereignty this is no more than a pious aspiration.

The meaning of 'liberty' is hardly more easy to define. In terms of a democratic ideal of justice, liberty means certain rights of personal freedom which must be secure from interference by government. They include legal protection from arbitrary arrest, freedom of opinion and association, of contract, labour, and many others. Briefly, they may be subsumed under the two broad categories of the freedom of the person and the freedom of the mind. But there is perhaps only one legal and constitutional maxim of general validity which can be deduced from this principle: that in so far as an individual is granted specific rights they should be secure from arbitrary interference.

This means that a judiciary as independent from interference by the executive as is possible, given the interlocking of State functions and the human factor in the judicial function, is an essential of the democratic ideal of justice. But it is impossible to lay down a generally accepted rule either as to the substance of these rights or as to the manner of their protection. The Declaration of Rights, adopted in 1948 by the United Nations, is vastly different from the Bill of

Rights embodied in the American Constitution. The Australian Constitution contains no individual rights other than the guarantee of religious freedom and perhaps – though this is still very much open to doubt – a protection of the individual from the restriction of free inter-State trade by State regulation (s. 92). A similar position obtains in Canada owing to the interpretation given by the Privy Council to the 'property and civil rights' clause of the British-North America Act. British law knows of no guarantees of individual rights other than the limited guarantee of personal freedom in the Bill of Rights of 1688 and the Habeas Corpus Acts. This leads to a more fundamental difference between two types of democratic constitution. In one type of democracy, a written constitution, which it is normally very difficult to alter, formulates and at the same time petrifies the meaning of the rule of law in a manner binding upon legislative and executive alike. Under these systems, a law court acquires the decisive function of an authoritative interpreter of the meaning of the rule of law, within the framework of the constitution. This conception of 'government under law', classically represented by the United States legal system, commends itself especially to federal democracies (though not to all of them) and the post-war Constitutions of West Germany and India have placed a court in a comparable position of ultimate arbiter, both of individual rights guaranteed in the Constitution, and of the respective rights and powers of Federation and States. It is difficult to exaggerate the difference between this system of ultimate judicial control, which gives way to political control only in the rare cases of constitutional amendment by referendum, and the purely political control of constitutional power which prevails in countries such as Great Britain.[8] There the rule of law leaves Parliament as the supreme law-giver, and the judge has the much more limited function of interpreting statutes, in so far as they come before him. If his interpretation differs too much from that of prevailing public opinion, a simple statute will alter the law. The difference between these two types of democratic systems is far more fundamental than that between English and Continental ideals of justice which Dicey exaggerated so much.[9]

Lastly, the principle of control by the people means that law must ultimately be the responsibility of the elected representatives of the people. This is, indeed, a vital principle but it can say little about the technique by which the modern legislator can discharge this function.

A more serious and universal danger to the principles of representative democracy arises from the decline of active civic participation – a product of the explosive increase of numbers, of urbanization, and of the dulling impact of modern mass media of communication. Some democracies – e.g. Australia – seek to solve the problem of apathy by statutory compulsion to vote. But even such a system – which many other democracies reject as basically undemocratic – cannot create an active sense of participation, beyond the occasional process of voting. On the national level, only a few small democracies, notably Switzerland, have been able to preserve something of a direct participation of the average citizen in national processes. The large democracies of today must seek to maintain or revive the average citizens' sense of responsibility and participation by a variety of devices: education in public and international affairs, which, of course, is meaningful only where freedom of press and other media of opinion is vigorously maintained; the decentralization of functions in the body politic, which enables the citizen to participate actively in the affairs of his local community (covering such vital fields as education, health, town planning, and the like), of his church, his trade union, or the various social services. None of these devices can counter the basic facts of our society, which tend to separate the elected representatives of the people more and more from the electors, because of numbers, distances, and the complexities of the modern machinery of government. It is all the more important that the law should be rigorous and vigilant in its watch over abuses, e.g. in assuring freedom from pressure in elections, in the standards of integrity imposed upon members of legislative bodies no less than those of the executive and the judiciary. By such preventive and curative devices, the law can help to maintain or restore the principles of control by the people – and the means by which it attempts to do so must vary from country to country and from one situation to another. The basic safeguard of this aspect of the 'rule of law' lies, however, in extra-legal elements: only a society whose members are imbued with their personal sense of responsibility can profit from legal safeguards.

### Modern Government and the Rule of Law

No contemporary analysis of the rule of law can ignore the vast expansion of government functions which has occurred as a result both of the growing complexity of modern life, and of the minimum postulates of social justice which are now part of the established public philosophy in all civilized countries.

Five different State functions call for analysis. They result from the activities of the State: first, as Protector; secondly, as Dispenser of Social Services; thirdly, as Industrial Manager; fourthly, as Economic Controller; fifthly, as Arbitrator.

The State acts first as a protector. This is its traditional function, and classical liberal thought regards it as the only legitimate function of the State. Older British and American decisions reflect this conception in describing defence, foreign affairs, police, and the administration of justice as the legitimate functions of the State.[10] To this may be added a limited taxing power confined to the efficient discharge of these functions. These are the traditional spheres of State sovereignty, and consequently, it is in this field that the inequalities which detract from the rule of law in Dicey's sense are most evident, though Dicey consistently attempted to belittle them for the sake of his principle. The immunities and privileges of the Crown, in regard to litigation, taxing, submission to statutes, and other fields, are survivals of feudal sovereignty; the special law and jurisdiction for military forces are an aspect of the defence power. The important prerogatives of the executive lie in the fields of foreign affairs and defence. The emergency defence powers of the executive in time of danger, the so-called acts of State, and other prerogatives which are above judicial scrutiny are all detractions from the principle of equality. They are bearable only as long as State functions are limited. As the activities of the State extend in the direction of industrial and commercial enterprise and of social services, the whole field of these privileges and immunities requires redefinition and limitation; otherwise it would gradually engulf a growing portion of the whole field of law.[11]

But three further and increasingly important functions of the modern State now look for adequate legal analysis. The first of these is the function of the State as dispenser of social services. Legally it expresses itself in two different ways. Many important social services are discharged through the imposition of compulsory duties and conditions on private relationships. A multitude of statutory duties affects both public and private law; their infringement leads to fines, as well as to remedies at the suit of persons protected by the statute. There is a parallel expansion of common-law duties of employers towards employees through the assimilation of new principles of public policy by the law courts.[12] At the same time, social minimum standards are enforced through compulsory conditions in contract. Service contracts are subject to many such compulsory terms. The Truck Acts invalidate provisions for payment in kind to defined categories of servants. Repatriation Acts compel the reinstatement of ex-servicemen. Agriculture Acts lay down compulsory terms of agricultural tenancies in the interests of agricultural efficiency. Employment contracts are subject to compulsory insurance terms.

The discharge of social-service functions also requires a multitude of active administrative and managerial functions by government departments or independent public authorities. Public and private law are intermingled. Catchment boards, regional hospital boards, repatriation commissions, forest commissions, discharge administrative functions of a social-service character. In doing so, they must make contracts, buy and sell large quantities of equipment and other goods, engage and dismiss staff, and undertake altogether a multitude of activities regulated by the law of property, tort, and contract. The main legal problem here is the adjustment of administrative discretion and private law obligations. The discussion of this problem has shown the need to bring the legal duties of public authorities into line with the general law, except where this would impair the fulfilment of overriding public duties.[13]

A supplementary and generally more important safeguard for the proper exercise of administrative discretion is provided by administrative law, through general directives and standards. An example is given by the Ministry of Education circulars or by the many public service regulations. This raises the twin problems of delegated legislation and administrative jurisdiction. It is necessary that administrative actions affecting the community as a whole or groups of individuals should as far as possible follow general directives and that these directives should be subject to parliamentary scrutiny. It is equally necessary that issues affecting important rights of the citizen should be subject to decision by an independent tribunal. The constitution of compensation tribunals to assess the compensation in the case of the nationalized industries, or of school tribunals to decide on the closing down of independent schools, are important moves in this direction.

It would, for instance, be a great step forward if the multitude of different compensation tribunals could be combined in a single compensation court, which should have general competence and should form part of a coordinated system of administrative jurisdiction.[14] Lastly, the growing practical and theoretical importance of administrative law should be recognized by the publication and systematization of the judgements of administrative tribunals. This would greatly assist the development of public-law principles, in which the administrative courts of the Continent have played an outstanding part.

Next, the modern State increasingly engages in the conduct of industrial and commercial activities. It does so either directly, through the State ownership of ships or railways or – increasingly – through independent corporate authorities, such as coal boards, transport commissions, atomic energy authorities, or State trading corporations. Sometimes, the State simply acquires a controlling interest in a company. The legal form of the enterprise, which is, from a sociological and economic point of view, a matter of accident, should not determine legal rights and liabilities. While the Crown must be made fully liable in tort and in contract, commercial and industrial activities should as a rule be carried on by incorporated public authorities. The Crown will always enjoy certain privileges, for example, freedom from certain taxes; but the incorporated public authority should be subject to the same rights and liabilities as any other legal person. It should be liable for taxes, rates, and other charges and be bound by general statutes. This is the legal position of the newly nationalized industries in Britain.

Subjection to ordinary legal liabilities need not prevent the fulfilment of economic, social, and other planning functions. Both government departments and separate public authorities operate in the service of public interests or national plans, to which the legal principle of security of transactions must be adjusted. As we have seen, the break clauses in government contracts safeguard the power of the government to terminate contracts which have lost their purpose, such as war supplies, subject to fair compensation and indemnification. This is no worse, and in some cases compares favourably with the standard terms contractually imposed by private industries on the other party. But the government should not be judge in its own cause. Disputes arising from such contracts should be justiciable, whether before the ordinary courts, an arbitration court, or an administrative tribunal.

An additional problem arises where public enterprise operates side by side with private enterprise. In Australia, for example, a decision of the High Court[15] has confirmed the constitutional power of the Commonwealth to establish a government-operated interstate airline, but has denied it the power to operate an interstate airlines monopoly. As a result, a government-controlled airline operates side by side with private airlines. Does the rule of law demand that the government should dispense its favours equally among its own instrumentality and the private operators? Is there anything objectionable, for example, in the government giving all air-mail contracts to the government enterprise or ordering civil servants to use no other air transport?[16] It seems that to hold so would be an impossible legal fetter on policy decisions in a democratic community. The establishment of public enterprises is the result of a parliamentary decision and subject to parliamentary control. It is a perfectly legitimate objective for the government of the day to encourage a form of enterprise which it regards as preferable to private enterprise, within the limits set by a constitution or other positive legal restrictions. It would be absurd to expect a Labour Government to allocate contracts equally among its own enterprise and private competitors if this is contrary to its avowed policy, and in the play of political forces it will be for any alternative government to reverse this policy if it wishes. For the sake of continuity, a wise government will act with moderation either way; but this is a matter of policy, not of law.

The dual role of the State which both enters into the field of government and industrial commercial management and, at the same time, acts as the general controller over the allocation of economic resources for the nation, leads, however, to a further and more subtle problem. The State as economic controller allocates scarce resources among different industries and for different purposes. This function of the State is becoming increasingly important in a world dominated by scarcity due to the aftermath of a previous war or the fear of another, and, at least in parts of the world, by overpopulation. Economic necessity may reinforce social policy. In a social democracy like modern Britain after the war or India at the present time, essential industries are favoured as against luxury industries, exports at the expense of home consumption. This means not only the allocation of essential materials according to a priorities plan, but also sometimes the direction of labour. In this capacity, the State can exercise a twofold vital influence which is not immediately apparent in individual legal transactions, but which regulates them by remote control. A State can thwart certain industries and encourage others. But it can also exercise a vital influence on the scope of individual liberties. Steel or coal are purely economic commodities; paper is not only an economic commodity which costs dollars, but also the material basis without which intellectual freedom is bound to wither. Again, the direction of labour threatens one of the most vital aspects of personal freedom, the right to choose one's job. It is true that both freedom of opinion and freedom of labour are severely restricted by existing social and economic conditions, by newspaper or broadcasting monopolies, economic compulsion, and other factors. But the threat is no less great if it comes from the State itself. The problem does not exist in a totalitarian planned economy, where any protection of individual freedoms is at best conditional and where such rights of private property and enterprise as remain are clearly subject to overriding State necessities. But it is acute in a planned economy of the democratic type which regards certain individual freedoms as essential and recognizes the existence of a private economic sector along with public enterprise.

The power of the government of the day to throttle criticism by its policy in allocating paper, or to curtail freedom of personal movement by direction of labour, certainly raises one of the gravest problems in modern planned democracy. Under the American Constitution, such action might result in complex legal controversies, about the interpretation of the Bill of Rights of the Constitution, in particular the First, Fifth, and Fourteenth Amendments. In Great Britain, this is a matter of purely political decision, for Parliament and public opinion. The vigilance of Parliament and public opinion may, in special cases, justify the setting up of representative commissions to investigate problems of urgent concern.[17] But, ultimately, it is the alertness and strength of conviction of a community on which the prevention of destruction of liberties by such eroding processes depends.

Finally, the State functions as arbitrator between different groups in society. The term 'collectivist' State is often used loosely. A social-service State need not be collectivist. It can be a parental or dictatorial State, dispensing social welfare among the citizens while forbidding them to engage in any autonomous collectivist association, like Nazi Germany or Fascist Italy or Franco's Spain. On the other hand, the State may take complete responsibility for all group activities going on within its borders, while regarding their quasi-autonomous organization as convenient and necessary from an administrative and managerial point of view. This is the position in Soviet Russia where the managements of State-operated industries face trade unions. But the trade unions are not genuinely autonomous collective organizations. They represent group interests, within a well-defined national plan, and subject to overriding State policy ensured by the one-party system, political pressure, and the many other sanctions at the disposal of the totalitarian State. In the modern democratic society, group associations are still permitted to develop freely in principle and to adjust their relations by mutual agreement, that is in the sphere of private law. This purely passive function of the State is proving increasingly insufficient. As the moral and legal authority of employers' associations and trade unions increases, their agreements become more and more a matter of national concern. The vast majority of States are now in a condition of more or less permanent economic crisis. They cannot afford a prolonged standstill of production, or a rise of prices, profits and wages which paralyses the economic capacity of the nation. Hence the State must intervene, by wage boards, conciliation commissioners, compulsory awards, arbitration courts, and other means designed to ensure industrial peace as well as a certain amount of public influence on the formation of prices and wages. It is almost impossible to reconcile a compulsory national wage policy with the recognition of full freedom of organized groups and the consequent right of unimpeded collective bargaining. The most desirable solution is voluntary agreement and persuasion, but this leaves the legal dilemma unsolved. Freedom of association must include the freedom not to associate. It is true that, increasingly, agreements made between the major employers' and employees' associations are applied to the whole industry so that even non-members join in the benefits of such agreements. Graver, however, than this situation would be the recognition of a general principle of compulsory union membership as a condition of employment. This would transform democratic industrial society into that of the corporate State. The practical difference is small, for the trend is towards powerful unions which hardly need coercion. The freedom of the occasional dissenter makes a difference of principle out of proportion to its economic significance.

In short, the State as arbitrator in a democratic society has three tasks: the maintenance of a rough balance between contending organized groups and the usually unorganized consumer; the protection of the individual freedom of association; and the safeguarding of overriding State interests, such as the maintenance of export capacity.

## CONCLUSIONS

We are free to construe a dream-world ideal of the rule of law. According to our predilections, this may correspond to the enlightened rationalism of the eighteenth-century aristocracy, to nineteenth-century Manchester middle-class Liberalism, to the Church supremacy in medieval Europe, or to the centrally directed economy of a Socialist State. But a meaningful definition of the rule of law must be based on the realities of contemporary society, and this means that we must recognize the irreducible minimum functions of modern government, as well as the ubiquitous strength of group power. This still leaves plenty of choice between different ideas. A meaningful formulation of the rule of law for a contemporary democracy can only set the sights. It cannot be spelt out in terms of nineteenth-century ideals, of the philosophy of the Founding Fathers, of a Bentham or a Dicey. The basic value remains the same: the fullest possible provision by the community of the conditions that enable the individual to develop into a morally and intellectually responsible person. But the means by which this goal is to be attained cannot but be deeply influenced by the social conditions in which we live. The ideal of social welfare, i.e. of the responsibility of the community for minimum standards of living and protection against the major vicissitudes that would leave the individual – except the fortunate few – destitute and degraded, provided only with the theoretical freedoms of contract, property, and trade, is now almost universally accepted. But welfare and work, without responsibility, can lead to the completely regimented and conditioned society. The rule of law in democracy must, therefore, safeguard the elementary rights of participation in the process of government. It must devise adequate protection against the abuse of both public and private power. How the balance is to be struck must, to a large extent, depend on the changing conditions of society. Today the elementary standards of living are, more than at any previous period, protected by social-security laws and the recognition of collective bargaining as the predominant instrument of regulation of labour conditions. Emphasis is therefore shifting to safeguards against administrative arbitrariness, the legal immunities of public authority, the excessive concentration of corporate power and abuses of union power over the individual. No less important are efforts designed to preserve effective, as distinct from nominal, freedom of opinion, and measures to preserve or restore the minimum possibilities of civic participation in public affairs without which democracy must wither. In all these fields the law has a vital part to play.

That the content of the rule of law cannot be determined for all time and all circumstances is a matter not for lament but for rejoicing. It would be tragic if the law were so petrified as to be unable to respond to the unending challenge of evolutionary or revolutionary changes in society. To the lawyer, this challenge means that he cannot be content to be a craftsman. His technical knowledge will supply the tools but it is his sense of responsibility for the society in which he lives that must inspire him to be jurist as well as lawyer.

# Notes

## PREFACE

1. Chaps. 3, 4, 5, 11, 12, and 13 are based on corresponding chapters in the earlier book, although they have been largely rewritten.
2. 70 *L.Q.R.* 115.
3. Professor Jaffe in 65 *Harv. L.R.* 1264.

## I. THE INTERACTIONS OF LEGAL
## AND SOCIAL CHANGE

1. For a more detailed account of their theories, see Friedmann, *Legal Theory* (4th ed., 1960), pp. 158 et seq. (Savigny) and pp. 267 et seq. (Bentham).
2. The evolution is brilliantly analysed in Dicey's *Law and Public Opinion in the Nineteenth Century* (2nd ed., 1914).
3. Ehrlich's principal work, *Grundlegung der Soziologie des Rechts*, 1912, has been translated and published under the title *Fundamental Principles of the Sociology of Law*, in the Twentieth-Century Series of Legal Philosophy, Vol. V. See further *Legal Theory*, pp. 191 et seq.
4. It should be noted that Ehrlich's approach was strongly influenced by his study of the social, and especially of the family, habits of the numerous nations and races combined at his time in the Austro-Hungarian Empire.
5. See John N. Hazard, *Law and Social Change in the U.S.S.R.*, 1953; Juins, *Soviet Law and Soviet Society*, 1954.
6. For details, see Hazard, op. cit., pp. 245–73
7. See pp. 182 et seq.
8. As has been demonstrated by the history of Prohibition in the U.S.A., or the indifferent success of various English statutes over the last century, invalidating betting transactions, in fighting the deeply ingrained national passion for betting.
9. See further below, Chap. 7.
10. The Qur'ān (the revelation of God) and the Sunna (the Practice of the Prophet)—see Vesey-Fitzgerald, 'Nature and Sources of the Sharī'a' in *Law in the Middle East*, pp. 85, 87 et seq.
11. See Anderson, 'Law Reform in the Middle East', *International Affairs*, Vol. 32, pp. 43 et seq. (1956).
12. Anderson, op. cit., p. 45.
13. See further on the role of the courts in response of law to social change, pp. 37 et seq.
14. *Brown* v. *Board of Education*, 347 U.S. 483 (1954).
15. See further pp. 42 et seq., 124 et seq.

16. See p. 304.

17. See further pp. 211 et seq.

18. See further pp. 195 et seq.

19. See, for a survey, the O'Connor Report, Ottawa, 1939, Annex 1, pp. 18–52.

20. *Bank of New South Wales* v. *Commonwealth* (1948) 16 *C.L.R.* 1; (1949) 79 *C.L.R.* 497.

21. *U.S.* v. *Darby*, 312 U.S. 100 (1941).

22. cf. Freund, *On Understanding the Supreme Court* (1951), pp. 9 et seq.

23. 163 U.S. 557 (1897).

24. *Brown* v. *Board of Education*, 347 U.S. 483 (1954).

25. In order to justify the resistence of the deep South against the Supreme Court decision, *Brown* v. *Board of Education*, an Appeal Court judge of Georgia in 1958 propounded a theory that the court was, indeed, empowered to give an authoritative interpretation to the Constitution once. Having done so, it was not entitled to depart from such an interpretation, and by doing so, it turned itself from an interpreter of the Constitution into a law-maker! See further pp. 50 et seq.

26. Only the Australian Constitution appears to imitate the U.S. Constitution, by composing the Senate of sixty members, ten from each of the six states. This has on more than one occasion resulted in political stalemates. Of the newer Federal Constitutions, the West German *Grundgesetz* of 1949 compromises between equality and proportionality by giving each of the ten *Länder* in the Upper Chamber, the *Bundesrat*, a minimum of three votes, with one additional vote for any *Land* with more than two million, and a second additional vote for any *Land* with more than six million, inhabitants. Under the Indian Constitution of 1949–51, the Council of States, which represents the federal element, has twelve members, nominated by the President from the fields of literature, science, art, and social service – a small concession to the 'corporative' idea – and the remaining number – at present exceeding 200, but not yet up to the constitutional maximum of 238 (art. 81) – fixed in proportion to the population of the different states (Fourth Schedule).

## 2. THE COURTS AND THE EVOLUTION OF THE LAW

1. *Méthode d'interprêtation et sources en droit privé positif*, Paris (1899).

2. In both cases, judicial creativeness was later supplemented by legislative action.

3. The first edition was published in 1905, the second in 1914.

4. *The Nature of the Judicial Process* (1921), pp. 112–13

5 (1868) L.R. 3 H.L. 330.

6. This is brought out in Professor Bohlen's classical essay on the rule in *Rylands* v. *Fletcher*, *Studies in the Law of Tort*, 1926, pp. 1 et seq.

7. *Mersey Docks Trustees* v. *Gibbs* (1866) L.R. 1 H.L. 93.

8. *McPherson* v. *Buick* (1916) 217 N.Y. 382, 111 N.E. 1050; *Donoghue* v. *Stevenson* [1932] A.C. 562.

9. *Parkinson* v. *Commissioners of Works* [1949] 2 K.B. 632; *British Movietonews* v. *London Cinemas* [1951] 1 K.B. 190. The latter decision was reversed by the House of Lords [1952] A.C. 166.

10. *Lloyds* v. *Murphy* (1944) 25 Cal. 2d 48, 153 P. 2d 47.

11. *Peerless Cash Co.* v. *Weymouth Gardens Inc.*, CCA 1st, (1954) 215 F. 2d 362.

12. *Priestley* v. *Fowler* (1837) 3 M. & W. 1.

13. Friedmann, *Legal Theory* (4th ed.), pp. 437–8.

14. See further pp. 204 et seq.

15. (1951) 25 *Aust.L.J.* p. 296.

16. [1951] 2 K.B. 164.

17. cf. further p. 222.

18. For an analysis of this whole process, see, among many others, Stone, *Province and Function of Law*, pp. 171 et seq. On the difficulties of discovering the *ratio decidendi* and the consequent opportunities of choice between different solutions, see Paton and Sawer (1947), 63 *L.Q.R.*, pp. 461 et seq.; on the problem in general, see Friedmann, *Legal Theory* (4th ed.), Chaps. 31, 32. See also the recent controversy between Montrose and Simpson in (1957) 20 *Mod.L.R.* 124, 413; (1958) 21 *Mod.L.R.* 155; Goodhart (1959) 22 *Mod.L.R.* 117.

19. H. L. A. Hart, 'Positivism and the Separation of Law and Morals', 71 *Harv.L.R.* 593 (1958), pp. 607–8 and 612.

20. Professor Fuller, in his reply to Professor Hart, op. cit., pp. 661 et seq., has rightly disputed the validity of the distinction between a 'core' and a 'penumbra' of meaning.

21. See the controversy between Hart and Fuller, op. cit., and the admission by Hart that 'the interpretations stigmatized as automatic have resulted from the conviction that it is fairer in a criminal statute to take a meaning which would jump to the mind of the ordinary man at the cost even of defeating other values, and this itself is a social policy (though possibly a bad one); or much more frequently, what is stigmatized as "mechanical" and "automatic" is a determined choice made indeed in the light of a social aim but a conservative social aim,' (p. 611).

22. cf. the observations by Judge Traynor, on 'Courts and Lawmaking' in the Columbia Law School Centennial Symposium (1959): 'Although the judge's predilections may play a part in setting the initial direction he takes towards the creative solution, there is little danger of their determining the solution itself, however much it bears the stamp of his individual workmanship. Our great creative judges have been men of outstanding skill, adept at discounting their own predilections and careful to discount them with conscientious severity. The disinterestedness of the creative decision is further assured by the judge's arduous articulation of the reasons that compel the formulation of an original solution and by the full disclosure in his opinion of all aspects of the problem and of the data pertinent to its solution.'

23. *Crofter Handwoven Harris Tweed Co.* v. *Veitch* [1941] A.C. 435.

24. *Morehead* v. *Tipaldo*, 298 U.S. 587 (1936).

25. e.g. *Smith* v. *Allwright* (1944) 321 U.S. 649; *Shelley* v. *Kraemer* (1948) 334 U.S. 1; and, in particular, *Brown* v. *Board of Education of Topeka*, 349 U.S. (1954), p. 294.

26. *Constantine* v. *Imperial Hotels, Ltd* [1944] K.B. 693.

27. See also Friedmann, *Legal Theory* (4th ed., 1960), p. 420.

28. *Canadian Wheat Board* v. *Nolan et al.* [1951] S.C.R. 81; [1951] D.L.R. 466.

29. *Ransom & Luck* v. *Surbiton* [1949] Ch. 180.

30. *Prochnow* v. *Prochnow*, 274 Wis. 491 (1957).

31. A. N. Carter (1950) 28 *Can.Bar Rev.* p. 946.

32. (1948) 26 *Can.Bar Rev.* 1277; for an incisive criticism of the literal approach to statutory interpretation, see also Willis, 'Statute Interpretation in a Nutshell' (1938) 16 *Can.Bar Rev.* 1.

33. See also the observations by Mr Justice McDonald, p. 46. Sir Carleton K. Allen (*Law in the Making*, 6th ed., 1958, p. 514) objects that: 'It is to be feared, however, that any such attempted classification would merely add a series of ambiguous adjectives to the existing difficulties of interpretation. Categories of this kind, and others which might easily be suggested, could not possibly be precise and would overlap at many points.' It cannot be denied that a precise delimitation of different categories of statutes is difficult. This is, however, a difficulty of any principle of interpretation. None can be more than a general guide to the understanding of the specific problem at hand. Some support for the approach suggested here has recently come from an American jurist: 'The unresolved conflict between the opposing approaches stems from the false assumption that all statutes are alike. All statutes are not alike, and, in fact, are not treated similarly. Yet judicial standards of construction and rationale of interpretation purport to apply a single approach to all statutes. What is required is an acknowledged pluralistic treatment. The close application approach is appropriate to one kind of statute, and the creative elaboration approach to another kind of statute. There are intermediate variations suitable to statutes of intermediate kinds.' (Judge Breitel, in a paper published in the Columbia University Law School Centennial volume, 1959.)

34. [1925] A.C. 578.

35. [1942] A.C. 206.

36. *Nakkuda Ali* v. *Jayaratne* (1950) 66 *T.L.R.* (pt. 2) 214.

37. (1948) 26 *Can.Bar Rev.* 21, p. 23. See also, apart from the authorities already mentioned, Richard (1940), 18 *Can.Bar Rev.* 243; Kennedy (1937) 15 *Can.Bar Rev.* 393; Laskin (1947) 25 *Can.Bar Rev.* 1054; and *Canadian Constitutional Law* (2nd ed., 1960) pp. 24–5; also McInnis, *Canada: Political and Social History* (1947) pp. 641–3.

38. See p. 30.

39. *Hood* v. *DuMond* 336 U.S. 525 (1949).

40. The High Court of Australia, in March 1951, by a majority of six

to one, invalidated the Government Act outlawing the Australian Communist Party. None of the judges representing the majority could be suspected of any sympathy for the Communist Party and some of them quite probably approved the political objectives of the Act. cf. Beasley, 'Australia's Communist Party Dissolution Act' (1951) 29 *Can.Bar Rev.* 490.

41. *West Coast Hotel* v. *Parrish*, 300 U.S. 379 (1937), holding valid a minimum wage statute; *N. L .R. B.* v. *Jones & Laughlin Steel Corp.*, 301 U.S. 1 (1937), sustaining the National Labour Relations Act; and *Steward Machine Co.* v. *Davis*, 301 U.S. 548 (1937), sustaining the Social Security Act.

42. See, in elaboration of Holmes's celebrated dictum that 'the Fourteenth Amendment does not enact Mr Herbert Spencer's Social Statistics', *Lochner* v. *New York* (1904) 198 U.S. 45, Stones' dissenting judgement in *Morehead* v. *Tipaldo* 298 U.S. 587 (1936), which invalidated a New York Minimum Wages Act: 'It is not for the courts to resolve whether the remedy by wage regulation is as efficacious as many believe, or is better than some other, or is better even than the blind operation of uncontrolled economic forces. The legislature must be free to choose unless the government is to be rendered impotent. The Fourteenth Amendment has no more embedded in the Constitution our preference for some particular set of economic beliefs than it has adopted, in the name of liberty, the system of theology which we may happen to approve.' (p.636).

43. *Brown* v. *Board of Education* (1954) 347 U.S. 483, 349 U.S. 294. *Cooper* v. *Aaron*, *U.S.Sup.Ct.Bulletin*, vol. 19, p. 3 (1958).

44. 163 U.S. 537 (1897). The Court softened the effect of the decision by leaving its implementation to the supervision of the U.S. District courts. Their power to approve schemes which would bring about integration in gradual stages 'with all deliberate speed' has not prevented seven Southern states from defying the decision by an act of political rebellion, thinly disguised by quasi-legal justification, such as the doctrine of 'interposition' or the contention that the Court had usurped legislative functions and therefore acted *ultra vires*.

45. See pp. 32, 42.

46. Under which Federal Statutes, e.g. in matters of sedition or regulation of labour relations, 'pre-empt' the field, and thus invalidate or suspend incompatible state legislation. See, in particular, *Pennsylvania* v. *Nelson*, 350 U.S. 497.

47. cf. *Sweezy* v. *New Hampshire*, 354 U.S. 234 (1957).

48. *Watkins* v. *U.S.* 354 U.S. 178 (1957); but see *Barenblatt* v. *U.S.*, 79 S.Ct. 1081 (1959) where the court restored to Congress some of the freedom of investigation which it had appeared to restrict severely in *Watkins*.

49. See, among many others, a statement by Chief Judge Felton of the Court of Appeals of Georgia – issued by the Georgia Commission on Education: 'When is a Supreme Court Decision the Law of the Land?'

50. Learned Hand, *The Bill of Rights* (1958), p. 34.

51. Cited here from the *Harvard Law Record*, 23 October 1958.

52. See note 43 to p. 49 on p. 391.

53. op. cit., p. 71.

54. Perhaps on the model of the *Dred Scott* case, which is universally held to have been a major contributing cause to the American Civil War of the 1860s.

55. Dean Ribble, 'Policy Making Powers of the Supreme Court and the Position of the Individual', 14 *Washington and Lee L.R.* (1957) 167, at 184–5.

56. See above, pp. 27 et seq.

57. *U.S.* v. *Carolene Products Company*, 304 U.S. 144 (1938), 152. A similar approach is inherent in the observation by Cardozo J. (in *Palko* v. *Connecticut* (1937) 302 U.S. p. 327) that freedom of thought and speech is 'the matrix, the indispensable condition', of nearly every other form of freedom'.

58. *A. F. of L.* v. *American Sash and Door Co.*, 335 U.S. 538 (1949), p. 555.

59. *Kovacs* v. *Cooper*, 336 U.S. 77 (1949), p. 95.

60. Judge Learned Hand, *The Bill of Rights* (1958), pp. 50–1.

61. 73 *Harvard Law Review* 1 (1959).

62. *Shelley* v. *Kraemer*, 334 U.S. 1. (1948). (Non-enforceability of covenants restricting land transfers to persons of designated race.) See also *Pennsylvania* v. *Board of Trusts*, 353 U.S. 230 (1957). (Illegality of refusal by City Board as trustees of a will establishing a college for 'poor white male orphans' to admit Negro orphans.)

63. One technical way of helping towards greater consistency might be the abandonment of the frequent practice of the Court simply to grant or deny certiorari *per curiam*, without a reasoned decision. See Brown, foreword: 'Process of Law', 72 *Harvard L.R.* 77 (1958).

64. This is supplemented by another provision permitting analogous punishment 'in accordance with those articles of the criminal code which deal with crimes most closely approximating, in gravity, and in kind, to the crimes actually committed. . . . ' It should be added, however, that many Soviet jurists have for a number of years been critical of such provisions and have maintained that their practical significance was always limited, while the incorporation of the provision in the Penal Code gave an excuse to the enemies of the Soviet Union to attack its principles of administration of justice. The new 'basis', as published in 1958, incorporating the general principles for new criminal codes to be adopted by the Soviet Republic seems to abolish the analogy principle by saying that 'no one may be held criminally responsible and be subjected to punishment except for acts constituting a crime provided by the criminal law'. Another article of the new basis says that 'criminal punishment may be applied only by court sentence in accordance with law'. To what extent this would outlaw the continuation of the powers of the police courts to imprison citizens in work camps as 'socially dangerous', without regard to the rules of the criminal code or the

Code of Criminal Procedure, is not certain. But the trend in Soviet legal thinking appears at present to be in favour of the 'legality' principle. (See for a discussion of the Draft of 1958, John N. Hazard, 'Soviet Codifiers Release the first Drafts', in 8 *Am. Journal of Comparative Law* 72 (1959). See also Berman, 'Soviet Law Reform in Dateline Moscow 1957', 66 *Yale L.J.* 1191 (1957).)

65. *Bagg*, 11 Co.Rep. at 98a, 77 E.R. at 1277.

66. *Jones* v. *Randall*, Lofft 383, 98 E.R. 706.

67. [1933] 1 K.B. 529.

68. 2 East 5.

69. See the survey and discussion in Williams, *Criminal Law* (2nd ed., 1961), pp. 606 et seq.

70. s. 8.

71. [1961] 2 A.E.R. 446.

72. See his statements in *Jacobs* v. *L.C.C.* [1950] A.C. 361, at p. 361: 'to determine what the law is, not what it ought to be, is the present task'; or, in *Scruttons* v. *Midland Silicones* [1962] 2 *W.L.R.* 186, at p. 191: 'to me heterodoxy, or, as some might say, heresy, is not the more attractive because it is dignified by the name of reform'. On *Jacobs* see further p. 125. And see generally Dworkin *'Stare decisis* in the House of Lords' 25 *M.L.R.* [1962] 163 et seq.

73. H. L. A. Hart, *Law, Liberty and Morality*, (1963), p. 12.

74. It may well be argued that a totalitarian régime with a sub-servient judiciary could use the crime of sedition for the complete suppression of liberties and opposition, without any new drastic legislation.

75. In the civilian sphere, codifications of criminal law appear to be universal. In the common-law sphere, the state of the English criminal law, in which most offences are defined by statute, but not codified, contrasts with the Canadian Criminal Code of 1954.

76. As held by the Supreme Court of the United States in *McBoyle* v. *U.S.*, 283 U.S. 25 (1931), *per* Holmes J.

77. Livingston Hall in 48 *Harv.L.R.* (1935), p. 760.

78. So held in the English cases as quoted in Livingston Hall, op. cit., p. 760; *contra* a Californian decision of 1874.

79. In 'Common Law and Legislation' (1908) 21 *Harv.L.R.* 383, at 407: 'The public cannot be relied upon permanently to tolerate judicial obstruction or nullification of the social policies to which more and more it is compelled to be committed.' See also Waite, *Criminal Law in Action* (1934) p. 16, bitterly criticizing the widespread judicial policy 'to utilize casuistic plausibility or any dubiety of the situation for the benefit of the accused rather than for the immediate safety of society'.

80. See, for a survey of the different types, Livingston Hall, op. cit., pp. 752 et seq. and Appendix p. 771.

81. See pp. 167 et seq.

82. *State* v. *Longino* (1915) 109 Mis. 125, 67 SO 902.

83. *Howell* v. *Falmouth Boat Construction, Ltd* [1951] A.C. 837.

84. See Williams, op. cit., Chap. 8, pp. 302 et seq.

85. For an example of analogical extension of a statute, no doubt under the influence of war-time emotions, see the famous case of *William Joyce* [1946] A.C. 347, where the statutory law of treason was applied to an alien – although he was not on British soil at the time and had declared the intention of renouncing British nationality – on the sole ground that he still possessed a British passport.

86. This would seem to be close to the approach of Professor Livingston Hall in the above quoted article, in which he suggests, p.770, that: 'A penal statute may be construed strictly where such construction is necessary (1) to make the words of the statute not misleading to persons acting in good faith and honestly attempting to comply with all provisions of law regulating their conduct; or (2) to prevent the imposition of a penalty which is so disproportionate to other penalties imposed by law or which is so clearly inappropriate in view of changed social or economic conditions in the state that it is reasonable to believe that the legislature did not intend such a result.'

87. The extent of the reservations attached by most States to this general commitment under the optional clause has assumed such proportions that Judge Lauterpacht, in a separate opinion delivered in the 'Norwegian Loans Case' (*I.C.J. Reports*, 1957, p. 9, pp. 55 et seq.) regarded reservations that leave freedom to decide whether a particular dispute is justiciable or not to the party concerned (and by virtue of the principle of reciprocity, correspondingly reduce the extent of the obligation of the other party) as nullifying the acceptance altogether.

88. For a searching analysis of the function of the International Court of Justice in the development of international law, see Sir Hersch Lauterpacht's *The Development of International Law by the International Court* (1958), in particular Part V, dealing with the 'Court and State sovereignty'. See also Dr Schwarzenberger's *International Law*, Vol. I (3rd ed. 1957), an analysis of the practice of international courts.

89. 'Reparation for Injuries suffered in the Service of the United Nations' *I.C.J. Reports*, 1949, p. 174.

90. 'Effect of Awards of Compensation made by the U.N. Administrative Tribunal', *I.C.J. Reports*, 1954, p. 47.

91. 'Fisheries Case (*United Kingdom* v. *Norway*)', *I.C.J. Reports*, 1951, p. 116.

92. See the above-mentioned works of Lauterpacht and Schwarzenberger, also Cheng, *General Principles of Law as applied by International Courts and Tribunals*, 1953.

93. See further pp. 345 et seq.

94. It is likely to prove far more important than the isolated decision of the Permanent Court of Justice in the case of the jurisdiction of the courts of Danzig. *Advisory Opinion* No. 15, Series B (1928), p. 17, or even decisions of the Nuremberg and Tokyo Tribunals dealing with war criminals and establishing thereby the direct personal legal responsibility of individuals in international law. In this writer's opinion, the

law-making importance of the latter decisions is severely curtailed by the composition of the courts, and the linking of their jurisdictions with authority derived from victory in the Second World War.

95. (1922) 1 *Camb.L.J.* 1, p. 8.

96. See further pp. 278 et seq.

97. The high-water mark is the decision of the Court of Appeal in *R.* v. *Electricity Commissioners* [1924] 1 K.B. 171.

98. cf. in particular *Franklin* v. *Minister of Town and Country Planning* [1948] A.C. 87; *Robinson* v. *Minister of Town and Country Planning* [1947] K.B. 702.

99. *Lee* v. *Showmen's Guild* [1952] 2 Q.B. 329; *Bonsor* v. *Musicians' Union* [1956] A.C. 104.

100. Judge Breitel, 'Courts and Lawmaking', *Columbia Law School Centennial Symposium* (1959).

## 3. PROPERTY

1. In the medieval scholastic philosophy of St Thomas Aquinas, and even centuries later of Suarez, the right of property was not proclaimed as a 'natural' law, but as a matter of social utility and convenience. See further on this subject, *Legal Theory* (4th ed.), pp. 59 et seq.

2. For a recent presentation to that effect, cf. Pashkov in *Transactions of the Third World Sociological Congress* (Amsterdam, 1956), pp. 213 et seq.

3. In the words of the U.S. Patent Code 35 U.S.C., para. 261 (1952), a patent has 'the attributes of personal property'.

4. Kahn-Freund, Introduction to Renner, *The Institutions of Private Law and Their Social Functions* (1949), p. 19.

5. Harding in 'Free Man versus His Government,' *Southern Methodist Studies in Jurisprudence*, V (1958), p. 81.

6. e.g. Cheshire, *The Modern Law of Real Property*, 7th ed., p. 27.

7. e.g. Hargreaves in 19 *Mod.L.R.* (1956), pp. 14 et seq.

8. cf. Art. 823 of the German Civil Code, and the voluminous jurisprudence defining the meaning of a '*Sonstiges Recht*', the violation of which engenders tort liability in the same way as the violation of the right of property.

9. See Morin, '*Le Sens et l'évolution contemporaine du droit de propriété*' (*Études Ripert*, II, p. 7); Ripert, *Les forces créatrices du droit* (1955), Section 86.

10. Ripert, op. cit., pp. 215–16.

11. D. Bastian, '*La Propriété commerciale en droit français*', *Travaux de l'Association Henri Capitant*, Vol. 6. (1950), pp. 76 et seq.

12. *Statut du Fermage; loi du 1 septembre 1948.*

13. Agricultural Act, 1947, which gives the Minister powers to dispossess the owner on grounds of bad management or husbandry (ss. 12, 16).

14. Vinding Kruse, *The Community of the Future* (1950), pp. 435 et seq.

15. op. cit., p. 436.

16. From a sociological point of view, Renner, half a century ago, pursued a similar line of thought when he spoke of the 'Konnexinstitut' of property, as drawing off more and more of the substance of the property function.

17. See further pp. 344 et seq.

18. On this aspect, see p. 82

19. Kahn-Freund, op. cit., p. 26.

20. op. cit., *passim*.

21. See p. 74.

22. Berle and Means, *The Modern Corporation and Private Property* (1932).

23. Berle and Means give as an example the Brothers van Sweringen. In 1930, an investment of less than $20,000,000 was able to control eight Class I railroads, with combined assets of over two billion dollars.

24. *Bradford Corporation* v. *Pickles* [1895] A.C. 597.

25. For detailed discussion, cf. Gutteridge, 5 *Camb.L.J.*, pp. 22–45.

26. Notably *Hollywood Silver Fox Farm* v. *Emmett* [1936] 2 K.B. 468, where the defendant was restrained from firing his gun repeatedly in order to interfere with the plaintiff's breeding of silver foxes.

27. Prosser, *Handbook of the Law of Torts* (2nd ed.), p. 412.

28. See authorities quoted in Prosser, op. cit., p. 413, note 49.

29. Professor Gutteridge in 5 *Camb.L.J.*, pp. 22 et seq., felt certain that the German court would restrain such an action. For some criticism of this view, see (1943) 21 *Can.Bar Review*, p. 374.

30. It is not often that the fantastic situation arises which occupied the Dutch courts some years ago. A determined engineer, feuding with his neighbour, a lawyer, erected a mock water-tower at a place where it obstructed his neighbour's view of the sea. When enjoined to refrain, the ingenious engineer converted the mock water-tower into an effective water supply. He was restrained none the less because the Hooge Raad, in a decision of 13 March 1936, held that he could equally well have erected this water-tower on a different part of his property where it did not obstruct the neighbour's view. (This account is based on oral information given to the author by a Dutch lawyer.)

31. See Bastian, op. cit., p. 68, note 11, p. 87.

32. s. 1, Civil Code of the R.S.F.S.R.: cf. Gsovski, *Soviet Civil Law* (1948), Vol. 1, pp. 314–38.

33. On these, see further pp. 167 et seq.

34. Following *Donoghue* v. *Stevenson* [1932] A.C. 562.

35. *Monk* v. *Warbey* [1935] 1 K.B. 75.

36. *Read* v. *Croydon Corporation* (1939) 108 L.J.K.B. 72.

37. For a concise survey, see Prosser, *Handbook of the Law of Torts* (2nd ed., 1954), pp. 154 et seq.

38. See Prosser, op. cit., p. 156.

39. R. Savatier, *Les Métamorphoses économiques et sociales du droit civil d'aujourd'hui* (2nd ed., 1952).

40. *Ordinances du 17 octobre 1945*, Law of 13 April, 1946, *sur le statut des Baux Ruraux.*

41. For details, see Agriculture Act, 1947, Pt. II.

42. Dr Kahn-Freund has analysed different ways in which ownership in land and agricultural lease can, in English law, cover widely different economic situations. His comparison is particularly valuable (see op. cit., pp. 9, n. 1, 33 et seq.). The forms of tenancy in English law here account for many differences from Continental law, but this does not affect the importance, in either system, of the developments outlined in the text.

43. *Ransom & Luck, Ltd* v. *Surbiton Borough Council* [1949] 1 Ch. 180.

44. For an illuminating concise survey, see Howard R. Williams, 'The Continuing Evolution of the Land', in *Transactions of the Third World Congress of Sociology*, Vol. II, pp. 196 et seq. (1956).

45. See *Suring State Bank* v. *Giese*, 210 Wis. 489, 246 N.W. 556 (1933).

46. Every one of the States now has zoning enabling legislation, and at least 90 per cent of the cities with a population exceeding 10,000 now regulate through zoning ordinances such matters as the use of urban land (Williams, op. cit., p. 198).

47. See *Lyon's Head Lake Inc.* v. *Township of Wayne*, 10 N.J. 165, 89A Sec. 693 (1952), appeal dismissed, 344 U.S. 919 (1953).

48. Cross, 'Diminishing Fee', *Law and Contemporary Problems* (1955), summer issue, pp. 517 et seq.

49. cf. Chap. 9.

50. See Kahn-Freund, in Renner, op. cit., p. 186.

51. See Chap. 4, pp. 108 et seq.

52. Harding, in *Free Man versus his Government* (1958), p. 106.

### 4. CONTRACT

1. By-products of the former immobility and non-commercial characterization of land ownership remained, e.g. in the rule in *Cavalier* v. *Pope* [1906] A.C. 428, under which the landlord was exempt from liability to his tenant for dangers existing on the premises. But see now Occupiers' Liability Act, 1957, s. 4 (1).

2. e.g. West Australian Crown Proceedings Act, 1947.

3. See further on the relations of government and governed, pp. 291 et seq.

4. For a survey of the different theories, cf. Paton, *Textbook of Jurisprudence*, s. 80; M. Cohen, *Law and the Social Order*, pp. 69–111; Pound, *Introduction to the Philosophy of Law*, Chap. VI.

5. *Liesbosch Dredger* v. *Edison S. S.* [1933] A.C. 449.

6. Between the decisions of the House of Lords in *Rose* v. *Ford* [1937] A.C. 826 and *Benham* v. *Gambling* [1941] A.C. 157. In the latter case, the House reduced the amount of damages to be awarded for loss of expectation of happiness in respect of a child two and a half years old from £1,200 to £200.

7. [1917] 1 K.B. 305.

8. French law accords with English law in invalidating agreements that subject one party to the will of another (Planiol, *Traité élémentaire de droit civil*, II, § 43; III, § 1123). But French law is much stricter than English law in the condemnation of contractual restrictions on freedom of marriage and religion. For a detailed comparison, see Lloyd, *Public Policy* (1953), pp. 30 et seq. Any condition obliging a person to follow a particular religious belief would be counter to the secular and tolerant approach to religion which has dominated French law since the Revolution. English law regards these matters traditionally more as legitimate conditions of the disposal of property. That Quebec law, which generally is closely modelled on French law, has in this matter followed English public policy – in a decision declaring valid a clause revoking the legacy of a (Catholic) legatee if the legatee married a Jew (*Renaud* v. *Lamothe*, 32 S.C. 357) – is certainly due to the rigidly Catholic character of Quebec. In the matter of 'radical covenants' – sales of property subject to a covenant, prohibiting sale or lease to persons of Jewish, Negro, or coloured blood, the English courts would presumably regard them as a legitimate part of a property transaction. The Ontario Court of Appeal – which closely follows English law – has declined to invalidate such a covenant as contrary to public policy (*Re Noble and Wolfe* [1949] 4 *D.L.R.* 375, reversed by the Supreme Court of Canada on another ground). The U.S. Supreme Court, on the other hand, more conscious of the issue of radical discrimination, has declared such covenants unenforceable (*Shelley* v. *Kraemer*, 334 U.S. 1 (1947)). These divergences reflect not only different approaches to the relation of basic human freedoms, to the right to dispose of property, but also different conceptions about the role of the courts in the enforcement of freedom through their jurisdiction over contracts.

9. *Wyatt* v. *Kreglinger* [1933] 1 K.B. 793.

10. For a criticism of this extremely questionable use of the notion of public interest, see (1933) 49 *L.Q.R.* 465–7.

11. This is brilliantly analysed in Dicey's *Law and Public Opinion in England during the Nineteenth Century* (2nd ed. 1914).

12. The most recent English textbook, by Cheshire and Fifoot, first published in 1945, in the 4th ed., 1956, does not even refer to the term or meaning of 'standard contracts', or 'contract of adhesion' (except for a note on the interpretation of 'standard terms') or to the impact of law on contract. This is all the more regrettable, as Eastwood and Wortley drew attention, in 1938, to some of the impacts of administrative law on contract ([1938] *J.S.P.T.L.* 23–31).

13. See, e.g. Fuller, *Basic Contract Law* (1947); Kessler and Sharp, *Cases and Materials on Contract* (1953); and the excellent symposium in 43 *Col.L.R.* (1943), pp. 565 et seq., in particular, Hale, 'Bargaining Duress and Economic Liberty' (pp. 605 et seq.); and Kessler, *Contracts of Adhesion*, pp. 629 et seq.

14. 236 U.S. 1, 17 (1915) cf. also Dodd, 43 *Columbia Law Review*, 667:

'It is impossible to uphold freedom of contract and the right of private property without at the same time recognizing as legitimate those inequalities of fortune that are the necessary result of the exercise of those rights ... Indeed, a little reflection will show that whenever the right of private property and the right of free contract co-exist, each party, when contracting, is inevitably more or less influenced by the question whether he has much property or little or none: for the contract is made to the very end that each may gain something he needs or desires more urgently than that which he proposes to give in exchange.'

15. cf., among others, Schwartz, 'The Changing Role of the United States Supreme Court' (1950) 28 *Can.Bar Rev.* 48; Mason, *Security Through Freedom; American Political Thought and Practice* (1955); Friedmann, 'Property, Freedom, Security and the Supreme Court of the United States' (1956) 19 *M.L.R.* 461, and see further, pp. 53 et seq.

16. *United States* v. *Bethlehem Steel Corporation* 315 U.S. 289. (1942).

17. cf. Kessler and Sharp, op. cit., p. 274.

18. See pp. 224 et seq.

19. *Crofter Harris Tweed Co.* v. *Veitch* [1942] A.C. 435.

20. For a short account, cf. Salmond, *Law of Torts* (13th ed., Heuston), § 198.

21. *Nordenfelt* v. *Maxim Nordenfelt Guns and Ammunition Co.* [1894] A.C. 535.

22. *Mason* v. *Provident Clothing Co.* [1913] A.C. 724.

23. Employees' covenants are generally valid if they prohibit the use of trade secrets acquired in the employment: cf. *Morris* v. *Saxelby* [1916] 1 A.C. 688.

24. Law Reform (Personal Injuries) Act, 1948.

25. cf. Friedmann, *Legal Theory* (4th ed.), Chaps. 31 and 32, and above, pp. 37 et seq.

26. On the public-law element in contract, see further pp. 101 et seq.

27. See Prausnitz, *Standardisation of Commercial Contracts in English and Continental Law* (1937); Llewellyn, 'What Price Contract?' 40 *Yale L.J.* 704; Book Review, 52 *Harv.L.R.* 700; Kessler, 'Contracts of Adhesion', 43 *Col.L.R.* 629.

28. See pp. 294 et seq.

29. Morris R. Cohen, *Law and the Social Order*, p. 106.

30. *Henson* v. *L.N.E.R.* [1946] 1 All E.R. 653.

31. e.g. in the typical shipping or air-transport contract.

32. Frequent clause in Landlord and Tenant agreements.

33. *Standard Conditions of British Government Contracts for Store Purchases* (1947 ed.).

34. Note 63 *Harv.L.R.* 504.

35. See pp. 224 et seq.

36. cf. Cheshire and Fifoot, *Law of Contract* (1945), pp. 83–7; Kahn-Freund, *Law of Inland Transport* (3rd ed. 1956), pp. 432–4; 'Contract Clauses', 62 *Harv.L.R.* 594, 2504.

37. For details of the rather complex legislation, see Kahn-Freund, *Law of Inland Transport* (3rd ed. 1956), pp. 438 et seq.

38. *Fairfax Gas & Supply Co.* v. *Hadary*, Circuit Court of Appeals of the United States, Fourth Circuit, 1945, 151 F. 2d 939.

39. Lenhoff, 43 *Col.L.R.* 595 (1943).

40. See, generally, on the major public enterprises in different countries, Friedmann (ed.), *The Public Corporation* (1954); Hanson, *Public Enterprise* (1955). Socialization, as such, is not, however, a sufficient safeguard against exploitation. Legislation may still be needed to protect the user against abuse of superior power. (See, e.g. the British Transport Communication Passenger Charges Scheme, 1954).

41. cf., for a slight different classification, Eastwood and Wortley [1938] *J.S.P.T.L.*, pp. 23–4.

42. Cooper, *Outlines of Industrial Law*, pp. 256 et seq.

43. cf. *Pratt* v. *Cook* [1940] A.C. 437.

44. cf. *Industrial Relations Handbook* (1944), pp. 133–8; Kahn-Freund (1948) 11 *M.L.R.* 269, 429.

45. For details, see *Industrial Relations Handbook*, § VIII; Kahn-Freund, 97 *Penn.L.R.* 778, 784 et seq.

46. cf. Kahn-Freund, 'Collective Agreements under War Legislation' (1943) 6 *M.L.R.* 112, 121. On the position in legal systems outside the common law, cf. Lenhoff, *Labour Law, Cases and Materials*, Vol. 2 (preliminary ed.), pp. 44–62.

47. See pp. 294 et seq.

48. Arthur S. Miller, 'Government Contracts and Social Control: A Preliminary Inquiry', 41 *Va.L.R.* (1955), pp. 56–7; Friedmann, *Law and Social Change in Contemporary Britain* (1951), p. 71, and Cohen, *Law and Social Order* (1933), pp. 102–11.

49. Berman (1947) 35 *Cal.L.R.*, p. 225.

50. For details, cf. Berman, loc. cit., pp. 191–234.

51. cf. the Soviet authorities quoted by Berman, *Justice in Russia*, p. 65.

52. Thus, in a case reported by Berman, 35 *Cal.L.R.* 230, a factory, operating under the paper machine construction trust, which was insufficiently equipped for the manufacture of pergament machines, had contracted to manufacture such a machine. It was rejected as faulty by the plaintiff, a Siberian paper factory of the People's Commissariat of Timber. Not only were the defendant factory and its superior administration held liable for the breach of contract, but the court also notified the People's Commissariat of General Machine Construction that no steps had been taken by the defendant administration to remedy the position.

53. cf. Decree of the Council of Ministers of 21 April 1949; Berman, *Justice in Russia*, p. 72.

54. cf. the case reported in 35 *Cal.L.R.* p. 234, where the defendant was ordered to pay 13,915 roubles penalty for delaying the conclusion of a local contract by one month.

55. Berman, *Justice in Russia*, p. 74.

56. cf. the comparative survey in *Journal of Comparative Legislation*, Vol. 28, pp. 1–25 (Scots law, French law, and German law); Vol. 29, pp. 1–18 (American law and Soviet law); Vol. 30, p. 55 (Swiss law). Also Zepos, 'Frustration of Contract in Comparative Law and the new Greek Code of 1946' (1948) 11 *M.L.R.* 36–46; Smit, 'Frustration of Contract', 58 *Col.L.R.* 287 (1958).

57. For details, see the articles quoted in *J.C.L.*, above, n. 67.

58. Greek Civil Code, article 388, cf. Zepos, loc. cit., pp. 36, 42.

59. The latter is the normal effect of *imprévision* in French law; German courts have applied similar principles under s. 242, German Civil Code; s. 388 of the Greek Civil Code of 1946 specifically empowers the court to reduce the promisor's obligation, or decree the discharge of the contract, where because of a change due to extraordinary and unforeseen events the obligation has become excessively onerous.

60. *Sir Lindsay Parkinson & Co., Ltd* v. *Commissioners of Works & Public Buildings* [1949] 2 K.B. 632.

61. *British Movietonews* v. *London & District Cinemas, Ltd* [1950] 2 All E.R. 390.

62. [1951] 2 All E.R., p. 623.

63. Smit, 'Frustration of Contract', 58 *Col.L.R.* 287 (1958).

64. In the U.S.A., as well as in the British Dominions, the share of both has been considerably greater.

65. Cooper and Wood, *Outlines of Industrial Law* (4th ed., 1962).

66. cf. Kahn-Freund, 'Collective Agreements under War Legislation' (1943) 6 *M.L.R.* 112; cf. also the same author in Flanders and Clegg, *The System of Industrial Relations in Great Britain* (1954).

67. As Kahn-Freund points out, this has mainly happened in weakly organized industries, where employees' organizations cannot take care of themselves; cf. Agricultural Wages Act, 1948; and, for the general machinery, Wages Councils' Act, 1945.

68. e.g. in a recent agreement made between the British Transport Authority and the Transport Workers' Union.

69. cf. Kahn-Freund (1943) 6 *M.L.R.* 112; Thomson, 1 *University of West Australia L.R.* 80; Lenhoff, *Labour Law Cases and Materials*, Vol. 2. (preliminary ed.), compiled by a group of teachers of labour law.

70. *Holland* v. *London Society of Compositors* (1923) 40 *T.L.R.* 440.

71. cf. Kahn-Freund, 6 *M.L.R.*, p. 118.

72. cf. Cox and Dunlop, 63 *Harv.L.R.* (1950), 389–432.

73. cf. Teller, *Labour Disputes and Collective Bargaining*, Vol. 1, § 157.

74. cf. *Moody* v. *Model Window Glass Company*, 145 Ark. 197, 224 S.W. 436 (1920).

75. *Wilson* v. *Airline Coal Company*, 215 Iowa 855, 246 N.W. 753 (1933).

76. *Schlesinger* v. *Quinto*, 201 A.D. 487, 194 N.Y.S. 401 (1922).

77. *J. I. Case Company* v. *N. L. R. B.* (1944) 321 U.S. 332.

78. The practical difficulties of this theory are shown in *Shelley* v. *Portland Tug and Barge Company*, 76 P. (2d) 477 Oregon (1938).

79. cf. authorities quoted in Teller, § 168, note 83. Further, *Leahy* v. *Smith*, 290 P. 2d 679 (1955) (action under collective agreement granted to non-union employee).

80. See, in particular, Shulman, 'Reason, Contract and Law in Labour Relations', 68 *Harv.L.R.* 999 (1955); Cox. 57 *Mich.L.R.* 1.

81. *Young* v. *Canadian Northern Ry* [1931] A.C. 83.

82. e.g. *Aris* v. *Toronto, Hamilton and Buffalo Ry* [1933] O.R. 142; *Wright* v. *Calgary Herald* [1938] 1 *D.L.R.* 111.

83. cf. the Federal Industrial Relations and Disputes Investigation Act, 1948, and, among others, the Ontario Labour Relations Act, 1950. Under the 1950 Ontario Act, for example, the sanctions for violation of a collective agreement consist in the right of either party to call for arbitration, in the power of the arbitrator to make awards which are sometimes tantamount to damages, and in the power of criminal prosecution for non-observance of the arbitrator's award.

84. The precise classification of the Australian and New Zealand systems is not easy. Recent developments in the Australian practice tend to reduce the collective bargaining element in industrial relations, and to emphasize increasingly the part of the Arbitration Court in laying down minimum terms for an entire industry or even all industries. The main share of the parties in that procedure lies in setting the machinery in motion (through application of a registered association of employers or employees). Once the conciliation and arbitration machinery has started to operate in a particular dispute, it is doubtful how far any right to collective action (e.g. by strike or lock-out) still remains. On this point, recent decisions are conflicting. For a brief survey of the general position, cf. Thomson, 'Voluntary Collective Agreements in Australia and New Zealand', 1 *University of Western Australia L.R.* 80–90. Further, *Industrial Regulation in Australia* (1947).

85. cf. Soviet sources quoted in Hazard and Weisberg, *Cases and Readings on Soviet Law* (1950), pp. 144 et seq.

86. cf. Berman, *Justice in Russia*, p. 262.

87. Berman, op. cit., pp. 263–9; cases quoted in Hazard and Weisberg, op. cit., pp. 156–60, 164–74.

88. *The Common Law* (1881), p. 301.

89. See, among others, Buckland, 8 *Camb.L.J.* 247; Cohen, *Law and the Social Order*, p. 100; Paton, *Textbook of Jurisprudence* (2nd ed.), p. 359.

90. cf., for example, the German Civil Code, s. 249. For a comparison of the Anglo-American and the Continental (French, German, and Swiss) approach, see Szladits, 'The Concept of Specific Performance in Civil Law', 4 *Am.J. of Comp.Law* (1955), pp. 208 et seq.

91. e.g. in the supply of a rare picture or the performance of an artist or the supply of a manuscript.

92. See p. 95.

93. cf. Cahn, *The Sense of Injustice* (1949).

## 5. TORT AND INSURANCE

1. *The Common Law* (1881), 144–5.

2. See, for a concise survey of this shift, Seavey, '*Candler* v. *Crane, Christmas & Co.*' (1951) 67 *L.Q.R.* 466, 469 et seq.

3. See, for recent examples, Leflar, 'Negligence in Name Only' (1952) 27 *New York University L.R.* 564; Pound, 'The Rule of the Will in Law' (1954) 68 *Harv.L.R.* 1.

4. A. A. Ehrenzweig in a book published under this title in 1951.

5. R. A. Leflar in the article quoted above, note 3.

6. Judicial awareness of the fact that the defendant had indemnity insurance caused a West Virginia Appeals Court to discard the rule of parental immunity from liability for children's injury (*Lusk* v. *Lusk* (1932) 113 W.Va. 17, 166 SE 538). But more recently, a New Hampshire court refused to concede 'that the existence of liability insurance should create a right of action where none would otherwise exist' (*Levesque* v. *Levesque* (1954) 99 N.H. 147, 106A 2d 563).

7. This is so in the United States and Canada, but not in the United Kingdom, where the civil jury has ceased to play any significant part since the procedural reforms of 1933. See, on the significance of the jury for the law of torts, Fleming, *Law of Torts* (1957), pp. 29 et seq.

8. e.g. a reduction from twelve to six, as enacted in 1955 in Ontario.

9. This was suggested by the so-called Columbia Plan of 1932 and substantially adopted by the Automobile Accident Insurance Act, 1947, of the Canadian Province of Saskatchewan. For a recent proposal to that effect, see Ehrenzweig, *Full Aid Insurance for the Traffic Victim* (1954), pp. 20 et seq., who also surveys the relevant literature. This view has recently received powerful support from Dean Leon Green (*Traffic Victims: Tort Law and Insurance*, 1958), who demonstrates 'the obsolescence and futility of common-law jury trial and liability insurance as a remedy for traffic casualties' and advocates 'compulsory comprehensive loss insurance as a substitute' (Preface). See also in the same sense the warning by Judge Schaefer, in his recent talk to the Chicago Bar Association, 39 *Chic.Bar Rev.* 265 (1958)

10. The number of people injured on the American continent by automobile, railway, or airplane accidents now considerably exceeds the number of accidents, estimated at about two million annually, in factories and workshops. cf. Pound, op. cit., note 1, p. 18.

11. Green, op. cit., p. 81.

12. cf. Esmein, 'Liability in French law for Damages Caused by Motor Vehicle Accidents' (1953) 2 *Am. J. of Comp.Law* 156; Tunc, 'Establishment of *Fonds de Garantie* to Compensate Victims of Motor Vehicle Accidents', ibid., 232.

13. This is particularly clear where, as in France, workmen's compensation started as a judicial innovation, an application of the principle of '*le risque créé*' which the French *Cour de Cassation* developed from the

end of the nineteenth to the middle of the present century in ever-widening spheres, especially the fields of industrial accidents and motor-car accidents. In the former, a statute of 1898 displaced the judge-made creation. In the latter, French law has so far failed to lead on from the principle of strict liability to that of insurance, except for the recent introduction of an Unsatisfied Judgement Fund for motor-car accidents. cf., on the whole development, Planiol et Ripert, *Traité pratique du droit civil* (2nd ed., 1952), Vol. 6, § § 476 et seq., 700 et seq.

14. For a discussion of this matter, see pp. 130 et seq.

15. cf. Riesenfeld, 'Contemporary Trends in Compensation for Industrial Accidents Here and Abroad' (1954) 42 *Cal.L.R.* 531.

16. Riesenfeld, op. cit., pp. 559 et seq.

17. Larson, 'Changing Concepts in Workmen's Compensation' (1954) *Nacca L.J.* 23.

18. This does not necessarily mean socialization in the narrow political sense, which may or may not be an aspect of such development.

19. It is in this sense that negligence is defined in a recent Canadian judgement (*J. P. Porter Co.* v. *Bell* [1955] 1 *D.L.R.* 62, p. 64): 'Negligence is a pervading cause to action which comes into play whenever the relation between parties is such as to produce a risk of foreseeable harm so as to create in law a duty of care appropriate to that risk, and the appropriate degree of care is not taken with consequent loss to the plaintiff. It is in no way restricted to loss caused by activities on land or to dangerous or harmful things escaping from land on the one hand; nor is it restricted to interference with proprietary right in land or its enjoyment'.

20. See *Candler* v. *Crane, Christmas & Co.* [1951] 2 K.B. 164.

21. *Guay* v. *Sun Publishing Co.* [1953] 4 *D.R.L.* 577.

22. See pp. 72 et seq.

23. cf. Morison, 'A Re-examination of the Duty of Care' (1948) 11 *Mod.L.R.* 9 et seq.

24. *Candler* v. *Crane, Christmas & Co.* [1951] 2 K.B. 164.

25. (1789) 3 *T.R.* 51.

26. It is interesting to compare these words with those used by Ashhurst J. in *Paisley* v. *Freeman* (1789) 3 *T.R.*, p. 69: 'Another argument which has been made use of is, that this is a new case, and there is no precedent of such an action. Where cases are new in their principle, there I admit that it is necessary to have recourse to legislative interpretation in order to remedy the grievance; but where the case is only new in the instance, and the only question is upon the application of a principle recognized in the law to such new case, it will be just as competent to courts of justice to apply the principle to any case which may arise two centuries hence, as it was two centuries ago; if it were not, we ought to blot out of our law books one fourth of the cases that are to be found in them.'

27. *Hedley Bryne* v. *Heller* [1963] 3 *W.L.R.* 101.

28. (1931) 255 N.Y. 170

29. Professor Seavey, op. cit. on p. 403 note 2.

30. *Glanzer* v. *Shephard* (1922) 233 N.Y. 236.

31. Restatement § 552. (1938).

32. loc. cit., above, p. 403, note 2, at p. 481.

33. [1945] K.B. 216, affd. [1947] A.C. 156.

34. *Restatement*, § 520 (1938).

35. [1945] K.B. 216, 231–2.

36. ibid., 238.

37. (1866) L.R. 1 C.P. 274.

38. See, for a recent critical survey of British and Commonwealth cases, Fleming, *Law of Torts* (1957), Chap. 19; on the generally corresponding U.S. cases, Prosser (2nd ed., 1955), Chap. 15.

39. Some years ago, I suggested ('Liability of Visitors to Premises' (1943) 21 *Can.Bar Rev.* 79) that the general principle of negligence would cover 'all types of visitors', other than those entering 'as of right' and by contract. Paton, in 21 *Can.Bar Rev.* 440, 444, suggests a reclassification into four categories, ranging from the duty to use reasonable care to make the premises reasonably safe, owed by contractors, public utilities, and invitors, to the duty not intentionally to injure owed to trespassers. Prosser, 20 *Can.Bar Rev.* 357, sees the unifying principle in the assumption of responsibility by the occupier for the safe condition of premises thrown open to the public as distinct from situations where an individual enters the premises for the performance of contracts or other economic purposes from which an assurance of safety can be implied.

40. [1950] A.C. 361.

41. [1951] A.C. 737.

42. [1891] A.C. 325.

43. See, e.g. Lord Wright (himself an eminent member of the House of Lords when it took a more constructive part in the evolution of the law) in (1951) 67 *L.Q.R.* 532; Lloyd, 14 *M.L.R.* 496; Fleming, *Law of Torts*, pp. 448 et seq.

44. Mr C. E. Griffith, in his article 'Fault Triumphant' (28 *N.Y.U.L.R.* 1069) appears to attach more significance than warranted to the recent swing of the pendulum in English decisions.

45. 'Hazardous Enterprises and Risk-Bearing Capacity' (1952) 62 *Yale L.J.* 1172. cf. also G. Williams, criticism of the extension of liability for the acts of independent contractors, in *Camb.L.J.* (1956), 180.

46. cf. pp. 122 et seq.

47. For brief survey, and reference to the cases, see the note in (1949) 63 *Harv.L.R.* 333 et seq.

48. *U.S.* v. *Standard Oil Co. of California* (1947) 332 U.S. 301.

49. cf. 63 *Harv.L.R.* 334–5.

50. cf. for a survey, James, 'Social Insurance and Tort Liability' (1952) 27 *New York U.L.R.* 552 et seq.

51. Final Report of the Departmental Committee on Alternative Remedies (1946) Cmd. 6860.

52. Law Reform (Personal Injuries) Act, 1948.

53. ibid., s. 2 (1).

54. (1947) 152 *H.L.Deb.* 1202.

55. As shown (p. 140), comparative study would have revealed that 'gross negligence' and 'wilful misconduct' criteria play an increasingly important part not only in civil but also in common-law systems.

56. Which has since the Report replaced the earlier Coal Mines Act, 1911.

57. (1946) Cmd. No. 6860, para. 82.

58. (1948) 449 *H.C.Deb.* 2161–6.

59. *Negligence without Fault*, 1951.

60. 'Full Aid' Insurance (1954).

61. 27 *New York U.L.R.* (1952), pp. 537 et seq.

62. op. cit., p. 556.

63. Ussing, 'The Scandinavian Law of Torts', 1 *American Journal of Comparative Law*, 359 et seq. (1952).

64. cf. Ussing, op. cit., p. 369.

65. (1925) 19 Cr. App.R. 8.

66. [1937] A.C. 576.

67. *People* v. *Dunleavy* [1948] Ir.R. 95.

68. For recent illustrations of this provision, see the decisions of the Supreme Court of Canada in *Kerr* v. *Cummings* [1953] 2 D.L.R. 1 and in *Walker* v. *Enders* [1955] 2 D.L.R. 66.


# 6. CRIMINAL LAW

1. See for a recent survey, Williams, 'The Definition of Crime' in *Current Legal Problems*, 1955, pp. 107 et seq.

2. Wechsler, 'The Criteria of Criminal Responsibility', 22 *Un. of Chicago L.R.*, 374. (1955).

3. Report of the Royal Commission on Capital Punishment, 1949–53, H.M.S.O., Cmd. 8932, hereafter cited as 'Report'.

4. (1843) 4 *St. Tr.* (N.S.) 847.

5. See the survey in the Report, pp. 105 et seq.

6. e.g. Fitzjames Stephen, *History of Criminal Law*, II, 157 (1883).

7. Report, p. 80.

8. *State* v. *Pike*, 1870, 49 N.H. 399; *State* v. *Jones*, 1871, 50 N.H. 369.

9. For up-to-date surveys, see Report, Sections 263 et seq., and, in regard to the law and practice in other countries, Section 298, 2307. See also the references in *Durham* v. *United States*, 214 F. 862, and further Wechsler, 1956, Supp. to Michael and Wechsler, *Criminal Law and its Administration*, Notes to pp. 834, 835, 840.

10. Sheldon Glueck, 'Psychiatry and the Criminal Law', 12 *Mental Hygiene* 575, 580 (1928) as quoted in *Durham* v. *U.S.*, above note 9.

11. *Durham* v. *U.S.*, 214 F. 2d 862.

12. e.g. *Smith* v. *U.S.*, 1929, 36 F. 2nd 548: 'In cases where insanity

is interposed as a defence, and the facts are sufficient to call for the application of the rule of irresistible impulse, the jury should be so charged'. And see the various conflicting views of witnesses before the Royal Commission, Report, Sections 264–70.

13. Report, Section 314. This criticism was specially endorsed in *Durham* v. *U.S.*, note 9 above.

14. *Durham* v. *U.S.*, 214 F. 2nd 862 (1954). This test has, however, been rejected in subsequent decisions of other U.S. Appeal Courts, which felt bound by the 'right and wrong test' adopted by the *U.S.* Supreme Court in *Davis* v. *U.S.*, 165 *U.S.* 373 (1897), but also doubted the correctness of the Durham test (e.g. *Sauer* v. *U.S.* (1957) 241 F. 2d 640; see also *Andersen* v. *U.S.*, 237 F. 2d 118 (1956)).

15. Report, para. 317.

16. Report, p. 117.

17. See the ten types classified by Schneider as described in the Report, Section 396.

18. See Report, Appendix IX, at p. 413.

19. Homicide Act, 1957, s. 2. This was contrary to the recommendation of the Royal Commission.

20. In cases of homicide, some American jurisdictions have accepted mental abnormality as justifying a reduction from first degree to second degree murder, e.g. *People* v. *Moran*, 249 N.Y. 179, 163 NE 553 (1928), but a majority of the cases dealing with these questions have rejected the test. See the Brief for the United States in *Fischer* v. *U.S.*, 328 U.S. 463, 747 (1945).

21. Art. 17.

22. Report, p. 93, Section 264.

23. e.g. a minority of the Royal Commission, Report, Section 333, and Memorandum of Dissent at p. 285.

24. cf. the reply given by an eminent Scottish judge, Lord Cooper, when asked whether it was not desirable to have some yardstick to guide the jury: 'I do not think so, for this reason. . . . . However much you charge a jury as to the M'Naghten Rules or any other test, the question they would put to themselves when they retire is – "Is this man mad or is he not?".' There was, in fact, considerable divergence of opinion among legal witnesses as to whether the M'Naghten Rules were, in practice, applied at all. The degree of elasticity left under the cover of a legal formula induced many of the most influential legal witnesses before the Royal Commission, such as the Lord Chief Justice of England and the Director of Public Prosecutions, to counsel against any alteration of the Rules at all. Report, Sections 268 et seq.

25. Section 325.

26. Report, Section 325.

27. e.g. the accused in *Durham* v. *U.S.*, above, note 14 to p. 147.

28. cf., e.g. Flügel, *Man, Morals and Society* (1945), pp. 168 et seq.; Reiwald, *Society and Its Criminals* (1950).

29. cf. the *New Yorker*, 19 April 1958, p. 85.

30. See for a recent survey, Gardiner, 'The Purposes of Criminal Punishment', 21 *M.L.R.* 117, 221 (1958).

31. These two aspects are, in the German terminology, called *Generalprävention* (deterring others) and *Spezialprävention* (deterring the individual concerned). See, on this distinction, Andenaes, 'General Prevention – Illusion or Reality', 43 *J.Crim.L.*, 176, 179 (1952).

32. Report of the Royal Commission on Capital Punishment, 1953, Section 65. See also for a thorough comparative statistical survey, Appendix 6 ('The Deterrent Value of Capital Punishment') in the same Report.

33. See Report, Sections 50–61.

34. cf., for example, the sternly moralistic view expressed by Lord Justice Denning (as he then was) in his evidence before the Commission – contrasting with the same eminent judge's progressive views in regard to the M'Naghten Rules, or the matrimonial relationships, and the function of law in social change in general: 'The punishment inflicted for grave crimes should adequately reflect the revulsion felt by the great majority of citizens for them. It is a mistake to consider the objects of punishment as being deterrent or reformative or preventive and nothing else. . . . The ultimate justification of any punishment is not that it is a deterrent, but that it is the emphatic denunciation by the community of a crime: and from this point of view, there are some murders which, in the present state of public opinion, demand the most emphatic denunciation of all, namely the death penalty.' See also the similar view expressed by the Archishop of Canterbury, ibid.

35. Notably the Scandinavian countries and, following the proposal of the American Law Institute in 1940, California, Wisconsin, and Minnesota.

36. The steady progress in scientific measurement of the factors on the basis of which the probability of the commission of further offences by those committed to corrective institutions can be predicted, is shown by the recent work by Mannheim and Wilkins on *Prediction in Relation to Borstal Training* (1955). From the dossiers of 700 juveniles sentenced to Borstal training, some 60 background factors were obtained, and their relationship to subsequent conduct was measured. From these data, a small number of significant factors were isolated, and from these a prediction table of behaviour for new cases was calculated, which is reported to have proved nearly four times as accurate as the opinion of Borstal governors and housemasters. See Gardiner, op. cit., p. 224.

37. See Sheldon and Eleanor Glueck, 'Unravelling Juvenile Delinquency', and the analysis by Thompson in *British Journal of Delinquency*, Vol. 3 (1953), pp. 289 et seq.

38. See, for example, the English Children Act, 1948.

39. See Gardiner, op. cit., pp. 226 et seq.

40. See Gardiner, op. cit., p. 230.

41. Civil Liberties Record of the Greater Philadelphia Branch, A.C.L.U., Feb. 1956.

42. Olney, 'Juvenile Courts – Abolish Them', 13 *Cal. State, B.J.* 1, 2 (1938).

43. See, for a critical analysis and survey, Paulsen, *Fairness to Juvenile Offenders*, 41 *Minn.L.R.*, 547 (1956); Allen, 'The Borderland of the Criminal Law', *The Social Service Rev.*, Vol. XXXII (1958), p. 107.

44. See Norval Morris, *The Habitual Criminal* (1951), Chap. III, and Chap. IV, pp. 234 et seq.

45. See, for instance, s. 21 of the English Criminal Justice Act, 1948, and the Memorandum of the Secretary of State on Preventive Detention, printed in Morris, op. cit., pp. 257 et seq.

46. *White* v. *Reid* 125 F.Supp. 647 (D.D.C. 1954).

47. ibid. 650.

48. See for a discussion of this test, Paulsen, op. cit., pp. 574 et seq.

49. *People* v. *Higgins* 10 Misc. 2d 42T (1958).

50. e.g. Radzinowicz, *The Persistent Offender in the Modern Approach to Criminal Law*, p. 165; Grünhut, *Penal Reform*, p. 393.

51. H. Mannheim, *Criminal Justice and Social Reconstruction*, p. 213; Morris, op. cit., pp. 241 et seq.

52. See further on this problem, pp. 280 et seq.

53. See, e.g. the wartime agricultural legislation in England, consolidated in the Agricultural Act, 1947.

54. See, for example, art. 14 (2) of the West German Constitution of 1949: 'Property shall involve obligations. Its use shall also serve the common good.'

55. Art. 131, Soviet Constitution of 1936.

56. Art. 128 of the Criminal Code of the R.S.F.S.R. imposes imprisonment for periods up to two years on directors of public enterprises who, through negligence or unconscientious attention to duty, cause waste or irretrievable harm to the property of the enterprise or office. A wartime decree of 1940 went even further in making it an offence for managers and other responsible officers to produce goods of substandard quality. See Hazard, *Law and Social Change in the U.S.S.R.* (1953), pp. 90 et seq.

57. See p. 84.

58. Of 26 July 1949, amended 25 March 1952, and 9 July 1954.

59. Section 1 (author's translation).

60. On this, see Friedmann, 'Monopoly, Reasonableness and Public Interests in the Canadian Anti-Combines Law', 33 *Can.Bar Rev.* 133 (1955); also Blair in Friedmann (ed.), *Anti-Trust Law* (1956), pp. 3 et seq.

61. See pp. 222 et seq.

62. See Chap. 9.

63. Even in the more extreme versions of the organic theories of corporate personality (on which see Friedmann, *Legal Theory*, 4th ed., Chap. 33).

64. For recent illuminating discussions of various parts of this problem, see Williams, *Criminal Law* (2nd ed.,1961), para. 281; Welsh 'Criminal Liability of Corporations' (1946) 62 *L.QR.* 345; Wechsler,

(1956) Supp. to Michael and Wechsler, *Criminal Law and Its Administration*, pp. 159–62.

65. *Moore* v. *Bresler* (**1944**) 2 All E.R. 515; see Welsh, op. cit., p. 360.

66. See Wechsler, **op. cit.**, p. 161: 'no cases have been found in which a corporation was thought to be held criminally liable for such crimes as murder, treason, rape, or bigamy'.

67. See *I.C.R. Haulage, Ltd* [1944] K.B. 551 (C.C.A.); *Moore* v. *Bresler*, above; and Wechsler, op. cit., p. 161.

68. cf. Wechsler, op. cit., p. 159.

69. *Lennard's Carrying Co., Ltd* v. *Asiatic Petroleum Co., Ltd* [1915] A.C., p. 713.

70. *Cain* v. *Doyle*, 72 *C.L.R.* 409 (1946).

71. The above criticism of *Cain*'s case, made in more detail in *Law and Social Change in Contemporary Britain* (pp. 102 et seq.), has been endorsed by Williams, *Criminal Law*, § 282.

72. James Goldschmidt, *Verwaltungsstrafrecht* (1902).

73. See Sayre (1933) *Col.L.R.* 71; Hall, *Principles of Criminal Law* (1947), pp. 281 et seq.; Williams, *Criminal Law* (2nd ed., 1961), § 81; Schwenk, 'The Administrative Crime' (1943) 42 *Mich.L.R.* 51.

74. Section 2.07 2(a).

75. See, e.g. the English Sale of Food (Weights and Measures) Act, 1926, s. 12 (2) which directs the discharge of a defendant, where he can prove 'that such deficiency was due to a bona fide mistake or accident, or other causes beyond his control, and in spite of all reasonable precautions being taken and due diligence exercised by the said defendant to prevent the occurrence of such deficiency, or was due to the action of some person over whom the defendant had no control . . . '

76. See, e.g. Hall, *Principles of Criminal Law*, p. 331. The opposite argument against strict liability, i.e. that the imposition of a fine on a shopkeeper or chemist for a statutory offence may have disasterous consequences, is put forward by Edwards, *Mens Rea in Statutory Offences*, p. 245.

77. *R.* v. *St Margaret's Trust, Ltd* (1958) 2 All E.R. 289.

78. The title of a monograph by A. Ehrenzweig discussed at p. 135.

79. See the survey of public-welfare offences in Williams, op. cit., sections 76 to 81; Hall, *General Principles of Criminal Law*, pp. 327 et seq.; Edwards, *Mens Rea in Statutory Offences*, pp. 80 et seq.

80. Hall, op. cit., p. 343. For a similar view see now Henry M. Hart, 'The Aims of the Criminal Law', 23 *Law and Contemporary Problems* (1958), pp. 422 et seq.

81. 342 U.S. 246 (1952).

82. 18 U.S.C., § 641.

83. *V.S.* v. *Behrmann*, 258 U.S. 250 (1922)

84. Hall, op. cit., p. 352.

85. Tentative Draft No. 2, sec. 1.05 (1954).

86. For suggestions of 'civil offences', see also Gausewitz, 12 *Wis. L.R.* 365 (1937) and Perkins, 100 *U. of Pa.L.R.* 832 (1952).

## 7. FAMILY LAW

1. *Republic*, Book V, 457, tr. Lindsay.

2. See, e.g. the statement of the Christian view of marriage by the Federal Council of Churches of Christ in America (reprinted in *Selected Essays on Family Law*, p. 118) or the Encyclical on Christian Marriage (Pope Pius XI) (ibid., pp. 132 et seq.).

3. e.g. the strong protests against the second marriages entered into some years ago by a Prime Minister of Pakistan and the President of the Indonesian Republic.

4. The formal sanction is now increasingly civil, i.e. by the authority of the State, rather than the Church, even in many Catholic States, such as France and Italy. How strong the moral authority of Church sanction remains in many communities is shown by the libel action brought (and won) in 1958 in Italy by a civilly married couple against a bishop, who had condemned the lack of religious marriage as sinful and depraved.

5. See further pp. 211 et seq. For a survey of the major developments in English law since the Matrimonial Causes Act, 1857, see the Symposium, *A Century of Family Law* (1957), ed. Graveson and Crane, and especially the introductory and concluding chapters, pp. 1 et seq., 411 et seq., by Graveson.

6. ibid.

7. However, the ecclesiastical courts have considerably extended grounds of nullity, in particular for impotence and for wilful refusal to consummate the marriage. The latter is really a failure to fulfil a marriage once validly concluded. When the secular courts took over jurisdiction from the ecclesiastical courts, as happened in England in 1857, they also took over some of these classifications. (For details, see Scott, *Nullity of Marriage in Canon Law and English Law*, 1938, 2 *U. of Tor.L.J.* 319–43.) It is only in its *Report* of 1956 that the British Commission on Marriage and Divorce recommended that wilful refusal to consummate the marriage should be made a ground of divorce rather than nullity. In 36 American jurisdictions, impotence now is a statutory ground of divorce. (See Table 3, Appendix II, *Report of the British Royal Commission on Marriage and Divorce*, Cmd. 9678, H.M.S.O. 1956.)

8. Among them are most of the Latin American Republics, Eire, Spain, Italy, and the Canadian Province of Quebec.

9. Matthew 19:6.

10. The compatibility of this 'existentialist' conception of marriage with Christian ethics and religion has been argued, for example, by Canon Carpenter (*Listener*, 21 August 1958).

11. According to the report of the British Royal Commission (Table 2, Appendix II), dissolubility of marriage by mutual consent is today openly recognized only in Bulgaria and in Portugal (for non-Catholics). However, the Swedish Marriage Code of 1920 goes a considerable way

towards recognition of the dissolubility of marriage by consent. Under this Act, a judicial decree of separation may be granted in cases of 'profound and lasting disruption' due to 'diversity of temperament and opinions or other causes'. Alternatively, two married people can obtain a separation decree if both of them apply jointly. Divorce can be obtained after one year of judicial separation, on application by either spouse if, after the separation decree, they have lived separated for one year. In other words, judicial separation can be obtained by mutual consent at any time, and divorce one year afterwards by unilateral application, where factual separation has taken place. (The author is obliged to Professor Ake Malström of Uppsala University for information on the Swedish law.)

Japanese law, before the modernization effected by the Civil Code of 1898, recognized a unilateral right by the husband to divorce his wife by a simple letter. The Civil Code of 1898 provided for divorce by mutual consent, along with judicial divorce. Where there are children, the parties must accompany their notification to the municipal office with the terms of agreement on custody. If the parties reach no agreement, the family court decides on guardianship and custody, but it has no power to halt the divorce itself. This state of the law has remained unchanged, except that a reform of 1947 has added to the grounds of judicial divorce (unchastity; malicious desertion; absence for three years or more; and severe mental disease) a broad judicial discretion to grant divorce for 'any other grave reason'. The admission of divorce by consent is attributed by Professor Toru Ikuyo, of Nagoya University – to whom I am obliged for this information – to the religious philosophy of the Japanese (Buddhism, Shintoism, Confucianism), which has not condemned divorce as a religious or moral sin. The main progress of the reform of 1898 has been to put the wife, at least in theory, in a position equal to that of her husband. Such equality is still far from being a social reality, although a reform of 1947 provides for a right for either spouse to demand distribution of property in any case of divorce, whether by consent or judgement.

12. *Ehegesetz*, Section 48.

13. See Hazard, *Law and Social Change in the U.S.S.R.*, 1953, p. 247

14. See Hazard, op. cit., p. 270. According to personal information given to the writer by Professor Hazard, the present practice of the Soviet courts is still guided by these principles.

15. Eighteen American states now have laws permitting divorce after separation for periods varying from two to ten years. Most of these do not require absence of 'fault' or consent by both parties. See McCurdy, 'Divorce – A Suggested Approach' (1956) 9 *Vanderbilt L.R.* 701 et seq.

16. See Vernier, *American Family Laws* (1931), Vol. II, para. 78; *Stewart* v. *Stewart* (1946) Fla. 326; *A.L.R.* 1073.

17. *Blunt* v. *Blunt* [1943] A.C. 517, *per* Lord Simon L.C.

18. See the survey in the Report of the Royal Commission, p. 376 (Commonwealth), p. 380 (17 European countries), p. 384 (U.S.A.).

19. See Tables 1, 2 and 3, Appendix III, pp. 375 et seq.

20. C. P. Harvey, Q.C., 'On the State of the Divorce Market' (1953) 16 *M.L.R.* p. 130.

21. Among others, see a series of Essays in *Selected Essays on Family Law* (published by the Association of American Law Teachers in 1950), in particular, Bradway, 'The Myth of the Innocent Spouse', pp. 937 et seq.; and an anonymous note entitled 'Collusive and Consensual Divorce and the New York Anomaly', ibid., pp. 1121–33; further, Jacobs and Angell, *Research in Family Law* (1930), *passim*; and, for a sociological analysis, Lichtenberger, *Divorce: A Sociological Interpretation* (1931). See also the symposium in (1956) 9 *Vanderbilt L.R.* 633 et seq., and, in particular, the articles by Rheinstein (633 et seq.), Bradway (665 et seq.), and McCurdy (685 et seq.). For the most authoritative recent British survey, see the *Report of the Royal Commission on Marriage and Divorce* (1956) Cmd. 9678, Part I, and for critical comments thereon, Kahn-Freund: 'Divorce Law Reform?' (1956) 19 *M.L.R.* 573–600; also McGregor, 'The Morton Commission: A Social and Historical Commentary', *Br. Journal of Sociology*, Vol. VII (1956), p. 171.

22. See the analysis by C. R. McGregor, *Divorce in England* (1957), pp. 41 et seq., of the reasons for the post-war increase in divorce petitions, especially those alleging cruelty 'largely, though not entirely, a husband's offence' (p. 43).

23. Interesting conclusions can be derived from the Table annexed to the Report of the Royal Commission on p. 359. Between 1938 and 1954 the number of divorce decrees based on adultery in England and Wales increased from 5,349 to 11,794. At the same time, divorce decrees given for desertion (including 'constructive desertion') increased from 1,874 to 11,640 and those based on cruelty from 306 to 3,593. Whereas, in 1938, desertion and cruelty together accounted for far less than half the divorce decrees based on adultery, in 1954 they considerably exceeded adultery as a cause for divorce. That, in many cases of desertion and cruelty, adultery may also be present, though not pleaded, does not affect the point made here.

24. McGregor (op. cit., p. 47) concludes from the statistics published in the annual Reports of the Law Society that 'approximately 45 per cent of the total number of divorce petitions in 1954 were filed by assisted persons'.

25. *Report,* Sec. 69, p. 16.

26. ibid., p. 23.

27. McGregor, *Divorce in England* (1957).

28. op. cit., pp. 39 et seq.,

29. Barbara Wootton, 'Holiness or Happiness' (*The Twentieth Century*, Nov. 1955), p. 415.

30. Rheinstein, 'The Law of Divorce and the Problem of Marriage Stability' (1956) 9 *Vanderbilt L.R.*, p. 643.

31. Save for the above-mentioned evasion by somewhat extended grounds of nullity of marriage, and the existence of thousands of Catholic marriages which are separate and, in effect, dissolved, except for the

legal bond which prevents remarriage. The Anglo-Catholic wing of the Church of England adopts the same philosophy as the Church of Rome. On matters of divorce and birth control the Church of England is deeply split. But a resolution passed at the 1958 Lambeth Conference accepted birth control as compatible with Christianity.

32. This is the law in a substantial number of American States; and the subject of recent British reform proposals. See p. 178.

33. op. cit., p. 17.

34. McCurdie, 'Divorce – A Suggested Approach' (1956) 9 *Vanderbilt L.R.*, p. 706.

35. For an effective criticism of the 'fault' principle in support cases, as applied in the United States, see Paulsen, 'Support Rights and Duties' (1956) 9 *Vanderbilt L.R.* 709, 727 et seq.

36. op. cit., p. 138.

37. A proposition supported by six members of the Commission, ibid., p. 138.

38. The freedom of the married woman to choose a profession or trade or paid employment without the consent of the husband is now more and more generally recognized in the Western world. It is now universal in the common-law world (for a statutory formulation of this right, see sec. 51, New York Domestic Relations Act), including, with certain reservations, the majority of the American community property states (Clark in Friedmann (ed.), *Matrimonial Property Law*, pp. 107 et seq.), West Germany (Sec. 1356 BGB, as amended in 1957), the Scandinavian states, and, of course, the legal systems of the Soviet type. But progress is far from universal. In France, the exercise by the wife of a separate profession is still subject to the husband's veto (Conseil d'État, Dalloz 1945, 60, quoted in Ancel in Friedmann (ed.), *Matrimonial Property Law*, p. 21). In Quebec and South Africa – both strongly traditionalist countries still largely dominated by the religious and social concepts of the French and Dutch immigrants of several centuries ago – the husband, as lord and master, can still forbid his wife to engage in a trade or profession (ibid., Turgeon, p. 172; Price, p. 196). This marital power may be excluded by marriage contract.

39. Jacobs and Angell, *Research in Family Law* (1930), pp. 37–8.

40. O. M. Stone, 19 *M.L.R.*, p. 601.

41. The Report altogether gives welcome emphasis to 'preventive law' in family affairs. It emphasizes the need for marriage guidance and reconciliation and premarital education. It recommends greatly increased State support for existing agencies and, in particular, substantial extension of the probation service.

42. For a powerful recent criticism of the inadequacy of the adversary divorce court procedure as a means of eliciting the facts of family life, see Bradway, 'Divorce Litigation and the Welfare of the Family', 9 *Vanderbilt L.R.* 665 et seq. (1956).

43. Judge Paul W. Alexander of Toledo, Ohio, 'The Family Court of the Future', 31 *Journal Am.Jud.Soc.* 38 (1952).

44. See the Report by a special Committee of the Association of the Bar of the City of New York, based on a study by W. Gellhorn, published in 1954.

45. With jurisdiction over the following matters: '(a) all cases over which the Children's Court now has jurisdiction; (b) crimes and wayward behaviour of minors over 16 years of age *except:* (1) crimes punishable by death or life imprisonment; (2) such felonies committed by youths 19 to 21 as the legislature may exclude; (3) cases of youths pleading not guilty of any crime who wish a trial in the appropriate criminal court; (4) cases of minors charged with felony which, after investigation, the integrated court in its discretion may see fit to refer to the criminal court; (c) simple assaults and disorderly conduct involving members of an immediate family unit; (d) proceedings to establish paternity; (e) all claims for support, including those for support of children born in or out of wedlock; (f) matters involving custody of children; (g) proceedings for divorce, dissolution, annulment, and separation; (h) proceedings to authorize adoption.'

46. See the concurrent resolution of the Senate and Assembly of the State of New York introduced in 1958, as reproduced in the Report of the Joint Legislative Committee on Matrimonial and Family Laws, Legislative Document No. 26 (1958).

47. See the whole problem, Harper, *Problems of Family Life* (1952), Chap. VII.

48. For a recent survey of the New Jersey experiment and those of other states, see the above-mentioned Report of the Joint Legislative Committee on Matrimonial and Family Laws, New York State, 1958.

49. See Himes, *Medical History of Contraception*, 1936.

50. In Japan, whose population will soon reach 100 million, on a small and already fully cultivated and developed island, the official encouragement of birth control in recent years has led to a drastic decline in the birth-rate in a generally educated population. In India, the Government is encouraging birth control clinics, but so far with indifferent success among a still overwhelmingly illiterate peasant population. Recently, the Government of Communist China, hitherto addicted to the Communist and totalitarian philosophy of encouraging the maximum number of children on a mixture of stategic grounds and the Marxist faith in unlimited opportunities in a Socialist society, has urged the use of contraceptives on the recently emancipated women of that country.

51. This opposition accounts, for example, for the practical impossibility of officially sponsored family-advice centres in many American states, or for the total absence of discussions on such matters in public communication media, such as radio and television, in Canada or the U.S.A. The City of New York, in 1958, after a bitter controversy, decided to permit doctors in city hospitals to fit contraceptive devices to non-Catholic patients whose health would be gravely endangered by the birth of a child.

52. 'The Apostolate of the Midwife', in *Moral Questions Affecting Married Life*, The Paulist Press, New York, p.7.

53. 'The Apostolate of the Midwife', No. 36, in op.cit., p. 15.

54. *Baxter* v. *Baxter* [1948] A.C. 274.

55. *Knott* v. *Knott* [1955] 3 *W.L.R.* 162.

56. *Report*, Table 3, p. 384.

57. 'The Apostolate of the Midwife', No. 27, in op. cit., p. 13.

58. ibid., No. 51, p. 20.

59. See Glanville Williams, *The Sanctity of Life and the Criminal Law*, pp. 130 et seq.

60. For the considerable legal literature dealing with these problems, see Glanville Williams, op. cit., p. 129. and Tallin, 34 *Can.Bar Rev.* 1, 166 (1956).

61. See 'The Apostolate of the Midwife', No. 12, in op. cit., p. 7.

62. Pope Pius XII, in 'The Apostolate of the Midwife', No. 19, p. 10.

63. Code of Ethical and Religious Directives for Catholic Hospitals, as quoted by Glanville Williams, op. cit., p. 202.

64. See *R.* v. *Dudley and Stephens* (1884) 14 Q.B.D. 273; *U.S.* v. *Holmes*, 26 Fed. Case 360 (CCED Pa. 1842).

65. For a survey, see Williams, op. cit., pp. 160 et seq.

66. *R.* v. *Bourne* [1939] 1 K.B. 687.

67. In a Massachusetts decision, *Commonwealth* v. *Wheeler*, 53 N.E. (2d) 4 (Mass. 1944), the court acquitted where the physician, who, in accordance with the general opinion of competent practitioners, had had a bona fide belief in the necessity of abortion in order to prevent serious impairment of the mother's health, and this despite the fact that Massachusetts is one of a few states that do not, by statute, recognize abortion to save even the *life* of the mother.

68. Taking an average of the various semi-official and authoritative estimates made, Dr Williams, op. cit., pp. 210 et seq., concludes 'that there is not in England more than one prosecution to every thousand criminal abortions'.

69. See Berman, *Justice in Russia* (1950), p. 286, and the documents printed in Schlesinger, *The Family in the U.S.S.R.* (1949), pp. 254 et seq.

70. For a discussion, with reference in particular to Ekblad, *Induced Abortion on Psychiatric Grounds*, Stockholm, 1955, see Williams, op. cit., pp. 236 et seq.

71. See Glanville Williams, op. cit., pp. 232 et seq.

72. Perhaps the most vivid, though poetic, description of a typical rural household of the late eighteenth century is found in the poem *Die Glocke* by Freidrich Schiller.

73. See, e.g. for the community of acquest systems prevalent in Louisiana and seven Western states of the United States, the articles by Clark and Morrow in Friedmann (ed.), *Matrimonial Property Law*, op. cit., pp. 29 et seq. and 89 et seq. On the contemporary law of Quebec, see Turjeon, ibid., pp. 139 et seq.

74. Book I, Chap. XV; Book II, Chap. XXIX.

75. See Kahn-Freund, in Friedmann (ed.) *Matrimonial Property Law*, p. 275.

76. e.g. the Domestic Relations Law of New York, section 50: 'Property, real or personal, now owned by a married woman, or hereafter owned by a married woman at the time of her marriage, or acquired by her as prescribed in this chapter, and the rents, issues, proceeds, and profits thereof, shall continue to be her sole and separate property as if she were unmarried, and shall not be subject to her husband's control or disposal nor liable for his debts.' See W. Tucker Dean in Friedmann (ed.) *Matrimonial Property Law*, p. 326.

77. For an account, see Dean, ibid., pp. 315 et seq.

78. i.e. common ownership of all property earned by the spouses during the continuation of the marriage, as distinct from property belonging to the spouses before entering upon marriage – which remains separate property.

79. The West German *Gleichberechtigungsgesetz* of 1957, like the earlier Scandinavian statutes, which give full equality to husband and wife, have essentially abandoned the community concept. See p. 203.

80. John N. Hazard in Friedmann (ed.) *Matrimonial Property Law*, p. 219.

81. Henri Turgeon in ibid., p. 157.

82. For Louisiana, see C. J. Morrow in Friedmann (ed.) *Matrimonial Property Law*, pp. 50 et seq.; for the Western states, see Clark, ibid., pp. 98 et seq.

83. For details, see Clark, op. cit., pp. 101 et seq.

84. For details, see Malmström in Friedmann (ed.) *Matrimonial Property Law*, pp. 410 et seq.

85. For details, see Franz Massfeller in Friedmann (ed.) *Matrimonial Property Law*, pp. 378 et seq.

86. This should not, however, be overstated, for the vast majority of families everywhere operate with limited property comparable to that of (sec. 392) the average Soviet family. It is only in the limited field of considerable estates derived either from investments or business operations that the differences become marked.

87. Planiol-Ripert, *Traité Élémentaire du droit civil*, 4th ed., 1951.

88. See, for the relevant Canadian legislation, Clyde Auld in Friedmann (ed.) *Matrimonial Property Law*, pp. 259 et seq.

89. In a number of other states, e.g. certain financial privileges are granted to married women on account of 'homesteads', but here the homestead is merely an accounting item. Moreover, the exemption is usually very low.

90. This is due to the political impossibility of confining the more favourable rate, applicable through the splitting of the joint income of husband and wife on a fifty-fifty basis, to community-property systems. After a number of hasty legislative changes, introducing community property in traditionally common-law jurisdictions, the Federal Tax Law was amended so as to make the income of husband and wife

optionally joint throughout the country. After this reform, the common-law states promptly reverted to the common-law system of matrimonial property.

91. [1952] 2 Q.B. 466.

92. In later decisions (*Woodcock* v. *Hobbs* [1955] 1 W.L.R. 152, C.A.; *Westminster Bank* v. *Lee* [1956] Ch. 7), this right of the deserted wife has been held to be an equity binding a third party only in so far as it has knowledge or constructive notice. See Kahn-Freund, 'Matrimonial Property – Some Recent Developments', 22 *M.L.R.* 241, 260 (1959).

93. e.g. *Rimmer* v. *Rimmer* [1953] 1 Q.B. 63.

94. The similarity between this judicial reform and the more systematic statutory reform of the German *Gleichberechtigungsgetz* is a remarkable indication of the way in which different legal concepts can be made to respond similarly to a social challenge.

95. They were, however, very vague on the details, and in their belief that a community system is at present in operation in the Scandinavian countries (sec. 653) they were mistaken.

96. Some modern States, like India, have clearly adopted the principle of the equality of sexes, of equal opportunity for all and of the care, maintenance, and education of children, in accordance with the principles of modern Western societies. (See Indian Constitution, Arts. 15, 23, 24, and others.) But the translation of these principles into reality, in a society struggling against a centuries-old tradition of caste, sex, and other discriminations, will, of course, take a long time.

97. See New York Domestic Relations Law, para. 70, giving the court power to determine, on habeas corpus, for a child detained by a parent, in regard to the custody of the child, 'what is for the best interest of the child, and what will best promote its welfare and happiness and make award accordingly'. See also the English Guardianship of Infants Act of 1925, s. 1. which regulates the powers of custody in similar terms.

98. Sec. 1626 BGB as amended.

99. Sec. 1631 BGB as amended.

100. *Campbell* v. *Campbell* (1942) 200 S.C. 67, 20 S.E. 2nd 237.

101. See the survey in *Porter* v. *Powell*, 79 Iowa 151, 44 N.W. 295 (1890).

102. *Report of the Royal Commission on Marriage and Divorce*, 1956, Section 560.

103. e.g. the Summary Jurisdiction (Separation and Maintenance) Acts, 1895 to 1949, the Matrimonial Causes Act, 1950, s. 26, or the National Assistance Act, 1948, s. 42, under which the National Assistance Board may take over the liability for maintenance and recover the cost of assistance from the parents.

104. Sections 1360, 1360a BGB as amended. In Scotland, as distinct from England, the common law imposes upon the parents the liability to aliment their children in so far as they are able.

105. See *Kehey* v. *Kehey*, 200 Ga. 41, 36 S.E. 2nd, 155 (1946) and the

note in Jacobs and Goebel, *Cases and Materials on Domestic Relations*, 3rd ed., 1952, p. 1040.

106. *Bonner* v. *Surman*, 215 Ark. 301, 220 S.W. 2nd, 431 (1949).

107. See note in Jacobs and Goebel, op. cit., p. 1041.

108. The wife conducts the household in her own responsibility. She is entitled to engage in gainful work (*erwerbstätig*), in so far as this is compatible with her obligations in marriage and in the family.

109. Section 1356 BGB as amended in 1957.

110. Section 1360 BGB as amended in 1957.

111. Though not under the National Assistance Act of 1948.

112. loc. cit. n. 7, *supra*, Section 568.

113. loc. cit., Section 567.

114. R.S.F.S.R. Code, 1926, Sections 42, 48 to 50, 54 to 55.

115. See Hazard, *Law and Social Change in the U.S.S.R.*, p. 258

116. Robbins and Deak, 'The Familial Property Rights of Illegitimate Children, A Comparative Study' (1930) 30 *Col.L.R.* 308; reprinted in *Selected Essays on Family Law*, op. cit., pp. 728 et seq.

117. Report, Sec. 1180.

118. No exclusion of children conceived or born in adultery appears to be considered in any of the American statutes. See, e.g. New York Domestic Relations Law, para. 24: 'all illegitimate children whose parents have heretofore intermarried or who shall hereafter intermarry shall thereby ... become legitimate for all purposes ... ' In France, various laws from 1907 to 1924, revoked by legislation of the Vichy Republic, and restored in 1945, have introduced the legitimation of children of adultery, though some writers, like the majority of the Royal Commission, deplore such laxity (see the note in Carbonnier, *Droit Civil*, Vol. I, 1955, p. 554). No restriction exists in German law (sec. 1719 BGB) except where the husband of a wife who conceives in adultery omits to contest the legitimacy. In that case, the child is a fully legitimate issue of the former marriage and suffers no hardship.

119. For details, see Magnusson, *Norwegian Law of Illegitimacy* (1918), U.S. Children's Bureau, Legal Series No. 1, Pub. No. 31; also, Robbins and Deak, op. cit., pp. 745 et seq.

120. See, for example, the various procedures available for applications for adoption orders under the British Adoption Act, 1950.

121. In German law, this whole sphere of judicial activity is termed *freiwillige Gerichtsbarkeit*.

122. Married Women's Property Act, 1882, s. 17.

123. See, for example, Section 1631, German Civil Code, as amended in 1957.

124. New Zealand, Sweden, the United Kingdom, the U.S.S.R.

125. While voluntary group insurance, through Blue Cross schemes and the like, now covers substantial parts of the population in Canada and the United States, it does not cover, at least in the U.S.A., ordinary doctor's or dentist's bills. Moreover, many forms of diseases are excluded from coverage. The burden for the individual family

remains very considerable. Why it should be beyond the province of the State to insure a minimum health standard for its people – as maintained by the organized medical profession in both countries – is no more intelligible than opposition to compulsory school education.

126. cf. Kahn-Freund, op. cit., p. 305. See, however, the Report of the Royal Commission, above, p. 201, n. 75.

127. For details, see Kahn-Freund (1953) 16 *M.L.R.* 148 et seq., 164.

128. W. Tucker Dean in W. Friedmann (ed.) *Matrimonial Property Law*, p. 361.

## 8. FREEDOM OF TRADE AND POLICY

1. The ambiguity of the concept was dramatically illustrated in the *Australian Bank Nationalisation Case* (76 *C.L.R.* 1 (1948); 79 *C.L.R.* 497 (1949)), where the Australian High Court interpreted sec. 91 of the Australian Constitution: '... shall be absolutely free' as meaning not just lack of restriction on the volume of trade between the states of Australia, but freedom from Government restriction, and therefore entailing invalidity of Commonwealth legislation nationalizing the banks, despite the power of the Commonwealth to legislate in matters of banking. The Privy Council refused to disturb the judgement.

2. See for further details, Hazard in Friedmann (ed.), *The Public Corporation* (1954), pp. 374 et seq.

3. ibid., pp. 108 et seq. (Drago), pp. 162 et seq. (Friedmann), and pp. 542 et seq.

4. New Zealand attempted, in the Commercial Trust Act, 1910, entitled 'An Act for the Repression of Monopolies in Trade or Commerce', a more direct attack on monopoly and restrictive practices. The Act, which was inspired by distrust of foreign oil and meat interests and comparable in conception to the Sherman Act, was effectively killed by the judgement of the Privy Council in *Crown Milling Co.* v. *The King* [1927] A.C. 394. In that case, the Privy Council held that a flour mill cartel in the form of a company empowered to fix prices, regulate production, eliminate competition between flour mills, and apply coercive measures against outsiders had not been shown to be 'contrary to the public interest'. The irony of this judgement, which did of course, by implication, strike a decisive blow for restrictive practices, lies in the celebrated phrase of Lord Finlay that 'it is not for this tribunal nor for any tribunal, to adjudicate as between conflicting theories of political economy' (ibid., p. 402). For an analysis, see Robson, in Robson (ed.), *New Zealand, the Development of its Laws and Constitution* (London, 1954), pp. 197 et seq.

5. Grünfeld in Friedmann (ed.), *Anti-Trust Laws, A Comparative Symposium* (1956), pp. 342 et seq.

6. Until the end of 1955 it had delivered ten major Reports dealing with dental goods, cast iron, rainwater goods, supply of electric lamps, insulated electric wires and cables, insulin, matches, imported timber,

calico printing, and supply of buildings in the Greater London Area. The last Report, as distinct from the others, dealt with a general practice, that of collective discrimination, exclusive dealing, collective boycotts, aggregated rebates, and other discriminatory practices.

7. This new principle of compulsory registration of listed restrictive practices follows the example of the Scandinavian countries, in particular Norway, which have for some years made this principle of publicity the cornerstone of their anti-cartel legislation. See for details Eckhoff, in Friedmann (ed.) *Anti-Trust Laws* (1956), pp. 281 et seq.; further on Sweden, Bolin, ibid., at pp. 319 et seq.; and on similar laws in the Netherlands, Verloren van Themaat, ibid., pp. 258 et seq. Registration of restrictive agreements, under the auspices of the Cartel Office, has also become a major feature of the German Anti-trust Act (*Wettbewerbsgesetz*) of 1957, replacing in part the principle of absolute invalidity of agreements in restraint of trade, which dominated the earlier drafts.

8. A similarly mixed court is established by the South Africa Act of 1955; see Friedmann (ed.) *Anti-Trust Laws* (1956), pp. 308 et seq.

9. *Re The Agreement between the Members of the Chemists' Federation* [1958] 3 All E.R. 448.

10. *Re The Yarn Spinner's Agreement* [1959] 1 All E.R. 299. For a similar decision on the minimum-price scheme of blanket manufacturers, see *Re Blanket Manufacturers' Association* [1959] 1 All E.R. 1.

11. A similar effect may flow from the new German *Wettbewerbsgesetz*, which compels the notification or registration of thousands of agreements that have never been challenged before.

12. See pp. 26 et seq.

13. '(1) Every one who conspires, combines, agrees or arranges with another person

    (*a*) to limit unduly the facilities for transporting, producing, manufacturing, supplying, storing or dealing in any article,

    (*b*) to restrain or injure trade or commerce in relation to any article,

    (*c*) to prevent, limit or lessen, unduly, the manufacture or production of an article, or to enhance unreasonably the price thereof, or

    (*d*) to prevent or lessen, unduly, competition in the production, manufacture, purchase, barter, sale, transportation or supply of an article, or in the price of insurance upon persons or property is guilty of an indictable offence and is liable to imprisonment for two years.

'(2) for the purposes of this section, "article" means an article or commodity that may be a subject of trade or commerce.

'(3) This section does not apply to combinations of workmen or employees for their own reasonable protection as workmen or employees.'

14. For a detailed survey and analysis, see Timberg, op. cit., pp. 403 et seq.

15. On this point, see Friedmann, 33 *Can. Bar Rev.* 133, pp. 142 et seq.

16. For a detailed analysis, see the articles of D. Gordon Blair and S. Timberg in Friedmann, op. cit., pp. 3 et seq., 403 et seq.; also,

Friedmann, 'Monopoly, Reasonableness and Public Interest in the Canadian Anti-Combines Law' (1955) 33 *Can.Bar Rev.* 133.

17. *U.S.* v. *Standard Oil Co.*, 221 U.S. 1 (1911).

18. *U.S.* v. *Aluminium Co. of America*, 148 F. 2d 416 (C.C.A. 2nd 1945).

19. *American Column and Lumber Co.* v. *United States*, 257 U.S. 418 (1921), pp. 418–19.

20. The Australian Commonwealth Court of Arbitration, composed of three judges, has, however, never hesitated to take and appraise voluminous economic evidence before coming to its decisions on such momentous matters as a forty-hour week or a minimum wage. See on the organization and function of the court, Sawer in Paton (ed.), *The Commonwealth of Australia*, Vol. 2 of *The British Commonwealth, The Development of Its Laws and Constitutions* (London, 1952), pp. 289 et seq.

21. See the figures given by Adelman, 'The Measurement of Industrial Concentration', *Review of Economics and Statistics*, Vol. 32, No. 4, p. 289.

## 9. CORPORATE POWER, THE LAW, AND THE STATE

1. Maitland, 'The Unicorporate Body', in *Selected Legal Essays* (1936), 135–6.

2. Maitland, 'Trust and Corporation', in ibid., 182–3.

3. ibid., 207.

4. In a recent sample, taken in the United States, 2,262 out of 2,981 foundations were found to be incorporated, Rich, *American Foundations and Their Fields*, xvii (7th ed., 1955). For an analysis of the developments which have, despite the partial approximation of the status of an unincorporated association to that of a corporate legal person and despite the versatility of the trust, led in England to the increasing use of the incorporated charity (company limited by guarantee), see Gower, *Modern Company Law* (2nd ed., 1957), pp. 12, 172.

5. See Carnegie, *Share the Wealth* (1895).

6. According to an article, 'How to Have your Own Foundation', *Fortune* (Aug. 1947), pp. 108, 109, the Treasury Department estimated that there were then in the United States more than 10,000 foundations. Six years later, a *Report of the Select Committee to Investigate Foundations*, H.R. Rep. No. 2514, 82d Cong., 2d Sess. (1953), estimated the number of tax-exempt foundations and organizations at over 30,000, and their gross endowments at about 7 billion dollars. But only between 60 and 100 were estimated to have assets of 10 million dollars or more (excluding colleges, universities, and religious organizations), ibid., at 2. Rich, op. cit., *supra*, note 4, xix–xxii, estimates that 78 foundations, each with assets of more than 10 million dollars, had a total capital of 3.1 billion dollars. This is almost certainly an underestimate, as the assets of the Ford Foundation, are listed as below 500 million dollars. They are now estimated at more than twice this amount.

7. There are, however, also numerous examples of smaller foundations

whose main purpose is to secure an income for dependants from a less highly taxed capital fund.

8. cf. *Fortune, supra,* note 6; also an excellent note, 34 *Va.L.Rev.* 182 (1948).

9. The limit is 10 per cent or, in certain cases not generally applicable to foundations, 20 per cent for individual donors and 5 per cent for corporate donors.

10. cf. Gower, op. cit., *supra,* note 4, 171 et seq.

11. Political rivalries have led to such legislation in the Province of Ontario, Canada. 13 Geo. 6, c.10 (1949). The owner of a successful Liberal newspaper established a charitable foundation in which he vested the bulk of his shares. The founding members and controllers were the management and editors of the newspaper. Political opposition was largely responsible for an Act providing that, except for religious organizations:

> Wherever any interest in any business that is carried on for gain or profit is given to or vested in any person in any capacity for any religious, charitable, educational or public purpose, such person shall dispose of such portion thereof that represents more than a ten per centum interest in such business.

Such disposal must be carried out within seven years after the interest was vested, unless the Supreme Court extends the period.

12. For detailed calculations, see *Fortune, supra,* note 6, at 109, 140.

13. 'It is this peculiar circumstance – *retention of control* – which largely explains the emergence of family foundations as the dominant feature on the foundation scene today. Men who have built successful enterprises and seen the value of their equity swell have sought, naturally, to keep control with the family. They have accordingly established charitable family foundations, minimized their tax, enjoyed the satisfaction of promoting good works, and retained practically all but the dividend benefits of ownership. Such persons, it has been said, actually do not give away their property at all, but only the income thereon – though this is perhaps an overstatement.' Note, 34 *Va.L.Rev.* 182, 188 (1948).

14. cf. in particular Berle and Means, *The Modern Corporation and Private Property* (1932); Renner, *Institutions of Private Law* (Kahn-Freund ed., 1949); and such more general analyses as Arnold, *The Folklore of Capitalism* (1937), and Burnham, *The Managerial Revolution* (1941).

15. cf. the examples given in *Fortune, supra,* note 6. Recent legislation has, however, put obstacles in the way of certain obvious devices of this kind. See Int. Rev. Code of 1954, §§ 503–14.

16. For a discussion of tax reform proposals, see Latcham, 'Private Charitable Foundations, Income Tax and Policy Implications', 98 *U.Pa.L.Rev.* 617 (1950).

17. Note, 34 *Va.L.Rev.* 182, 193–4 (1948); see Latcham, *supra,* note 16. The advantages of incorporation for the American type of foundation have been formulated as follows:

'The advantages of the corporate form are many. In several states exemption of the property of charitable institutions from taxation is limited to incorporated organizations. Also, corporations may generally be created for perpetual duration, thus eliminating questions as to reversion or the difficulties occasioned by death of an individual trustee. Furthermore, where there are restrictions upon the investment of trust funds, they may be found inapplicable to corporations or subject to removal by charter or by-laws. The principal advantage, however, is undoubtedly the insulation of the "trustees" from personal liability.' Note, *supra*, at 195.

18. A testator devised to a foundation established by his will a ceramics manufacturing business. The income of the foundation was to go to the promotion of the ceramic arts, but a sum actually exceeding its average income was to be paid to the testator's wife for five years. The foundation was held charitable. Edward Orton, Jr, 'Ceramic Foundation', 9 *T.C.* 533 (1947), 34 *Va.L.Rev.* 225 (1948).

19. In this respect the combined effect of the numerous small foundations established by small and medium-sized business firms or wealthy individuals should not be underestimated. In the United States thousands of small firms and affluent individuals establish 'research' foundations with small amounts of capital. Both the initial capital and the annual appropriations, even if they only amount to a few thousand dollars, are diverted from the coffers of the State into a multitude of private or semi-private channels.

20. See text at note 13, *supra*.

21. See Berle, *The 20th Century Capitalist Revolution*, Chap. III (1954).

22. Many research foundations set up by major industrial corporations are largely devoted to the training of scientists and may well be regarded as a kind of self-insurance, though the benefits are not likely to be confined to the one corporation. Insurance of the maintenance of a flow of trained scientists and engineers is one of the basic requisites for the further development of industry.

23. In that respect they differ from the many small foundations which, as described above, are often thinly disguised ways of diverting income from the tax collector to the family.

24. cf. *The Report of the Select Committee to Investigate Foundations, supra*, note 6.

25. Thus a number of grants made by the Ford Foundation have undoubtedly a major share in the remarkable increase of cultural and social relations between the United States on the one part and India and the Middle East on the other.

26. The eight points on which the educators concurred are: (1) colleges and universities have a deep obligation to society; (2) they have an obligation to give to corporation executives an adequate understanding of their nature, purposes, and internal operations; (3) the form of corporate giving most useful to the college or university is unrestricted gifts; (4) gifts for special projects should not impose a hidden cost upon

the institution; (5) corporation gifts for any purpose other than the advancement of learning through independent teaching and research should not be accepted; (6) scholarship programmes can be operated more effectively by universities and colleges than by corporations themselves; (7) gifts of equipment are most welcome but should not be tied to advertising programmes; (8) corporations deserve and should receive appropriate and public acknowledgement of their support from the beneficiary institutions.

27. Some time ago there was some concern whether the actions of the Fund for the Republic, a $15,000,000 foundation established as an independent institution by the Ford Foundation and accused repeatedly of excessive 'liberalism' and promotion of 'subversive' causes, might affect the sale of Ford automobiles.

28. *United States* v. *Aluminium Co.*, 148 F. 2d 416, 423 (2d Cir. 1945).

29. In recent years the tendency has been to conclude five-year or at least three-year agreements in which the right to strike is suspended for the duration in consideration of a number of benefits, including pensions and social security.

30. For a more detailed account and criticism of the Hegelian philosophy of State and law, see Friedmann, *Legal Theory*, 114-27 (4th ed. 1960).

31. The most brilliant analysis of the social basis of the Nazi State is that of Neumann, *Behemoth* (2nd ed. 1944). See also Fraenkel, *The Dual State* (1941).

32. In the overwhelmingly Catholic environment of such countries as Italy, Portugal, and Spain, the influence of the Church is vital. Apart from its own organization, it operates largely through the other major social groups, such as landowners and industrialists.

33. See Galbraith, *American Capitalism* (1925).

34. Latham, *The Group Basis of Politics*, 37 (1925).

35. This approach, suggested in an earlier version of this chapter, published in 57 *Col.L.R.* 155 (1957), is developed by Miller in 'The Constitutional Law of the Security State', 10 *Stanford L.R.*, pp. 645 et seq.

36. See the example given in Berle, *The 20th Century Capitalist Revolution*, 54 (1954).

37. See the English wartime decisions of *Howard* v. *Inland Revenue Commrs* [1942] 1 K.B. 389, 397; *Latilla* v. *Inland Revenue Commrs* [1943] A.C. 377.

38. See *Levene* v. *Inland Revenue Commrs.* [1928] A.C. 217.

39. For further discussion of this problem, see pp. 369 et seq.

40. It is not believed that the analysis of the relationship between State and social groups in modern democracy given above is basically at variance with Earl Latham's brilliant analysis of 'Group Conflict and the Political Process' given in his *Group Basis of Politics*, Chap. 1 (1952). Rather, it stresses a different aspect of that relationship. In Professor Latham's analysis, the 'public groups', while endowed with 'officiality',

i.e. the power to exercise against all groups and individuals certain powers which they, in turn, may not exercise against the official groups, themselves form a social force, or rather a conglomerate of social forces struggling with each other as well as providing compromises between the conflicting pulls of private social groupings. To that extent, Latham's analysis seems to agree with the theory of the pluralists that the State is, itself, one of a number of social associations, such as churches, corporations, and trade unions, with which it has to compete for the allegiance and obedience of the individual. That each of the various groups of officialdom has its own social pull within the fabric of organized democracy is indeed evident from Professor Latham's own analysis of the struggle about the basing point legislation of a few years ago or, again, from the melancholy history of the proposed Missouri Valley Authority, which, despite the obvious need for official action, has been defeated time and again not only by the pressure of the private power lobby, but also by conflicts between various governmental organizations, each jealous of its own prerogatives. What is stressed in the text is that granted all the conflicting pulls between social groups and within the official family of the State, it becomes at times, though usually only in times of emergency, the articulate expression of something more than a compromise between the various social groups within the State, the articulation of a national public policy. We have tentatively called this the 'reserve function' of the State. This is probably not far removed from the recent analysis of Kenneth S. Carlston which describes the State as 'the ultimate organization of the national society, since it is characterized by a common acceptance of a certain authority and by the fact that its members identify themselves with it': Carlston, *Law and Structures of Social Action*, 65 (1956).

41. Drucker, *The Concept of the Corporation* (1946).

42. ibid., 6–7.

43. Lilienthal, *Big Business* (1952).

44. This view of competition won an important judicial triumph when a four to three majority of the Supreme Court dismissed a suit brought under sec. 2 of the Sherman Act by the Department of Justice charging du Pont with the monopolization of interstate commerce in cellophane: *United States* v. *E. I. du Pont de Nemours & Co.*, 351 U.S. 377 (1956). The majority held that, although du Pont controlled 75 per cent of United States cellophane production, and the only other producer had cross-licensing agreements with du Pont, the availability of alternative products such as glassine or wax paper, whose combined sales greatly outstripped cellophane in the 'relevant market', excluded monopolization in the sense of sec. 2. The minority denied that the alternative products were in any way competitive with cellophane.

45. Galbraith, *American Capitalism* (1952).

46. Berle, *The 20th Century Capitalist Revolution* (1954).

47. On the other hand, the rise of automobile prices during a serious depression in 1958 was attributed by many economists to the ability of

the Big Three 'to impose administered prices' on the community in 'partial disregard of' the laws of supply and demand. The industry countered by pointing to the inflexibility of labour costs in the age of collective bargaining. See 'Administrative Prices', Hearings before the Sub-Committee on Antitrust and Monopoly of the Committee on the Judiciary, U.S. Senate, 85th Congress, Second Session, 1958 (S.Res. 57 and S.Res. 231).

48. For a striking British counterpart of this philosophy, see the remarks of Lord Citrine, Chairman of the British Electricity Authority, a statutory public monopoly, and a former prominent trade union leader, as reported in *The Economist*, 14 July 1956, p. 149. Industrial statesmanship and the community's insistence on proper disclosure of the operations of huge undertakings – public or private – are, according to Lord Citrine, reasonable guarantees against abuse of power.

49. See further on this point Section VIII, *infra*.

50. For a stinging criticism of the apotheosis of the modern corporation, implicit in the oversimplifications of the theories of Galbraith, Lilienthal, and Berle, see Latham in 47 *Am.Econ.Rev.* (1957), pp. 303 et seq.

51. See Jaffé, 'Law Making by Private Groups', 51 *Harv.L.Rev.* 201 (1937); Wirtz, 'Government by Private Groups', 13 *La.L.Rev.* 440 (1953).

52. A term used by the late Austrian jurist, sociologist, and statesman, Karl Renner, in Renner, *The Institutions of Private Law and Their Social Function* (Kahn-Freund ed. 1949).

53. As Professor Berle points out, the giant corporations today increasingly finance themselves out of their own capital assets. They are less and less dependent on investment bankers, although the latter play a decisive role for small businessmen and farmers. Berle, *The 20th Century Capitalist Revolution*, 35 (1954).

54. See text at note 29, p. 239, *supra*.

55. In West Germany the powerful central trade union organization has begun to make major industrial investments, for example, in the film industry. In Great Britain, the trade unions have, for many years, held 49 per cent of the shares in a national Labour daily, the *Daily Herald*. On the whole, however, the financial (and general) influence of organized labour in press, radio, the film industry, and other opinion-making media of communication is remarkably weak. It should, however, be noted that, outside the United States, radio and television are almost everywhere either wholly or in part operated by the government or public corporations. These media of public communications are not, therefore, under the financial control of private entrepreneurs and, indirectly, of the sponsors of programmes. In 1956 the mine owners and the United Mine Workers – which is outside the A.F.L.-C.I.O. organization – set up a joint shipping company to promote export of American coal overseas. This is a remarkable joint capital venture, but one which remains strictly within the traditional objectives of American unions – namely, the promotion of immediate economic interests. That this is now

sometimes done by joint action between employers and union is in line
with many other current developments.

56. In so far as the A.F.L. has a political philosophy, it is strongly
anti-Socialist. See the manifesto issued by the New York State Association of Electrical Workers-A.F.L. against the Niagara Public Power Bill,
*N.Y. Times,* 8 July 1956, § 4, p. E7.

57. cf. the conflicting statements by Meany (A.F.L.) and Reuther
(C.I.O.) on Indian 'neutralism'.

58. In Great Britain the Trades Union Congress is the major organizational and financial backbone of the Labour Party. In pre-war Germany,
the larger 'Free Trade Unions' were linked with the Social Democratic
Party, the smaller 'Christian Unions' with the Catholic Centre Party.
Since the last war, the reorganized and unified Trade Union Organization has had no direct links with any party, but the indirect and personal
links with the Social Democratic and Christian Democratic Parties
respectively are strong.

59. For a detailed account of the Soviet public corporation, see Hazard
'The Public Corporation in the U.S.S.R.', in *The Public Corporation,*
374–409 (Friedmann ed. 1954).

60. In June 1956 a report made for the International Bank for Reconstruction and Development by an economic mission led by Mr Thomas
H. McKitterick, Vice-President of one of America's leading banks,
acknowledged that economic development in India would, at the present
stage, be impossible without a great deal of government enterprise,
although the share of private enterprise should be increased.

61. On the other hand, its parent, Canadian National Railways, is a
product of necessity: the amalgamation, in 1919, of a number of bankrupt railway lines which the State had to take over in order to maintain
an essential national service.

62. For detailed analyses of the place and organization of the public
corporation, see *The Public Corporation* (Friedmann ed. 1954), in particular Hodgetts, 51–107 (Canada); Drago, 108–37 (France); Friedmann,
162–89 (Great Britain); *Comparative Survey,* 539–94.

63. For a good survey and data, see a recent German study, Hoffmann,
*Die ländlichen Elektrizitätsgenossenschaften in den U.S.A.* (1954).

64. India, Burma, Turkey, Mexico, among others, are undertaking a
number of development projects through joint ventures with American,
British, German, and Japanese industrial interests. An example of a
partnership between a government, foreign private interests, and international agencies, is the recently established International Credit and
Investment Corporation of India.

65. For details, see Muggia, 'The Public Corporation in Italy', in
*The Public Corporation,* 244–66 (Friedmann ed. 1954).

66. For a recent account, see Fischer, 'Problems Arising From Co-
determination in Western Germany', *Transactions of the Third World
Sociological Congress, International Sociological Association,* 204 (1956). See also
MacPherson, 'Co-determination: Germany's Move Toward a New

Economy', 5 *Ind. & Lab.Rel.Rev.* 20 (1951); MacPherson, 'Co-determination in Practice', 8 *Ind. & Lab.Rel.Rev.* 499 (1955), and Shuchman, *Co-determination* (1957), for a generally positive appraisal of the effect of co-determination on management-worker relations. The statutes governing this matter are of 21 May 1951 (*Bundesgesetzbl.* I, 347) and 7 August 1956 (*Bundesgesetzbl.* I, 707).

67. It is doubtful that this German experiment will have any appeal in other countries (especially in the Anglo-American world), although Professor Carlston thinks otherwise. Carlston, *Law and Structures of Social Action*, 269–71 (1956). The British trade-union movement would see in it a threat to its party position in the collective bargaining process, which it has maintained even in regard to the public corporations. This would apply even more emphatically to the American labour unions. The so-called 'partnership' arrangements which have resently been the subject of some public discussion in Great Britain are only profit-sharing arrangements, giving employees either a bonus or a limited capital share in the enterprise. Unlike the German *Mitbestimmungsrecht*, they do not purport to alter the pattern of management and control. Nor is it likely that the Pension Funds established by a growing number of corporations in the United States will greatly affect the power of management. Although these Funds, created for the benefit of employees, are becoming increasingly important institutional investors in the common stock of the leading corporations, few of them have acquired controlling interests. The tendency has been either to abstain from voting, or to vote with the management. Certainly there have been few signs of employee ownership of stock through pension funds leading to a form of *Mitbestimmungsrecht*. (See Tilove, *Pension Funds and Economic Freedom* (*Fund for the Republic, 1959*), p. 64 and *passim*.)

68. See pp. 222 et seq.

69. According to an estimate made by Professor Adelman, 'The Measurement of Industrial Concentration', *The Review of Economics and Statistics*, No. 4, November 1951, p. 289, in the United States – the one country that has consistently enforced anti-trust legislation for sixty-five years – 139 corporations as of 1947 owned 45 per cent of all industrial assets.

70. According to the *Report of the Attorney-General's Committee to Study the Anti-Trust Laws*, 354 (1955), there are only twenty-four litigated cases in which decrees requiring divorcement, divestiture, or dissolution were entered. Three of these involved single firm monopolies, twenty a combination of corporations united by common-stock control, and one a combination of separate corporations. In the most important of the monopoly case, the *Alcoa* cases, the 'divestiture' part of the judgement was not executed, because the equity decree considered that the advent of two competitors had eliminated the monopoly and the abuse against which the judgement was directed: *United States* v. *Aluminium Co.*, 91 F.Supp. 333 (S.D.N.Y. 1950), *on remand from* 148 F. 2d 416, 445–8 (2d Cir. 1945).

## 10. INDIVIDUAL FREEDOM, GROUP CONTROL, AND STATE SECURITY

1. See pp. 231 et seq.

2. This problem was adumbrated in the present author's *Law and Social Change in Contemporary Britain* (1951), pp. 142 et seq., and the beginnings of a new trend were noted at pp. 46 et seq.

3. See, for comparative data, Friedmann (ed.), *Anti-Trust Laws* (1956), pp. 329 et seq. (Sweden); pp. 368 et seq. (U.K.); pp. 444 et seq. (U.S.A.). Anti-trust does, however, apply where labour colludes with employers in exclusionary practices. See Timberg, ibid., p. 444.

4. The British Nationalization Statutes recognize this position by conferring upon the Boards or Commissions power and the duty 'to seek consultation with any organization appearing to the Commission to be appropriate, with a view to the conclusion between the Commission and that organization of such agreements as appear to the parties to be desirable, ... for the settlement by negotiation of terms and conditions of employment'. (e.g. Transport Act, 1947, s. 96.)

5. The distinction between 'closed shop' – which is now prohibited – and 'union shop' – which is normal in most industries requiring skilled labour – is a fine one and hardly intelligible to Europeans. A 'closed shop' requires the employer to hire his employees exclusively from the bargaining union (which, in some cases, as in the printing and building trades, combines in effect the functions exercised by trade unions and Handicraft Chambers on the Continent, somewhat like a modern version of the medieval guilds; for it is a bargaining agent as well as the exclusive trainer and judge of the skill required in the particular trade). A 'union-shop' agreement permits the employer to recruit employees anywhere, provided they join the bargaining union within thirty days. The latter would be regarded as a 'closed shop' outside the United States, and certainly be considered illegal in the Continental systems noted at p. 257. For an American view to the effect that there is 'precious little difference' between the two types of agreement, see Mulvoy, 'The Taft-Hartley Act in Action', 15 *U of Chicago L.Q.* (1948), p. 619. However, the distinction is of considerable importance in cases of monopolistic control over a certain trade by a combination of a closed union and a closed shop. For, in such cases, the 'union-shop' agreement, but not the 'closed-shop' agreement, permits the outsider to obtain employment by joining the union.

6. cf. the cases quoted at 64 *Harv.L.R.* (1951), pp. 829 et seq.

7. cf. *Reynolds* v. *Shipping Federation* [1924] Ch. 28.

8. Such a view is endorsed by Lord Justice Denning (as he then was) in his speech to the American Bar Association as reported in *U.S. News & World Report*, 16 September 1955, p. 142. It is, however, contrary to the *Reynolds*'s case (see note 8), and to certain dicta of Lord Wright in *Crofter Hand Woven Harris Tweed Co.* v. *Veitch* [1942] A.C. 435. See further, Kahn-Freund in *System of Industrial Relations in Great Britain* (ed. Flanders & Clegg, 1954), p. 113.

9. 'Compulsory Unionism in Europe', 5 *American Journal of Comparative Law* (1956), pp. 18 et seq., 26.

10. For a comprehensive survey and appraisal of this problem in European labour law, see Lenhoff, op. cit.

11. Nebraska Constitution (Art. XV, para. 13). For a comprehensive survey of state legislation designed to curb 'unfair labor practices' by unions, see Millis and Katz, 'A Decade of State Labor Legislation', 15 *U of Ohio L.R.* (1952), pp. 282 et seq. In November 1958, six states held referenda on constitutional amendments introducing 'right to work' provisions. In all (including the important industrial States of California and Ohio) but one of these (Kansas), the amendment was rejected.

12. *Railway Employees Department, A.F. of L.* v. *Hanson*, 351 U.S. 225 (1956).

13. For the different traditions and approaches of European labour laws, see p. 257.

14. It was foreseen by Brandeis, a strong champion of Labour, in a letter written in 1912 to Lincoln Steffens (quoted from Mason, *Brandeis, A Free Man's Life* (1946), p. 303).

15. Clyde W. Summers, 'Legal Limitations on Union Discipline' (1951), 64 *Harv.L.R.*, pp. 1049 et seq., p. 1051.

16. J. S. Williams, 'The Political Liberty of Labor Union Members', 32 *Texas Law Review* (1954), pp. 826 et seq., p. 829. For American judicial authority to that effect, see the footnotes to the above-quoted articles.

17. See *General Medical Council* v. *Spackman* [1943] A.C. 627, where the House of Lords reversed the removal of a doctor from the medical register by the Council on the ground of lack of 'due inquiry'.

18. *Selected Essays*, p. 237.

19. *Free Church* v. *Overton* [1904] A.C. 515.

20. [1919] A.C. 606.

21. [1929] 1 Ch. 602.

22. [1951] 2 All E.R. 435.

23. The case and the whole situation had been analysed in detail by Whitmore, 'Judicial Control of Union Discipline – The *Kuzych* Case', 30 *Can.Bar Rev.* 1 (1952). For a more recent survey of British and Canadian cases, see Sherbaniuk, 'Actions by and against Trade Unions in Contract and Tort'. 12 *Univ.of Toronto L.J.* (1958), 151 et seq.

24. It should be emphasized again that the widespread lack of impartial procedures and adequate safeguards for disciplined members is not confined to labour unions, but probably general among all kinds of clubs. But, as stated earlier, the public significance of union rules and their impact on the livelihood of their members is vastly greater than that of the normal club.

25. Professor Summers has given a most informative survey of constitutional provisions regarding disciplinary powers in his two articles on 'Disciplinary Powers of Union', 3 *Ind.Lab.Relations Rev.* 483 (1950); 4 *Ind.Lab.Relations Rev.* 15 (1950).

26. It should be stressed that, by virtue of the Taft-Hartley Act (61 U.S.C., Chap. 120), the economic penalty of expulsion from the union is less severe in the United States than in countries which, like Great Britain, have little legislative regulation in this field. Under s. 8 (*a*) (3), *only* expulsion for refusal to pay dues can result in the loss of a job. Violation of this limitation may entail reinstatement, back-pay, and, generally, *restitutio in integrum*.

27. [1954] Ch. 479 (C.A.); [1955] 3 *W.L.R.* 788 (H.L.).

28. They have been analysed by D. Lloyd, 'Damages for wrongful expulsion from a trade union', 19 *Mod.L.R.* 121 et seq. (1956), and by K. W. Wedderburn, 'The Bonsor Affair, A Postscript', 20 *Mod.L.R.* 105 (1957).

29. *Taff Vale Ry* v. *Amalgamated Society of Railway Servants* [1901] A.C. 426.

30. In Great Britain or the Dominions there would probably be strong opposition to any compulsory incorporation of unions, or, indeed, any association. A considerable number of American states have enacted statutes under which the unions are treated as legal entities for certain purposes. (See Millis and Katz, 15 *U. of Ohio L.R.* (1948), pp. 282 et seq., 306.) A typical provision is that of the Louisiana statute of 1947: 'Both labor organization and employer shall be bound by the acts of its duly authorized agents and may sue or be sued as an entity and in behalf of those whom they represent in the courts of the State of Louisiana, provided that any money judgement against such labor organization, whether under this section or otherwise, shall be enforced only against the organization as an entity and against its assets and funds, and shall not be enforceable against the property of an individual member.' Such provisions produce legal results similar to those obtained in Britain by the *Bonsor* case.

31. *Huntley* v. *Thornton* [1957] 1 All E.R. 234.

32. Summers, 64 *Harv.L.R.*, p. 1101.

33. He has apparently since given up this view (34 *Texas L.R.* 612 (1956)) and opposes the proposal made by Professor Williams (32 *Texas L.R.* 826 (1954)) for adjudication of union discipline cases by impartial arbitrators, or, failing agreement by the union, by the National Labor Relations Board.

34. Professor Paul Hays, in a note to the author. In a recent paper (*The Union and Its Members: The Uses of Democracy*, New York University 11th Annual Conference on Labor, 1958), the same author has warned against expecting too much of increased legal safeguards for internal union democracy. While corruption in unions is widespread, the remedy, in Hay's opinion, lies 'not so much in improving democracy in unions as in improving the operation of the democratic process in the communities where these criminals operate, to the end that public officials will be elected who cannot be overawed, intimidated or bribed' (p. 46). The same paper illustrates vividly the practical importance of the 'right to representation' by many instances where the union representatives

deliberately work against the interests of certain individual members or groups whom they dislike.

35. This can, however, be defeated by amendments of union by-laws, specifically precluding remedies for breach of contract. See Wedderburn, op. cit., pp. 118 et seq.

36. This does not, of course, affect the legal treatment of discrimination on racial, religious, or other grounds offensive to the Constitution (Fifth and Fourteenth Amendments) or public policy (*Shelley* v. *Kraemer*, 334 U.S. 1 (1948); *Re Drummond Wren* [1945] 4 *D.L.R.* 674).

37. For a survey, see Timberg, in Friedmann (ed.), *Anti-Trust Laws* (1956), pp. 425 et seq.

38. For example, in the relations between newspaper proprietors and newspaper vendors. See the English case of *Sorrell* v. *Smith* [1925] A.C. 700.

39. This lack of equality increases greatly, of course, in times of economic depression, somewhat comparably to, but probably less so than in, the relations between employers and labour. The large unions are usually now able to accumulate in times of prosperity large reserves which enable them to hold out in major disputes until either the companies feel the strain as much as the unions or national interests become so strongly involved that public authority intervenes with a compromise settlement. But such retailers as automobile dealers or the usual middle- or small-type business man have seldom reserves large enough remotely to equal the vast capital reserves of large corporations, which can tide them over periods of crisis.

40. The recent Report of the Special Committee on the Federal Loyalty Security Programme, set up by the Association of the Bar of the City of New York (Dodd, Mead & Co., New York, 1956) reports the number of private employees covered by the Defense Department's Industrial Security Programme as nearly three million. This is based on official testimony. To these must be added over 800,000 long-shoremen and seamen, who, under the Port Security Programme – a survival of the Second World War security operations – have been subjected to security clearance (op. cit., p. 115).

41. See op. cit., n. 67, p. 142.

42. In present Soviet law private law is important. But its field of application is not in the vital sphere of economic relationships. It is in the sphere of relationships that surround the daily incidents of life, such as accidents (tort), or the sale of products of small-scale activities (surplus vegetables, etc.), transfer of private land, or family relationships.

43. See pp. 249 et seq.

44. *Shelley* v. *Kraemer*, 334 U.S. 1 (1948).


## II. THE GROWTH OF ADMINISTRATION AND THE EVOLUTION OF PUBLIC LAW

1. e.g. the Swedish railways.
2. See further pp. 306 et seq.

3. Such as the Interstate Commerce Commission established in 1884, followed in the present century by the Federal Trade Commission, the Federal Communications Commission, the Security and Exchange Commission, the Civil Aeronautics Board, and the National Labor Relations Board, not to speak of the many non-permanent wartime agencies.

4. Both these quotations are from a thoughtful address by Richard B. McIntyre, Commissioner, Securities and Exchange Commission, 1946–53 given before the National Association of Securities administrators in 1947, and reprinted in Gellhorn and Byse, *Administrative Law, Cases and Comments*, 1954.

5. McIntyre, loc. cit.

6. See *Soviet Legal Philosophy* (ed. Hazard), pp. 120 et seq.; Friedmann, *Legal Theory* (3rd ed.), pp. 255 et seq.

7. Letter to Kurskii, as quoted in Yudin, *Soviet Legal Philosophy* (ed. Hazard), p. 292.

8. See further pp. 309 et seq.

9. See his *Law of the Constitution*, 10th ed., by Wade (1959), Chap. 4.

10. *Constitutional History of England* (1887), p. 415.

11. Such as Jennings (*Law and the Constitution*), Robson (*Justice and Administrative Law*), Wade (9th ed. to Dicey's *Law of the Constitution*), Allen (*Law in the Making*), Hamson (*Executive Discretion and Judicial Control*), and others.

12. For a criticism of this narrow conception of 'ordinary' courts, see, e.g. Jennings, op. cit., (5th ed.), pp. 312–13.

13. See, for England, e.g. *Ransom & Luck, Ltd* v. *Surbiton B. C.* [1949] 1 Ch. 180; and the discussion in the Supreme Court judgements and in literature about the scope of the 'discretionary' exemption from federal tort liability under the Federal Tort Claims Act, 1946, on which see further pp. 303 et seq.

14. See the famous controversy in German between Baehr, *Der Rechtsstaat* (1864), who wanted to subject all public law to civil law and procedure, and von Gneist, *Der Rechtsstaat* (1st ed., 1868), who advocated a system of administrative justice.

15. Among many other examples, we might mention, from the judicial practice of the Conseil d'État, the doctrine of *imprévision*, from which, unlike the jurisprudence of the Supreme Civil Court, the Cour de Cassation has developed a system of compensation in public contracts, where the equilibrium of the contract has been disturbed by certain outside events (see further p. 292), or the decision in the *affaire Barel* (R.D.P. 1954, 509), which quashed the exclusion, by the Minister, from admission to the Concours of the École Nationale de l'Administation of candidates suspected of Communist sympathies. No less significant is the retention and strengthening of the system of administrative justice in West Germany, after the Second World War, as a means of restoring the rule of law. This was done under the guidance of British and American Military Government authorities.

16. See, for the United States, among others, the treatise on *Administra-*

*tive Law* by K. C. Davis (1951) or *Cases and Comments on Administrative Law* by Gellhorn and Byse (1954); for England, Griffith and Street, *Principles of Administrative Law* (3rd ed., 1963); for Australia, Friedmann, *Principles of Australian Administrative Law* (1950).

17. See Davis, op. cit., p. 2: 'Administrative law, as the term is here used, is limited to law concerning powers and procedures; it does not include the enormous mass of substantive law produced by the agencies.' This limitation is accepted by all the leading case-books.

18. Such as Waline, *Droit administratif* (6th ed., 1957) or Forsthoff, *Lehrbuch des Verwaltungsrechts* (1st vol. Allgemeiner Teil, 7th ed., 1958).

19. Discussion of such matters can be found, incidentally, in the corresponding American works, e.g. in the discussion of the scope of government immunities.

20. 103 U.S. 168 (1881).

21. It should not, perhaps, be taken too seriously. Madison, one of the principal architects of the Constitution, displays a far more realistic understanding of the interplay of the different branches of government, in his analysis of Montesquieu and the British Constitution (*The Federalist*, Letter No. XLVII).

22. Wilson, *Constitutional Government in the United States*, pp. 56 et seq.

23. Davis, *Administrative Law*, para. 7.

24. Parker, 'The Historic Basis of Administrative Law: Separation of Powers and Judicial Supremacy', 12 *Rutgers L.R.* (1958), pp. 449 et seq.

25. Miller, 'The Constitutional Law of the "Security State",' 10 *Stanford L.R.* 620, 639.

26. cf. Frankfurter J. in *Youngstown Sheet & Tube Co.* v. *Sawyer*, 343 U.S. 579 (1952).

27. See Jaffé, 'The Effective Limits of the Administrative Process: A Revaluation', 67 *Harv.L.R.* 1105 (1954).

28. *Individual Freedom and Government Restraints*, pp. 14 et seq.

29. [1942] A.C. 206.

30. For a survey, see the Report on the Federal Loyalty-Security Programme, prepared under the chairmanship of Professor Elliott Cheatham for the Association of the Bar of the City of New York (1956) and Ralph S. Brown, *Loyalty and Security Employment Tests in the United States* (1958). See pp. 267 et seq.

31. For the development of judicial countermoves, see pp. 262 et seq.

32. See Gellhorn, op. cit., Chap. 3.

33. On which see Friedmann (ed.), *Anti-Trust Laws* (1956).

34. Forsthoff, op. cit., pp. 67 et seq.

35. Waline, op. cit., §§ 703 et seq.

36. See the list of decisions quoted in Waline § op. cit., § 704, and, in particular, the *affaire Barel*, quoted above, note 15.

37. Lord MacDermott, *Protection from Power* (1957), p. 81.

38. *National Broadcasting Co.* v. *United States*, 319 U.S. 190, 224 (1943).

39. Waline, *Droit administratif* (7th ed., 1957, § 683).

40. Jellinek, *Verwaltungsrecht* (1932), pp. 37 et seq.; Forsthoff, *Verwaltungsrecht* (7th ed., 1958), pp. 87 et seq.

41. See Trotabas, '*Les Actes de gouvernment en matières diplomatiques*', in *Revue critique de législation et de jurisprudence* (1925), 342, and, for a more recent discussion, Waline, op. cit., §§ 322 et seq.

42. For a critical discussion of various recent views, see Waline, op. cit.

43. *Rederiaktiebolaget Amphitrite* v. *The King* [1921] 3 K.B. 500.

44. Keir and Lawson, *Cases on Constitutional Law* (3rd ed.), pp. 491 et seq.; see also Mitchell, *The Contracts of Public Authorities* (1954), pp. 28 et seq.

45. See Street, *Governmental Liability* (1953), p. 73.

46. *Youngstown Sheet & Tube Co.* v. *Sawyer*, 343 U.S. 579 (1952).

47. That this still leaves much scope for divergent judicial interpretations is shown by *Liversidge* v. *Anderson* [1942] A.C. 206.

48. *Horowitz* v. *U.S.* (1924) 267 U.S. 458.

49. [1949] 1 Ch. 180.

50. *William Cory & Son, Ltd* v. *City of London Corpn* [1951] 2 K.B. 476.

51. 'Any claim based upon an act or omission of an employee of the Government, exercising due care in the execution of a statute or regulation, whether or not such statute or regulation be valid, or based upon the exercise or performance or the failure to exercise or perform a discretionary function or duty on the part of a federal agency or an employee of the Government; whether or not the discretion involved be abused is withheld from jurisdiction of the courts'. (S. 2680 (*a*).)

52. *Dalehite* v. *U.S.*, 346 U.S. 15 (1953).

53. *Indian Towing Co.* v. *U.S.*, 350 U.S. 61 (1955).

54. *Rayonnier* v. *U.S.*, 352 U.S. 315 (1957).

55. 346 U.S., p. 42.

56. K. C. Davis, 'Tort Liability of Governmental Units', 40 *Minn. L.R.* 751, 785.

57. *East Suffolk Catchment Board* v. *Kent* [1941] A.C. 74.

58. *Indian Towing Co.* v. *U.S.*, 350 U.S. 61 (1955).

59. *Roberts* v. *Hopwood* [1925] A.C. 578.

60. The House was apparently unaware that at the time, as now, the basic wage had already become the corner-stone of Australian industrial law.

61. [1925] A.C., at 594.

62. This, in contemporary Britain, rather exceptional exhibition may be compared to the long line of decisions in which the Supreme Court of the United States, for many decades, interpreted the 'due-process' clauses of the Constitution so as to invalidate social legislation – Federal and state – which regulated conditions of labour by minimum wages, maximum hours, etc.

63. See, e.g. the wartime decision in *Re Decision of Walker* [1944] 1 K.B. 644, and the postwar decision of the Court of Appeal in *Associated Provincial Picture Houses, Ltd* v. *Wednesbury Corpn* [1948] 1 K.B. 223.

64. *Prescott* v. *Birmingham Corpn* [1954] 3 *W.L.R.* 990 (C.A.).

65. See, among other criticisms, Benjafield, 'Statutory Discretions', 2 *Sydney L.R.* (1956), p. 7.

66. On the question of remedies, see further Chap. 13, pp. 309 et seq.

67. See p. 290.

68. See Davis, 40 *Minn.L.R.* pp. 786 et seq.; Fleming James, 10 *U.of Fla.L.R.*, pp. 187 et seq.

69. *Fisher* v. *Ruislip U. D. C.* [1945] K.B. 584.

70. This analysis is in accord with the suggestion made by the present author shortly before the decision of the Court of Appeal; see Friedmann, 'Statutory Powers and Legal Duties of Local Authorities' (1945) 8 *Mod.L.R.* 31, 48.

## 12. GOVERNMENT LIABILITY, ADMINISTRATIVE DISCRETION, AND THE INDIVIDUAL

1. Dall.Pér. 1873, 3, 17.

2. Mitchell, *The Contract of Public Authority* (1954) 167, 179–80; see also Street, *Governmental Liability* (1953); and for a French analysis, Waline, *Droit administratif* (6th ed. 1957) S. 132 et seq.

3. *Affaire époux Bertin*, D. 1956, 433; *Affaire Soc. française de Transports Gondrand frères*, *C.E. 20 avril et 11 mai 1956.* ibid., both with note by de Laubadère.

4. The so-called *clause exorbitante du droit commun*.

5. See Mitchell, op. cit., p. 184.

6. See, for example, *Affaire Storch*, S. 1907, III, 33.

7. Conclusion de M. Corneille in *Soc. Déclarage de Poissy*, S. 1924, III, 2.

8. *Soc. Le centre électrique*, D. 1932, III, 60.

9. Waline, op. cit., § 974.

10. S. 1916, III, 17.

11. For the whole development, see Waline, op. cit. §§ 979 et seq.

12. It has been noted by the advocates of the French *droit administratif* that the Cour de Cassation, the highest French civil court, has never recognized anything equivalent to *imprévision*, or, indeed, any form of frustration of contract as developed by Continental courts in other countries. See Mitchell, op. cit. p. 190.

13. See the comparative studies by Langrod, 'Administrative Contracts', 4 *Am. J. of Comp. Law* (1955), 325, 347 et seq., and by Imboden, *Der verwaltungsrechtliche Vertrag* (1958), 9–37, which detects a gradual growth of the administrative contract in German post-war practice.

14. Forsthoff, op. cit., p. 253; Langrod, op. cit., p. 354.

15. ibid., p. 221.

16. Langrod, op. cit., p. 362.

17. Street, op. cit., pp. 81 et seq. But see Mitchell, *Contracts of Public Authorities* (1954).

18. See, for example, Cherne, *Government Contract Problems* (1941); the chapter 'Government Contracts' in Williston, *Law of Contracts*, Vol. IX,

Chap. XII; the recent Symposium on Various Aspects of Government Contracts in the *George Washington L.R.*, Vols. 24, 25, 26 (1956–8) and the articles by Miller, 'Government Contracts and Social Control', 41 *Va.L.R.* 27 (1955); Pasley, 'The Interpretation of Government Contracts', 25 *Fordham L.R.* 211 (1956).

19. For the United States, see the Tucker Act of 1887; for the United Kingdom, see s. 1 of the Crown Proceedings Act, 1947; and for the Commonwealth, see the brief survey in Street, *Government Liability*, pp. 6 et seq. Since then the Canadian Crown Liability Act, 1952–3 (*Statutes of Canada*, Chap. 30, s. 3), and the Petition of Rights Act (RSC. 1952, Chap. 158), have made the Federal Government in Canada generally liable in contract and tort.

20. Major extracts from the *General Government Contracts for Building and Civil Engineering Works* (7th ed.), and from the *R.I.B.A. Standard Form of Building Contract*, adapted for use by local authorities (1950 ed.) are reprinted in the Appendix to Mitchell, op. cit., pp. 245 et seq.

21. See, for example, the elaborate terms of the *Government Contracts for Building and Engineering Works*, § 3 (A).

22. e.g. *Reading Steel Casting Co* v. *U.S.*, 268 U.S. 186 (1925) and some of the opinions in the *Bethlehem Steel Case*, 315 U.S. 289.

23. Pasley, 'The Non-Discrimination Clause in Government Contracts', 43 *Va.L.R.*, at pp. 846 et seq.

24. *U.S.* v. *Wunderlich*, 342 U.S. 98 (1951).

25. *U.S.* v. *Moorman*, 338 U.S. 457 (1950).

26. 41 U.S.C., para. 321 (Sup. III, 1956). See the Note on 'Remedies against the United States', 70 *Harv.L.R.* (1957), p. 887. The difficulties of distinguishing between questions of fact and law have, in the light of recent court practice, been analysed by Pasley, 'The Interpretation of Government Contracts', 25 *Fordham L.R.*, pp. 219–22.

27. *Lynch* v. *U.S.*, 292 U.S. 571, 579 (1934).

28. 70 *Harv.L.R.*, p. 884.

29. See 70 *Harv.L.R.*, p. 886.

30. [1949] 1 K.B. 227.

31. *Turberville* v. *West Ham Corpn* [1950] 2 K.B. 203.

32. *William Cory & Son* v. *City of London* [1951] 2 K.B. 476.

33. Professor Street, after a lucid comparative discussion of government liability in England, the United States, and France, criticizes the French jurisprudence for 'the lack of precision consequent upon a denial of the binding force of precedent'. loc. cit., p. 77. Whatever the weaknesses and uncertainties of French jurisprudence, it can hardly exceed that of the corresponding jurisprudences of the common-law countries. Indeed, elsewhere in his book, Professor Street concedes that the main objection to the present English system is the lack of certainty (p. 104).

34. cf. Street, op. cit., pp. 104 et seq.; Note in 70 *Harv.L.R.*, pp. 886 et seq.

35. See above, p. 95.

36. On which see Mitchell, op. cit., pp. 68 et seq.

37. On the position of the government corporation (public corporation in English terminology), see further pp. 306 et seq.

38. For a discussion of the conditions governing the appointment and removal of federal officials in the United States, see Gellhorn and Byse, op. cit., pp. 160 et seq.; for comparative surveys of the position in Great Britain and the United States, with brief observations on the comparative French position, see Griffith and Street, op. cit., pp. 32 et seq., 41 et seq.; also Street, op. cit., pp. 111 et seq.

39. The leading cases are, for Britain, *Dunne* v. *R.* [1896] 1 Q.B. 116; and for the United States, *Myers* v. *U.S.*, 272 U.S. 52 (1926). But in *Wiener* v. *U.S.* (357 U.S. 349 (1955)), the Supreme Court denied the President's power to remove at will a member of an adjudicatory commission.

40. See, for Britain, the contradictory dicta in *Reilly* v. *R.* [1934] A.C. 179 (Lord Atkin); *Rodwell* v. *Thomas* [1944] K.B. 602; and *Robertson* v. *Minister of Pensions* [1949] 1 K.B. 231. For the United States, see *Morgan* v. *T.V.A.*, 115 F. 2nd 990 (C.A.6, 1940), cert., denied, 312 U.S. 701; *Wiener* v. *U.S.*, 357 U.S. 349 (1958).

41. For a recent summary of the legal position of the Crown, see Griffith and Street, op. cit., p. 276.

42. *Fisk* v. *Jefferson Police Jury* (1885) 116 U.S. 131; *O'Leary* v. *U.S.* (1933) 77 Ctcl. 635; contrast *Lucas* v. *Lucas and High Commissioner for India* [1943] P. 68, and the critical article by D. W. Logan, 'A Civil Servant and His Pay' in 61 *L.Q.R.* (1945), pp. 240 et seq.

43. However, there is a growing army of temporary public servants in a variety of government programmes, often dependent on shifting policies (e.g. in the field of foreign information services and broadcasting) and the whims of appropriation committees.

44. See, for example, the decision of the United States Supreme Court in *Bailey* v. *Richardson* (1951) 71 S.Ct. 669, affirming by an evenly divided vote the majority judgement of the lower court that a civil servant could not claim that she had been denied due process in a loyalty order proceeding, because she had no legally protectable interest to which the due process could apply.

45. See the *Bundesbeamtengesetz* of 1953 in conjunction with the *Bundesdisziplinarordnung* of 1952, and the express constitutional provision, both in the Weimar Constitution and the Bonn Constitution, that no statute must exclude the ability of a civil servant to sue for his pay in the ordinary civil courts.

46. See the Law of 19 October 1946.

47. Dicey, *Law of the Constitution* (9th ed., 1939), p. 193.

48. See, for example, Jennings, 'Tort Liability of Administrative Officers', 21 *Minn.L.R.* 263 (1937); Davis, *Administrative Law* (1951), para. 231; Schwartz, *French Administrative Law and the Common Law World* (1954), pp. 250 et seq.

49. See Davis, op. cit.; Gellhorn and Byse, op. cit., pp. 350 et seq.

50. 152 Mass. 540 (1891).

51. Waline, op. cit., § 1096.

52. e.g. *Affaire Pastor*, C.E. 28 Nov. 1947.

53. Authorities cited in Waline, op. cit., §§ 1099 et seq.

54. For this and other reasons, the leading modern textbook (Waline, *Droit administratif* ) rejects the terminology of '*faute de service*' and '*faute personnelle*', for which the concept of '*faute détachable de l'exercice des fonctions*' is substituted.

55. Examples in Waline, *op. cit.*, § 1102.

56. Attribution of the whole field of State liability for damages to private individuals to the administrative courts goes back to the decision of the Cour des Conflits in the *Pelletier* case of 1873.

57. Para. 839 BGB.

58. See article 839 BGB, article 34 (*g*).

59. For an illuminating comparative survey, see Schwartz, op. cit., Chap. 9, and regarding the present state of the French law, in particular, pp. 276 et seq.

60. The extension of modern tort liability is, in fact, largely derived from the widening of the notion of responsibility, which makes the transition between presumed fault and actions or omissions apt to cause damage without 'fault' a fluid one.

61. H. and L. Mazeaud, *Traité de la responsabilité* (4th ed.), No. 353.

62. The Mazeaud theory is quoted with evident approval by Waline, op. cit., §§ 1267 et seq.

63. *Cie. du gaz de Lyon*, 1919, and subsequent decisions quoted in Waline, § 1191.

64. Waline, op. cit., pp. 696 et seq.

65. *L'arrêt Regnault-Desroziers*, S., 1919.3.25, note Hauriou; D., 1920. 3.1, note Appleton; *R.D.P.*, 1919.239, concl. Corneille, note Jèze.

66. The Commonwealth of Australia had established the principle of tort liability in the federal sphere as early 1903.

67. s. 2.

68. Some of these relate to the position of the semi-autonomous public corporation with the Government; see further pp. 306 et seq.

69. Lord MacDermott, *Protection from Power* (Hamlyn Lectures, 1957), p. 107.

70. Lord MacDermott, op. cit., p. 108.

71. e.g., *Chisholm* v. *Ga.*, 2 U.S. 419 (1793).

72. (1866) L.R. 1 H.L. 93.

73. See in detail 28 U.S.C., para. 2680(*a*) (1952).

74. ibid.

75. See 28 U.S.C., para. 1346 (1952).

76. See p. 286.

77. 40 *Minn.L.R.*, pp. 785, 789.

78. Leflar and Kantorowicz, 'Tort Liability of the States', 29 *NYU L.R.* (1954), pp. 1363 et seq.

79. As Leflar and Kantorowicz observe (op. cit., p. 1366), this distinction has not, in general, been applied to tort suits against the states or to other subdivisions of states, such as townships, school districts, highways

departments, universities, and the like, for no rationally discernible reason.

80. This is comparable to the desire to protect charitable medical institutions from liability by the now equally discredited distinction of 'administrative' and 'medical' functions.

81. *Indian Towing Co.* v. *U.S.*, 350 U.S. 61, 65.

82. *Hoogart* v. *City of Richmond*, 172 Va. 145, 200 SE 610 (1939).

83. See Gellhorn and Lauer, 'Congressional Settlement of Tort Claims Against the United States', 55 *Col.L.R.* 1 (1955); Gellhorn and Lauer, 'Federal Liability for Personal Property Damage', 29 *N.Y.U.L.R.* 1325 (1954); Davis, 'Tort Liability of Governmental Units', 40 *Minn. L.R.* 751, 757 et seq.

84. During the 82nd Congress (1951–3), for example, 123 tort claims were recognized by statutory settlement. Gellhorn and Lauer, 29 *N.Y.U.L.R.*, p. 1330.

85. A well-known example is *U.S.* v. *Causby*, 328 U.S. 256 (1946), where the owner of a chicken farm recovered damages from the United States for the injury done to his property, i.e. to the airspace immediately above his land, by very low flying, considered as 'an invasion of the surface'.

86. Liability insurance is, in most cases, the best answer to the argument that liability and tort would burden smaller authorities to an undue and unforeseeable extent.

87. The term 'public corporation', used in the countries of the British Commonwealth, where this institution has been developed to great theoretical and practical significance, is used here, rather than the usual American term: 'government corporation'. As will be seen, the difference in terminology reflects to some extent a difference in legal theory.

88. President Roosevelt's message to Congress in 1933 recommending the formation of the T.V.A.

89. For comparative surveys of the role and legal status of the public corporation, see Friedmann (ed.), *The Public Corporation* (1954) and Hanson (ed.), *Public Enterprise* (1955).

90. e.g. in certain German State-controlled coal mines, and the French nationalized banks, or the Italian industrial holding company for State interests, the Instituto per Reconstruccione Industriale (I.R.I.).

91. Staff Report on Public Authorities under New York State, issued by the Temporary State Commission on Co-ordination of State Activities, Albany, 1956.

92. Friedmann, 'International Public Corporations' (1942) 6 *Mod.L.R.* 185; Schmitthoff, 'International Corporations', *Grotius Society* (1946); Glazer, 'A Functional Approach to the International Finance Corporation', in 57 *Col.L.R.* 1089 (1957).

## 13. THE PROBLEM OF ADMINISTRATIVE REMEDIES AND PROCEDURES

1. See Schwartz, op. cit., pp. 120 et seq.

2. See article 19, para. 4, *Gerichtsverfassungsgesetz*.

3. See further, Forsthoff, op. cit., § 28.

4. Which, in France, is, since the *Blanco* decision, handled by the administrative courts, but in Germany by the civil courts. See p. 309.

5. How far the injunction can be used in administrative proceedings is doubtful. Legal opinion in Germany is divided, since a number of writers argue that the preliminary injunction (*einstweilige Verfügung*) is not appropriate to administrative proceedings. See Forsthoff, op. cit., p. 505.

6. K. C. Davis, *Administrative Law* (1951), pp. 718 et seq.

7. *R.* v. *Metropolitan Police Commissioner* [1953] 1 W.L.R. 1150.

8. *Ex p. Fry* [1954] 1 W.L.R. 730.

9. *R.* v. *L. C. C., ex p. Entertainments Protection Association* [1931] 2 K.B. 215.

10. *Mount Hope Development Corpn* v. *James*, 25 A.N.Y. 510; 180 N.E. 252 (1932).

11. For a discussion of this subject, see, among innumerable other discussions, Davis, op. cit., Chap. 17 (U.S.); Griffith and Street, op. cit., p. 222 (U.K.); Davis, 'Forms of Proceeding', 44 *Ill.L.R.* 565 (1949); de Smith, 'Wrongs and Remedies in Administrative Law', 15 *Mod.L.R.* (1952), 189; Wade, 'Courts and the Administrative Process', 63 *L.Q.R.* 164 (1947); Carrow, 'Types of Judicial Relief from Administrative Action', 58 *Col.L.R.* (1958), pp. 1 et seq.; Benjafield, 'Statutory Discretions', 2 *Sydney L.R.* (1956), pp. 1 et seq.

12. (1888) 21 Q.B.D. 313.

13. See *Harmon* v. *Brucker*, 358 U.S. 579 (1958).

14. *R.* v. *Northumberland Compensation Appeal Tribunal, ex p. Shaw* [1952] 1 Q.B. 338.

15. ibid.

16. Hughes C.J. in *Consolidated Edison Co.* v. *N.L.R.B.*, 305 U.S. 197 (1938).

17. See decisions collected in Gellhorn and Byse, op. cit., pp. 424 et seq. But see *Harmon* v. *Brucker*, 358 U.S. 579 (1958) for a stronger exercise of review powers by the Supreme Court over a decision by military authority endowed with statutory finality.

18. See pp. 287 et seq.

19. *Degge* v. *Hitchcock*, 229 U.S. 162 (1913).

20. See Carrow, 58 *Col.L.R.*, pp. 2 et seq.

21. *Boyce* v. *Paddington B. C.* [1903] 1 Ch. 109; [1903] 2 Ch. 556 (C.A.); [1906] A.C. 1 (H.L.).

22. See Yardley, 'Remedies in Administrative Law', in 3 *British Journal of Administrative Law* (1957), pp. 69 et seq., 76.

23. *Barnard* v. *National Dock Labour Board* [1953] 2 Q.B. 18.

24. Denning L.J., p. 43.

25. Carrow, op. cit., p. 20.

26. For a survey of the various forms of appeal in Australia, see Friedmann and Benjafield, *Principles of Australian Administrative Law* (2nd ed., 1962).

27. London, H.M.S.O. (1957), Cmnd. 218.

28. See the trenchant criticism by Davis, op. cit., pp. 685 et seq.

29. ibid., at p. 647.

30. 342 U.S. 485 (1952).

31. 'Standing, Ripeness and Civil Liberties: A Critique of *Adler* v. *Board of Education*', 38 *A.B.A.J.*, 924 et seq. (1952). As an example of an interest 'undeserving of legal protection', Professor Davis gives the interest of a business in freedom from new competition.

32. For details of the procedural reforms, see Waline, op. cit. (7th ed., 1957), pp. 136 et seq.

33. For details, see Forsthoff, op. cit., § 28.

34. Except for Rheinland-Pfalz where the court of second instance consists of three professional judges and two lay assessors.

35. 'No officer, employee or agent engaged in the performance of investigative or prosecuting functions for any agency in any case shall, in that or a factually related case, participate or advise in the decision, recommended decision, or agency review pursuant to section 8 except as witness or counsel in public proceedings' (s. 5 (*c*)).

36. s. 403.

37. i.e., the National Insurance Commissioner, the Industrial Injuries Commissioner, and the National Assistance Appeal Tribunal.

38. This Act also establishes a Council on Tribunals to keep under review the constitution, working, and procedure of administrative tribunals. It also tightens up the methods of appointment and qualifications of the chairman of administrative tribunals, so as to promote greater uniformity of standards.

39. *Report*, §§ 121 to 126.

40. *French Administrative Law and the Common Law World* (1954), pp. 73 et seq. For an apparent change of view, see the same author's proposal for the creation of an Administrative Court of the United States, to exercise the functions now exercised by the six Commissions. (Schwartz, *The Professor and the Commissions* (1959), p. 274.)

41. *Executive Discretion and Judicial Control* (1954), p. 213.

42. cf. the observations of Professor Robson in *Journal of Public Law*, Spring 1958, pp. 12 et seq.

## 14. SOCIAL ORGANIZATION AND INTERNATIONAL LAW

1. See Wilfred Jenks, 'The Scope of International Law', 31 *British Year Book of International Law*, 1–48 (1954), revised version in *The*

*Common Law of Mankind* (1958), Chap. I. Mr Jenks, like the present writer, emphasizes the interpenetration of international and national law, and the consequent importance of incorporating in the study of international law 'the common law of mankind'. Such a study would include, side by side with the law governing the relations between States, the law of treaties, and the law governing international arbitration and judicial settlement (all of which are dealt with in the usual treatises and case-books on international law), the structure and lawmaking processes of the international community, as well as human rights, property rights, and common rules regarding services in so far as they are of an international character.

2. cf. further pp. 324 et seq.,

3. This does not, of course, imply any judgement on the effectiveness of these rules. Recent controversies over the Continental shelf, for example, show much disagreement on the physical extent of national sovereignty, and the limitations imposed by the principle of freedom of the seas. But the disagreements arise from conflicts of national interests, not of State organization.

4. For a comparative survey, see Friedmann (ed.), *The Public Corporation* (Toronto and London, 1954).

5. Such countries as France, which has nationalized her basic industries, or Italy, where nearly 50 per cent of the total industrial production is controlled by State-owned companies, must probably be put in the same category.

6. 293 U.S. 360.

7. See, in particular, *New York* v. *U.S.* (the *Saratoga Spring* case), 326 U.S. 572 (1946); *The Pesaro*, 271 U.S. 562 (1926).

8. e.g. by Lord Wright in *The Cristina* [1938] A.C. 485; and by Lord Denning in the *Nizam of Hyderabad Case* [1957] 3 All E.R., at p. 463.

9. [1949] 2 All E.R. 274.

10. [1957] 3 All E.R. 441.

11. The 1952 letter announced that the Department would no longer favour claims to immunity on the part of foreign governments in respect of their commercial transactions (see Bishop in 47 *A.J.I.L.* 93–106 (1953)). But in an action before a District Court in 1955 (*New York and Cuba Mail S.S. Co.* v. *Republic of Korea*, 132 F. Supp. 684 (1955)), an American company sued the Republic of Korea for damage caused to the libellant's steamer by a lighter belonging to the respondent which had assisted in unloading the steamer's cargo of rice in a Korean port. The Department of State – and the United States Attorney-General – affirmed that the property of the Republic of Korea was not subject to attachment in the United States, though it did not file a suggestion of immunity 'inasmuch as the particular acts out of which the cause of action arose are not shown to be of purely governmental character'. The court (Weinfeld J.) deduced from this statement that the principle of the immunity of a foreign government's property from attachment was unconditionally

affirmed, and vacated the suit. It seems that this reduces any judgement denying foreign governments immunity for commercial transactions in the United States to a kind of declaratory judgement.

12. See p. 291.

13. It is not the purpose of this article to restate in detail a problem that has been so amply discussed in legal literature. cf., for the most recent survey of the state of the doctrine, and the alternative criteria, Lauterpacht in 28 *B.Y.I.L.* 250–72 (1951), and Schmitthoff, 'Sovereign Immunity in International Trade', 7 *Int. & Comp. Law Quarterly* 452 (1958).

14. cf. *The Pesaro*, 271 U.S. 562, where the Supreme Court declared: 'We know of no international usage which regards the maintenance and advancement of economic welfare of the people in time of peace as any less a public purpose than the maintenance and training of a naval force.'

15. See pp. 294 et seq.

16. See 176 *L.N.T.S.* 199.

17. See pp. 291 et seq.

18. *R.* v. *The International Trustee for the Protection of Bondholders Aktiengesellschaft* [1937] A.C. 500.

19. [1937] A.C. 500, 531 (*per* Lord Atkin).

20. Fawcett, 'Legal Aspects of State Trading', 25 *B.Y.I.L.* 35 (1948).

21. See F. A. Mann, 'The Law Governing State Contracts', 21 *B.Y.I.L.* 11–33 (1944).

22. cf. Fawcett, loc cit., 45.

23. *Re Investigation of World Arrangements*, 13 F.R.D. 280 (1952).

24. 3 F. 2d (1929).

25. This case was distinguished in the Anglo-Iranian decision on the remarkable ground that there was 'a vast distinction between a sea-faring island-nation maintaining a constant supply of maritime fuel and a government seeking additional revenue in the American markets and causing a direct injury in the United States to our domestic commercial structure'. (13 F.R.D. 291).

26. See p. 325 at note 9.

27. See Drago, in Friedmann (ed.), *The Public Corporation*, 108 et seq.

28. Unfortunately, this very distinction is suggested in the judgement of Cohen L.J. in the *Tass Agency* case (note 9, above). The decision rests, however, on the different ground that the Tass Agency was not clearly a corporate entity separate from the government. But in *Baccus S.R.L.* v. *Servicio Nacional del Trigo* [1956] 3 *W.L.R.* 948, the Court of Appeal definitely applied immunity to a Spanish Government corporation charged with the import and export of grain for the Government.

29. e.g., the British Government in the British Petroleum Co., or the French Government in the Compagnie Française des Pétroles.

30. McDougal, 'International Law, Power and Policy: A Contemporary Conception', 82 *Academy of International Law, Recueil des Cours, Hague,* 137 (1953).

31. Jessup, *Transnational Law* (1956), 71. See also Timberg, 'Inter-

national Combines and National Sovereigns', 95 *U.Pa.L.R.* 575, 577 (1947).

32. e.g., the Iranian Oil Agreement.

33. The approximation of the status of such transactions to public international law has been acknowledged by some modern writers, such as Reuter (*Institutions internationales* (1955), pp. 57, 295 et seq.) or Schwarzenberger (*International Law*, Vol. I (3rd ed., 1957), p. 578), who describe agreements between a State and a foreign corporation as 'quasi-international treaties'. Verdross, '*Die Sicherung von ausländischen Privatrechten*', Z. *für ausl u. öffentl. Recht u. Völkerrecht*, Vol. 48 (1958), p. 638 treats them as a third category, governed neither by private nor by public international law, but by the *lex contractus* of the parties.

34. See, for a recent critical survey of these measures and of their impact on international trade, Miller, 'Foreign Trade and the Security State', 7 *Journal of Public Law* 37 (1958). And, for a survey of British State trading agencies, see Fawcett, 'Legal Aspects of State Trading', 25 *B.Y.I.L.* 34 (1948).

35. For a cautious, but telling, expression of the dilemma, see, for example, the speeches of the Chairman of the United States Export-Import Bank, and of the President of the – strongly American-influenced – International Finance Corporation at the New Delhi meeting, in October 1958.

36. See, for a recent survey, V. A. Seyid Muhammad, *The Legal Framework of World Trade* (1958), Chap. 5.

37. cf. Domke and Hazard, 'State Trading and Most Favored Nation Clause', 52 *A.J.I.L.* (1958), pp. 55 et seq., 57.

38. Lord Runciman in *Parl.Deb.*, *Commons*, Vol. 286, Cols. 1291–2, 1 March 1934.

39. Hazard, 'Commercial Discrimination and International Law' 52 *A.J.I.L.* 495 (1958).

40. Economic Commission for Europe, *U.N. Doc. E/ECE/*270, 12 March 1957.

41. See the arguments as reported by Hazard, 52 *A.J.I.L.*, pp. 495 et seq.

42. Although the Finnish-Soviet Treaty of 1947 contains the most-favoured-nation clause, the really important provision is that 'the Governments of the Contracting Parties will from time to time enter into negotiations for the purpose of concluding agreements defining the size and character of mutual delivery of commodities . . .' (Art. 1).

43. Domke and Hazard, op. cit., p. 68.

44. Schwarzenberger, 'The Most-Favoured-National Standard in British State Practice', 22 *B.Y.I.L.* 96, 113 (1945); Robert R. Wilson, *The International Law Standard in Treaties of the United States* (1953), p. 246.

45. cf. Muhammad, op. cit., p. 240.

46. British-Soviet Commercial Agreement of 1930.

47. For detailed substantiation, see among others, Preuss, 28 *A.J.I.L.* 649–68 (1934); Friedmann, 19 *B.Y.I.L.* 142 et seq. (1938).

48. In India conditions may change without any revolution, as in the case of Pakistan, where, during the first few years, the Muslim League enjoyed an overwhelming position, which has collapsed in the last few years.

49. See Oppenheim-Lauterpacht (8th ed., 1955), Vol. I, para. 127a.

50. ibid., 292.

51. See, among others, Hyde and Wehle, 27 *A.J.I.L.* 1 et seq. (1933); Lauterpacht, 14 *B.Y.I.L.* 125–140 (1933); Bouvé, 28 *A.J.I.L.* 19 et seq. (1934); Preuss, ibid., 667 et seq.; Friedmann, 19 *B.Y.I.L.* 142 et seq. (1938); Walz, *Nationalboykott und Völkerrecht* (1939).

52. *Crofter Hand Woven Harris Tweed Co.* v. *Veitch* [1942] A.C. 435.

53. cf. Prosser, *Law of Torts*, 754 et seq. (2nd ed., 1955).

54. Bouvé, loc. cit., 24.

55. For the United States, see the Sherman Antitrust Act (1890), the Clayton Act (1914), and the other extensive legislation, including the establishment of such regulatory authorities as the Federal Trade Commission, etc. For England, see the Monopolies Act (1948) and Amendments.

56. 14 *B.Y.I.L.* 125–40 (1933).

57. Preuss, 28 *A.J.I.L.* 667 (1934); Friedmann, 19 *B.Y.I.L.* 144 (1938).

58. For details, see Oppenheim-Lauterpacht, op. cit., paras. 197 et seq.

59. See *League of Nations Official Journal* (1936), p. 1437; 186 *L.N.T.S.* 301.

60. For a general survey of the most important case collections and literature, see among others, Bishop, *Cases and Materials on International Law*, Chap. VII, p. 626 (2nd ed; 1962); Briggs, *The Law of Nations*, Chap. IX (2nd ed., 1952); Oppenheim-Lauterpacht, *International Law*, Vol. I, pp. 360 et seq. (8th ed.).

61. The term is used, for example, by Borchard, 'The Minimum Standard of the Treatment of Aliens', 38 *Mich.L.R.* 445 (1940); Freeman, *The International Responsibility of States for Denial of Justice*, 497 et seq. (1938); Roth, *The Minimum Standard of International Law Applied to Aliens* (1949); Briggs, op. cit., 618 et seq., speaks of an 'International Standard of Justice'.

62. This does not necessarily mean a numerical majority of States. In this, as in many other fields, the nations which, by their history, the importance of their international relations, and their consequent weight in international affairs, have been chiefly articulate in the development of such standards, count for more than a small State with a minimum of international contacts. On the other hand, many of the challenges to established international minimum standards come from nations that struggle out of isolation or dependence towards a more independent international position and, in the course of that process, challenge established positions.

63. For a detailed discussion of this problem and a substantiation of this position, see Friedmann, *Legal Theory*, Chap. 3 (4th ed., 1960).

64. See Art. 38, para. 3, of its Statute.

65. Elihu Root, 'The Basis of Protection to Citizens Residing Abroad', *Proceedings, American Society of International Law* (1910), p. 16, at pp. 20–2.

66. *A.J.I.L.Supp.* 75 (1934).

67. cf. the *de Sabla Claim* (*U.S.* v. *Panama*), Hunt's *Report*, 379, 447 (1933); cf. also the note by Bishop, op. cit., 690 et seq.

68. For opposing viewpoints, see, among many others, Fachiri, 'Expropriation in International Law', 6 *B.Y.I.L.* 159 (1925), in favour of the compensation principle; on the other hand, Fischer Williams, 'International Law and the Property of Aliens', 9 ibid., 1 (1928), against any duty of compensation in the case of general legislative measures; and, for a general survey, Roth, *International Minimum Standards* (1949), and S. Friedman, *Expropriation in International Law* (1953). See further pp. 344 et seq. The majority of writers consider expropriation without compensation as an international delinquency. An intermediate view is taken by Lauterpacht, in the 8th ed. of Oppenheim, Vol. I, p. 352, where 'the granting of partial compensation' is advocated.

69. For a principle of law to be regarded as 'generally' recognized, it is not necessary to show that it should be *universally* accepted. 'If any real meaning is to be given to the words "general" or "universal" and the like, the correct test would seem to be that an international judge before taking over a principle from private law must satisfy himself that it is recognized in substance by all the main systems of law, and that in applying it he will not be doing violence to the fundamental concepts of any of those systems.' Gutteridge, *Comparative Law*, 65 (2nd ed., 1949).

70. It is an established principle of the international law of treaties that changes in the government – as distinct from changes in the international status – of one of the parties can have on influence on the binding force of treaties. (See McNair, *The Law of Treaties*, Chap. 41 (1961). Oppenheim-Lauterpacht, op. cit., 925 (8th ed., 1955).) The rationale is that internal political decisions – whether of an administrative or a legislative character – cannot affect international obligations once validly entered in accordance with constitutional process.

71. There has been surprisingly little discussion on this principle in the literature of public international law. (See, however, Schwarzenberger, *International Law*, Vol. I, pp. 214–16 (1945).) That the principle of unjust enrichment is one generally recognized, though with many differences in detail, in both the common and civil-law systems, can no longer be doubted. It is specifically embodied, for example, in the German, Swiss, Italian, Spanish, and Russian Civil Codes, while the French courts have developed similar principles. The principle of restitution is now sufficiently firmly established in American law to justify a separate *Restatement on Restitution*. In English law, the various actions for money had and received *quantum meruit*, constructive trust, etc., constitute the elements of a principle of unjust enrichment (cf. Lord Wright, *Legal Essays and Addresses*, Chaps. I and II). For a com-

parative analysis of the principle of unjust enrichment, see, among others, Dawson, *Unjust Enrichment* (1952); Friedmann, 'The Principle of Unjust Enrichment', 16 *Can.Bar Rev.* (1938), pp. 243 et seq., 365 et seq., and *Legal Theory*, 354 et seq. (3rd ed.); David and Gutteridge, 'Unjust Enrichment', 5 *Camb.L.J.* 223 et seq.; O'Connell, 'Unjust Enrichment', 5 *A.J.Comp.Law* 2 et seq. (1956).

72. *Annual Digest* (1929-30), Case No. 1.

73. See, in particular, Lauterpacht, *Private Law Sources and Analogies of International Law*, 203 et seq. (1927); Cheng, *General Principles of Law*, 141 et seq. (1953); Schwarzenberger, 'The Fundamental Principles of Law', *Hague Recueil* 87 (1955), pp. 312 et seq.; MacGibbon, 'Estoppel in International Law', 7 *I.C.L.Q.* (1958), pp. 468 et seq.

74. See for details the respective country studies in Friedmann and Pugh (eds.) *Legal Aspects of Foreign Investments* (1959), and, in particular, Fatouros, ibid., pp. 699 et seq.

75. Treaty between the U.S.A. and Japan, 1953, art. VI, para 3. On the whole subject, see Walker, 'Treaties for the Encouragement and Protection of Foreign Investment', 4 *Am.J.Comp.Law* (1956), pp. 229 et seq.

76. See, for some details, the article by A. A. Fatouros on 'Legal Security for International Investment', in op. cit., note 74, above.

77. (Art. 112.)

78. (Art. 127.)

79. (Art. 128.)

80. These minimum standards of 'due process', on which judicial precedent and literature are voluminous, have been summarized by Professor Orfield in 12 *U. of Pittsburgh L.R.* 35, 41-4 (1950) in eleven principles embodying the elements of a fair trial.

### 15. NATIONAL SOVEREIGNTY AND WORLD ORDER IN THE NUCLEAR AGE

1. In the process, the Assembly produced a most important and valuable by-product, the U.N. Emergency Force, which still does duty in the Gaza strip and the Straits of Tiran.

2. Racial and national tensions between Greeks and Turks threatened to divide even the small island of Cyprus into two separate political units, until early in 1959, Greece, Turkey, and Britain (the present sovereign) worked out a settlement that gave Cyprus political independence with constitutional safeguards for the (Turkish) minority and the maintenance of a British naval base.

3. *I.C.J.* (1951), p. 116.

4. See the Geneva Convention on the Continental Shelf of 1958. In the process, the right to exploit natural resources of the sea bed and subsoil has been extended to sedentary living organisms. (Geneva Convention, art. 2.)

5. See MacDougal and Burke, 'Crisis in the Law of the Sea: Community Perspectives versus National Egotism', 67 *Yale L.J.* 540-89 (1958).

6. As expressed in the wishful formula of 'sovereign equality', employed in the Preamble to, and various other provisions of, the United Nations Charter.

7. See pp. 332 et seq.

8. 'The Parties will contribute toward the further development of peaceful and friendly international relations by strengthening their free institutions, by bringing about a better understanding of the principles upon which these institutions are founded, and by promoting conditions of stability and well-being. They will seek to eliminate conflict in their international economic policies and will encourage economic collaboration between any or all of them.'

9. The European Court of Human Rights was created in September 1958, after eight members had declared their acceptance of its jurisdiction as compulsory. Most of these have not, however, extended the acceptance to complaints by individuals, and some signatories, including the United Kingdom, have not yet accepted the compulsory jurisdiction of the Court. See Robertson, 8 *I.C.L.Q.* (1959), pp. 396 et seq.

10. These are defined in the Convention and include the usual freedoms, of person, expression, assembly, equality, and fairness in the administration of justice, and peaceful enjoyment of possessions, subject to law.

11. Clark and Sohn, *World Peace through World Law* (1958).

12. See, for such a view, Granville Clark, in Clark and Sohn, op. cit., p. xxxi.

13. See Chicago Convention, 1944, art. 1.

14. See Jenks, op. cit., p. 389.

## 16. THE RULE OF LAW, THE INDIVIDUAL, AND THE WELFARE STATE

1. See above, Chap. 4.

2. cf. Goodhart, 'The Rule of Law and Absolute Sovereignty', 106 *U.of Pa.L.R.* 943 et seq. (1958) who distinguishes 'rule by law which can be the most efficient instrument in the enforcement of tyrannical rule' from 'rule under the law which is the essential foundation of liberty'. See also the present writer's earlier discussion in *The Planned State and the Rule of Law* (1948) and in *Law and Social Change in Contemporary Britain* (1951), Chap. 13.

3. See for a recent example of the colloquium on 'The Rule of Law as Understood in the West', held in September 1957 at the University of Chicago under the sponsorship of the International Association of Legal Science and the International Committee of Comparative Law. For a general survey, see Marsh, 'Defining the Rule of Law', 'Freedom and Legislative Power', *Listener*, 28 May, 4 June 1959.

4. See p. 276.

5. The following reformulation of Dicey's ideas as applicable to the

modern welfare State eliminates the equation of arbitrary and wide discretionary power:

'There are, I believe, ideas of universal validity reflected in Dicey's "three meanings" of the rule of law. . . . (1) in a decent society it is un-thinkable that government, or any officer of government, possesses arbitrary power over the person or the interests of the individual; (2) all members of society, private persons and government officials alike, must be equally responsible before the law; and (3) effective judicial remedies are more important than abstract constitutional declarations in securing the rights of the individual against encroach-ment by the State.' (Harry W. Jones, 'The Rule of Law and the Welfare State', in 58 *Columbia Law Review*, 1958, 149.)

6. For a more detailed criticism of Hayek's concept of the rule of law, see *Law and Social Change in Contemporary Britain* (1951), Chap. 13; also, Jones, 'The Rule of Law and the Welfare State', pp. 143 et seq.

7. For an important attempt to analyse the meaning of the rule of law, and especially the tension between economic liberties and public interest in contemporary American law, see Robert L. Hale, *Freedom through Law* (1952). For a briefer analysis of contemporary British developments, see Lord Denning's *Freedom under Law* (1949).

8. See, for an interesting brief comparative appreciation, Hamson, '*La Notion de l'égalité dans les pays occidentaux*', *Revue internationale de droit comparé*, January–March 1958, p. 54.

9. The new French Constitution of 1958 gives to the Conseil Con-stitutionnel the power (and duty) to rule on the constitutionality of laws and regulations before their promulgation. (Art. 61.)

10. cf. *Ohio* v. *Helvering*, 292 U.S. 366; *Coomber* v. *Berks Justices* (1883) 9 App.Cas. 61.

11. cf. pp. 299 et seq.

12. See, in particular, *Wilsons & Clyde Coal Co.* v. *English* [1938] A.C. 57.

13. cf. pp. 280 et seq.

14. In a Supreme Administrative Court of the Continental type, one senate would normally deal with all compensation matters; this greatly helps the development of constant judicial principles.

15. *Australian National Airways* v. *Commonwealth* (1946) 71 *C.L.R.* 29.

16. The latter, but not the former, is, at present, the case in Australia.

17. Such as discrimination in the allocation of paper, extent of news-paper monopolies, abuses of patents, and so forth.

# Bibliography

Adelman, 'The Measurement of Industrial Concentration', *The Review of Economics and Statistics*, Vol. 32, No. 4 . . 230

Alexander, Paul W., 'The Family Court of the Future', 31 *Journal Am. Jud.Soc.* 38 (1952) . . . . 190

Allen, 'The Borderland of the Criminal Law', *The Social Service Review*, Vol. XXXII, 107 (1958) . . . 156

Allen, C. K., *Law in the Making* (6th ed., 1958) . . . 45, 276

Ancel, 'French Matrimonial Property Law', in Friedmann (ed.), *Matrimonial Property Law* (1955) . . . 187

Anderson, 'Law Reform in the Middle East', *International Affairs*, 43 (1956) . . . . . 26

Arnold, *Folklore of Capitalism* (1937) . . . . 235

Auld, 'Canadian (Common Law Provinces) Matrimonial Property Law', in Friedmann (ed.), *Matrimonial Property Law* (1955) . . . . . . 204


Baehr, *Der Rechtsstaat*, 1864 . . . . . 277

Bastian, '*La Propriété commerciale en droit français*' *Travauxç de l'Association Henri Capitant*, Vol. 6 (1950) . . 74, 80

Beasley, 'Australia's Communist Party Dissolution Act', 29 *Can.Bar Rev.* 490 (1951) . . . . 47

Benjafield, 'Statutory Discretions', 2 *Sydney L.R.* 7 (1956) . 288

Berle, *The Twentieth Century Capitalist Revolution* (1954) 237, 243, 245, 247

Berle and Means, *The Modern Corporation and Private Property* (1932) . . . . . . . 77, 78, 235

Berman, 'Commercial Contracts in Soviet Law', 35 *Cal.L.R.* 225 (1947) . . . . . . 105

—, *Justice in Russia* (1950) . . . . 105, 113, 197

—, 'Soviet Law Reform in Dateline Moscow', 66 *Yale L.J.* 1191 (1957) . . . . . . 56

Bishop, *Cases and Materials on International Law* (2nd ed. 1962) 343, 345

Blackstone, *Commentaries on the Law of England* . . 200

Blair, 'Canadian Anti-Trust Law', in Friedmann (ed.), *Anti-Trust Laws* (1956) . . . . . 162, 226

Bohlen, *Studies in the Law of Torts* (1926) . . . 37

Bolin, 'Swedish Anti-Trust Law', in Friedmann (ed.), *Anti-Trust Laws* (1956) . . . . . 223, 256

Borchard, 'The Minimum Standard of the Treatment of Aliens', 38 *Mich. L.R.* 451 (1940) . . . . 343

Bouvé, 'The National Boycott as an International Delinquency', 28 *A.J.I.L.* 79 (1934) . . . . . 339
Bradway, 'Divorce Litigation and the Welfare of the Family', 9 *Vanderbilt L.R.* 665 (1956) . . . . . 180, 189
Bradway, 'The Myth of the Innocent Spouse', in *Selected Essays on Family Law* (1950) . . . . . 180
Breitel, 'Courts and Law-Making', in *Columbia Law School Centennial* (1959) . . . . . . . 45, 67
Brown, Ernest J., 'Process of Law', in 72 *Harv.L.R.* 77 (1958) 54
Brown, Ralph S., *Loyalty and Security Employment Tests in the United States* (1958) . . . . . . 281
Burnham, *The Managerial Revolution* (1941) . . . 235

Cahn, *The Sense of Injustice* (1949) . . . . 115
Carbonnier, *Droit civil* (1955) . . . . . 210
Cardozo, *The Nature of the Judicial Process* (1921) . . 36
Carlston, *Law and the Structure of Social Action* (1956) . 244, 253
Carnegie, *Share the Wealth* (1895) . . . . 233
Carrow, 'Types of Judicial Relief from Administrative Action', 58 *Col. L.R.* 1 (1958) . . . . . 310, 311, 312
Cheng, *General Principles of Law* (1953) . . . 65, 347
Cherne, *Government Contract Problems* (1941) . . 294
Cheshire, *The Modern Law of Real Property* (7th ed., 1954) . 73
Cheshire and Fifoot, *Law of Contract* (5th ed., 1960) . 93, 99
Clark, E., 'Matrimonial Property Law in Western United States', in Friedmann (ed.), *Matrimonial Property Law* (1955) . . . . . . . 187, 200, 203
Clark and Sohn, *World Peace through World Law* (1958) . 363, 364
Cohen, M., *Law and Social Order* (1933) . . 90, 98, 104
Cooper and Wood, *Outlines of Industrial Law* (4th ed., 1962) . 101, 109
Cox and Dunlop, 'The Duty to Bargain Collectively', 63 *Harv. L.R.* 389 (1950) . . . . . . 110
Cross, 'The Diminishing Fee', *Law and Contemporary Problems* (1955) . . . . . . . . 84

David and Gutteridge, 'Unjust Enrichment', 5 *Camb.L.J.* 223 (1935) . . . . . . . . 347
Davis, *Administrative Law* (1951) . . 278, 279, 299, 300, 310
—, 'Tort Liability of Governmental Units', 40 *Minn.L.R.* 751 (1955) . . . . . . . 304, 305
—, 'Forms of Proceeding', 44 *Ill.L.R.* 565 (1949) . 310
—, 'Standing Ripeness and Civil Liberties', 38 *A.B.A.J.* 924 (1952) . . . . . . . . 313
Dawson, *Unjust Enrichment* (1952) . . . . 347
Deák, *The Hungarian-Roumanian Land Dispute* (1928) . . 344

Dean, 'New York Matrimonial Property Law', in Friedmann
   (ed.), *Matrimonial Property Law* (1955) . . . . 201, 214

Denning, Lord, *Freedom under Law* (1949) . . . 375

Dicey, *Law and Public Opinion in England in the Nineteenth Century*
   (2nd ed., reissued 1960) . . . . 36, 93

—, *Law of the Constitution* (10th ed., 1959) . . . 276, 299

Dodd, 'From Maximum Wages to Minimum Wages', 43 *Col.
L.R.* 667 (1943) . . . . . . . 93

Domke and Hazard, 'State Trading and Most Favoured
   Nation Clause', 52 *A.J.I.L.* 55 (1958) . . 334, 335

Drago, 'French Public Corporations', in Friedmann (ed.), *The
Public Corporation* (1954) . . . . 220, 251, 330

Drucker, *The Concept of the Corporation* (1946) . . 244


Eastwood and Wortley, 'Administrative Law and the Teaching of the Law of Contract', *J.Soc.P.T.L.* (1938), Chap. 3    101

Eckhoff, 'Norwegian Anti-Trust Law', in Friedmann (ed.),
   *Anti-Trust Laws* (1956) . . . . 223

Edwards, *Mens Rea in Statutory Offences* (1955) . . 168, 169

Ehrenzweig, *Negligence without Fault* (1951) . . 119, 135, 169

—, *Full Aid Insurance for the Traffic Victim* (1954) . 120, 135

Ehrlich, 'Fundamental Principles of the Sociology of Law', in
   the *Twentieth Century Series of Legal Philosophy*, Vol. V    20

Ekblad, *Induced Abortion on Psychiatric Grounds* (1955) . 198

Esmein, 'Liability in French Law for Damages Caused by
   Motor Vehicle Accidents', 2 *Am.J.of Comp.Law* 156 (1953)    121


Fachiri, 'Expropriation in International Law', 6 *B.Y.I.L.* 59
   (1925) . . . . . . . 346

Fatouros, 'Legal Security in International Investment', in
   Friedmann (ed.), *Legal Aspects of Foreign Investment* (1959) . 347, 349

Fawcett, 'Legal Aspects of State Trading', 25 *B.Y.I.L.* 35
   (1948) . . . . . 328, 329, 332

Fischer, 'Problems Arising from Co-Determination in West
   Germany', *Transactions of the Third World Sociological Congress*,
   International Sociological Association (1956) . . 252

Fleming, *Law of Torts* (1957) . . . 120, 128

Flügel, *Man, Morals and Society* (1945) . . . 150

Foenander, *Industrial Regulation in Australia* (1947) . 112

Forsthoff, *Lehrbuch des Verwaltungsrechts* (7th ed., 1958)278, 282, 283, 294
   309, 310, 314

Fraenkel, *The Dual State* (1941) . . . . 240

Freeman, *The International Responsibility of States for Denial of
Justice* (1938) . . . . . . 343

Freund, *On Understanding the Supreme Court* (1951) . . 32

Bibliography 457

Glueck, Sheldon, and Eleanor, 'Unravelling Juvenile De-
linquency', 3 *British Journal of Delinquency* 289 (1953) . 155
Gneist, von, *Der Rechtsstaat* (1868) . . . . 278
Goldschmidt, James, *Verwaltungsstrafrecht* (1902) . . 167
Goodhart, 'The Rule of Law and Absolute Sovereignty', 106
*U.of Pa.L.R.* 943 (1958) . . . . 373
Gower, *Modern Company Law* (2nd ed., 1957) . . 233, 234
Graveson and Crane (ed.), *A Century of Family Law* (1957) . 173
Green, Leon, *Traffic Victims: Tort Law and Insurance* (1958) . 121
Griffith, 'Fault Triumphant', 28 *N.Y.U.L.R.* 1069 (1953) . 129
Griffith and Street, *Principles of Administrative Law* (3rd ed.,
1963) . . . . 278, 283, 284, 310
Grünfeld, 'U.K. Anti-Trust Law', in Friedmann (ed.), *Anti-
Trust Laws* (1956) . . . . . 221
Grunhut, *Penal Reform* (1950) . . . . 158
Gsovski, *Soviet Civil Law* (1948) . . . . 80
Gutteridge, 'The Abuse of Rights', 5 *Camb.L.J.* 22 (1936) . 79, 80
—, *Comparative Law* (2nd ed., 1949) . . . . 346


Hale, 'Bargaining Duress and Economic Liberty', 43 *Col. L.R.*
605 (1943) . . . . . . 93
—, *Freedom Through Law* (1952) . . . . 375
Hall, J., *General Principles of Criminal Law* (2nd ed., 1960) . 168, 169
Hall, L., 'Strict or Liberal Construction of Penal Statutes', 48
*Harv.L.R.* 748 (1935) . . . . 60, 61, 62
Hamson, *Executive Discretion and Judicial Control* (1954) . 276, 316
—, '*La Notion de l'égalité dans les pays occidentaux*', *Revue inter-
nationale de droit comparé* (1958) . . . . 376
Hand, *The Bill of Rights* (1958) . . . 50, 52, 53
Hanson (ed.), *Public Enterprise* (1955) . . . 100, 306
Harding, *Free Man Versus his Government*, (Southern Methodist
Studies in Jurisprudence, V) (1958) . . . 72, 88
Hargreaves, 'Modern Real Property', 19 *Mod.L.R.* 147 (1956) 73
Harper, *Problems of Family Life* (1952) . . . 190
Hart, Henry M., 'The Aims of the Criminal Law', *Law and
Contemporary Problems* (1958), 422 . . . 169
Hart, H. L. A., 'Positivism and The Separation of Law and
Morals', 71 *Harv.L.R.* 607 (1958) . . . 41
Harvey, 'On the State of the Divorce Market', 16 *Mod.L.R.*
130 (1953) . . . . . 180
Hays, 'The Union and its Members: The Uses of Democracy'
(paper delivered at N. Y. U. 11th Annual Conference on
Labor, 1958) . . . . . 264
Hazard, *Law and Social Change in the U.S.S.R.* (1953) .22, 160, 177, 209
—, 'The Public Corporation in the U.S.S.R.', in Friedmann
(ed.), *The Public Corporation* (1954), 374 . . . 220, 249

Hazard, 'Soviet Codifiers Release the First Drafts', *American Journal of Comparative Law* 72 (1959) . . . 56

—, U.S.S.R. Matrimonial Property Law', in Friedmann (ed.), *Matrimonial Property Law* (1955) . . . . 201, 202

—, 'Commercial Discrimination and International Law', 52 *A.J.I.L.* 495 (1958) . . . . . 334

Hazard and Weisberg, *Cases and Readings on Soviet Law* (1950) 112, 113

Himes, *Medical History of Contraception* (1936) . 191

Hodgetts, 'Canadian Public Corporations', in Friedmann (ed.), *The Public Corporation* (1954) . . . . 251

Hoffmann, *Die ländlichen Elektrizitätsgenossenschaften in den U.S.A.* (1954) . . . . . . . 251

Holmes, *The Common Law* (1881) . . . 113, 117

Hyde and Wehle, 'The Boycott in Foreign Affairs', 27 *A.J.I.L.* 1 (1933) . . . . . . . 339

Imboden, *Der verwaltungsrechtliche Vertrag* (1958) . . 294

Jacobs and Angell, *Research in Family Law* (1930) . . 180, 188

Jacobs and Goebel, *Cases and Materials on Domestic Relations* (3rd ed., 1952) . . . . . . 207, 208

Jaffe, 'The Effective Limits of the Administrative Process: A Revaluation', 67 *Harv.L.R.* 1105 (1954). . . 280

—, 'Law Making by Private Groups', 51 *Harv.L.R.* 201 (1937) . . . . . . . . 247

James, Fleming, Jr, 'The Federal Tort Claims Act and the "Discretionary Function" ', 10 *U.of Fla.L.R.* 187 (1957). 289

—, 'Social Insurance and Tort Liability', 27 *N.Y.U.L.R.* 552 (1952) . . . . . . . . 131, 136

Jellinek, *Verwaltungsrecht* (1932) . . . . 283

Jenks, *The Common Law of Mankind* (1958) . . 321, 365

Jennings, *Law and the Constitution* (5th ed., 1959) . 276, 277

—, 'Tort Liability of Administrative Officers', 21 *Minn.L.R.* 263 (1937) . . . . . . . 299

Jessup, *Transnational Law* (1956) . . . . 331

Jones, Harry W., 'The Rule of Law and the Welfare State', 58 *Col.L.R.* 149 (1958) . . . . . 374

Juins, *Soviet Law and Soviet Society* (1954) . . . 22

Kahn-Freund, 'Collective Agreements under War Legislation' 6 *Mod.L.R.* (1943) . . . . . . 102, 110

—, Introduction to Renner, *The Institutions of Private Law and their Social Function* (1949) . . . 72, 76, 83, 85

—, 'Divorce Law Reform?' 19 *Mod.L.R.* 573 (1956) . . 180

—, 'Matrimonial Property – Some Recent Developments', 22 *Mod.L.R.* 241 (1959) . . . . . . 204

McDermott, Lord, *Protection from Power* (1957) . . 283, 290

McDonald, 'Constitution in a Changing World', 26 *Can.Bar Rev.* 21 (1948) . . . . . . . 46

McDougal, 'International Law, Power and Policy: A Contemporary Conception', 82 *Hague Recueil* 137 (1953) . 331

McDougal and Burke, 'Crisis in the Law of the Sea', 67 *Yale L.J.* 540 (1958) . . . . . . . 358

McGregor, *Divorce in England* (1957). . . . 181, 183, 184

—, 'The Morton Commission: A Social and Historical Commentary', *Br.Jour.of Sociology*, Vol. VII (1956), 171 . 180

McInnis, *Canada's Political and Social History* (1947) . 46

McIntyre, 'Address to National Association of Securities Administrators', in Gellhorn and Byse, *Administrative Law, Cases and Comments* . . . . . . 247

McNair, *The Law of Treaties* (2nd ed., 1961) . . . 346

MacGibbon, 'Estoppel in International Law', 7 *I.C.L.Q.* 468 (1958) . . . . . . . . 347

MacPherson, 'Co-Determination: Germany's Move Toward a New Economy', 5 *Ind.& Lab.Rel.Rev.* 20 (1951) . 252

—, 'Co-Determination in Practice', 8 *Ind.& Lab.Rel.Rev.* 499 (1955) . . . . . . . . 252

Magnusson, *Norwegian Law of Illegitimacy* (1918), U.S. Children's Bureau, Legal Series No. 1, Pub. No. 31 . 210

Maitland, *Constitutional History of England* (1887) . 276

—, *Selected Legal Essays* (1936) . . . . 232, 261

Malmstrom, 'Swedish Matrimonial Property Law', in Friedmann (ed.), *Matrimonial Property Law* (1955) . . 203

Mann, F. A., 'The Law Governing State Contracts', 21 *B.Y.I.L.* 11 (1944) . . . . . . . 329

Mannheim, H., *Criminal Justice and Social Reconstruction* (1946) 158

Mannheim and Wilkins, *Prediction in Relation to Borstal Training* 155

Marsh, 'Defining the Rule of Law', *Listener*, May and June 1959 . . . . . . . . 374

Mason, *Brandeis, A Free Man's Life* (1946) . . . 259

—, *Security through Freedom: American Political Thought and Practice* (1955) . . . . . . . 94

Massfeller, 'German Matrimonial Property Law', in Friedmann (ed.), *Matrimonial Property Law* (1955) . . 203

Mazeaud, H. and L., *Traité de la responsibilité* (4th ed.) . 301

Miller, 'The Constitutional Law of the Security State', 10 *Stanford L.R.* 645 . . . . . . 242, 279

—, 'Foreign Trade and the Security State', 7 *Journal of Public Law* 37 (1958) . . . . . . . 332

—, 'Government Contracts and Social Control: A Preliminary Inquiry', 41 *Va.L.R.* 27 (1955) . . . . 104, 294

Millis and Katz, 'A Decade of State Labor Legislation', 15 *U.of Ohio L.R.* 282 (1952) . . . . . . 258

Paulsen, 'Support Rights and Duties', 9 *Vanderbilt L.R.* 709
(1956) . . . . . . . . 187
—, 'Fairness to Juvenile Offenders', 41 *Minn.L.R.* 547 (1956)   156, 157
Pius XII, 'The Apostolate of the Midwife', in *Moral Questions
Affecting Married Life* (1951) . . . 192, 193, 194, 195
—, Encyclical on Christian Marriage . . . 172
Planiol, *Traité élémentaire de droit civil* (4th ed., 1962) . 92
Planiol et Ripert, *Traité pratique du droit civil* (2nd ed., 1952) . 122, 203
Plato, *The Republic* . . . . . . 172
Pound, *Introduction to the Philosophy of Law* . . . 90
—, 'The Rule of the Will in Law', 68 *Harv.L.R.* 1 (1954) . 118, 121
—, 'Common Law and Legislation', 21 *Harv.L.R.* 383 (1908) 60
Prausnitz, *Standardisation of Commercial Contracts in English and
Continental Law* (1937) . . . . . 98
Price, 'South African Matrimonial Property Law', in Fried-
mann (ed.), *Matrimonial Property Law* (1955) . . 187
Preuss, 'International Responsibility for Hostile Propaganda
Against Foreign States', 28 *A.J.I.L.* 649 (1934) . 337, 339
Prosser, *Handbook of the Law of Torts* (2nd ed., 1955) . .80, 81, 339


Radzinowicz, 'The Persistent Offender', in *The Modern Ap-
proach to Criminal Law* . . . . . 158
Reiwald, *Society and its Criminals* (1950) . . . 150
Renner, *The Institutions of Private Law and Their Social
Functions* (1949) . . . . . . 234, 247
Reuter, *Institutions Internationales* (3rd ed., 1962) . . 331
Rheinstein, 'The Law of Divorce and the Problem of Marriage
Stability', 9 *Vanderbilt L.R.* 633 (1956) . . 180, 185
Ribble, 'Policy Making Powers of the Supreme Court and the
Position of the Individual', 14 *Washington and Lee L.R.* (1957) 52
Rich, *American Foundations and their Fields* (1955) . . 233
Riesenfeld, 'Contemporary Trends in Compensation for In-
dustrial Accidents', 42 *Cal.L.R.* 531 (1954) . . 123
Ripert, *Les Forces créatrices du droit* (1955) . . . 74
Robbins and Deak, 'The Familial Property Rights of Illegiti-
mate Children, A Comparative Study', 30 *Col.L.R.* 308
(1930) . . . . . . . 209, 210
Robertson, 'The European Court of Human Rights', 8 *I.C.L.Q*
396 (1959) . . . . . . . 362
Robson (ed.), *New Zealand, the Development of its Laws and
Constitution* (1954) . . . . . 220
Robson, W. A., *Justice and Administrative Law* (3rd ed., 1951) 276
Root, 'The Basis of Protection to Citizens Residing Abroad',
*Proceedings, American Soc. of Int. Law* 16 (1910) . . 344
Roth, *The Minimum Standard of International Law Applied to
Aliens* (1949) . . . . . . 343

Salmond, *Torts* (13th ed. by Heuston, 1961) . . . 96

Savatier, *Les Métamorphoses économiques et sociales du droit civil d'aujourd'hui* (1952) . . . . . . 82

Sawer, 'Industrial Law', in Paton (ed.), *The Commonwealth of Australia* (1948) . . . . . . 227

Sayre, 'Public Welfare Offences', 33 *Col.L.R.* 71 (1933) . 167

Schlesinger, *The Family in the U.S.S.R.* (1949) . . 197

Schmitthoff, 'International Corporations', *Grotius Society* (1946) . . . . . . . . 308

—, 'Sovereign Immunity in International Trade', 7 *Int.& Comp.Law Quarterly* 452 (1958) . . . . 325

Schwartz, 'The Changing Role of the United States Supreme Court', 28 *Can.Bar. Rev* (1950) . . . . 94

—, *French Administrative Law and the Common Law World* (1954) . . . . . . 299, 301, 402

—, *The Professor and the Commissions* (1959). . . 316

Schwarzenberger, 'The Fundamental Principles of International Law', 87 *Hague Recueil* (1955) . . . 347

—, *International Law* (3rd ed., 1957) . . . 63, 65, 331

—, 'The Most-Favoured-Nation Standard in British State Practice', 22 *B.Y.I.L.* 96 (1945) . . . . 335

Schwenk, 'The Administrative Crime', 42 *Mich.L.R.* 51 (1943) 167

Scott, 'Nullity of Marriage in Canon Law and English Law', 2 *U.of Tor.L.J.* 314 (1938) . . . . . 174

Scrutton, 'Work of the Commercial Courts', 1 *Camb.L.J.* 6 (1922–4) . . . . . . . 42

Seavey, '*Candler* v. *Crane, Christmas & Co.*', 67 *L.Q.R.* 466 (1951) . . . . . . . 118, 126

Sherbaniuk, 'Actions by and against Trade Unions in Contract and Tort', 12 *U.of Toronto L.J.* 157 (1958) . . 261

Shuchman, *Codetermination* (1957) . . . . 252

Shulman, 'Reason, Contract and Law in Labor Relations', 68 *Harv.L.R.* 999 (1955) . . . . . 111

Smit, 'Frustration of Contract', 58 *Col.L.R.* 287 (1958) . 106, 108

Smith, de, 'Wrongs and Remedies in Administrative Law', 15 *Mod.L.R.* 189 (1952) . . . . . . 310

Stephen, *History of Criminal Law*, II (1883) . . . 145

Stone, J., *Province and Function of Law* (1950) . . 40

Stone, O. M., 'Royal Commission on Marriage and Divorce: Family Dependents and their Maintenance' 19 *M.L.R.* 188

Street, *Government Liability* (1953) . . 285, 292, 294, 298

Summers, 'Disciplinary Powers of Unions', 3 *Ind.Lab.Relations Rev.* 483 (1950); 4 *Ind.Lab.Relations Rev.* 15 (1950) . 262

—, 'Legal Limitations on Union Discipline', 64 *Harv.L.R.* 1049 (1951) . . . . . . 260, 262, 263

—, 'The Political Liberties of Labor Union Members – A Comment', 33 *Texas L.R.* 602 (1955) . . . 264

Szladits, 'The Concept of Specific Performance in Civil Law',
4 *Am.J.of Comp.Law* 208 (1955) . . . . . 113

Tallin, 'Artificial Insemination', 34 *Can.Bar Rev.* 1, 166 (1956) 194
Teller, *Labour Disputes and Collective Bargaining*, Vol. I . 111
Thomson, 'Voluntary Collective Agreements in Australia and
New Zealand', 1 *U.of W. Australia L.R.* 80 . . . 112
Tilove, *Pension Funds and Economic Freedom* (1959) . . 253
Timberg, 'International Combines and National Sovereigns',
95 *U.of Pa.L.R.* 575 (1947) . . . . . 331
—, 'U.S. Anti-Trust Law', in Friedmann (ed.), *Anti-Trust
Laws* (1956) 225, 226, 256, 266
Traynor, 'Courts and Law-Making', in Columbia Law
School Centennial Symposium . . . . . 42
Trotabas, '*Les Actes de gouvernement en matières diplo-
matiques*', *Revue critique de législation et de jurisprudence* (1925) 284
Tunc, 'Establishment of *Fonds de Guarantie* to compensate
Victims of Motor Vehicle Accidents', 2 *Am.J.of Comp.Law*
232 (1953) . . . . . . . . 121
Turgeon, 'Quebec Matrimonial Property Law', in Friedmann
(ed.), *Matrimonial Property Law* (1955) . . . 187, 200

Ussing, 'The Scandinavian Law of Torts', 1 *Am.J.of Comp.
Law* 359 (1952) . . . . . . . 137, 138

Verdross, '*Die Sicherung von ausländischen Privatrechten*', *Z. für
ausl. u.öffentl.Recht u.Völkerrecht*, Vol. 48 (1958) 331
Verloren van Themaat, 'Netherlands Anti-Trust Laws', in
Friedmann (ed.), *Anti-Trust Laws* (1956) . . . 230
Vernier, *American Family Laws* (1931) . . . . 179
Vesey-Fitzgerald, 'Nature and Sources of the Sharī'a', *Law
in the Middle East* . . . . . . . 26

Wade, 'Courts and the Administrative Process', 63 *L.Q.R.*
164 (1947) . . . . . . . . 310
Waite, *Criminal Law in Action* (1934) . . . . 60
Waline, *Droit administratif* (6th ed., 1957) 278, 282, 283, 284, 293, 300,
302, 314
Walker, 'Treaties for the Encouragement and Protection of
Foreign Investment', 4 *Am.J.Comp.Law* 229 (1956) . 348
Walz, *Nationalboykott und Völkerrecht* (1939). . . 339
Wechsler, Supp. to Michael and Wechsler, *Criminal Law and
its Administration* (1956) . . . . 145, 163, 164
—, 'The Criteria of Criminal Responsibility', 22 *U.of Chicago
L.R.* 374 . . . . . . . . 143
—, 'Toward Neutral Principles of Constitutional Law', 73
*Harv.L.Rev.* 1 (1959) . . . . . . . 54

Wedderburn, K. W., 'The Bonsor Affair, a Postscript', 20
  *Mod.L.R.* 105 (1957) . . . . . . . 263, 264
Welsh, 'Criminal Liability of Corporations', 62 *I.Q.R.* 345
  (1946) 163
Whitmore, 'Judicial Control of Union Discipline – The *Kuzych*
  Case', 30 *Can.Bar Rev.* 1 (1952) . . . . 261
Williams, Glanville, *Criminal Law* (2nd ed., 1961) 57, 62, 163, 166, 167,
  169
——, *Sanctity of Life and the Criminal Law* (1957) 194, 195, 196, 197, 198, 199
——, 'Liability for Independent Contractors', *Camb.L.J.* 180
  (1956) 130
——, 'The Definition of Crime', *Current Legal Problems* (1955) 143
Williams, Howard R., 'The Continuing Evolution of the
  Land', *Transactions of the Third World Congress of Sociology*
  (1956) . . . . . . . . . 84
Williams, J. Fischer, 'International Law and the Property of
  Aliens', 6 *B.Y.I.L.* (1928) . . . . . . 346
Williams, J. S., 'The Political Liberty of Labor Union Mem-
  bers', 32 *Texas L.R.* 26 (1954) . . . . 260, 264
Willis, 'Statute Interpretation in a Nutshell', 16 *Can.Bar Rev.* 1
  (1938) . . . . . . . . . 44
Williston, *Law of Contracts* . . . . . . 294
Wilson, Robert R., *The International Law Standard in Treaties
  of the United States* (1953) . . . . . 335
Wilson, Woodrow, *Constitutional Government in the United States*
  (1908) . . . . . . . . . 279
Wirtz, 'Government by Private Groups', 13 *La.L.R.* 440 (1953) 247
Wootton, Barbara, 'Holiness or Happiness', *Twentieth Century*
  (November 1955) . . . . . . . 184
Wright, Lord, *Legal Essays and Addresses* . . . 347


Yardley, 'Remedies in Administrative Law', 3 *Br.Jour.of Administrative Law* 69 (1957) . . . . . 312


Zepos, 'Frustration of Contract in Comparative Law and the
  New Greek Code of 1946', 11 *Mod.L.R.* 36 (1948) . . 106, 107

# Index

*Other Pelican books on the law are described
on the following pages*

# The Law in Pelicans

Considering how often the ordinary citizen, as householder, parent, businessman, or traveller, is involved in the law, it is remarkable how little has been done to explain to him what the law is; how it has come to be what it is; and how it might be improved.

Pelicans have embarked, therefore, on a bold, new attempt to explore for the general reader a variety of legal topics of wide public interest.

*In addition to the book described overleaf, the titles which have already been published are:*

THE ART OF THE ADVOCATE
Richard du Cann

THE CONSUMER, SOCIETY AND THE LAW
Gordon Borrie and Aubrey L. Diamond

THE CRIMINAL LAW
F. T. Giles

THE FAMILY AND THE LAW
Margaret Puxton

THE IDEA OF THE LAW
Dennis Lloyd

JOHN CITIZEN AND THE LAW
(Fifth edition, revised) Ronald Rubinstein

*Future titles will include:*

A SHORT HISTORY OF ENGLISH LAW
Alan Harding

THE WORKER AND THE LAW
K. W. Wedderburn

# Freedom, the Individual and the Law

Harry Street

Civil Liberties are very much in the news. At the heart of every incident that concerns the rights and obligations of the individual lies a conflict, sometimes muted, sometimes violent, between competing interests: freedom of speech *v.* security of the state, freedom of movement *v.* public order, the right to privacy *v.* professional integrity. Every day brings fresh reports of 'punch-up' politics, banning of controversial posters, curious corners of theatre censorship, abuse of telephone tapping, contempt of Parliament . . . the headlines never stop.

Yet Professor Street's *Freedom, the Individual and the Law* is the first comprehensive survey of the way English law deals with the many sides of Civil Liberty. After an introductory description of the powers of the police, Professor Street addresses himself in detail to the main areas of freedom of expression, freedom of association, and freedom of movement.

'For anyone who values his liberty this book is a must' – *Tribune*

'Imaginative, fresh and compelling, his book brings alive the liberties we enjoy and those we are in danger of losing . . . minor masterpiece' – *Observer*

*For a complete list of books available please write to Penguin Books whose address can be found on the back of the title page*